FIFTY YEARS ON

FIFTY YEARS ON

A Prejudiced History of Britain Since the War

ROY HATTERSLEY

LITTLE, BROWN AND COMPANY

A *Little, Brown* Book

First published in Great Britain in 1997
by Little, Brown and Company

Copyright © 1997 by Roy Hattersley

A CIP catalogue record for this book
is available from the British Library.

ISBN: 0 316 87932 0

Typeset in Bembo by M Rules
Printed and bound in Great Britain by
Clays Ltd, St Ives plc

Little, Brown and Company (UK)
Brettenham House
Lancaster Place
London WC2E 7EN

CONTENTS

———•—•———

Contents

Chronology of
General Elections

———•———

LABOUR	GENERAL ELECTION	CONSERVATIVE
Labour leader: *Clement Attlee*	pre-1945	*Conservative leader:* *Winston Churchill*
Attlee defeats Churchill; Labour majority 146	**26 July 1945**	
Attlee defeats Churchill; Labour majority 5	**23 February 1950**	
	25 October 1951	Churchill defeats Attlee; Conservative majority 17
		Churchill resigns 5 April 1955; Anthony Eden PM 6 April 1955
	26 May 1955	Eden defeats Attlee; Conservative majority 58

LABOUR	GENERAL ELECTION	CONSERVATIVE
Attlee resigns 7 December 1955; Hugh Gaitskell Labour leader 14 December 1955		
		Eden resigns 9 January 1957; Harold Macmillan PM 10 January 1957
	8 October 1959	Macmillan defeats Gaitskell; Conservative majority 100
Gaitskell dies 18 January 1963; Harold Wilson Labour leader 14 February 1963		
		Macmillan resigns 10 October 1963; Alec Douglas-Home PM 18 October 1963
Wilson defeats Douglas-Home; Labour majority 4	**15 October 1964**	
		Douglas-Home resigns 22 July 1965; Edward Heath Conservative leader 27 July 1965
Wilson defeats Heath; Labour majority 96	**31 March 1966**	
	18 June 1970	Heath defeats Wilson; Conservative majority 30
no clear majority; Wilson forms minority government 5 March 1974	**28 February 1974**	

LABOUR	GENERAL ELECTION	CONSERVATIVE
Wilson defeats Heath; Labour majority 3	**10 October 1974**	
		Heath resigns 4 February 1975; Margaret Thatcher Conservative leader 11 February 1975
Wilson resigns 16 March 1976; James Callaghan PM 5 April 1976		
	3 May 1979	Thatcher defeats Callaghan; Conservative majority 43
Callaghan resigns 15 October 1980; Michael Foot Labour leader 10 November 1980		
	9 June 1983	Thatcher defeats Foot; Conservative majority 144
Foot resigns 12 June 1983; Neil Kinnock Labour leader 2 October 1983		
	11 June 1987	Thatcher defeats Kinnock; Conservative majority 101
		Thatcher resigns 22 November 1990; John Major PM 28 November 1990
	9 April 1992	Major defeats Kinnock; Conservative majority 21

GENERAL
ELECTION

LABOUR

CONSERVATIVE

*Kinnock resigns 13 April
1992; John Smith Labour
leader 18 July 1992*

*John Smith dies 12 May
1994; Tony Blair Labour
leader 21 July 1994*

Blair defeats Major;
Labour majority 179

**1 May
1997**

*Major resigns 2 May 1997;
William Hague Conservative
leader 19 June 1997*

FIFTY YEARS ON

I

WINNING THE PEACE
Attlee's Post-war Britain

———•————

It was Field Marshal Montgomery who best reflected the mood of the nation. On the evening of the German surrender on Lüneburg Heath, he drafted what, with his usual sense of drama, he called 'My last message to the armies'. Montgomery had no great literary talent, and he later admitted that the brief valediction had been hard to compose. But when it was finished, his eight short paragraphs expressed all the emotions that the British people felt at the news of victory. First was gratitude to our 'comrades who died in the struggle'. There followed great joy and thankfulness that 'we have been preserved to see this day'. Relief gave way to pride: 'In the early days of the war the British Empire stood alone . . .' The message ended with the mixture of hope and apprehension that characterised what the country felt about the future: 'We have won the German war. Let us now win the peace.' Few people doubted the ferocity of the battles that lay ahead.

Four days later, after victory had been officially declared, King George VI said much the same in a statement which – since it was the work of a committee – failed to reflect the emotions of his people. He recalled 'the knowledge that everything was at stake; our freedom, our independence, our very existence as a people; but the knowledge that in defending ourselves we were defending the liberty of the whole world . . .' The Archbishop of Canterbury's call for 'rejoicing without excess' was generally ignored. Winston Churchill – the hero of the hour and the 'lion's roar', who had inspired the nation with his oratory – broadcast at three o'clock, made a statement in the House of Commons immediately afterwards, spoke from the Ministry of Health balcony in Whitehall and addressed, impromptu, the adoring crowds which mobbed him wherever he went. He orated more successfully than he extemporised. One group was told Britain's achievements would be remembered 'wherever the bird of freedom chirps in human hearts'.

Characteristically, the man who was to dominate British politics for the next five years said nothing at all. Clement Attlee was on the west coast of America, at the United Nations' founding conference. His description of the day makes the moment of triumph sound like an anti-climax: when the news came through that the war against the Nazis was ended, the delegates 'gathered to celebrate the event in a room at the top of a skyscraper. In San Francisco, the Japanese war was nearer and of greater concern.'

Three months later – largely because of the combination of optimism and anxiety which Montgomery had detected in his soldiers – Clement Attlee became Prime Minister of the United Kingdom. In May, when the praise of a rightly grateful people was ringing in Winston Churchill's ears, no one had doubted that the British electorate would want the 'Greatest Living Englishman' to lead them in peace as he had led them in war. Indeed the Tories in the coalition government were astonished by Labour's insistence on an early General Election and what they saw as the consequent sacrifice of any claim to credit for the victory over Japan. Attlee himself took the return of a Conservative government for granted. In a rare moment of presumption, he told 'Jock' Colville, the Prime Minister's private secretary, that he hoped to reduce the Tories' parliamentary majority to double figures.

Even on 5 July, when the votes were cast, commentators – without opinion polls to guide them – assumed that the government would not change. The votes of British soldiers, sailors and airmen in occupied Europe, India and South-east Asia, North Africa and the South

Atlantic had to be collected and counted, so it took three weeks for the result to be announced. On 26 July, the day of the declaration, Attlee's daughter – on her way home from school – was surprised to read on the billboards that Labour had won and her father was destined for Downing Street. The victorious party leader later confessed that when he went to Buckingham Palace to kiss hands, 'the king pulled my leg a bit . . . He told me that I looked more surprised than he felt.' When the last result was declared, Labour had a majority of 146 over all other parties.

It now seems extraordinary that even the Labour Party should attempt to depose the man who had, two days before, led them to an unexpected and historic victory. But, within hours of the 1945 election result being declared, Herbert Morrison began his campaign to unseat Clement Attlee. In 1983, after recording his contribution to the television profile which marked the centenary of Attlee's birth, George Strauss (almost fifty years in the House of Commons and a Morrison lieutenant from their days together on the London County Council) confessed, in the privacy of the green room, that he had conspired to change leader. 'If we had been allowed a vote, Attlee would have been defeated. It would have been a terrible mistake, but that is what would have happened.' Attlee forestalled the coup by accepting the King's Commission while the plot was still being hatched: 'If the King asks you to form a government you say "Yes" or "No", not "I'll let you know later"!' He went straight from Buckingham Palace to the victory rally in Westminster Central Hall and told the ecstatic audience that, for the first time in history, there was a Labour majority government in office.

There were many reasons for Labour's unexpected victory. The contributory causes of the Conservatives' defeat were both obvious and prosaic. Labour's leaders – represented before the war as red revolutionaries – had become comfortable household names. Ernest Bevin had been transformed from the aggressive union leader of the General Strike into the much-loved Minister of Labour. Herbert Morrison – before the war, the tyrant of the London County Council – was the Home Secretary who had been photographed in the ruins of every blitzed city in Britain. Attlee himself – excoriated

3

by Tory newspapers during the Spanish Civil War for giving the clenched-fist salute to the republican International Brigade – had become Churchill's deputy in the victorious coalition. The newspaper which had once denounced him as a Communist stooge spent the war years extolling his virtues as the essential partner in the triumph of a united nation. Labour had played a crucial part in the creation of the coalition in which Churchill replaced the discredited Neville Chamberlain in May 1940. The Conservative campaign broadcast, which claimed that a Labour government would 'fall back on some form of Gestapo' only had the effect of making the Tories seem extreme, ridiculous and desperate.

Even the Soviet Union – which, it was once claimed, illustrated the sort of repressive society that Labour wanted to build in Britain – had become admirable, if not benign. The war had cleared the skeletons out of Labour's closets. But there was more to their victory than the death of pre-war prejudices, more than the radical propaganda of the Army Bureau of Current Affairs and more than the historic *Mirror* campaign that urged the women at home to 'vote for them', in the certainty that 'they' (the soldiers, sailors and airmen who had won the war) would vote Labour. Britain voted Labour out of pride and because of hope.

Ever since the creation of something that could be called Great Britain, boys and girls within that nation's boundaries had been brought up to believe that their country possessed unique virtues. And being English was, in the words of one patriot, 'to be dealt a winning hand in life's game of cards'. Nothing that happened during the Second World War changed that perception. At the South Yorkshire Boy Scouts' service of thanksgiving for victory, the chaplain, introducing the hymn 'I Vow To Thee My Country', said that the words were written by an American who was almost good enough to be an Englishman. His error about the verse's authorship is less important than what his opinion signified about the British psyche. Certainly, the British Establishment had been slow to recognise and respond to the threat posed by Nazi Germany, so the battle for civilisation had begun badly. But the common people – G. K. Chesterton's men and women 'who have not spoken yet' – asserted themselves and won a crushing victory. And by their efforts, they saved the world. Everyone knew that Russia had endured years of slaughter and destruction which had been spared the other Allies, and nobody doubted that without the belated intervention of the USA, the war might never have been won. But if Britain had surrendered after the capitulation of France, there would have been nothing left of Western Europe for Russia and America to save. The explanation of Britain's greatness had changed, but the claim to greatness had not diminished. Indeed, it had become more plausible since the days when popular songs claimed that 'we always won' and school atlases boasted that 'the sun never sets on the British Empire'. The justifiable certainty that Britain had a special place in history was illustrated by five words in Field Marshal Montgomery's valedictory message. For a year, 'The British Empire stood alone.' The men and women who had saved the world deserved something better than the poverty, ill-health and unemployment that had characterised Britain before the war. The way that the war had been fought and won convinced the British people that there was a way of building a better life for themselves and their children.

It had been a people's war – a conflict so total that women had been recruited for jobs which had previously been thought only suitable for men, and working men had been promoted to positions which were once the preserve of gentlemen. Clerks had become colonels and discovered that, basically, the officer class was very similar to the ranks. If Waterloo was won on the playing fields of Eton, then Alamein, Monte Cassino and Normandy were victories for the concrete yards of municipal elementary schools. Nostalgia for the imaginary past of noble instincts and elegant manners was generally confined to the novels of Evelyn Waugh. Despite their undoubted literary superiority, *Brideshead Revisited* and the *Sword of Honour* trilogy did not capture the national mood in the way that it was caught and, for a year or two, held by the calls for a new beginning that characterised J. B. Priestley's post-war plays and stories. Both men recorded the passing of an old order. Waugh resented the ascendancy of men in badly-fitting 'demob suits'. Priestley, in *An Inspector Calls*, prophesied the destruction of 'old England'. Millions of men and women – servicemen home from the wars, their wives, their sweethearts and their children – hoped that Priestley's prediction (made in a play which was more popular in Moscow than in London) would be fulfilled.

The change in attitude between the two world wars was illustrated in the poetry. Certainly, by the time of the slaughter on the Somme, the romanticism of Rupert Brooke had given way to the bitterness of Isaac Rosenberg and Wilfred Owen. But, with the exception of Rosenberg, the First World War poets fought an officer's war. The conscripts of 1940, however, composed unheroic verse for the ranks. Herbert Read's *Lessons of War* included 'Unarmed Combat', 'learned not in the hope of winning but rather of keeping something alive'. The mood was best illustrated by the four lines of the John Pudney poem which were made famous by *The Way to the Stars* – a film which for all its patriotic sentimentality came to the conclusion:

> Better by far
> For Johnny-the-bright-star,
> To keep your head,
> And see his children fed.

The working men and women who had won the war knew that in order to 'win the peace', in Montgomery's phrase, radical changes had to be made in the way the old country was run. The Labour Party looked like the engine of change for more reasons than its innocence of all responsibility for the failures and frustrations of the 1930s. In 1945, there was a real belief that the war had been won on the principles which inspired Clement Attlee and his party.

On the eve of the 1945 General Election, A. V. Alexander – First Lord of the Admiralty in the wartime coalition – told a startled Sheffield public meeting that Britain's battle for survival had been fought 'according to the example of the two wise donkeys'. The donkeys in question were the heroes of a co-operative cartoon. Tied together by a six-foot stretch of rope, they realised that if they pulled against each other they would not reach either of the bales of hay which the thoughtless and brutal farmer had left ten feet apart. But when they moved together, in the same direction, they could share each feast in turn. All over Britain, more sophisticated versions of the same theory were being advanced as the prescription for 'winning the peace'. The comparison with the humble donkey underestimated the British working classes' self-esteem. But in 1945, they certainly did not identify with the farmer who already owned the hay. The middle classes consisted of professionals at the top of that social stratum and commercial travellers (despised by the solicitors and doctors) at the bottom. In between, there were relatively few industrial and commercial managers, hardly any technicians, and no technologists. Even comparatively prosperous families still rented their houses, found doctors' bills hard to pay and feared the poverty which came with old age. Socialism – at least the benign form which was implemented by the Labour government – had direct benefits to offer a country which had yet to develop either a dominant middle class or middle-class prejudices.

When the country had been in mortal danger, the British Establishment had abandoned the shibboleths they had once pretended were the only prescription for prosperity. The hidden hand of competition had been replaced by ministerial direction. Faced with special demands for vital war materials, or chronic shortages of vital supplies, the government had simply stepped in and taken over. If it had been sensible to plan the production of aircraft and munitions, why was it foolish to do the same with coal, gas and electricity, the essential weapons in the battle for greater output? The wartime coalition would not have contemplated leaving the development of the jet engine or the production of radar to private industry. Why, the argument ran, do we leave the profit motive to dominate the extension of new techniques and technologies which are essential to our peacetime success?

Above all, there was the question of unemployment. Conscription, and the direction of labour, had ensured that the war produced at least one benefit. Everybody had a job. Few people wanted the old regime of rigid regulation to continue, and there was immediate agitation for early demobilisation. But men and women with memories of 1918 were fearful of a swift return to the old free market in labour. They believed that the most likely result of that freedom would, for many ex-servicemen, be the liberty to sign on the dole.

7

There was something very near to a consensus that the economic dangers which lay ahead would only be overcome by a new view of economic management – or at least an attitude which, although not original, had been unacceptable to pre-war governments. Labour's great attraction was its determination to implement economic policies which, thanks to the war, had changed from the minority preoccupation of Fabian intellectuals and street-corner orators into what was generally regarded as the obvious way ahead.

The Labour government of 1945 was reinforced in its enthusiasm for a new start by what reforming politicians always need to give them confidence – an intellectual justification for the policies to which they were emotionally committed. In 1936, John Maynard Keynes had published his *General Theory of Employment, Interest and Money*. His prescription for full employment seemed – indeed, in the days of generally self-contained national economics, was – undeniably effective. All that was needed was a government which was prepared to accept the role of job creation. In 1942, Sir William Beveridge had published his *Report on Social Insurance and Allied Services*. It was both a product of the spirit of community which, by then, the war had begun to engender, and confirmation of the belief that nothing was impossible for a united nation. Between them the two texts became the social manuals of the age. Both pointed to the same political moral: improvement depended on active government.

The way ahead was certain to be hard. The failing economy of pre-war Britain had been devastated in the pursuit of victory. The once-greatest maritime nation in the world – hugely dependent on its invisible earnings – had lost 18 million tons of shipping, and many of the losses had not been replaced. In 1939, Britain and its colonies had owned 21.1 million tons; by 1945, the merchant fleet had shrunk to 15.9 million tons. Domestic capital had been depleted even more quickly. Over 210,000 houses had been destroyed by enemy action and 250,000 more made uninhabitable. Altogether four million homes – one-third of the total stock – had been destroyed, damaged or (because of no more than time's wear and tear) needed urgent repairs which had been postponed, in the phrase of the time, 'for the duration'. External assets, to the value of £1,000 million, had been sold to finance the war effort and, as a result, external liabilities had risen by £3,000 million. Most dangerous of all, potentially, consumption had been reduced by something between a fifth and a quarter. Personal living standards were lower in 1945 than they had been in 1939. The spirit of sacrifice and the belief that 'we can take it' had survived the victory over Nazi Germany. But little boys who longed for a banana and mothers who had grown tired of sacrificing their sweet rations to sons, believed that when the troops came home they would bring the end of austerity with them. The new government had to decide how long the mood of willing sacrifice would survive the war and the pressures of the pent-up demand which six years of siege economy had created.

The price which had been paid for victory – loss of the invisible earnings which had sustained Britain for so long, and the destruction of so much national capital – made the achievement of Labour's economic aims doubly difficult. The aims were modest. The preservation of wartime full employment was a moral imperative that the whole nation took for granted. The achievement of a balance of payments surplus on current account was a less emotionally charged, but no less urgent, objective. And the replacement of physical assets lost during the war was essential if the fourth aspiration – the restoration of living standards to their pre-war level – was to be achieved. Unfortunately, in the short term, the aims conflicted with each other. Concentrating resources on investment in plant and machinery, hospitals, houses and schools meant that consumption had to be held back. Rationing – which some optimists had assumed would end on the day of victory – had to be continued and, as it turned out, extended and intensified. But at least it was possible to draw a rough map of the road to recovery – assuming that there were no unexpected catastrophes along the way to victory over Japan. On 21 August, seven days after VJ Day, the unexpected catastrophe occurred. The British economy was the victim of what in more modern times has come to be called 'friendly fire'.

On 21 August 1945, Lee Crowley, head of the United States Foreign Assistance Administration, told President Harry S. Truman that Lend-Lease – America's financial help to her ally – was no longer legal. Congress had voted to finance economic aid to America's allies until the war was over, and it had been over for a week. Truman signed the order to cancel the programme without hesitation, discussion or consultation. Knowing that Lend-Lease could not last for ever, John Maynard Keynes was discussing, in an Anglo-American working party, what should take its place. American envoys in London, considering the economic rehabilitation of Europe, were told by the Foreign Office of their President's decision. Their deliberations were interrupted with the news that it was too late to negotiate a gradual run-down. Lend-Lease was over.

For Britain the consequences were potentially disastrous, and the damage was not purely economic. Lend-Lease had been an acceptable form of help – the debt that the British nation was owed for its special contribution to the war. When it came to a sudden end, a choice had to be made between two equally unpalatable alternatives. The government could have rejected all foreign aid and asked the people to accept a further fall in their already diminished standard of living, or it could have accepted charity from its more prosperous ally in the knowledge that American help was no longer a contribution to the war effort but alms for a poor relation. The decision to accept United States largesse intensified the psychological condition which was to prejudice British international policy for the next fifty years. Britain had come down in the world, and the injustice of the reduced status festered. The absolute belief in British superiority was unshakable. But there was a persistent fear that – since that special status was less visible than it had been during the reign of Victoria – there was no longer a universal recognition of how great that superiority was. Britain became a national version of Oscar Wilde's ingrate – incapable of forgiving those to whom it owed a debt of gratitude.

There was no choice but to accept American charity. The immediate loss of Lend-Lease was the equivalent of a sudden £2,000 million reduction in Britain's annual purchasing power – a near mortal blow to a damaged economy which was already having to balance the rival demands of investment and consumption. There were, however, ways of softening the impact. It was possible to reduce the gold and dollar reserves, and the rest of the Sterling Area (the countries of the Commonwealth and Empire who held their reserves in London) had the strongest possible vested interest in a healthy pound and could be relied on to underwrite a loan. But the Treasury estimated that, even when all the help was gathered in, another £1,000 million would still have to be found if Britain was to finance any sort of recovery programme. Truman – bitterly regretful that he had 'signed without asking' – was prepared to ask Congress to authorise a loan. Attlee had no choice. Keynes negotiated its terms in Washington during the autumn of 1945.

By the time the deal was done, the war against Japan was won and the peace was complete. An atomic bomb had been dropped on Hiroshima on 6 August 1945. Three days later a second bomb was dropped on Nagasaki. Mr Attlee made a brief announcement on the midnight news. The bomb had been an essentially American innovation, and Britain had been no more than notified of the intention to devastate the two Japanese cities. The morality of President Truman's decision has become one of history's great arguments. Critics claim that it was done for no better reason than to prevent the Soviet Union from enjoying a part in the certain victory, while the President insisted that more lives would have been lost in months of savage conventional warfare. One thing is, however, certain – the development and use of an atomic bomb changed the world. Once nuclear weapons began to proliferate – proving wrong the arrogant assertion that only American technology could split the atom – foreign policy was never the same again. A new terror, and a new symbol of international status, had to be accommodated within conventional diplomacy. And the economies of East and West had to finance both innovations.

The American loan was, by many standards, a generous deal. A $3,750 million credit was to be repaid over fifty years at an annual rate of interest of 2 per cent – a comparatively modest figure even in the age of cheap money. All outstanding Lend-Lease debts were cancelled, and an extra $650 million was provided to pay for aid in transit since or promised on VJ Day. There was even a waiver which allowed Britain to default on interest payments in years when they were greater than the UK's earnings in foreign exchange. But there was a price to be paid. The pound had to become fully convertible with the dollar within a year of the loan agreement being signed. For good or ill Britain was becoming – if not part of America's economic empire – a semi-autonomous dominion.

There was no alternative to accepting the loan other than to ask a war-weary nation to continue the years of unremitting, and perhaps deepening, austerity, and the British people might well have regarded that request as intolerable. Between 1939 and 1945, post-tax savings had risen from 5 per cent to 25 per cent of disposable income, and the people believed that the time had come to spend their money. Demand, which had willingly been held back when the Germans were in Calais, could not be restrained indefinitely. Attempting to depress it even further by exhortation and regulation was, in 1945, regarded as too great a risk. In any case, the Labour government had a duty to maintain, and if possible improve, living standards. The nation which had stood alone had suffered enough.

Enlightened opinion was firmly in favour of convertibility. It was a step towards the integration of the Sterling Area and the dollar bloc. Sooner or later, Britain would have to emerge from the collapsing cocoon of the Commonwealth and Empire. But – as the British government was to discover time after time during the next fifty years – the chance to change gear and status rarely comes at the right time. Long-term benefits have to be reconciled with short-term penalties. Keynes, echoing St Augustine, advised convertibility – but not yet.

Britain had edged towards an integration of the dollar and the pound since the early years of the war. In 1941, the Atlantic Charter had promised 'equal access, on equal terms, to trade raw materials'. The Bretton Woods agreement of 1944 had included (among its plans for a New World Economic Order) the promise of a reduction of tariffs and an integration of currencies. But it was more politics than precedents that made convertibility irresistible. Truman was convinced that only the promise of a liberalisation of trade would persuade Congress to endorse a massive loan to a government which – at least according to the *Wall Street Journal* – was determined to abolish private enterprise. Attlee, as was his habit, did his best in the circumstances. When he visited Washington in November 1945, he addressed a joint session of Congress, and his speech there included a child's guide to democratic socialism:

> I think that some people over here imagine that the socialists are out to destroy freedom, freedom for the individual, freedom of speech, freedom of religion and freedom of the press. They are wrong . . . We in the Labour Party declare that we are in line with those who fought for Magna Carta and *habeas corpus*, with the Pilgrim Fathers and with the signatories of the Declaration of Independence. There is, and always will be, scope for enterprise; but when big business gets too powerful, so it becomes monopolistic, we hold it not safe to leave it in private hands.

It was the sort of *apologia pro vita sua* that mendicant Prime Ministers have to make and, as such things go, it was a remarkably dignified plea for understanding and $3,750 million. The loan was agreed with the proviso that Britain accepted the obligation to implement all the clauses of the Bretton Woods accords – including the creation of the World Bank and the International Monetary Fund. Keynes judged that the eventual outcome would be a new era of international economic stability. The loan became effective on 15 July 1946 on the understanding that the pound and the dollar would be convertible one year later. Hugh Dalton, the Chancellor of the Exchequer, was certain that he would not have to invoke the postponement clause, for 'the pound could look the dollar in the face'.

Dalton's mindless optimism undoubtedly appealed to the British people, who wanted to believe that Britain could soon recover its economic independence. The enthusiasm for a change in domestic policy was overwhelming. But when Britain looked at the rest of the world there was a natural, though disastrous, inclination to re-live the glories of the past rather than face the dangers of an uncertain future. Nobody could reasonably expect the first post-war government to redefine Britain's international role immediately. The extraordinary fact is that there was no lonely prophet preaching the importance of accepting the status of a medium-sized power which could no longer, either militarily or economically, go it alone.

Despite the predictable howls of rage from the extreme left wing of the Labour Party, when the House of Commons debated the American loan, the Tory Opposition seemed far more divided than the government. Churchill, to the fury of the Tory die-hards (who could never be reconciled to the end of the tariff on 'foreign' food euphemistically called Commonwealth Preference), advised his supporters to abstain. They split three ways – eight voted for, seventy-one against and one hundred and eighteen sat on their hands, as their leader had recommended. Robert Boothby announced: 'We have sold the empire for a packet of cigarettes.' But his flamboyant patriotism was more of an embarrassment to Winston Churchill (his old mentor) than it was to his natural adversary, Clement Attlee. Labour was lucky that, at a moment of unavoidable vulnerability, it faced a Tory party in total disarray.

There are many different explanations of why the Tory party performed so badly during the autumn and winter of 1945. But much of the blame undoubtedly lies with Churchill himself who, despite urging new Tory MPs 'never to give the enemy any respite', was not suited either by temperament or experience to sustain a continuous assault on a government which, after its first year in office, was able to boast that it had introduced seventy-three Bills and that fifty-three of them were already law. He attended the House only spasmodically, held irregular Shadow Cabinet meetings over lunch at The Savoy, and intervened in debates without warning his colleagues who had been nominated to speak for the Opposition or bothering about whether what he said was consistent with what passed for Tory policy. Not that much policy existed – a normal problem for the Tories when they are suddenly and unexpectedly ejected from office. But Churchill had to deal with a unique political liability. The Labour Party, for the first time in its history, reflected popular opinion.

The welfare programme, which – together with Indian independence and freedom for Pakistan – marked out the Attlee government as the great reforming administration of the twentieth century, was part of a trend towards comprehensive social security which had begun almost fifty years earlier. Destitute children had received free school meals since 1906. Trade boards had been established to fix minimum wage levels in 'sweated' industries as early as 1908. 'Old-age pensions' dated back to 1909, and the 1911 National Insurance Act introduced the notion of contributory payments which financed unemployment benefit 'as of right' and provided medical care for workers 'on the panel'. The Family Allowance Act (implemented by Labour at the rate of twenty-five pence for the second and every subsequent child) was the product of legislation introduced while the wartime coalition was in office. The Beveridge Report – on which the plans for post-war social security had been based and built – was written in anticipation of Allied victory over the Axis powers, not the Labour triumph which followed the defeat of Nazi Germany. Labour's two great welfare Bills were the climax, though not the culmination, of a process that had begun shortly after the party had been founded.

The National Insurance Act of 1946 – pensions as well as sickness and unemployment benefit – made social security genuinely comprehensive. And the National Assistance Act (passed two years later) offered help to those families which, for one reason or another, were not adequately protected by national insurance. They were both historic contributions to the creation of a civilised society. And the decision to make payment in full from the day that the scheme came into force – rather than phasing-in the benefits, as Beveridge himself had recommended – confirmed Attlee's willingness to decide his own priorities and, when he believed the risk to be justified, give precedence to conscience and compassion over financial probity. But they were not the product of sudden original thinking – one of the 'big ideas' so much admired and so often demanded by fashionable commentators in the 1980s. Labour was finishing a task which had begun – tentatively and haphazardly – many years before 1945.

The same was true of medical care. The wartime coalition's White Paper had promised a health service which ensured that 'every man, woman and child can rely on getting the advice and treatment they need', irrespective of the ability to pay. That promise was made good by Aneurin Bevan. And it is highly unlikely that, in the economic circumstances of the mid-1940s, a Tory government would have done the same. But the idea – whether or not it had been implemented in 1948 – was not new. It can be plausibly argued that Bevan's character was crucial to Labour's success. He charmed some of the doubting doctors and he intimidated the rest. But the British Medical Association recalcitrants knew that their militant members were not just in conflict with the Minister of Health. They were standing out against history. Even before the 1945 General Election, the idea of 'free' medical care had grown in popularity to a point at which it was irresistible. Within a couple of years of its creation, the National Health Service had achieved the special position in the national imagination that provokes myths and encourages fantasies. Opponents of socialised medicine told stories of bogus patients stuffing cushions with free cotton wool obtained on prescription. More dangerously, supporters prophesied with sublime certainty that, as the population grew more healthy, the cost of the NHS would fall. Within weeks of its creation, the Health Service was second only to the royal family as Britain's most popular institution.

Churchill approached that truth – in a grudging, biased and typically partisan fashion – when he told a Tory women's conference in April 1948 that 'all these schemes were devised and set in motion in the days before the socialists came into office'. It was a grotesque exaggeration. For, as every politician knows, there is an immense difference between floating a popular idea and, by implementing it, accepting the costs and consequences. But the claim to have been the only true begetter of the welfare state was an admission of how popular the government's programme had become. Socialism, in its modest Labour Party pattern, seemed tailor-made to suit the British taste. And the approval extended far beyond the social programme – there was genuine support for Labour's economic prescription as well.

The Labour government which led Britain into the perilous peace was reformist, not revolutionary. Its leader, although in domestic affairs a genuine radical, took a wholly pragmatic view about the best way to build a better society. Believing that Labour was 'the one party most nearly that reflects in its representation and composition all the main streams that flow through the great rivers of our national life', he took it for granted that his view on economic management

16

reflected the innate common sense of a practical people: 'Private interest and public interest should be mingled in our planning. We are not suggesting that the profit motive should not happen at all. On the contrary, we have two great sectors of industry. One sector is nationalised and the other is in private hands.' It was a view of economic management which owed very little to ideology, and it represented a judgement about the proper balance of ownership towards which Britain had been edging since the turn of the century.

At the 1944 Labour party conference, the National Executive – with the smell of an election already in its nostrils – had proposed no more public ownership than the nationalisation of the Bank of England. But the rank and file had felt differently. An amendment, moved by Ian Mikardo, who was to be a thorn in the leadership's flesh for the next forty years, was carried by an overwhelming majority. It ensured that, when the manifesto was written, coal, gas, electricity, civil aviation, the railways and steel would all be added to the list. Herbert Morrison – who is now regarded as the principal advocate of the 'state corporation' – told Mikardo that he had 'just lost us the General Election'. Presumably, Morrison feared that Clause IV of the Labour Party's constitution ('To secure for the workers by hand or by brain the full fruits of their industry and the most equitable distribution thereof that may be possible on the basis of the common ownership of the means of production, distribution and exchange . . .') was too dogmatic for the voters' taste. The founder of the London Passenger Transport Board had forgotten that Britain was already on a slow march to a mixed economy.

In 1919, the Sankey Commission (chaired by a High Court Judge of Conservative inclination) had produced four reports on the future of the coal industry. The one which Lord Sankey himself had signed recommended nationalisation. The 1921 Railway Act amalgamated 120 railway companies into four regional enterprises, and the new corporations were effectively subsidised by rate reductions. The Chancellor of the Exchequer (one Winston Churchill) required them to pass on their subsidy to coal and steel producers by way of reduced freight tariffs. The Heyworth Committee (over which the chairman of Unilever presided) recommended public ownership for gas, and the

Scott Report (delivered to the coalition government) proposed nationalisation of electricity. It was more than the size of Labour's majority that carried the nationalisation legislation through the House of Commons – in the case of the Bank of England Bill, without the Tories even voting against the Second Reading and Robert Boothby (the scourge of the American loan) actually voting in favour. Had the Tories fought a sustained rearguard action against the advance of the mixed economy, they would have alienated thousands of the voters who, although they remained loyal to the Conservative party even in Labour's landslide victory of 1945, had been seduced by the ideas for which Labour stood. Obvious though the Conservative dilemma was, it was not recognised by many of the knights of the shires who sat on the opposition back-benches.

In November 1945, complaints from the 1922 Committee of Tory back-benchers provoked Churchill into reluctant yet precipitous action. The Tories announced that they would move a motion of 'No Confidence' in the government. When it was debated on 5 December, Attlee treated Churchill like an ignorant and argumentative schoolboy. Even Labour MPs were astounded by the spectacle of the great wartime leader being not so much beaten as thrashed in debate by the man whom he had described as 'modest, and with a lot to be modest about'. Churchill had nothing constructive to say. Although he understood that time had passed his policies by, he was not personally equipped to invent new ways of taking his party back into the political mainstream. His most radical suggestion was a change of name – always the last refuge of beleaguered party leaders. Conservative, he feared, sounded too like a commitment to re-create a dead and discredited past. Unfortunately 'Unionist', the alternative which he believed emphasised a belief in one nation, had already been appropriated by Ulstermen who wanted to preserve the link between Great Britain and Northern Ireland. So the idea was abandoned. Had it been adopted, it might have helped the ageing giant to remember which party he led and avoided the lapse of memory which caused him to declare, 'Socialists attack capital, Liberals attack monopoly.' Fortunately for the Tories, there were also more constructive suggestions of ways by which the party could ease to the left.

At moments of crisis, the Conservative instinct is always to steal its opponents' policies. The problem was how to do it without the more bone-headed members of the 1922 Committee complaining that their party was drifting to the left. The Tories needed a man who was clever, subtle and piously devious.

Cometh the hour, cometh R. A. Butler. The man whom Churchill had despised during the war for wanting to be Minister of Education was invited to reinvigorate the moribund Conservative Research Department. Among the men he recruited – partly to work on new policies and partly to form a Shadow Cabinet secretariat – were three future Cabinet ministers, Iain Macleod, Reginald Maudling and Enoch Powell. 'Rab' Butler's aim of bringing the Tory party 'to terms with the mixed economy' was further assisted by his appointment as chairman of the Industrial Policy Committee. The inclusion among its members of both genuine Tory grandees and Harold Macmillan, the unrepentant author of *The Middle Way* – the restatement of 'one-nation' Conservatism which some of his colleagues regarded as blatant socialism – proved less of a handicap to progress than the modernisers feared. The main problem was Churchill's own injunction that 'no detailed policies are to be published' – a prohibition that made a Somerville undergraduate (by the name of Margaret Roberts) complain that 'at the moment, Conservative means no more than anti-socialist'. Thirty years before she became Prime Minister, Margaret Thatcher was a conviction politician.

In May 1947, her hope of a 'clear and unified statement of policy' was at least partially gratified. Butler published the party's Industrial Charter. With the exception of steel and road haulage (the two profit-making industries in Labour's public ownership programme), it accepted the government's nationalisation plans as necessary to the national interest. When the young Reggie Maudling was asked to provide five lines on the Charter for the leader's conference speech, the draft which he prepared was examined by the great man in sullen silence. Then, looking over his glasses, Churchill announced, 'But I don't agree with a word of it.' Notwithstanding his reservations, he included in his address the endorsement of Butler's conversion to public ownership. Maudling noticed that he read the passage with an obvious lack of conviction. But he read it. So for the next three years, Conservative attacks on the Labour government were almost always concerned with the performance of men rather than the propriety of measures. Afraid to attack the Labour government's ideas, Churchill chose to question the competence with which they were carried out. Fate provided him with three perfect opportunities to claim that socialists were, by nature, unfit to govern.

Britain, proudly bearing the burden of both imperial and occupying power, was responsible for the supply of grain to India and Germany. In the spring of 1946, German stocks of wheat were within fourteen days of running out, and India was at the edge of widespread famine. Sir Ben Smith, Labour's Minister of Food, resigned – officially because of age and overwork. But it was widely known that he believed that bread rationing in Britain was necessary to prevent 'widespread disaffection and discontent and possibly, in some places, bread riots'. He was also offended by the Cabinet's decision that Herbert Morrison should be the government's emissary to Washington and negotiate, 'at Prime Minister level', for more American grain.

Opponents of bread rationing within the Cabinet – notably Morrison himself and Ernest Bevin, who believed that he understood the psychology of the British working man – argued that rationing was probably unnecessary and certainly politically disastrous. Almost two years after the end of the war, Britain was so short of food that Sir William Early, a senior Treasury official, had offered to barter the British-owned Argentine railways in return for beef. Bananas had become such a national joke that sightings were reported in national newspapers and exotically-named tinned fish had become a much sought-after staple food. Bread rationing seemed likely to be the last straw.

Certainly there were a number of uncharacteristically charitable men and women who were positively anxious to make a further sacrifice. Victor Gollancz – speaking with the special authority of a Jew – founded the 'Save Europe Now' movement and told a packed meeting at the Albert Hall that the German people could not be left to starve. Sixty thousand supporters of Gollancz's initiative volunteered to accept a cut in their war rations so that more food parcels could be sent to the defeated enemy. But they were not typical. Morrison believed that the Washington negotiations were crucial to the government's future.

The Americans agreed to send grain to India and accepted that the supplies which they sent to Germany should be available, according to greatest need, in both the US and British zones. But the United Kingdom had a price to pay. A 200,000-ton shipment of wheat scheduled for September would be cancelled. The crisis had been postponed, but bread rationing had become inevitable. On 27 June 1946, John Strachey, the new Minister for Food, announced that a month later all adults – with the exception of some manual workers – would receive nine ounces of bread a week. At the Bexley by-election a month later, the Conservative candidate, Colonel Lockwood, cut the Labour majority from almost 11,000 to barely 2,000.

Naturally the Conservatives blamed the need for bread rationing on 'socialist ineptitude'. But the damage to the government's reputation would have been minimal had it not been for a second crisis, which began as an Act of God and was prolonged by an act of folly. Emmanuel Shinwell, the Minister of Fuel and Power, had been warned that the gap between the demand and supply of coal might grow to two or even three million tons. Instead of pressing the pits to increase output, he gambled on a mild winter.

In the last week of January 1947, blizzards followed by eight days and nights of continuous frost marked the beginning of the worst spell of weather since 1881. Coal supplies ran out. The crisis could not have come at a worse political moment. On the first day of the year, crowds had stood outside pit yards all over England to watch the unfurling of the flags which marked 'vesting day'. Notices, fastened to the gates, proclaimed: 'This colliery is managed on behalf of the people, by the National Coal Board.' Nationalisation, which had only come into force a couple of weeks before the big freeze, took the blame for the closed factories and cold homes.

The House of Commons debated the fuel crisis on 5 February. Shinwell, instructed by Attlee to abandon his usual vacuous optimism and tell the country the hard facts, set out emergency measures which echoed round Parliament and the country 'like a thunder-clap'. Some power stations would close so that available coal supplies could be concentrated on others. 'Control orders' rationed the supply of domestic electricity to limited hours each day. As an immediate result, two million workers were laid off. Within a fortnight, unemployment had risen to 2.5 million. Then the weather improved, coal was mined and moved and, five weeks after the February debate, unemployment was down to three-quarters of a million. But the political damage had been done. The most damaging slogan was 'Starve with Strachey and Freeze with Shinwell'. When the Minister of Fuel and Power became Secretary of State for War, the *Daily Express* offered a note of hope: 'If he maintains his record, we won't have any war, either.'

The brief shortages of bread and coal might well have been forgotten had they not been followed by a more lasting crisis which, being inevitable, the government should have anticipated. The pound and the dollar had been edging towards convertibility throughout the early months of 1947. Indeed the movement had been so swift and so smooth that Hugh Dalton, the Chancellor of the Exchequer, saw no reason to invoke the clause in the agreement which allowed the free market in pounds and dollars to be postponed. But the drain on sterling could not be sustained indefinitely. With the reserves running low and getting perilously near to running out, Dalton resisted calls to suspend convertibility on the principle that government intervention would do immense long-term harm to confidence. On 6 August, a Transitional Powers Bill prepared the way for improved long-term economic performance (Labour governments always hope to expand the economy out of trouble). The pits were to work longer hours. Steel production was to be expanded. Unessential imports were prohibited. Demobilisation was accelerated so that 80,000 ex-servicemen joined the overstretched labour market. But it was not enough. On 20 August, convertibility was suspended.

The sequence of three 'crises' at roughly six-month intervals – bread, coal and sterling – was certainly damaging to the government's reputation. And although Churchill continued to mount his assault on Labour's competence rather than the concept of common responsibility and collective action, some of the blame rubbed off on to the ideas of planning and partnership. As always, the opponents of planning and partnership blurred the distinction between the conflicting definitions of socialism. But Labour's attacks on Russian foreign policy were themselves so strident that the intellectual assaults on Soviet Communism – Arthur Koestler's *The Yogi and the Commissar*, Victor Kravchenko's *I Chose Freedom* and George Orwell's *Animal Farm* – did little or nothing to harm the still good name of social democracy. And Churchill's reaction to Friedrich von Hayek and *The Road to Serfdom* was that although the author was 'a clever chap' it 'couldn't happen here'. However, the fuel crisis did either provoke or coincide with the first great assaults on the 'new politics' of the Labour government – John Jewkes's *Ordeal by Planning* was a frontal attack on the notion of the regulated economy; Roy Harrod's *Are These Hardships Necessary?* appealed to those men and women who had grown impatient with sacrifice. The rush to publish marked the end of the ideological truce. The case for collectivism was still accepted by the vast majority of the British people, but the annoyance caused by three brief emergencies – critics of the government called them 'crises' – made it possible for a brave minority to dispute an idea which, since the end of the war, had been beyond question.

The government, untroubled by such doubts, continued to advocate the merits of co-operation and consensus. 'What we require,' said Attlee, 'are not plans conceived by a government in isolation, implemented by compulsion, but plans worked out in consultation with both sides of industry and willingly carried out under the general guidance of the government.' It was the beginning of what came to be called 'democratic planning' – the process by which government co-operates with industry in defining economic aims and working towards their achievement. Although the three crises had tarnished the government's sparkling reputation, the idea of collective, indeed corporate, action was strong enough to survive the temporary unpopularity of the ministers who proposed it. Sir Clive Baillieu, the President of the Federation of British Industry, was explicit about the need for co-operation: 'We want a broad measure of agreement' between all the parties to economic recovery.

Over the next four years, the government created the institutions through which that broad agreement might be achieved. Fifteen joint working parties were set up to examine the performance of individual industries. Anglo-American Productivity Councils compared efficiency on the two sides of the Atlantic. A National Production Advisory Council was created. Regional Boards for Industry and Development Councils were founded. They were the institutions of co-operation, the bureaucratic manifestations of the mixed economy. In one form or another – NEDYs and NEDOs, Three Wise Men, Guiding Lights and NEDCs – they continued for forty years and, while they remained, the idea of economic consensus prospered.

The idea that working together was the secret of success seemed, in the years which followed the war, too obviously true to be a matter of political controversy. The spirit – not to say the economic and social organisation – of the age conspired to confirm that collective effort and action was the national pattern of life. Mutual endeavour seemed less the pattern of the good life than the normal instinct of the human race. After the war, men and women worked together not because of a pious belief that they were all 'members one of another' but because – as even the trivia of their daily lives confirmed – *homo sapiens* is a gregarious species.

Fifty years earlier, the grandparents of the men who came home from the Second World War had made their entertainment at home. Forty years later, the grandchildren of the women who kept the home fires burning enjoyed themselves by sitting in front of flickering television screens. But in the ten years which followed the war, pleasure was a collective activity. Families queued outside cinemas and then sat in row on row in circle and stalls. Football grounds were filled with spectators who stood, shoulder to shoulder and well behaved, in the rain. Holiday camps were the summer rage. Campers ate together in huge dining-rooms, danced together in the evenings and left their children in the nurseries and crèches so that they could enjoy all the fun of a giant party. The collective pleasures – and the collective spirit which they encouraged – were essentially part of working-class life. In the late 1940s British society was neither equal nor mobile. Both home life and work encouraged the belief in pulling together. The cult of individualism – like the political domination of the middle classes – was still a quarter of a century away.

At work, women – 'emancipated' by the war – sat in front of great conveyer belts and picked bad peas from the crop that rolled its way into the canning plants, or wrapped copper wire round the armatures which would become the hearts of starter-motors. The men who came home from the battlefields worked in factories, collieries and shipyards, often earning bonuses which were dependent on the performance of a whole department or shift and, as trade unionists bound by collective agreements, almost always negotiating their pay as a group rather than as individuals. It was the age of solidarity. Working together was not so much the essential recipe for success as the obvious way to behave.

Economically, the three crises of 1947 had widely different effects. The bread shortage did not even have a passing influence on national prosperity. The fuel crisis – which seemed at the time to be a major industrial disaster – almost turned out to be as beneficial to the economy as it was damaging to the government. Shortage of power grievously reduced industrial output during that spring, and the effects of the slow-down were felt well into the summer. But once the generators were working again, the spirit of the time (which included years of pent-up demand) ensured that massive efforts were made to recover the lost production. Industrial output showed what economists called an 'exaggerated increase' in 1948, and the boost given by that sudden stimulus helped to prime the pump for the great post-war up-swing in production which, looking back, we now know began in the summer of 1947.

It did not seem so at the time. In the summer of 1947, foreign bankers, anticipating devaluation, began to sell sterling. Britain's gold and dollar reserves withstood the pressure without much difficulty. It was the earliest example of the price that Britain had to pay for overvaluing the pound on the international market. And therein lies the tragedy of the hot summer in which Denis Compton scored 3,816 runs. Neither party learned the lesson that a country of Britain's size cannot isolate itself from the rest of the world. Until the revolution in information technology made exchange control literally impossible, it was within the government's power to influence the exchange rate and protect the reserves. But that show of independence carried with it enormous penalties. Keeping the pound strong and free involved the constant depression of the economy. Britain should have found that out three years after the war ended, but it was almost impossible to accept the idea that we must play a permanently subservient role to countries with stronger currencies. Accepting a few years' help as recompense for our good war was just about politically acceptable. Abandoning sterling's special place in the world economy was not.

Despite the national desire to preserve Britain's world role, in 1945 the British people were at least prepared to lose the jewel in the imperial crown. It may be that they were weary of the trouble and apparent expense involved in retaining that restless outpost of Empire. It is even possible that in that radical hour, they believed it right that a whole sub-continent should decide its own destiny. Whatever the reason, the end of the Raj was accepted with hardly a dissenting voice. Not even Winston Churchill – the great India rebel of the 1930s – voted against the proposition. It was a tactical triumph for the Labour government, which completed the move to independence at such a speed that the deed was done before the national mood changed. Its long-term historical significance was as important for Britain as it was for India and Pakistan. A nation, obsessed with its glorious past, began to look realistically towards its uncertain future. The processes by which independence was agreed and granted illustrated the Labour government's determination, in at least this one international particular, to move with the times.

For most of the war, the coalition government had thought of India in purely strategic terms. The Japanese, marching westward, had captured Burma and, for a time, it was feared that they would strike towards Assam. Although thousands of Indians, most of them Sikhs and Muslims, fought with the British Army, the predominantly Hindu Congress Party had called for a total boycott of the war effort, and Mahatma Gandhi – dismissed by Winston Churchill as a 'half-naked fakir' – had traded insult for insult by describing the offer of future independence in return for military co-operation as 'a post-dated cheque to be drawn on a failing bank'. In August 1942, the Congress leaders were interned – with the full support of Clement Attlee, who believed them to be 'in a state of treason against the Crown'. However, the Labour leader never flinched from the long-held conviction that India must be free. In the House of Commons in October 1942, he summed up the dilemma of self-government in two typically succinct and characteristically sardonic sentences: 'Running through all political life in India there is a desire for self-government with which we all sympathise. The trouble is, they do not all desire to be governed by the same people.'

When the Japanese threat to India abated, Whitehall and Westminster lost, or at least temporarily mislaid, their interest in the sub-continent. Field Marshal Sir Archibald Wavell – the hero of the first North African campaign who had been kicked upstairs into the Viceroy's palace – began first to fret and then to agitate. In early 1945, the Congress leaders were released from gaol to allow the creation of a constitutional conference. Five weeks before the British General Election, twenty-one delegates met in Simla with authority to examine ways of progressing towards Dominion Status. After three weeks of desultory discussion, the conference foundered on Mohammed Ali Jinnah's insistence that all the Islamic members should be nominated by his Muslim League. The sub-continent which Labour inherited was hungry, divided and on the point of open revolt. To the new government 'giving India its freedom' was an article of faith.

Attlee's interest in India, and his commitment to independence, dated back to 1927, when he was appointed a member of the Simon Commission, set up to examine the working of the 1919 India Act. The Labour Party of the day was deeply suspicious of his willingness to serve on an all-party enquiry, and Attlee himself – for both public and private reasons – was reluctant to spend months away from Britain. But he believed in duty and service and, concluding that it was his duty to serve, he joined the Commission and developed views on India which, twenty years later, began the slow dissolution of the British Empire.

The new Prime Minister despised the old Viceroy, whose plans, Attlee believed, had always failed because they offered India far too little and, even then, offered it grudgingly. Wavell himself got near to admitting his unsuitability for the mighty task which confronted him. Political negotiation was 'entirely foreign to military training', and despairing of ever finding a solution acceptable to all the parties, he prepared what he openly entitled the 'Breakdown Plan'. Although it was built around the assumption that attempts to negotiate a settlement would continue, it anticipated the moment when there would be no alternative to a British evacuation, leaving India in anarchy and chaos. True to character, Attlee found the Breakdown Plan 'utterly repugnant'. India, he explained, needed a new Viceroy because 'we weren't getting anywhere. Both parties were asking for everything and blaming us for getting nothing when they should have blamed themselves.'

The new Viceroy was Viscount Mountbatten of Burma, sometime Supreme Allied Commander in South-east Asia, cousin to the King and a glamorous figure of the sort that Attlee usually suspected and disliked. But throughout his life he regarded the choice of Mountbatten as a master-stroke which, with uncharacteristic lack of modesty, he later described as 'my own thought entirely'. He explained with admirable clarity why: 'Mountbatten had been the obvious choice. The so-called experts had been wrong about Aung San and Dickie had been right.' Aung San was a Burmese nationalist who, accepting the promise of post-war independence, had sided with the Japanese invaders and commanded a battalion of Burmese irregulars in the war against the Allied forces. Despairing of either Japan keeping its word or the Allies losing the war, he changed sides and organised an underground resistance movement. Then, with encouragement from Mountbatten, he overthrew the puppet government. Despite being told to keep Aung San at arm's length, the Supreme Commander had prepared him to be the figure around which independence was built – a policy which showed courage, magnanimity, foresight, pragmatism and cool judgement. It also demonstrated a willingness to accept the world as it is rather than as he would like it to be. That willingness was essential to speedy progress towards Indian independence. And Attlee was determined on speed. Although the Viceroy was brand-new, the policy which he had first to pursue was essentially second-hand. Attlee had not quite abandoned hope of granting independence to a single state – Muslim, Hindu and Sikh. And while he was certain that a deadline must be set for the end to negotiations, he had not decided how early that deadline should be.

Mountbatten became one of the most controversial characters in post-war Britain. Detractors have blamed him for the tragedies which followed independence – particularly the massacres of something like half a million men, women and children. Admirers have claimed that most of the crucial decisions – the date of Indian independence and the creation of Islamic Pakistan – were, if not his alone, at least the result of his inspiration. Attlee was not a man to take part in demeaning competitions for the plaudits of history. The facts speak for themselves and for him.

Certainly Mountbatten asked for what Attlee described with some surprise as 'plenipotentiary powers'. They were granted because they were essential to the speed of action on which the government insisted. Almost immediately after his arrival in New Delhi on 22 March 1947, Mountbatten telegraphed the government: 'Unless I act quickly, I may find a real civil war on my hands.' But by 19 April, he had given up all hope of maintaining 'one India'. So he drew up a partition plan as his 'last shot'. It exploded in his face.

Mountbatten's original idea was to allow each Indian state to decide its own destiny by referendum. Prudently or recklessly – the adverb depends on individual judgement – the Viceroy gave early sight of his plan to Jawaharlal Nehru, the leader of the Congress Party and his personal friend. Nehru described his proposals as 'the Balkanisation of India' and they were swiftly dropped. So Mountbatten fired one more shot. His final plan was to have two states, one India and the other Pakistan ('the land of the pure'). The boundary between the two (which, in deference to the 'last-shot plan' and the principle of self-determination, was initially to be decided by plebiscite) was drawn up by a Commission under the chairmanship of Sir Cyril Radcliffe, an English barrister.

It has since been argued by Mountbatten's detractors that because of his close (and his wife's even closer) friendship with Nehru, the boundary between India and Pakistan was gerrymandered. The truth will never be known. It is, for example, easy enough to demonstrate that Firozpur was an Islamic city. But it is impossible to be sure if its destiny and destination was changed between the provisional map and the Commission's final recommendation because of Mountbatten's prejudiced determination to keep the military arsenal away from the Muslims, or Radcliffe's rational judgement that irrigation of the Hindu state of Bikaner could not be left dependent on rivers that rose across the borders in a foreign land. With Mountbatten it is always hard to separate the myth from reality. The important fact is that the government was prepared, for the sake of speed, to leave such questions to the Viceroy.

The controversy continues about the date which was decided for partition and independence, even though the basic facts are beyond dispute. As early as December 1946, the India Committee of the Cabinet – convinced by Attlee of the need for swift action – agreed 'that Parliament shall be asked to hand over power to India not later than 31 March 1948'. It happened more than seven months before that date.

Mountbatten, having abandoned hope of a united India and having obtained Cabinet approval for partition, announced the government's intention during a radio broadcast on 3 June and held a press conference in New Delhi on the following day. Inevitably, he was asked the date of the hand-over. To the surprise of his audience (and the consternation of the India Office when the news reached London), he replied, 'I think that the transfer could be about 15 August.' He was later to claim that he chose the date himself. And he got very near to admitting that he chose it on the spot. Neither the claim nor the admission tells the full story.

Mountbatten's aide recorded in his diary: 'Mr Attlee . . . has assumed full personal responsibility for the government's India policy and any action arising from it [and] has successfully injected a sense of the utmost urgency into his colleagues.' When the Secretary of State for India proposed repudiating the August deadline, the Prime

Minister wrote on the bottom of his draft telegram 'Accept Viceroy's proposal'. Perhaps 15 August was a date plucked out of the Delhi air. But the idea of concluding the business by the high summer was undoubtedly Attlee's. He felt no more obligation to tell his Secretary of State about the date of independence than he had felt a duty to consult or inform him about the appointment of the new Viceroy. He was a practical man and he had to increase the pressure on political leaders – in India and Britain.

The House of Commons gave the India Bill an unopposed Second Reading on 10 July. Four days later, its Committee Stage having been completed, it was given an unopposed Third Reading. It became law after Royal Assent on the 18th, and the date of Independence was set as 15 August. Parliament had taken a little more than a week to end the Raj which had lasted for almost three hundred years and, because of the speed with which the government had acted, Aneurin Bevan's hope – set out to the Cabinet on New Year's Eve, 1945 – had been achieved:

> Withdrawal from India need not appear to be forced on us by our weakness . . . On the contrary, the action must be shown to be the logical conclusion, which we welcome, of a policy followed by successive governments for many years. There was no occasion to excuse our withdrawal. We should rather take credit for claiming these initiatives.

The Labour government had done what it did best. It had caught the post-war mood of the nation, built on it and moved Britain along towards a new view of its future. Tragically, it did not act with the same open-minded courage when it considered other aspects of Britain's place in the post-war world.

India was – as far as the United States was concerned – essentially Britain's own affair, a topic which did not even appear on its foreign policy agenda. Notwithstanding that, American isolationism was over – certainly for the next fifty years and possibly for ever. Nineteen forty-five was the year when the United States became a European power as Britain had been an African power in the nineteenth century. Washington no longer simply sent men and materials to protect friends against sudden aggression or to maintain stability. America accepted – indeed insisted – that it had a permanent interest in both the military balance and economic performance of half the world. It has never been possible to decide where the economic commitment ended and the military involvement began, but the permanent extension of both sorts of influence began with an act of admirable British realism.

On 21 February 1947, His Majesty's Ambassador in Washington officially notified the State Department of a policy decision which the Americans had anticipated and feared for some months. The United Kingdom – desperate to cut military expenditure – was to withdraw its forces from Turkey and Greece immediately. Two years earlier, Greece had been engulfed in a bitter civil war between Royalists and Communists. The United States government was not prepared to leave a vacuum in the Mediterranean. It set in train a series of initiatives which climaxed and culminated in the Marshall Plan.

Three weeks after Britain announced that it was to leave the east Mediterranean, President Truman asked Congress to approve an assistance payment of $400 million for Greece and Turkey. The argument with which he justified his request – 'The United States must support free people who are resisting subjugation by armed minorities or outside pressure . . . primarily through economic and financial aid' – came to be called the Truman Doctrine. On 8 May 1947 it was expanded in a speech at Cleveland by Dean Acheson, Under-Secretary of State, Europhile and constant advocate of American involvement in Europe. It promised to make the 'stricken countries of Europe . . . self-supporting'. Undoubtedly, credit or blame for *Pax Americanus* – dollar imperialism or altruistic sacrifice – lies with Acheson. But, as is so often the case when the deputy does the thinking, the definitive speech – which set out the principles and described the future practice – was made by his superior. At Harvard on 5 June, Secretary of State George Marshall promised that any government willing to assist in the task of recovery will find full co-operation . . . from the United States . . . Our policy is directed not against any country or doctrine, but against hunger, poverty, desperation and chaos. It would be neither fitting nor efficacious for this government to undertake to draw unilaterally a programme designed to place Europe on its feet economically. This is the business of the Europeans. The initiative must come from Europe.

According to the myth, British Foreign Secretary Ernest Bevin knew nothing of Marshall's Harvard speech until, listening in bed to his radio, he heard it reported on the BBC's late-night news. Certainly the British Embassy in Washington did not send a copy of the advance news release to London. But Bevin knew that such an offer was to be made, and he had been warned that Marshall would expect a near-immediate response.

Bevin took the initiative in co-ordinating Europe's reaction. But he judged it best that Britain should not assume the public leadership of the assorted mendicants. So he suggested that Georges Bidault, the French Foreign Minister, should arrange a meeting of the European 'big three' allies in Paris. When Vyacheslav Molotov, Foreign Minister of the Soviet Union, arrived, he described the Marshall Plan as 'an imperialist plot for the enslavement of Europe'. Bidault and Bevin went ahead without Russian support or approval, and the Organisation for European Economic Co-operation (OEEC) was formed the following year. Twenty-two European democracies co-operated in the implementation of the Marshall Plan. Cominform, the Communist Information Bureau, was established in Moscow in October to combat the threat of an 'imperialist peace'. The Cold War had developed an economic dimension.

Gratitude was not the universal emotion, even in the British Parliament. A pamphlet entitled 'Keep Left' – endorsed by a group of radical Labour MPs – argued that, if the Marshall Plan had not revived European capitalism, Britain would have applied a socialist solution to its economic problems. It went on to assert that economic dependence on the United States put Europe in the front line of the next world war. Aided by the hindsight of almost fifty years, it is still not

33

easy to be certain if, in the words of its preamble, Marshall Aid 'rescued Europe from poverty and economic stagnation' or if it merely encouraged those nations which were psychologically so inclined to rely on American investment, American innovation and, wherever possible, American products. But in two particulars, the Marshall Plan had a crucial effect on the history of Europe.

After its formation in April 1948, the OEEC's immediate task was to co-ordinate the American-financed recovery. But from it, there evolved the idea that Western Europe might become more prosperous if the rival economies co-ordinated their attempts to improve investment, output and trade. The second undoubted effect of the Marshall Plan was more malign. Europe was already divided. American aid to the West widened and deepened that division.

The division of Europe had been anticipated even before the war had ended. There had been much talk of accelerating the Anglo-American advance from the west, simply in order to deny the Soviet Union the occupation of captured territory and – whether or not wartime experience justified such an unfriendly act – the USSR's behaviour after the German capitulation confirmed how wise it would have been to hold back the frontiers of the Russian Empire. Timidity, incompetence and a mistaken view of military propriety combined to allow the Soviet armies to occupy not only Poland, Czechoslovakia, Hungary, Albania, Bulgaria and Yugoslavia, but also Austria and Germany as far west as the Elbe – surrounding Berlin.

The folly of allowing the Soviet Union so far west was confirmed almost immediately. At Yalta in 1945, the 'big three' – Churchill, Roosevelt and Stalin – had formally agreed to establish independent democratic governments in all the countries which were liberated from Germany. Russia made clear within weeks of victory that it had no intention of applying that policy to Bulgaria and Romania. For the next two years the Soviet Union seemed determined to confirm Winston Churchill's view – expressed at Fulton, Missouri, as early as 5 March 1946 – that an 'iron curtain' had descended on Europe.

In January 1948, Soviet troops surrounding Berlin began to delay and harass convoys carrying food supplies to the city. Gradually, the noose was tightened until the city was in the stranglehold of a total blockade, which went on to last 325 days. A month later, in February, Communists seized power in Czechoslovakia. The response was swift, obvious and inevitable. The Treaty of Brussels – uniting France, Britain and the Benelux countries in a non-aggression pact – was signed in March. Formal American association with European defence was delayed for another year, but in April 1949, the North Atlantic Treaty – establishing not simply the principle of collective security, but also the structure by which the defences of the West would be co-ordinated – was signed. Europe was divided for the next forty years into two armed camps – both of them spending more on their military budgets than they could afford.

It would be wrong to say – as was said by dissentient Labour MPs – that Britain was dragged into the Cold War by the United States, and that the costs and risks involved could have been avoided. With the Soviet Union in its post-war mood, collective security was right and unavoidable. And the idea that Britain was dragged in against its government's will is contradicted by all the evidence. Both Attlee and Bevin were instinctive and passionate opponents of Soviet Communism. Between 1945 and 1948, Attlee's speeches on the conduct and character of Britain's recent ally were far more virulent than anything which appeared in Churchill's florid foreign policy orations. The Prime Minister denounced 'an economic doctrine wedded to the policy of a backward state . . . which makes a strong appeal to backward people who have never known anything better'. He accused the Russian government of 'inverted Czarism' and showed every sign of feeling a personal animosity towards Stalin himself: 'Reminded me of a Renaissance despot. No principles, any methods but no flowing language. Always said yes or no – though you could only count on him when he said no.' Denis Healey, the young Secretary of Labour's International Department, defended the government's foreign policy in a pamphlet entitled 'Cards on the Table'. It argued that the 'major tragedy of socialist history was that the advent in power of a pro-Soviet Labour government in Britain coincided with the opening of a sustained offensive against Britain by her Soviet ally'. But the men who counted in Attlee's government never took such a sentimental view of the Soviet Union. Their antagonism, like their ready acceptance of collective security, was entirely justified, and the British government's decision to respond to the threat of Soviet aggression by participation in the Atlantic Alliance was clearly right and necessary. But the extent and nature of that participation is less easy to justify.

The hope of continual economic expansion was knowingly, if not willingly, sacrificed for membership of the nuclear club. Yet the reasons for paying the price remain in doubt. It seems impossible that Labour ministers genuinely believed that unless the United Kingdom possessed atomic weapons of its own, European defence would be incomplete. A more likely explanation is that resources were diverted away from crucial domestic investment because they imagined that a proud nation had to make a contribution to the defence of the West which was consistent with its history, status and prestige. There is some evidence to confirm that gloomy interpretation of events. When on 22 October 1945 the House of Commons debated foreign affairs, Anthony Eden, winding up for the Conservative Opposition, suggested that the world would only be made safe from nuclear war if the great powers 'modified their ideas of national sovereignty'. The suggestion was greeted with incredulity from the Labour benches and open hostility from the Tories.

There was no support in Britain for modified sovereignty, for it seemed indistinguishable from a loss of identity. And, in the years which immediately followed the war, the common preoccupation was not so much the discovering of a new national persona as the re-establishment of the old and distinct image of a unique Britain. If Anthony Eden had been a regular picture-goer, he would have understood the mood. Although Hollywood's cultural invasion was well under way, the films which were made in Britain were assertions of the exclusive national character. *Spring in Park Lane*, like *Maytime in Mayfair*, depicted England as illustrated in the pages of the *Tatler*. *Passport to Pimlico* celebrated working-class idiosyncrasies. *Whisky Galore* was a caricature of loveable Scottish weakness. *The Crowthers of Bankdam* portrayed the hard Victorian values which had made Britain great. *Holiday Camp* paid tribute to 'the little man' – the salt of the earth who had beaten the Jerries and would win the peace. Britain was different and Britain wanted to be distinct.

In any case, Britain had experimented in 'pooled sovereignty' during the war, and the results had been disastrous. The British government – having decided that it did not wish, or at least could not afford, to maintain an independent programme of nuclear research – had offered to share with the United States all the information which was already in its possession. In return, the United States agreed that the technology which was eventually developed – peaceful or military – should be available to both countries and that America, once it became a nuclear power, should never use its atomic weapons without the express agreement of its partners. The arrangements were formalised – and extended to include Canada – in the Quebec Agreement.

Within weeks of becoming Prime Minister, Attlee was told that America was not even pretending to keep its promise, and that the results of new research were being kept from Britain. When challenged, Truman replied that the Quebec accords had been an 'executive agreement' not a 'binding treaty'. Attlee responded in character by attempting to reason with the President. He personally wrote a 2,000-word memorandum which, as well as setting out details and dates of agreements and assurances, reminded his ally that Britain had regularly supplied America with the most up-to-date information on radar and jet propulsion – two vital areas of research in which British scientists were far ahead of their American counterparts. The Prime Minister's visit to Washington in November 1945 which secured the US loan was officially arranged 'to discuss world affairs in the terrible light of the discovery of atomic energy'. On his return to London, Attlee felt more certain about the pooling of nuclear information than the provision of the loan. The aid proposals had to be approved by Congress. The Quebec Agreement was a matter for the President alone. The Prime Minister felt sure that Truman would keep his word. He was wrong.

The President was, or said that he was, unable to keep his promise for two distinct but equally disreputably related reasons. He was struggling to shift control of the nuclear programme from the Defence Department, and a rumour which was circulating in Washington had convinced the administration's critics that unless a legal prohibition was placed on the exchange of information, the Soviet Union might be allowed to share America's atomic secrets. The rumour was probably started by the White House to ensure the success of the McMahon Bill, which both set up a civilian Atomic Energy Agency and forbade the transfer of atomic information to any other government.

Attlee solemnly warned the White House that, were Britain permanently to be denied access to American atomic research, the government would be left with no choice. Britain would embark on a nuclear programme of its own. Perhaps Harry S. Truman thought that a man as sensible as Attlee would never come to such a silly decision. If so, the President was mistaken. In January 1947, the Prime Minister secretly approved the creation of an independent nuclear capability financed by £100 million hidden in the estimates. Attlee had quarried a millstone which was to hang around the neck of the British economy long after the Russian threat had disappeared, and which is indeed still hanging round its neck today. The penalty of the independent nuclear programme was far greater than the immediate addition it made to government expenditure.

The case for British membership of the nuclear alliance – and the provision of bases for the nuclear superpower which dominated that partnership – was overwhelming. It remained incontrovertible for as long as the Soviet threat persisted. But there was no plausible strategic explanation for Britain's determination to possess an 'independent' capability. It was inconceivable that it *would* be used without the agreement of the USA, and for most of its life it *could* not be used without American assistance. The only real reason for the charade of nuclear independence was the feeling – which the French, unlike the inhibited British, were prepared to admit – that no country that does not possess its own atomic bomb can be a great power. So Britain was prepared to pay money which it could not afford to prove it had not come down in the world. Unfortunately, the most rational Prime Minister in history fell into a common, logical error. Perhaps the possession of a nuclear weapon was essential to superpower status – though thirty years later, Germany and Japan were to rival America in wealth and influence despite their lack of a nuclear capability. But the equation did not work in the other direction. Possession of a nuclear weapon does not, in itself, turn a medium-sized nation with chronic economic problems into a superpower. It merely gave it illusions of grandeur. And illusions of grandeur are notoriously expensive.

The first British atomic reactor went into full use at Harwell on 15 August 1947. Nine months later, A. V. Alexander – Minister of Defence and the Co-operative candidate for Hillsborough who, in the 1945 General Election, had told the parable of the foolish and sensible donkeys – announced in the House of Commons that Britain was to manufacture its own atomic bomb. He spoke on behalf of a government which, despite all its difficulties, felt both satisfied with its record and optimistic about its prospects.

India was free. The nationalisation programme was, with a remarkable lack of controversy, well under way. Marshall Aid was about to save Europe from starvation. The social security revolution had begun. Aneurin Bevan had worked out a system by which general practitioners would remain independent and self-employed within the Health Service, and the last barrier to medical care 'free at the point of use' had been broken down. The state of the economy still demanded self-discipline and sacrifice, but the acceptance of hardship had become an admirable aspect of the indomitable British character. 'We can take it' seemed to be the slogan by which Britain, having won the war, would win the peace.

2

THE PRICE OF VICTORY
Building the Welfare State

—— • ——

Fifty years ago psephology was still an infant science. So it is impossible to judge, with any degree of accuracy or sophistication, how long the Labour Party retained the positive support which swept it into power in 1945. But one thing is beyond dispute. In the summer of 1948, although the British people may not have been pleased with the government, the government was certainly pleased with itself.

Ministers rightly regarded the creation of the welfare state and the nationalisation of the public utilities as achievements of historic importance. And they could not imagine voters basing their judgement of the success of socialism on such trivial inconveniences as bread rationing or a fuel crisis which lasted for a couple of months of a uniquely severe winter. Rational men and women are notorious for their inability to understand the hopes and fears of more emotional mortals. But that common error was only part of the problem. The Cabinet never even considered the possibility that doubts about its competence had begun to undermine admiration for its legislative achievement. Aneurin Bevan, speaking on the day before the inauguration of the Health Service completed the implementation of the social programme – National Assistance, National Insurance, National Health – typified the government's mood:

The eyes of the world are turning to Great Britain. We now have the moral leadership of the world, and before many years we shall have people coming here as to a modern Mecca, learning from us in the twentieth century as they learned from us in the seventeenth.

The phrase for which that speech is now remembered is Bevan's announcement that he regarded Tories as 'lower than vermin'. But although that colourful expression inevitably caught the headlines, in terms of Labour's view of the challenge which faced Great Britain, it was nothing like as significant as his proclamation of Britain's new world role. Bevan's opinion of the Conservative party was not shared by his colleagues. Indeed, Attlee sent him a schoolmasterly (though entirely private) rebuke and – because of the doubts the speech raised about his discretion – forbade him to address the United Autoworkers of America in Detroit. But there is little doubt that the Prime Minister endorsed the main thrust of his argument. Attlee was temperamentally incapable of proclaiming the moral superiority of the government which he led. But he was personally modest, not politically insecure. He had total faith in the righteousness – and the consequent acceptance by a cognisant public – of the socialist cause.

In one sense, Attlee and his colleagues were right. The welfare programme was so widely accepted that when, in 1951, the Conservatives came back to power, the Tory government had no choice but to continue the social revolution of 1945. Labour's mistake was the belief that the country would never trust any other party to carry on the work which it had begun. We cannot be sure why Winston Churchill chose to attack the government for its incompetence rather than for its policy. Some of his critics at the time complained that he was reluctant to work out an alternative, but either by design or mistake, the tactic worked. For three years the Tories barely attempted to contest the Labour view of how society should be changed, and abdication from ideological dispute was the basis of their political recovery. At some point in the late 1940s, the political argument changed from 'Who supports the welfare state?' to 'Who will run the welfare state more efficiently?' By the beginning of the 1950s, half the population thought the answer was 'the Tories'.

The consensus over the need to protect and extend the social programme ensured that spending on health, education and social
security was adequately, if not generously, funded for the rest of the
decade, and that capital investment in housing was maintained at its
post-war level. During Labour's last year in office (1950–51), £27.6
billion (at 1995–96 prices) was spent on health, education and social
security. By 1960–61, the total had risen to £42.2 billion, 13.5 per
cent compared with 11 per cent of gross domestic product (GDP).
But the near-universal enthusiasm for the welfare state did have one
detrimental long-term effect. At a time when Britain needed, above
all else, to reassess its place in the world, and accept its status as a
medium-sized European power, the welfare state provided another
reason to perpetuate the myth of British superiority. Two years after
the Conservatives were returned to power, Aneurin Bevan in the
Hull Town Hall described the British Health Service as 'the best in
creation', and went on to boast about Labour's moral superiority over
the Tories and Britain's ethical leadership of the West. When asked
why Britain provided free medical care for visitors from abroad, when
such facilities were not available to the travelling British, he answered
without a moment's thought or hesitation: 'We are more civilised than
they are.' The 'lesser breeds without the law' were no longer the
Indians and Pakistanis over whose palms and pines Britain once ruled.
The barbarians were the Americans and Europeans who possessed
neither sufficient wisdom nor enough compassion to build a welfare
state. And when – during the next decade – the Europeans began to
match and better what had begun in Britain, the new myth of superiority made it almost impossible for the welfare pioneers to learn
from the foreign newcomers.

The Attlee government was entitled to rejoice at the success of the
domestic economy. Its full extent was not indisputably plain until
after the defeat of 1951, but when the statistics were published, they
revealed a record of remarkable achievement. Between 1946 and 1950,
employment in industry increased by 15 per cent; industrial production by 40 per cent; personal expenditure (at 1948 prices) by 8 per
cent; volume of exports by 77 per cent and volume of imports by 30
per cent. After the Kaiser was beaten in 1918, it took the British

economy almost ten years to return to 1913 levels of industrial production. But by 1950, five years after the defeat of Nazi Germany,
industrial output was almost 20 per cent higher than its pre-war level.
And, at the same time, other policy aims – most of them described by
free-market economists as incompatible with growth – were being
pursued with unparalleled success.

Chief among them was full employment. The speed of economic
growth was certainly held back by a cautious demobilisation programme which caused manpower shortages in the expanding
industries, but industrial output did rise by a steady 8 per cent per
year, and the dole queues – which had been a feature of the inter-war
economy long before the Great Crash of 1931 – remained part of folk
memory about the bad old days. The Labour government was enthusiastically Keynesian. It stimulated investment by tax incentives and
regulated the level of aggregate demand so as to strike an acceptable
balance between holding down the inflation which normally follows
war, and avoiding the slump which was the expected consequence of
changing gear to a peace-time economy.

Between 1945 and 1950, total employment increased by 12 per
cent. In industry the growth in jobs was 15 per cent. Apart from the
months which followed the fuel crisis of 1947, the level of unemployment never exceeded 400,000 and was, for most of the period,
substantially lower than any of the contemporary definitions of 'full
employment'. The 1944 White Paper had wisely avoided figures. But
it had widely been assumed that its recommendations were based on
the belief that 1.5 million men and women would always be without
jobs. The Beveridge Report suggested that the irreducible minimum
was 550,000. Nobody had ever aspired to keeping the dole queues to
the level which was consistently achieved by the Labour government.
To Clement Attlee and his Cabinet, the case for democratic socialism
seemed self-evident.

They were only partly right. The Labour government's recovery
programme was undoubtedly assisted by the rationing and regulation
which had been put in place (and accepted) during the war. And its
work was immensely helped by the spirit of the time. But during the
heady days of 1945 – and in the years that followed, as more and more

basic industries were 'managed on behalf of the people' after nation-alisation – it was assumed that all the workers in the socialised sectors of the economy would develop a whole new relationship with their bosses, even though the new managers were usually the same men who had managed the private companies.

The high hopes were not always realised. At Grimethorpe Colliery, in the summer of 1947, the Coal Board and the National Union of Mineworkers had agreed a change in working practices. The daily stint – the amount of coal to be cut in a single shift – was increased from nineteen to twenty-one feet. A hundred miners working on the Melton Field – one gallery in the Grimethorpe mine – refused to accept the new arrangement and went on strike. Two thousand five hundred other Yorkshire miners, who had endorsed the plan, came out in sympathy. The dispute spread. Before a compromise was reached, 90,000 miners – none of whom had any disagreement with the Coal Board – had joined the stoppage. A succession of Labour ministers who had been miners themselves pleaded with their comrades and friends. But the men chose to express their solidarity with the Grimethorpe dissidents, not with the Labour government. Democratic socialism had no easy answer to the irrationality of human nature.

But sometimes the government's clear call to comradeship and co-operation influenced even the most belligerent of workers. During the summer of 1948, a strike in London's docks escalated to a point at which the nation's food supply was in jeopardy. The Emergency Powers Act of 1920 – in effect making the continuation of the dispute illegal – was invoked for the first time since the General Strike of 1926, and a State of Emergency was declared. Nobody believed that the men would be driven back to work. Then Attlee broadcast on the Home Service of the BBC. He spoke not to the nation but to the dockers:

> The strike is not a strike against capitalism or employers. It is a strike against your mates, a strike against the housewife, a strike against the ordinary common people . . . I lived in the docklands for many years. I remember the horrible conditions. Do you remember what it was

like to go to work day after day and, when you arrived home, be met
with the question 'Any work today?' and the answer was 'No'?

The dockers remembered what it had been like before the Labour
government had 'decasualised' their industry with the National Dock
Labour Board Scheme. And they returned to work.

For at least a time, the whole nation was enthused by the idea that
we are 'members one of another'. The Oxford Economic Study of
the period concluded that the idea of full employment had 'taken a
strong hold on the popular imagination and will exercise a dominant
influence on all future economic policies in this country'. That
prophecy was not confounded for almost forty years – not least
because it was rightly believed that full employment was essentially a
contribution to social justice as well as to national prosperity. The
Rowntree/Laver survey into poverty in York reported a reduction
from 31 per cent in 1936 to 3 per cent in 1950. In 1936, one in three
of the families which lived below the subsistence line were poor
because the potential wage-earner was unemployed. In 1950 not one
able-bodied man in York attributed his family's poverty to unemployment. What was more, full employment improved wage levels.
According to the Rowntree survey, back in 1936 a third of the families in poverty were the victims of starvation wages. In 1950, the 3 per
cent of families below the poverty line were poor because they were
old or sick. It was an astounding achievement. But it is still generally
assumed that the Attlee government 'failed'.

Labour's 'failure' came to be expressed and epitomised in the single
word 'devaluation' – the formal reduction in the price at which
pounds can be exchanged for dollars. Devaluation (a single specific
act), like depreciation (a gradual erosion of value), is a perfectly legitimate instrument of economic policy. It has the overall effect of
reducing imports by making them expensive, and increasing exports
by lowering the price of domestically produced goods on international markets. It therefore promotes both employment and inflation,
and ought to be employed when jobs are more important than prices.
But the idea of devaluation has always been particularly offensive to
British opinion. In the patriotic mind, it seems that when sterling

loses value, British prestige is diminished by the same amount. Technical arguments about the need for, and advantage of, devaluation had gone on among the government's economic advisers since 1945. But although they had made careful and balanced calculations about the consequences for economic recovery, in the end the decision was political. The government chose not even to consider the possibility of planned devaluation. And it was not alone in regarding sterling as a symbol of national pride and prestige. As the Tory party struggled to find an alternative economic policy, Oliver Lyttelton – a senior member of the Shadow Cabinet – wrote to Winston Churchill advocating 'deflation, devaluation and decontrol'. It would, he argued, 'be necessary to unpeg the pound in relation to the dollar . . . and allow price rises to take place'. Churchill, the Leader of the Opposition – who, in 1925 as Chancellor of the Exchequer, had taken the pound back on to the Gold Standard – turned the suggestion down out of hand.

There is a penalty for not making a planned devaluation of an overpriced currency. A larger devaluation than was originally necessary is forced on a humiliated government. On 18 September 1949, the pound was devalued from $4.03 to $2.80. It is popularly supposed that Labour's terminal decline began that day, but, although it is never possible to pinpoint the exact moment when the pendulum of popularity starts to swing against a government, the likelihood is that the British people began to change their minds four months before the fateful summer announcement. The argument over sixteen weeks is not simply pedantic. For if it was the budget rather than the subsequent devaluation which moved opinion away from Attlee and his Cabinet, the cause of the alienation was less policy than performance. On 6 April 1949, the electors began to suspect that Labour had lost its way, its nerve or its convictions.

In his budget statement, Chancellor of the Exchequer Sir Stafford Cripps spoke of the 'baffling' economic problem which had come to be called 'the dollar gap'. There was nothing 'baffling' about the continued pressure on the pound. Indeed, it was inconceivable that Cripps – one of the most formidable intellects of the century – had any doubts about either its causes or the range of possible remedies.

International financial opinion had judged that, comparing the strengths of the British and American economies, the pound was grossly overvalued and that a realignment could not be long postponed. Naturally enough, there was little inclination to buy pounds for rather more than four dollars each, when it was taken for granted that they would soon be on sale for less than three.

The 'baffled' Chancellor did not introduce a harsh budget. The Prime Minister subsequently attributed its unpopularity to the unreasonable expectations which were excited by the press. Its least popular feature was a cut in food subsidies. But Cripps spoke openly of the need to switch policy from the redistribution of income to a growth in total earnings – implying, by intention or mistake, that the two goals were mutually incompatible. He warned that the development of the social services could not proceed at the pace which, in an ideal world, the government would have chosen. Oliver Stanley, speaking for the Conservative Opposition, announced 'the end of an era of socialist policy'. Rightly or wrongly, the British people believed him. Equally damaging for Labour was the fear that the government had lost control of events.

And so it had. Historians will argue whether it was reluctantly swept by international tides which it could not control or if – having mislaid its ideological compass – it was happy to float with the current. One fact is, however, certain. Between the spring of 1949 and the early months of 1950, events outside the United Kingdom forced (or at least caused) the government to change course. The defence commitment which was accepted in 1948 imposed a burden on the economy which made it impossible to fulfil the high hopes of 1945. All that remains in doubt is how hard ministers fought against being shackled to that millstone.

Two days before Cripps's 'baffled' budget, the North Atlantic Treaty was signed in Washington. No one can now seriously doubt the need for that alliance, and even those who challenged its necessity at the time – principally the 'Keep Left' group of the Parliamentary Labour Party – either chose to ignore the evidence of Russian intentions or could not bear to face the economic consequences of the decision to re-arm. But the diversion of essential resources back into an armaments programme held back the economy just at the moment when it was ready to leap forward. And the consequences for the government were equally damaging. Attention was diverted from domestic politics (where it seemed strong) to foreign affairs where, despite all the evidence, it was believed to be weak.

The Attlee government was re-elected at, more or less, the end of its statutory five years, but only just. It could – and perhaps should – have clung on for another few months before asking for a second mandate; certainly its prospects of a resounding re-endorsement would have been improved by delay. Some Labour dissidents described their leaders as having 'run out of steam', and there was no doubt that an essentially unideological party sometimes felt that it had done all that destiny intended. The result was a government which, by the end of its historic years in office, seemed unsure of its purpose and dubious about its prospects.

Despite the real achievements, by the time of the 1950 General Election, it was sometimes assumed – even by some Cabinet Ministers – that the Labour government's economic policies had failed. Some of the 'failure' was the result of international pressures which a single nation could not withstand. Marshall Aid put the defeated Axis powers back on their feet. The balance of payments – which, thanks to the acceptance of prolonged austerity, had moved into surplus on current account – was suddenly prejudiced by the return of Germany and Japan to the international export market. More damaging still was the effect of two events which were equally outside Britain's influence or control. The hopes of lasting recovery were destroyed by the crippling cost of rearmament and the international inflation which was caused by the United States stockpiling strategic raw materials. If the Labour government's economic policy 'failed', it was because the Soviet Union blockaded Berlin and tightened its grip on Eastern Europe, and then, four months after Labour was narrowly re-elected, North Korea advanced south over the 38th Parallel.

North Korean troops invaded South Korea on 25 June 1950. Kremlinologists could and did insist that Moscow and Peking held different views on the historical inevitability of world revolution, and that there was probably more animosity than solidarity between the two capitals. But Western politicians, recalling that the Soviet Union had boycotted the United Nations after its refusal to seat Communist China, feared that international communism was on the march. The only reasonable response was rearmament.

At first, Attlee resisted the American proposal to 'brand North Korea as an aggressor' in the United Nations. For he knew that the unavoidable result of such a declaration would be a massive Asian war into which the United Kingdom would be irresistibly drawn. But Hugh Gaitskell, the new Chancellor of the Exchequer, first warned of the financial consequences of a political breach with Washington, and then hinted that he could not continue at the Treasury if his advice was ignored. When amendments to the American resolution made it more moderate in tone and less bellicose in intention, the Prime Minister accepted the inevitable. Client nations cannot afford to quarrel with the benefactors who pay their regular remittance cheques. Britain had chosen, rightly or wrongly, to become America's remittance man. There was no choice but also to become its outpost in Europe.

Despite his doubts about supporting military action against North Korea, Attlee was intellectually – and indeed emotionally – wholly committed to the rearmament which he regarded as essential to the defence of Western liberty. On 28 January 1951 – unhappily, the day after a further reduction in the meat ration had been announced – he made a speech which was clearly intended to prepare the country for the rearmament programme that was to be set out on the following afternoon. He spoke with a passion which, although not as unusual as his reputation now suggests, certainly demonstrated the strength of his real feelings:

Our way of life is in danger, our happiness and the happiness and future of our children are in danger, and it is both our privilege and our duty to defend them if they are attacked . . . One power in the great alliance that overthrew Hitler did not turn back to the path of peace. It went down the road of conquest and imperialism . . . We have weighed up all factors in the situation which faces us today and decided that it is our duty to increase our armaments . . . We would far rather devote our resources to the things of peace and to the creation of a better life for us all. But peace and the better life are in danger . . .

The basic message of that speech – although intemperately expressed – was acceptable in most of the country and by a remarkably high proportion of Attlee's supporters in the House of Commons. But it contained no figures. The hard facts were revealed on the following day.

They were not as hard as they might have been. The original rearmament programme – drawn up by the British General Staff in co-operation with the Pentagon – would have increased the United Kingdom defence budget to £6,000 million. The Cabinet reduced that total to £4,700 million. But that figure was still £1,000 million more than the maximum which the previous September the Cabinet had agreed was the largest burden the economy could bear. Harold Wilson – then President of the Board of Trade – had no doubt that military spending of that size could not be sustained for long. He was vindicated when Winston Churchill, the 'war-monger' of socialist propaganda, came back to office in October 1951 and reduced Labour's defence budget. The basic figures demonstrated why the Tory cuts were unavoidable. In a little more than a year, defence expenditure had been doubled. When Labour left office, it soaked up 14 per cent – almost three shillings in the old pound – of national income and half of total government expenditure.

The short-term consequences were the resignation of three ministers – Aneurin Bevan, Harold Wilson and John Freeman – ten days after Hugh Gaitskell introduced his first budget. That year's Finance Bill proposed increases in income tax, purchase tax and petrol duty as well as abandoning the initial investment allowance by which the purchase of new plant and machinery was encouraged. Harold Wilson resigned – or later said he resigned – because he could not support the defence estimates. Aneurin Bevan resigned because the budget made provision for, though it did not actually introduce, charges for NHS dentistry and spectacles. The effect on Labour Party morale was catastrophic. The consequences for the British economy over the next forty years were worse.

Once defence estimates of that unreasonable level were accepted, it became virtually impossible to reduce the annual armed forces budget to a rational figure. Ever since 29 January 1951, the British government has accepted military expenditure which – as a proportion of gross domestic product – is substantially greater than most of its allies' contribution to collective security. Attempts to reduce that disproportionate share of Nato's costs were (and still are) attacked as defeatist, irresponsible, and lacking faith in Britain's capacity to meet its global obligation. The size of the defence budget became a symbol of virility – the ability to take continued economic punishment and still come out fighting. The sacrifice of other spending plans in favour of tanks, submarines and aircraft-carriers helped to perpetuate the myths which held the United Kingdom back. Britain was special, so it must spend more on defence than was spent by more prosperous countries. And because it spent more on defence than was spent by more prosperous countries, it was special. The argument was absolutely circular in its form and totally disastrous in its consequences.

Apologists claim that the Labour government had little choice but to increase its defence expenditure to something like the level which the United States thought necessary. Britain was a client nation, and it was no more free to break ranks with America over rearmament than it had been to take an independent view of aggression by North Korea. But the paradox of that position is now tragically clear. American support was essential to sustained recovery. It could only be maintained by spending one-seventh of national income on defence. Yet to spend one-seventh of national income on defence made sustained recovery impossible. Some British politicians willingly accepted the burden. They were men and women, in both parties, who still thought of Britain as a world power. Respect for that myth required the maintenance of a world-power defence budget.

There had been talk about a more closely integrated Europe ever since Winston Churchill's Strasbourg speech in September 1946.

Unfortunately, although Churchill had been unstinting in his enthusiasm for union, he had not thought it necessary to explain the form that union should take or how it might be brought about. In May 1949 the Council of Europe was created, but that was no more than a loose and formless alliance which gave its general support to democracy, civil liberty and the rule of law – and was glad to include Turkey among its number, a country which subscribes to none of the ideals on which the Council was founded.

There was virtually no politician of substance who regarded the idea of a 'federal Europe' as even remotely attractive. Although separated from France by less than twenty miles of sea, Britain still looked for hope, adventure and enterprise on more distant horizons. But, although Britain did not regard itself as a 'continental power', it did not see its island status as proof of its insularity. Opposition to a closer alliance with continental Europe had nothing to do with the fear of lost identity; Britain simply did not believe that it needed a partnership with its neighbours. The nation which had 'stood alone' could manage very well without assistance from the French, who capitulated, or the Germans, who were defeated. Pride and suspicion bred a determination that Britain should not act as a matchmaker to a Franco-German union which hoped to rival Britain's strength and status. The 'mother country' of the greatest empire that the world had ever known could still rely on trade from the Commonwealth. The centre of the Sterling Area could expect to enjoy the indefinite advantages of the City of London's invisible earnings. Perversely, even when it became clear that the United States was unreservedly in favour of Britain's integration with the continental powers, it was still believed that the 'special relationship' with America meant that a choice had to be made between Atlantic Alliance and continental union.

There is no doubt that the founders of the European Coal and Steel Community (ECSC) wanted British membership. But they did not want it at any price. The basic reasons for creating a Community were clear enough – the preservation of peace within Western Europe, and the reduction of East–West tension by the establishment of the Federal Republic of Germany as a full economic partner of the countries with which it had been at war. Without Britain, the Federation of Europe would be incomplete, but British membership was not essential to the achievement of Europe's basic aims.

The underlying objectives of union grew increasingly clear as the negotiations progressed. Konrad Adenauer, first Chancellor of the FRG, saw a European Community as Germany's way back to international respectability. France wanted to make sure that German industrial stagnation did not hold back French economic growth. The political objective, far from being hidden, was actually written into the announcement of the Anglo-German plan:

> By the pooling of basic production and the establishment of a new high authority whose decision will be binding on France, Germany and the countries which join with them, this proposal will lay the first concrete foundations of a European Federation which is indispensable to the cause of peace.

And that, of course, was Britain's principal objection.

The British attitude was hardened by the cynical (though sensible) way in which the French and Germans approached their objectives. They feared that if the United Kingdom was invited to take part in the initial discussion, it would somehow take the lead and use its domination of the proceedings to slow down the progress and water down the proposals. Britain was, therefore, presented with a *fait accompli* – a ready-made community with a firm commitment to federalism which it could join or not, according to taste.

It was the first occasion on which British politicians and diplomats experienced a technique with which they were to grow familiar (and infuriated) over the next forty years. It was a method of moving forward which owed nothing to the step-by-step approach of Cartesian logic in which the French took such pride. The long-term objective – in the case of the ECSC, eventual federation – was stated long before the prospects of its achievements were even examined. The response of the British Civil Service was typically pragmatic: 'Since we are still without any information about the practical details of the scheme . . . [we are] unable to estimate the possible effects on the progress of economic development.' The Cabinet brief listed the possible detriments of membership: the public-owned British utilities might find it impossible to co-operate with the private coal and steel companies of France and Germany; a European coal and steel plan might require a reduction in British output; and the notion of federalism would have to be accepted at the outset. At least that was an honest response: during the entry negotiations of the 1960s and '70s, advocates of membership chose to pretend that political union was an invention of the isolationists put about to frighten the ill-informed.

Britain – for the first time, though not for the last – asked for special terms. What amounted to associate membership was refused. On 1 June 1950 an ultimatum was issued. Ernest Bevin (in hospital) said that he would not be bullied and blackmailed. Herbert Morrison (in The Ivy restaurant in London's West End) insisted, 'It's no good. We can't do it. The Durham miners won't wear it.' On 2 June the Cabinet agreed that the Coal and Steel Community would have to struggle on without the United Kingdom.

That was the historic error of post-war Britain. It is possible to say, in defence of that decision, that the Conservative Opposition was equally in error. But that is not much of an excuse for a radical government to offer. Tories are expected to look to the past. Socialists should think of the future. Charitably, Jean Monnet – the true begetter of the plan which bore Robert Schuman's name – attributed Britain's lack of vision to the perverse fortunes of war. Neither occupied nor defeated, the British people felt 'no need to exorcise history'. Britain's rejection of the more prosperous future offered by the ECSC was 'the price of victory – the illusion that you can maintain what you have without change'.

It will never be possible to estimate the economic consequences of Britain's isolation. But the political results have become gradually clear. The Franco-German alliance – so feared in Whitehall and Westminster – was born. It continued to develop, through good times and bad, for the next forty years. During much of that time, Britain did not even offer itself as the potential third member of a politically and economically fruitful partnership. The process which began in May 1950, when the Schuman Plan was launched, achieved its apotheosis in the winter of 1993, when Chancellor Kohl and

President Mitterrand established a relationship which shifted the focus of European power and influence. When President Clinton made clear that he looked to the Bonn–Paris *rapprochement* to set the pace and give the lead in Europe, the process which began with the foundation of the Coal and Steel Community had come to its triumphant conclusion.

In the summer of 1950 the Labour Party in government and the Tories in opposition both believed, in their different ways, that the Commonwealth would see Britain through. But, like most other things in the post-war world, that unique institution was changing. So were British attitudes towards its citizens. Once the Commonwealth was not all white, the partnership developed problems. On 1 January 1949, the British Nationality Act became law and created two types of citizenship. But although the Act distinguishes between British and British Commonwealth citizens, the rights enjoyed by both groups – at least in Great Britain – were identical. Commonwealth citizens had the right to enter and reside within the United Kingdom. The creation of independent India and Pakistan made the redefinition of 'citizens' essential, and the Act was the inevitable result. In the days of the Raj the subjects of *Rex* (or *Regina*) *Imperator* had been free to travel and to live within the mother country – as indeed were the citizens of the other 'lands and dominions beyond the seas'. That right could have been exercised by millions of colonials, ranging in race from Anglo-Saxons through Sikhs, Ibbos, Boers, Parsees, Zulus, Pathans, Kikuyu and Maoris, to Celts of Scottish, Welsh and Irish origin. But it was never questioned by the British Parliament or people. The Establishment regarded the right of entry as part of the imperial obligation, and the working classes hardly knew of its existence. For it was only exercised by white settlers returning 'home' and the occasional Maharajah visiting England for Ascot and Cowes or Scotland for the grouse shooting. But by the time that the Labour government – devout believers in the Commonwealth ideal – decided to give the old colonial privilege the force of new law, a new sort of traveller was saving up to visit Britain. The *Empire Windrush*, landing its five hundred West Indian passengers at Tilbury in June 1948, was an augury of the future. It also proved the truth of Matthew Arnold's judgement that liberty poses no problems when its exercise is limited to the rich and powerful, but becomes 'inconvenient and productive of anarchy [when] the populace wants to do what it likes too'.

With the single exception of the Commonwealth Immigration Act of 1968, Labour, in government and opposition, has been on the side of the angels in every parliamentary debate on the subject of immigration control. It is even possible to argue that, on occasions, it has been sentimental to a fault and has failed to represent both the opinions and the interests of the indigenous urban poor. But since 1962 (when the first limitations were placed on the rights which the 1948 Nationality Act guaranteed), the only policy of which the party needed to feel ashamed was the sudden aberration brought on by Idi Amin's expulsion of the East African Asians. Yet twenty years earlier – when mass migration from the Commonwealth was barely in prospect – the commitment to unremitting virtue was not so absolute or universal. Shortly after the *Empire Windrush* docked, eleven Labour MPs wrote to the Home Secretary, claiming that 'an influx of coloured people, domiciled here, is likely to impair the harmony, strength and cohesion of public life'.

The overt reference to colour was typical of the time. The notion that black people were being kept out to safeguard race relations remains one of the most common excuses for racism. The Home Office – under Labour's James Chuter Ede – set up a working party to examine 'ways which might be adopted to check the immigration into this country of coloured people from British colonial territories'. There was not even a pretence that some matching limitation might have to be placed on the citizens of the white Commonwealth. The notion that the days of Empire were over and that the old imperial obligations need no longer be discharged seemed not to have passed through anyone's head. *Civis Britannicus sum*. The British Nationality Act had to encompass the Empire on which the sun had still not set. Only the undesirables – that is to say blacks and Asians – needed to be kept out. By the time Labour were removed from power in 1951, the Home Secretary's advisers had still not thought of a way of doing it.

That imperial obligation was discharged in a wide variety of ways. Incredible as it now seems, Seretse Khama – chief designate of the

Bamangwato tribe, grandson of the Great Khama King of All the Kaffirs and a law student of the Inner Temple – was exiled from what was then Bechuanaland by a Labour Commonwealth Secretary for the crime of marrying a white woman. A judicial enquiry had solemnly declared the union to be 'unsuitable', without explaining why. The general assumption was that the white settlers of what is now Botswana were mortally offended by the idea of a 'mixed marriage' receiving not only nationwide publicity but also the personal endorsement of the man to whom their house-boys and field labourers owed tribal allegiance. None of the European democracies was prepared to risk instability in south-west Africa; the uranium mines were there.

Imperial duty was sometimes done more honourably. Unfortunately, the most noble of all the government's colonial endeavours ended in total – and, worse still – risible failure. The Colonial Development Corporation was set up in 1947. Its chairman, Lord Trefgarne, warned, 'Expect little for three years . . . Then we should be really under way, employing hundreds of thousands of young workers in the colonies.' The newspapers built on the idea. 'Jungle lands will grow your food', promised the *Daily Herald*. The *Daily Express* made the same point in its own distinctive way: 'Chance for young Empire builders'. The greatest hopes were said to be in Africa, which the *People* believed provided 'The road back to plenty'.

So did the United Africa Company, which suggested that the government subsidise a scheme to clear 2.5 million acres of central Africa (at a cost of £8 million) and plant the whole area with *Arachis hypogaea*, or ground-nuts. Only a modest part of the plan was implemented. An area of bush, equal in size to Hampshire, Surrey, Sussex and Kent, was turned into 'the biggest government mechanical farm in history'. Henceforth a third of Britain's supply of fats would come from ground-nuts. But the principal beneficiaries would be the African people. Each worker would have 'a home and half an acre of garden and be encouraged to develop village crafts'. More than 10,000 British men and women applied to join what amounted to an early attempt to create Voluntary Service Overseas. A hundred miles of railways, mass-produced replicas of mud huts, schools, hospitals and reservoirs were all promised. And it all went wrong.

Tragically, from the government's point of view, it went wrong over a long period and in absurd ways. There was a shortage of tractors, and converted Sherman tanks – which had won the war in Europe – were defeated by the stumps of African trees. Drought killed most of the first crop and baboons dug up the rest at night. In 1949, Food Minister John Strachey – recovered from the trauma of bread rationing – was still confident enough to claim that 'the revenue from the scheme . . . may well add anything up to twice the original estimate'. But, by the end of that year, the £25 million that had been spent on the project had financed the production of 2,000 tons of ground-nuts – about half the amount which had been planted in the first year. Inevitably, the newspapers which had predicted and promised so much began to denounce and deride the scheme as another example of both the failure of utopianism and the incompetence of the Labour government – another reason why it was time for a change.

The Conservative party leadership began to believe in at least the possibility of victory when the pound was devalued in September 1949. It seemed that Labour had destroyed itself, so the tone which they were determined to set at that year's conference was consciously lofty. The Tory party's only concern was the 'national interest'.

It is arrogance, not loyalty, which is the real Conservative secret weapon. And the total absence of intellectual doubt encourages the genuine (though obviously indefensible) belief that, while other parties pursue narrow sectional interests, the Tories are only concerned with what is best for Britain. A month after the Labour government had reduced the value of the pound to $2.80 seemed the perfect opportunity for Winston Churchill to emphasise the selfless patriotism on which his whole political career had been built. So he told the party faithful, 'It would be far better for us to lose the election than to win on fake pretences.' It must have seemed, in the sombre autumn of that year, that the Conservatives had no need to offer the country a programme of its own. Labour had absolved the Tory leadership from the need to devise an alternative policy. What then appeared to be the certainty of victory provided Churchill with a welcome reply to the repeated demands for a detailed description of what a Tory government would do.

Winston Churchill was determined – for motives which were variously interpreted as 'a vision of national unity' and 'a pathological objection to new ideas' – that there should be no detailed statements of any sort. And although a secret opinion poll (commissioned by Tory party managers) suggested that the Conservatives would be no less popular were he to retire, Churchill's authority was still near to absolute.

So, the only remotely precise statement of policy which the 1949 Conservative conference was allowed to discuss was a combination of R. A. Butler's 'Industrial Charter' (written despite Churchill's reservations and published despite his doubts) and the 'Agricultural Charter' to which the party leader had agreed with little more enthusiasm. They were compressed into a single 'popular' document by Quintin Hogg (later to become Lord Hailsham) and published as 'The Right Road for Britain'. Despite that cumbersome title – less a liability in those more innocent times than it would be today – over two million copies were sold in three months. The party faithful, if not the party leader, longed for an alternative policy.

'The Right Road for Britain' was not much of an alternative, for it endorsed the principles of the mixed economy and accepted much of the legislation – including the nationalisation of basic industries – by which the Labour government had brought the mixture about. But it was the best policy the Tory party had. So it became, in even more 'popular' form, the manifesto for the General Election of February 1950. The ringing declaration with which the Tories went to the polls was a statement which might, equally well, have appeared on the Labour Party's platform: 'We regard the maintenance of full employment as the first aim of government.'

The last two years of the Labour government were not notable for what was once described as 'socialist advance'. Gas – a third of it already in municipal ownership – was nationalised in the spring of 1949. The Tories – who had supported the recommendations of the Heyworth Committee – announced their reconversion to private enterprise and voted against the Bill. From then on the young turks on the Opposition back-benches did their best to harry Attlee's ministers. But the Conservative leadership remained at best ambivalent about mounting an all-out ideological assault. And apart from the nationalisation of steel – once postponed and eventually achieved in February 1951 – there was not very much in the government's programme for them to be ideological about.

There is no doubt that, by the end, the government was beginning to show the scars of six years' hard pounding. Bevin was dead, Cripps too ill to serve, Morrison absurdly out of place at the Foreign Office and Bevan simmering on the back-benches. The economy – which had been managed so well in the early years – was reeling from the cost of the rearmament programme and the inflation caused by the Korean War. The three great social reforms – National Health, National Insurance and National Assistance – were in place. Undoubtedly, some ministers wondered what else there was to do – except weather the economic storm.

The intellectuals of the left began to argue that Labour – in the words of Dick Crossman, socialism's intellectual gadfly – had run out of ideas because it regarded 'ideological speculation best left to the exponents of American free enterprise and Russian communism'. If so, the government was paying the price for its particular sort of success. Even Crossman, in the middle of an essay devoted to the demand for a restatement of socialist first principles, conceded that 'it was largely because the party accepted the unphilosophical Fabian approach that it was able to become a national party and assume the national responsibilities of government more easily than any other socialist party in Europe'. Labour had come to power in 1945 as the people's party, with a policy based on common sense and compassion. The 'development from the liberalism of 1906 to the modern welfare state' was not 'explicitly socialist'. It needed neither socialist doctrine for its justification nor socialist vision to reveal the way ahead. It was for that reason that, according to Crossman, 'the post-war Labour government marked the end of a century of socialist reform and not, as socialist supporters had hoped, the beginning of a new epoch'.

The comparison with Margaret Thatcher's approach thirty years later is irresistible, though only partially apposite. In 1979 the Conservatives were elected on a manifesto which was, in its way, at least as radical as the Labour Party's 1945 programme. And the voters who put the Tories back in power believed – as their fathers and mothers had believed when they elected Clement Attlee – that they were doing more than exchanging one set of politicians for another. In 1979, no less than 1945, the result was decided by men and women who wanted to reject the established view of society, who believed that a new and clear ideology was necessary to end an era of failure and injustice.

Any comparison between the Tories' success in holding on to office in 1983, and Labour's failure in 1950 to consolidate its success of five years earlier, must make allowance for the one great difference in the circumstances which the two governments faced as they fought for re-election. After five years in power, Labour confronted a Tory party which had belatedly adjusted to defeat and spent at least its last two years in opposition preparing to return to government. The Conservatives in 1983 had only to defeat opponents who were divided, dispirited and visibly incapable of forming an effective administration. However she had chosen to behave, Margaret Thatcher would have been re-elected. But the size and certainty of victory was increased by the moral certainty of the campaign. Ideas are what makes politics exciting. If Labour after 1950 had evangelised for its ideas as enthusiastically as the Conservatives propounded theirs in 1983, Churchill would not have returned to Downing Street. Since Labour had lost heart and faith, he was re-elected on 25 October 1951 with an overall majority of seventeen seats.

The paradox of the Attlee government's last two years is that although the government seemed to have lost faith in the principles of democratic socialism, the people seemed still to support the ideas of co-operation and compassion. When the old Home Service of the BBC broadcast Lord Woolton's triumphant cry, 'After six years, we've beaten the socialists . . .,' the socialists were defeated, but socialism (of a sort) survived. Winston Churchill's Tory government implemented what, by any normal definition of the term, was a Labour programme. The country had begun to tire not so much of Labour's policies as

Labour's persona. In 1945, the zeitgeist had been indisputably solemn. On VE Day there had been a few hours of dancing in the streets, bonfires in parks and on village greens and the decoration of shop fronts with paper bunting. Then the nation got back to work. After five years, Britain began to want some fun, and Labour, notwithstanding (or perhaps because of) its undoubted virtues, seemed unlikely to provide it.

The government did not know, and had no way of knowing, the extent of the social revolution over which it was presiding, since the signs of great changes in attitude were small. They were typified by the 'New Look' which was in some of the shops and all of the magazines. After eight years of clothing coupons and 'utility' labels, British women adopted a Christian Dior style which seemed designed to express rejection of shortage and rationing. Hem-lines were lowered to ankle level and, as if to emphasise the determination to use as much material as possible, skirts were full, with pleat folding on pleat. Britain was beginning to grow weary of austerity. The rejection of shortage and sacrifice was soon to turn into a passion for consumption, portable property and the 'positional goods' which signify status. The individualism of the middle classes was beginning to replace the ethos of consensus and co-operation.

Excitement was not the Labour government's style. Six months before its defeat it did preside over the Festival of Britain – a celebration of British arts, science and industry which commemorated the centenary of the Great Exhibition of 1851. Herbert Morrison said that he would be happy to be remembered as the Father of the Festival and expressed particular pride in the futuristic 'skylon' – a giant metal cigar which stood next to County Hall, the home of the London County Council. But the slightly forced gaiety of the South Bank was not in character with the solemn integrity in which the government rejoiced. That integrity was expressed in many ways. John Belcher – an ex-railway clerk who had become Parliamentary Secretary to the Board of Trade – was suspected of accepting gifts from a small-time crook. He was not simply sacked. The unhappy recipient of a case of whisky was exposed, excoriated and publicly humiliated by his colleague, the Attorney General, at the public inquiry, set up by the government to enquire into 'black-market' operations which were eventually found to be within the law.

Labour's belief in its moral superiority was personified by Sir Stafford Cripps, the Chancellor of the Exchequer, who insisted that the election of 1950 should be held before budget day – just to make sure that he was not even tempted to bribe the voters with tax cuts. Jim Callaghan tells the story of how the Chancellor remained the sea-green incorruptible throughout the campaign. Three weeks before polling day, Cripps presided over a committee which considered a cut in the cheese ration. When John Dugdale, Parliamentary Secretary to the Ministry of Agriculture, asked if the decision could be postponed for a month, the Chancellor told him, 'Young man, I am not sure who you are, but if you take things like that into account, you are not fit to be one of His Majesty's ministers.'

The Labour Party had won the election of 1950 with an overall majority of five seats – a victory which, in more modern times, would have been regarded as big enough to keep the government in office for a full five years. But in 1950, as much because of the psychological condition of ministers as because of the problems of parliamentary management, it was generally assumed that Labour could not last for long. The Tories' preparation for the next General Election included the public announcement of at least one major policy objective – a target of 300,000 new houses each year. That single commitment resulted from neither careful economic analysis nor cynical political calculation: it was the product of the frustration felt by local activists and expressed at the 1950 party conference. The party workers – out in the country, canvassing in elections – were absolutely convinced of the need to promise something positive that would outflank Labour's social programme. There was nothing more likely to appeal to potential Conservative voters than the promise of houses.

The 1944 White Paper's estimate that, after the war, Britain would need to build 700,000 new houses, had turned out to be a considerable underestimate. By 1950, demand was so much greater than supply that the price of a family house was four times higher than it had been in 1939. Some experts predicted that, far from the demand being gradually met by new building, it was actually increasing.

Because of the change in the social climate, young couples wanted to start life in a home of their own. The back-to-back and terraced houses which had been built during the Industrial Revolution and tolerated in pre-war Britain were no longer regarded as fit for human habitation. A free-enterprise government ought, its supporters believed, to harness the building industry to what, for the party of the family, was a moral obligation: the creation of affordable homes.

There was no dispute among the Tory party leadership about the need to sound positive when discussing an improved house-building programme, but they believed that it was possible to be positive without being precise. The delegates at the party conference wanted a figure and, as the housing debate went on, it became increasingly clear that they would only be satisfied by a number which the platform regarded as wholly unrealistic. Believing that it was better to break their promises after the election than to split the party before the campaign had begun, party Chairman Lord Woolton (replying to the housing debate on behalf of the Shadow Cabinet) put on a remarkable show of enthusiasm for amending his own policy statement. 'This is magnificent! You want a figure of 300,000 put in. [Delegates: Yes!] Madam Chairman, I am sure that those of us on the platform will be very glad indeed to have such a figure put in.' The Tory party had at least one positive offer to make when the election was called.

It was called in the most absurd of circumstances. For the second time in two years, Clement Attlee was forced to dissolve Parliament on a date which was not of his choosing. King George VI, about to embark on a royal tour of Australia and New Zealand, told his Prime Minister that the 'uncertainty' which surrounded the government's future must be ended before he left the country. Attlee agreed. Polling day would be on 25 October 1951, the anniversary of the Battle of Agincourt. The King, in poor health for years, was immediately taken ill, and the state visit – though not the General Election – was cancelled.

The campaign was even more bizarre than the circumstances in which the election was called. The government stood on its record – National Health, National Insurance, National Assistance – and insisted, with considerable justification, that the nation's economic problems were international rather than domestic in origin. The Opposition seemed determined to prove that they were not Conservatives – at least, not Conservatives of the sort which had ruled Britain before the war. The policy statement 'Britain Strong and Free', which became the Tory manifesto, repeated the promise of full employment made in the 1950 election, and party spokesmen were even more ecumenical than they had been then. First, there was the promise of no trade union legislation during the lifetime of the next Parliament. Then, when the promise was interpreted as the threat of anti-union laws at some distant date, Winston Churchill – the miners' fiercest opponent during the General Strike – got very near to promising that no Tory government would ever legislate to prohibit, limit or discourage strikes. Perhaps even more improbably, the Conservatives proposed an Excess Profit Levy that at least reduced the fortunes which were being made out of defence contracts. There had been much talk during the war of Conservative connections with armament manufacturers; as the Korean conflict pushed up prices and held back the expansion of the social services, the Tories were determined not to be associated with the hard-faced men who did well out of the war.

The most extraordinary aspect of the campaign was the tacit pact which was agreed between the Conservative and Liberal parties. R. A. Butler and Lady Violet Bonham-Carter (daughter of H. H. Asquith, the Liberal Prime Minister from 1908 to 1916) had failed to come to any formal agreement about an anti-socialist common front. But, thanks to a combination of Liberal weakness and Churchill's personal friendship with the *grand-dame* of Liberalism, Tory candidates were given a free run against Labour in over 500 seats. Only 109 Liberals contested constituencies, compared with 475 in 1950. As if to solemnise the slightly irregular relationship, Churchill actually spoke for Violet Bonham-Carter in Colne Valley, one of the few seats in which the Conservatives had given precedence to the Liberals. As a by-product of that unusual event – the Leader of the Opposition drumming up support for a candidate of a theoretically antagonistic party – the *Manchester Guardian* abandoned its historical radicalism and urged its readers to vote Conservative.

The result was not a happy precedent for modern Liberals who believe in pacts. For the partnership, if partnership it was, did not provide equal benefits to the two participants. Inevitably, Liberal support fell from 9.1 per cent to 2.5 per cent of the total vote – a figure which destroyed, at least temporarily, its claim to be a national party. Liberal voters, without a candidate of their own to support, split by a ratio of three to two in favour of the Conservatives. The argument about how homeless Liberals divided between the two major parties has gone on ever since.

In the General Election of 25 October 1951, Labour won 48.8 per cent of the popular vote – 0.8 per cent more than the Conservatives and 1 per cent more than the party secured in the landslide of 1945. Labour's total vote was the biggest that it has ever secured – 800,000 greater than when Harold Wilson won a ninety-six seat majority in 1966. But 13,948,605 votes were not enough. The Conservatives, with only 13,717,538, won 321 seats to Labour's 295. The Liberals (whose vote fell from 2,621,548 to 730,556) won 6 seats, compared with 9 in 1950.

The contribution which the Liberals made to the Conservative victory was almost certainly crucial. But the pattern of voting on St Crispin's Day 1951 had another, and perhaps deeper, significance. The vote represented overwhelming support for the mixed economy and the welfare state. The people had not turned their backs on Labour, and remained in enthusiastic support of the policies for which Labour stood. The party which had pioneered those massive changes to society had won the popular vote and attracted increased support during its six years in government. And a high proportion of the new Conservative voters had been reconciled to the party by its conversion to the principles on which Labour had won its historic post-war victory. When Winston Churchill kissed hands at Buckingham Palace, he knew that the people he governed expected him to lead a shadow of the defeated government.

The Conservatives had no choice but to continue the economic policy of their defeated predecessors. Five days after the new government took office, R. A. Butler (the new Chancellor of the Exchequer) told the Cabinet that, having 'opened the books', he had discovered that the financial crisis was deeper than imagined. The estimated balance of payments deficit for the year was £200 million. With the reserves barely £1,000 million, immediate and drastic action was necessary. The Cabinet agreed to set the nation an example by cutting ministerial salaries. For the next two years, Churchill had nothing to offer by way of economic policy except blood, sweat, toil and tears.

The King's speech, with which the new Parliament opened, was (in Attlee's words) 'one of the thinnest' in modern history and 'exhibited no clear line of policy whatever'. It did, however, include the announcement that the meat ration was to be cut to 1s 5d a week – less in real terms than during the war. A month later, Butler announced that the Bank Rate – the minimum lending rate set by the Chancellor of the Exchequer and the return on absolutely secure government bonds – was to rise from 2 to 2.5 per cent – an increase from the low 'cheap money' base to a figure which looks modest by the standards of the 1970s and '80s but actually increased the cost of borrowing by 25 per cent. All building, except house construction, was prohibited for six months in order to reduce the import of timber. The screw was tightened again at the end of January 1952. The travel allowance was cut to £25 – an irritant to a nation which had just discovered foreign travel. However, there was also a direct assault on the welfare programme. Local education authorities were told to cut their expenditure by 5 per cent. Dental and prescription charges – foreshadowed by the Labour government – were introduced at the rate of a pound for teeth and a shilling for medicine. The nation knew that there was worse to come in the budget. Not surprisingly, the Conservative party fell badly behind in the opinion polls.

There was an alternative. It would, initially at least, have been very painful. But the more far-sighted Treasury civil servants were convinced that it would provide a permanent long-term solution. Their plan was known by the code word 'Robot' – an acronym constructed from the initials of the officials who advocated it most strongly. The plan was neither new nor particularly daring. It proposed a floating rather than a fixed exchange rate and the opening up of some (but not all) sterling holdings to cushion the economy against an immediate massive loss in sterling's value. The Chancellor was in favour, but to the Prime Minister, sterling was sacrosanct. To Churchill, reducing the value of the pound was a betrayal. Butler, slightly misunderstanding the old man's motives, complained that 'Winston is so brave in war and so cowardly in peace'. The chance to make sense out of sterling had been missed again.

So the deflation continued. In the 1952 budget, Bank Rate was increased to 4 per cent and the cost of borrowing therefore doubled in a year – an achievement which stood as an all-time record until 1992, when Norman Lamont did much the same in a single day. Food subsidies were cut from £250 million to £40 million and, to prove that the Conservatives were not reverting to the bad old habits and attitudes of the 1930s, an Excess Profits Levy (at a rate of 30 per cent) was imposed on all profits above the average levels of 1947 and 1949.

Then the world changed. The reserves, which the new Chancellor had been told would be less than £500 million in mid-1952, turned out to be much stronger than the Treasury had forecast. By the end of the year, they had risen to over £650 million. More important, at the end of the Korean War the terms of trade (the relative price advantage of imports and exports), which had turned against the Labour government, turned back to the Tories' advantage. The 1953 budget introduced no new taxes and increased none of those already in place. All rates of income tax were cut by six pence and all levels of purchase tax reduced by 25 per cent. The excess profits tax was abolished. The Minister of Housing and Local Government, Harold Macmillan, was provided with the resources he needed to fulfil the promise of the 1950 Conservative conference. On New Year's Eve 1953, he announced that 300,000 houses had been built since 1 January. The government had returned to the serious business of behaving like a worldly and money-wise replica of its predecessor.

In the early 1980s, some of Margaret Thatcher's most outspoken supporters openly condemned Harold Macmillan for, according to their interpretation of events, betraying Conservatism. It was Macmillan who was said to have compromised with public ownership, increased rather than restrained the power of government, and intensified the dependency culture by extending the welfare state. When Sir Keith Joseph spoke of 'the socialist ratchet' – the inability of reactionary governments to reverse the advance towards a society built on community rather than individualistic values – he was complaining about the conduct of the Macmillan government in which he had served as a high-spending minister. But an honest assessment of Conservative history leaves no doubt that the complaint should extend back beyond the years when we 'never had it so good'. Poor Harold Macmillan has become the hate figure of the extreme right. Anthony Eden was not Prime Minister long enough to be held responsible for anything except the Suez fiasco. And Sir Winston Churchill remains beyond criticism. But there is no doubt that he was the architect of Conservative consensus politics.

Although the Tories in opposition had voted against the nationalisation of the gas industry, in government they decided that it should remain in the public sector – together with the coal mines, electricity generators, the railways, the atomic energy agency, inland waterways, the two major airlines and the Bank of England. The denationalisation of road haulage was promoted to the top of the parliamentary agenda for reasons which had little to do with ideology or economics. Churchill received a letter from a widow which complained that, because of the British Road Service monopoly, she was prevented from hiring out the three lorries which her husband had left to her in his will. Thus are great political decisions taken. The Prime Minister was outraged. Hauliers were delighted to see his righteous anger given legislative effect. Road haulage had been one of the few profit-making industries which the Labour government chose to nationalise.

The other was steel. But, not withstanding the commercial potential of that state-owned industry, the Cabinet came very near to leaving it within the public sector. Butler, Macmillan and, incredibly, the Marquis of Salisbury (once the keeper of the High Tory conscience), were all openly in favour of leaving the British Steel Corporation undisturbed. In the end, a compromise solution turned into a Bill which was introduced in Parliament in November 1952 and made law in March of the following year. The legislation created an Iron and Steel Board, which supervised the organisation of the industry while its assets were sold off over an estimated period of ten years. The timetable proved propitious. Steel was denationalised just in time for it to be nationalised again by Harold Wilson's government in 1966.

Churchill was also responsible for the perhaps capricious continuation of social democracy, when it was suggested that a free market in rented houses would, according to the laws of competition, help to alleviate the shortage of accommodation. Churchill decreed, 'Any legislation amending the Rent Restriction Act must be designed so as to bring no financial benefit to the landlords. It must be made clear that the government has no other purpose but an increase in the number of habitable homes.' It was not his only flirtation with Labour policy. The Prime Minister told the Cabinet that he was 'impressed by the extent to which this country was falling behind others in the provision of up-to-date hospitals'. He considered that a great campaign should be undertaken to improve that part of our social services. When the Minister of National Insurance proposed to raise the retirement age as an economy measure, and to examine the likely increase in the cost of superannuation payments as a possible alternative, the Cabinet (under Churchill's guidance) concluded that: '. . . even if such an increase were to prove acceptable to the trade unions, it would still be widely misunderstood'. Churchill's desire not to offend the unions amounted to a near obsession.

Churchill – the hammer of the miners during the General Strike of 1926 – had changed his mind about organised labour. The unions had supported rearmament (and therefore, by implication, him) before the war. They had shown, with some deplorable exceptions, commendable patriotism once the war had broken out. And although they had supported the Labour Party, which had usurped his right to govern once the war was over, they had been commendably robust in their opposition to Soviet aggression. The Prime Minister's sentimental view about the nobility of the typical shop-steward may have owed something to the fact that he had never met one. But he was determined – whatever the reason – to be nice to the unions. He put that principle into practice by appointing Sir Walter Monckton as Minister of Labour.

Sir Walter was believed to be the most emollient man in London. He was a distinguished lawyer whose combination of charm, tact and intellect had resulted in his representing the Duke of Windsor during the abdication crisis. His style – indeed his way of life – was one of compromise. Ten years after his retirement from politics, officials at the Ministry of Labour still repeated, in reverential tones, the principle of conciliation and arbitration which he had laid down. 'Always give the lion the lion's share.' He interpreted his instructions from Churchill as the obligation to assist public-sector workers in obtaining wage levels which were comparable with pay in private industry, and made a point of never commenting on wage demands when he thought that the unions' claim was too unrealistic to receive his endorsement. Churchill's attitude was even more sympathetic towards the unions. Having expressed his 'alarm' at the prospect of a wage demand pushing up fares in the London commuter district, he suggested that, rather than encourage British Railways to resist the pay rise, the government should consider an increased subsidy. The Cabinet persuaded him to abandon the idea, but the White Paper which followed specifically rejected the notion that 'the railways should be required to cover all their costs'. Churchill remained conciliatory right to the end. In the autumn of 1954, when even Monckton wanted to persuade the Transport Commission to stand up to the railwaymen, Cabinet minutes note that the Prime Minister insisted on a compromise as a reflection of his view – expressed to Scottish Conservatives – that the unions were 'one of the outstanding institutions of our country'.

The contrast with the Conservative government which came into office twenty-five years later could not be more stark – particularly in its attitudes towards trade unions and employment. Churchill minuted the minister in charge of energy policy: 'The recent increase in the number of miners is encouraging and we must try to get even more. If necessary, we shall have to give them still greater privileges and wages.' When Monckton, in an uncharacteristic fit of reforming zeal, proposed a reconstruction of the Wages Council which then set minimum wages in the distributive trades, the Prime Minister himself saw the TUC and reassured them with the reminder that when he had been President of the Board of Trade over forty years earlier, he had been 'responsible for the legislation which established trade boards to protect conditions of employment of the lowest paid'. When economists forecast that unemployment would rise to 500,000, Churchill instructed that 'early consideration be given to measures which might be taken . . . including such measures as the reclamation of marginal land, highway development and the construction of a Severn Barrage'. The speech to the Scottish Conservative Rally, made on 17 April 1953, demonstrates that even when Churchill felt that his economic policies had won the support of the nation, he still wanted to emphasise a commitment to the welfare state which was as great, and more fruitful, than that of his socialist opponents. 'It is not Conservatives who would destroy the welfare state. It is national bankruptcy that would be its ruin . . . In spite of our grave financial problems we have improved the benefits under the various social insurance schemes, and we are actually spending more than the socialists did on education, health, and housing.'

There was no argument about which party had the best immigration policy, for although the subject became the obsessive concern of the inner cities to which the immigrants had come, senior politicians had nothing to say about the subject – in public. The Third World had moved on since Labour had passed the British Nationality Act, and Labour back-bench MPs had expressed their fears that the West Indians who landed from the *Empire Windrush* were the beginning of a mass migration. In 1952, the United States passed the McCarran–Walter Act, which prohibited Caribbean emigration to America. Conservative reaction to the prospect of West Indians setting sail for Britain was virtually indistinguishable from the position taken up by its Labour predecessors. Chuter Ede's committee, which in 1948 had examined 'ways which might be adopted to check the immigration into this country of coloured people from British colonial territories', was superseded by a Cabinet decision that the Home Secretary should 'examine the possibility of preventing any further increase in the number of coloured people seeking employment in this country'. There was not even the pretence that the government believed in equal treatment for all British citizens. The Chancellor of the Exchequer was requested to 'arrange for a concurrent examination of the possibility of restricting the number of coloured people obtaining admission to the Civil Service'. Like Labour, the Conservatives would not have hesitated to discriminate against black and Asian Britons if they had been able to think of an easy way of doing it.

In 1953, although there were no restrictions on entry, only 3,000 immigrants from the new Commonwealth made their homes in Britain. The total black population of the whole of the United Kingdom was about 40,000, yet the Cabinet – under pressure from MPs who feared mass entry into their constituencies – behaved as if the country had been invaded. Churchill summed up the Cabinet discussion with the prediction that 'the rapid improvement in communications is likely to [increase] the number of coloured people coming to this country'. But the neurotically nervous reaction of Westminster politicians – who never shrank from the overt identification of 'coloured' immigrants as the cause of their concern – was an early indication of Britain's diminishing self-confidence. A nation which had had no fears about losing its identity in a new pattern of international alliances started to fear that its character would be changed by the absorption of a few thousand Indians, Pakistanis and Afro-Caribbeans. From then on, there was an almost exact correlation between Britain's gradually diminishing world status and the British people's rapidly accelerating antagonism to men and women whom they regarded as foreign, alien or different.

The decline in national self-confidence was, from time to time, slowed down or even turned back by an event that renewed British memories of the past and hopes for the future. In February 1952, the accession to the throne of the 25-year-old Queen Elizabeth stimulated one remarkable, but regrettably only temporary, improvement in national self-esteem. Winston Churchill, broadcasting on the day of George VI's death, had not lost his capacity to touch the emotions of his audience. He ended on an almost personal note: 'You will understand the pride with which someone who was brought up in the high summer of Victorian England says once again, "God save the Queen".'

Leader-writers began to remind their readers that Britain's days of greatest glory had always coincided with the reign of a queen. Then the idea of coincidence was discarded, and the great achievements of England under the first Elizabeth and Britain in the time of Victoria were mystically linked with the monarch's gender. Sometimes Queen Anne was added to the list for good measure, and Marlborough's defeats of the Austrians and French were included alongside Drake's destruction of the Armada. The conclusion to which all this evidence pointed was that when a queen was on the throne, Britain was invincible – a fact which the French, Austrians and Spanish, not to mention the Germans, tacitly acknowledged throughout Victoria's sixty glorious years by following Rudyard Kipling's good advice and 'walking wide of the Widow of Windsor'.

In the weeks following the accession of the young queen, the talk was of a new Elizabethan Age. Its formal inauguration would be the coronation – an event in which Winston Churchill took a particular and personal interest, and the first great spectacle in the history of the country which a loyal people could watch in the comfort of their own homes – in the spring and summer of 1953, sales of television sets boomed.

So the sacred event of Elizabeth's anointment promoted one of the great secular changes in British society. The flickering pictures did more than provide a unique entertainment. To thousands of families they became what *Panorama* was later to call 'a window on the world'. Alongside *Animal, Vegetable and Mineral* and *What's My Line?* – the genteel panel games of the period – the BBC broadcast moving pictures of other lives in other lands. The American way of life had held British families enthralled ever since Hollywood had begun to export its films in the late 1920s. And the process had been accelerated after the war by the importation of American musicals which, whatever their plot and period, had been reflections of contemporary American life. *Annie Get Your Gun, Oklahoma!, Guys and Dolls* and *Brigadoon* all added to the feeling that America was mysterious, exciting, and above all, prosperous. But television made the whole nation – know it or not; like it or not – fall under the spell of the United States. The 1950s were the time when tins began to turn into cans, lorries became trucks and youths asked their barbers for 'DA' haircuts – often believing that the style was named after a District Attorney rather than a 'duck's ass', but realising that it was born in America. More important, their parents saw on the screen the images of an affluent society – working families which owned motor cars, washing machines and refrigerators. Television helped to educate Britain about glass-blowing, the life and habits of the wallaby, and the architecture of English cathedrals. It gave graphic meaning to stories about distant places which, although largely unknown to the viewers, had immense influence over their daily lives – Iran, which was still being difficult about oil; Japan, which had begun to take an interest in the manufacture of radios; and Germany, which was again building (and now exporting) motor cars. But most of all, television made British families want to enjoy a higher standard of living. It made the new Elizabethan Age the era of the consumer durables – the time in history when everyone wanted to join the middle classes.

3

SET THE PEOPLE FREE
Suez and Beyond

————•————

According to R. A. Butler's autobiography, 1954 was 'the year when, for the British trader and the British consumer, the war finally ended'. It had taken almost ten years, but

> nearly all State trade had been given back to private enterprise. Competition had been restored in the steel and road haulage industries. Most price controls were abolished . . . Import controls had been greatly relaxed . . . Above all, food rationing and restrictions upon consumption had been brought to an end.

The economic recovery had begun at the end of 1952, when Dwight D. Eisenhower's election as President of the United States heralded the end of the Korean War and the terms of trade turned in Britain's favour. Reserves rose to over £650 million rather than falling as the Treasury had predicted. It was the first, though by no means the last, example of economic policy being prejudiced by faulty official forecasting. But by the spring of 1953, it was clear to Butler that he could introduce the first budget since the war which neither proposed new taxes nor increased old ones. Every band of income tax was reduced by six (old pence) and purchase tax was cut by 25 per cent across the board.

Not everyone was satisfied with the progress that Butler made towards a truly Conservative economy. In February 1954, *The Economist*, speculating about the contents of that year's budget, invented 'Butskellism' as a description of what it claimed was the identical economic policy of the two major parties. The similarities had been noticed by Sir Norman Brook, the Cabinet Secretary. In March he wrote a memorandum to the Prime Minister with a complaint which was to become a familiar theme during the four decades which followed. 'Penal' rates of taxation were a disincentive to hard work and encouraged tax evasion. His memorandum ended thus:

> If, therefore, ministers concluded – as Mr Butler does – that we have to go on for years and years in a long slow grind with income tax at 9s 6d in the pound and surtax at its present levels, they will, in fact, be deciding that a Conservative government must perpetuate, or is at least powerless to alter, the pattern of society which the Socialists set out deliberately to create. It may be that this is inevitable. But ministers should look at this prospect squarely in the face before deciding that this is so.

It is difficult to decide what is most surprising about that memorandum – its attempts to bypass and undermine the Chancellor of the Exchequer; its overtly political tone; or the author's ignorance of tax levels. The standard rate was nine shillings in the pound, not nine and sixpence.

Although Butler had made the six-pence reduction which Sir Norman Brook had missed, there was much statistical evidence to support the view that taxes were higher than was consistent with traditional Tory views of individualism and enterprise. The standard rate was still twice as high as it had been in the 1930s. In the years which followed the war, Tory governments – despite protestations of belief in low taxation – accepted a marginal tax rate of 90 per cent on high incomes.

Thanks to the Brook memorandum, the Cabinet resolved to make a drastic reduction in public expenditures during the fiscal year 1954–55. A pattern was established which persisted down the years.

The cuts were made. But the £67 million which Butler pared off department budgets was not enough to enable the Chancellor to repeat the tax cuts of the previous year. Nor were more tax cuts likely in the foreseeable future without a massive review of defence expenditure – and that, in the early years of his return to office, Churchill would not even consider. So Tory strategists decided to concentrate on the election promise which they could keep. Harold Wilson, when he was Labour's President of the Board of Trade, had begun a 'bonfire of controls' and, as far as it went, it had proved highly popular. The Conservatives announced that they would finish the job; they would 'set the people free'.

The end of food rationing was a potent symbol of the government's determination. When the Tory party returned to power in 1951, Britain was living on what today would be called starvation rations – bacon and ham: 3oz; cheese: 1½oz; butter and margarine: 7oz; cooking fats: 2oz; sugar: 10oz; tea: 2oz; chocolate and sweets: 2oz. Presented with the list, Churchill thought it offered a 'reasonable level' of subsistence – until he discovered that the rations were supposed to last not for a day but for a week. Eighteen months after Labour's defeat, tea rationing ended. The process went on, item by item, until July 1954, when bacon and meat went back on to the open market. Then the ration books were thrown away.

And as well as bread, there were circuses. Part of the Tory campaign plan was to depict Labour as the party of grey austerity, and contrast the grim puritanism of socialist Britain with the happy hedonism of life under the Conservatives. The process came to its climax in 1956 with the introduction of Premium Bonds – described by Harold Macmillan as an 'innocent flutter' and Harold Wilson as a 'squalid lottery'. But the most appealing way of proving 'Conservative Freedom Works' was thought to be extending choice and, according to Labour's doomed propaganda, reducing the quality of television. On 30 July 1954 the Television Act became law. It established the Independent Television Authority and provided it with the power to license 'private franchise holders' to broadcast on a second channel. The new programme companies were scheduled to begin broadcasting on 22 September 1955. Estimates – which proved entirely correct – suggested that by November of that year, there would be more than five million licensed television viewers in Great Britain. The Tory party was almost ready to hold a General Election.

But in February 1955, it seemed that the preparations were going so badly wrong that the Labour Party – still divided by the disputes which had begun when Bevan left the Cabinet – might even win its way back to power. For the Tories the problem was the economy which, in the euphemism of the time, was 'overheating'. The Bank Rate was increased to 4.5 per cent (the highest level for twenty years) and hire-purchase restrictions (which had been relaxed as part of the determination to 'set the people free') were restored. The Labour Party, certain that it would win the General Election, feared that polling day would be delayed. It seemed to Attlee and Gaitskell that an unpopular budget was an economic necessity, and they naïvely assumed that the election would be postponed until the essential tax increases were reversed or forgotten. They were about to learn that Tory governments, determined to remain in office, decide when the election should be held and then construct a budget that – whatever its effect on the economy – improves the prospects of victory. The budget of April 1955 was recklessly expansionary. Another six pence was cut off the standard rate of tax, as part of a package which reduced the government's income by £146 million. The cynicism of the manoeuvre was made all the more obvious by the knowledge that the General Election was almost certainly only a month away. Butler made his budget statement to the House of Commons on 19 April. Thirteen days earlier Sir Anthony Eden had succeeded Winston Churchill as Tory leader. The new Prime Minister announced that, following the path of honour (as distinct from the tax reductions), he wished to win a specific mandate for his new administration.

The old man had left reluctantly – speeded on his way by Lord Woolton, who hoped that his demeanour, when the Prime Minister's future was discussed, had reminded his colleagues that 'Churchill had lost more elections than any Conservative in history'. Right to the end, the 'Greatest Living Englishman' hoped to devise some international initiative which would prolong his premiership and ensure that it ended on a high note. But when he could postpone his departure no longer, he left with good grace. The Cabinet minutes of 5 April 1955 record his valediction:

> The Prime Minister said that it remained for him to wish his colleagues all good fortune in the difficult but hopeful situation which they had to face. He trusted that they would be enabled to further the progress already made in rebuilding the domestic stability and economic strength of the United Kingdom and in weaving still more closely the threads which bound together the countries of the Commonwealth or, as he still preferred to call it, the Empire.

The General Election which followed was described by Hugh Dalton (sometime Chancellor, jovial trouble-maker and patron of bright, young intellectuals), as the dullest of the twelve campaigns which he had fought. Labour's manifesto, described by Bevan as 'cold porridge strained through a blanket', was as boring as its title – 'Forward With Labour'. The Tory alternative, 'United for Peace and Progress', was equally bland. The Conservative posters boasted that the government was 'Working for Peace'. Labour countered with 'You Can Trust Mr Attlee!', but despite the evidence of the billboards and hoardings, 1955 was not the last of the old-style elections; it was the first of the modern campaigns. The dominant issue was taxation.

Gaitskell's attack on the give-away budget was described by Eden as an example of the Shadow Chancellor's 'newly acquired class hatred'. The phrase was a reflection of the Prime Minister's distaste for what he regarded as social treachery. Gaitskell – who was educated at Winchester and New College, Oxford – should not, Sir Anthony believed, complain about the government offering a little help to the middle classes. But the phrase – although tailor-made to fit Eden's own instincts – was an early example of a technique which was refined and developed over the next thirty years. The allegation of class antagonism – 'the politics of envy' – became the standard method of diverting attention from the social and economic consequences of the Conservatives' fiscal policy.

In the 1980s and '90s a second indictment was added to the charge sheet. Labour, it was said, could only finance its programme by massive and sustained tax increases. The charge, repeated time after time on radio and television, was then taken up by the Conservative newspapers. In 1955 the accusation was made but not driven home. So in his election broadcast, Gaitskell was able to brush aside the idea that Labour was the profligate party. The Conservatives, he claimed, had 'thought of a number and multiplied it by ten'. There was, he said, 'no reason why a Labour government should put up taxes'; he had 'always argued against overloading programmes with expensive commitments'. That was the sum total of his response, and he got away with it. At least the Shadow Chancellor was not pursued with demands to explain how he would pay for promises that had never been made. Nor was he challenged to explain how specific income groups would be affected by tax increases which he did not intend to levy. Those were pleasures in store for his successors. But in the election on 26 May 1955, Labour still lost. However, thanks to his experiences in that doomed campaign, Gaitskell made a discovery which he seemed to find surprising: 'Whereas the middle classes do broadly fear the return of a Labour government . . . the working classes do not feel the same about the return of a Conservative government.' The need to reconcile the middle classes to socialism haunted the rest of his life.

Detailed analysis of the result should have taught Labour lessons which, much to its cost, were not fully learned until it had suffered six more defeats. Public ownership was crucially unpopular. Labour candidates did particularly badly in Middlesbrough and Cleveland – constituencies which would have been directly affected by the manifesto commitment to nationalise the steel and chemical industries. The median swing against Labour MPs said to be 'on the left' was 1.6 per cent, compared with 1.2 per cent against 'moderates'. Perhaps more important, the polls revealed that if Aneurin Bevan succeeded Attlee, 27 per cent of Labour supporters and 54 per cent of Liberals would have felt 'less inclined' to vote for the party. Bevan's national standing was important, because it was assumed that Attlee would soon follow Churchill into retirement. And Bevan believed himself to be the rightful heir to Labour's leadership.

When the new Parliament met, Hugh Dalton announced that he would stand down from the Shadow Cabinet, and urged other members of his age and generation to follow his example. But he was careful to exempt Attlee, who had been party leader for more than twenty years, from the call for early retirement. Indeed, at the first meeting of the new Parliamentary Labour Party, Dalton made a dramatic appeal for him to stay on 'indefinitely'. Bevan (who knew he could not win an early leadership contest) immediately spoke in support, and there was a rumble of agreement in which Herbert Morrison (who knew he could lose if there was a delay) did not join. Attlee accepted the wishes of his colleagues with an alacrity which suggested he had never even considered stepping down. But the battle for the succession had begun. Everyone assumed that when the election came, the contest would be between Morrison on the right and Bevan on the left.

But fate and fortune were to decide otherwise. Less than two months after the Conservative government's re-election, Butler introduced an emergency budget. To compensate for the increase in consumption which the pre-election tax cuts had stimulated, it restricted credit and capital expenditure. Gaitskell, still Shadow Chancellor, accused Butler of 'the biggest act of political deceit since . . . Stanley Baldwin sealed his lips on defence'. And although in the summer he regretted the personal attack, he repeated it in the autumn when the year's second emergency budget increased taxes by £138 million – almost exactly the amount by which they had been cut before the election. Butler's fiscal year, he said, 'began in folly and continued in deceit'.

Labour MPs – still depressed by defeat – were delighted by Gaitskell's recently acquired aggression. They began to forget that, according to Tory newspapers and the party's left wing, the economic policies of both front-benches were indistinguishably 'Butskellite'. The chance to denounce the Conservatives in language which he had never used before was not Gaitskell's only piece of good luck. In those days, the Labour leader was elected by Labour Members of Parliament – not, as was once supposed, the most sophisticated electorate in the world, but a collection of men and women who were always inclined to cast their vote for reasons which ranged from the hope of personal preferment, through the regional origins of the candidates, to the courtesy with which they had been treated by the rivals for office. Personal performance was, therefore, very important. At the 1955 party conference Bevan seemed to go out of his way to offend his parliamentary colleagues – many of whom already thought he treated them with too little respect.

At a 'private session' – which should have discussed the unideological subject of party organisation – Bevan attacked first his colleagues on the Labour front-bench (who were accused of being bad socialists and responsible for the election defeat) and then the trade unionists whose patronage he claimed kept the incompetent apostates in power. Inevitably, the private denunciations became public. Bevan was found guilty of both vanity and disloyalty – two of the greatest sins known to the Parliamentary Labour Party. In consequence, he lost essential support in the middle ground. At the same time, Gaitskell improved his reputation in a way which was to have a crucial effect on the future of the party.

On the afternoon of Bevan's indiscretions, Gaitskell spoke for the leadership on nationalisation. The speech began badly but ended in triumph – perhaps because some of the delegates recognised the strength of conviction with which the not altogether popular message was delivered:

> I became a socialist, quite candidly, not because I was a passionate advocate of public ownership but because . . . I came to hate and loathe social injustice, because I disliked the class structure of our society, because I could not tolerate the indefensible difference of status and income which disfigures our society . . . I am a socialist because I want to see fellowship, or if you prefer it, fraternity . . . Nationalisation . . . is a vital means, but it is only one of the many means by which we can achieve these objectives.

'Revisionism' – the belief that the application of the socialist principle must be relevant to the circumstances of the time – had found its champion.

Then Attlee changed his mind. During the last week of November 1955, he told the Labour Chief Whip that, because of the constant speculation about his future, he proposed to resign the party leadership. They decided that the announcement should be made on 7 December. 'Shall I tell the contenders in private?' the Chief Whip asked. Attlee replied, 'Tell Gaitskell'. There is now much argument about the reluctance with which Hugh Gaitskell agreed to stand. In the shadow of the General Election defeat he had certainly assumed that he would support Herbert Morrison and then become the natural successor. But in the months between July and September the calls for a younger man became increasingly insistent, and Gaitskell's intense dislike of Bevan made his candidature inevitable. His friends now claim that he was only persuaded to accept the nomination when he was warned that in a straight fight with Morrison, Bevan would win. But by late September, Attlee's mantle had been firmly placed on his shoulders. During a rare newspaper interview, the party leader had doubted the wisdom of trying 'to impress the nation by a futile left-wingism' and gone on to argue that 'we must have at the top, men brought up in the present age, not as I was in the Victorian age'. Bevan and Morrison were thus dismissed in a single paragraph.

The act of resignation was equally terse. Jim Callaghan recalls that at the fateful meeting of the Shadow Cabinet, Dr Edith Summerskill – famous for hats and aggressive feminism – appeared to be weeping behind a large silk handkerchief. No one had ever seen her weep before. After his announcement, and the tributes which followed, Attlee said he had one other item of business: 'Offered an Earldom . . .'. Dr Summerskill immediately recovered her composure and replied, 'Of course you must take it.' There was only a split second of silence before Attlee announced, 'That concludes the business.'

The meeting of the Parliamentary Labour Party which followed was taken by surprise. In Committee Room 12, high above the Thames, there was genuine weeping, spontaneous tributes and ragged singing of 'For He's A Jolly Good Fellow'. The stage was set for an election which can only be fully understood against the background of Labour Party history.

The Labour Party of 1955 was a loose coalition of men and women who ranged in opinion from orthodox Marxists to foot-loose Liberals. By instinct and philosophy they were all, whatever their ideology, dissenters. And the line between dissenter and dissident is often hard to draw. Constant and open disagreement among the Labour leadership was a major factor in ensuring that the Conservative party held office for thirty-five of the fifty post-war years. 'If they cannot agree among themselves,' Labour's opponents asked rhetorically, 'how can they hope to run the country?' And the need to present a united front to the nation often persuaded leaders who should have known better either to compromise with foolishness or to accept policies which they knew to be damaging to party and nation. Part of Attlee's peculiar talent was his perfunctory success in dealing with rebellion. Looking back on the ten years since the war, many Labour MPs wondered if anyone else could have held the disparate alliance together.

Herbert Morrison's unsuccessful putsch – attempted only days after Attlee had led Labour to the most spectacular victory in its history – was not even the first in the long line of rebellions and revolts which prejudiced Attlee's prospects of leading his party to power. During the 1945 election campaign, Harold Laski (who, because of 'Buggins turn' was that year's Party Chairman) issued the warning which became the catchphrase of his similarly self-important successors. He told Attlee to respect the sovereignty of the annual conference and the authority of the National Executive – in short, to know his place and govern according to the instructions of the party's rank and file. Attlee dealt with it in his own brusque way, ending his re-statement of parliamentary independence with the curt rebuke that 'a period of silence would be welcome'. Later party leaders found it difficult to reproduce his style with similar success.

Attlee himself turned the terse reproof into an art-form. When, in February 1946, Konni Zilliacus (the spokesmen for a group of far-left MPs) sent him a lengthy assault on government foreign policy, the Prime Minister replied, 'Thank you for sending me your memorandum, which seems to me to be based on an astonishing lack of understanding of the facts.' In the same month, Dick Crossman visited

Downing Street as leader of a delegation which believed (with some justification) that Attlee was less than enthusiastic about the conversion of Palestine into Israel. The Prime Minister, who had been a friend of Crossman's father, listened politely to a twenty-minute monologue before he asked a question. He then enquired, 'How's your mother, Dick?' Crossman replied that she was very well and that he was seeing her next week. 'Give her my regards,' Attlee said. The meeting was over.

But later opponents of his leadership were made of sterner stuff. And the contemptuous dismissal only worked when the Prime Minister enjoyed the authority which comes with leading a popular government. That hard fact was damagingly demonstrated by the resignations of Bevan, Wilson and Freeman in April 1951. And the demonstration was repeated time after time between that year's election defeat and Attlee's retirement.

In November 1952, J. P. W. Mallalieu – that most dangerous of political animals, the Member of Parliament and professional journalist – wrote a whimsical article in *Tribune* which compared the spirit of 'advance' in local Labour parties with the belief in 'consolidation' that characterised most MPs. The sting was in the tail. Votes at Parliamentary Labour Party meetings should, Mallalieu suggested, be recorded so that constituency activists could know what their representatives really believed. Dalton feared that 'the whole bloody Bevanite trouble is being brought up again'. And so it was, but the message which was inherent in the Mallalieu article was the herald of much more than a clash of personalities. It was the beginning of the demands for 'accountability' – the euphemism for the campaign which, throughout the 1970s and '80s, sought to limit the conscientious freedom of MPs.

The clash of personalities came two years later – in the year leading up to Attlee's retirement. It began with what started out as a comparatively good-natured disagreement about defence policy. But the mood changed during a Commons debate on the setting-up of the South-East Asia Treaty Organisation (Seato). In those days, there were no 'Shadow Ministers', each with specific responsibility for one area of policy and a single Department of State. Senior figures in the party spoke from the front-bench on a wide variety of subjects. Usually the freedom to range widely was used with discretion. But in April 1954, Bevan took advantage of his Shadow Cabinet status to push his way past Attlee to the Opposition despatch box and virtually disown his leader by describing Seato as created 'for the purpose of imposing European rule upon certain people of that area'. After days of damaging charge and counter-charge, denunciation and demand for apology, Bevan resigned from the Shadow Cabinet. To his chagrin, the runner-up in the elections filled the place he had vacated. The new Shadow Cabinet member was Harold Wilson.

Gaitskell and Bevan both announced that they would contest the vacancy for Party Treasurer – adding the risk of personal bitterness to the prospects of a Labour conference which was already certain to be torn apart by two foreign policy disputes. The creation of Seato – which had so angered Aneurin Bevan – was opposed with less passion than the leadership originally anticipated, and the amendment to oppose it was defeated by a million votes. It was the rearmament of Germany – initially proposed by the United States, barely five years after the war against Hitler was over – that raised real passion. In government, Gaitskell had reluctantly supported the proposal as the price that had to be paid for an American contribution to European defence. He was not the man to change his view in Opposition. In fact – partly in order to sustain his continuous challenge to Bevan – Gaitskell led the Labour leadership's 'education campaign'. It was not totally successful. The motion to support German rearmament was carried by only 200,000 votes, and only then because the delegate from the Woodworkers' Union was persuaded to change his mind and break his mandate. But the line was held and Gaitskell won the Treasurership with a resounding majority. However, as is so often the case with the Labour party conference, the trouble erupted not during the formal sessions but on the fringe. Attlee told the pre-conference rally that, 'Foreign affairs lend themselves to emotionalism, which is a bad guide.' Bevan replied the same evening at the *Tribune* meeting with an ironic admission, 'I know that I shall be accused of emotionalism. I know that the right sort of leader is a desiccated, calculating machine.'

The mixed metaphor has gone down in history, though it is still not clear whether Bevan meant to condemn Attlee or Gaitskell. It was, however, clear that he had a leadership election in mind and was interpreting every speech as a reflection on his prospects. Gaitskell seemed determined to challenge him head-on at every opportunity. Attlee – who had no intention of resigning before Winston Churchill – watched the party tearing itself to pieces even though it was generally agreed that the Prime Minister would soon step down and a General Election would follow within weeks.

Labour's crisis carried on into 1955, and came to a head in March during a debate on the hydrogen bomb – a weapon which Churchill promised would make 'safety the robust child of terror'. The Opposition's response was essentially unheroic. It accepted the need to manufacture advanced nuclear weapons and raised no objection to them being used in retaliation against conventional attack. But realising that what little hope of unity existed depended upon voting against the government, Labour put down an amendment which criticised the government's management of the defence budget. Not without justification, Bevan described the leadership's attitude as the 'monstrous evasion of a cataclysmic issue'. It was clear that he was going to lead the biggest Labour rebellion since the war.

When the vote came at the end of the hydrogen bomb debate, sixty-two Labour MPs rebelled either by voting against the government or abstaining on the official Opposition amendment. In order to encourage the others, the whip was withdrawn from Aneurin Bevan and there were attempts – stimulated and encouraged by Gaitskell but opposed by Attlee – to have him expelled from the party. Then, the whole sorry business was overtaken by Winston Churchill's retirement and the 1955 General Election.

But the scars remained. And when the time came for the Labour Party to choose its new leader, the campaign was dominated by the personal animosity between Bevan and Gaitskell – leaving poor Herbert Morrison, the heir-presumptive for so long, on the margin of the contest. As Gaitskell's popularity increased, Morrison's desperate supporters suggested that the other candidates should stand down so as to 'give Herbert his chance'. Bevan, knowing that he could not win, agreed. But it was too late. On 14 December 1955, a week after Attlee's resignation, Hugh Gaitskell was elected leader of the Labour Party with a landslide majority – 157 votes to Bevan's 70 and Morrison's 40.

Hugh Gaitskell was the overwhelming choice of Labour MPs. But because of his relentless battle against Bevan he had become the *bête noire* of party activists. For five of the seven years in which he led Labour, he was – in consequence – a leader who could not rely on the loyalty of those he led. Yet the second half of the 1950s was, perhaps more than any other period in post-war history, a time for the confident assertion of a radical alternative to the conventional view of Britain's place in the world. The country stood not so much at a crossroads as at a bewildering junction of alternative routes, and needed to take crucial decisions about the path it would follow into the future. Vital choices had to be made about the new relationships with continental Europe and the emerging nations of Asia and Africa. And the time had come for a hard examination of the United Kingdom's place in the Atlantic Alliance. Labour did its best to pioneer a new attitude towards Africa, and despite one or two stuttering false starts, ended the decade with an honourable and imaginative record on the Third World. But according to the text-books of political theory, a radical party with a new, young leader should have set the pace in the long march towards realism in Europe as well as in the colonies. Tragically, Labour failed to grasp the initiative. Instead of arguing for Britain to seize the leadership of Europe, it argued for the pursuit of the impossible – Britain as leader of a multi-racial Commonwealth. Much of the failure was the result of pressures put upon the leader by the party members he led.

The tragedy of Labour's failure to seize the initiative was made all the greater by the probability that the second half of the 1950s should have been one of Britain's rare periods of radical inclination. It was certainly a time of growing impatience among the young – most of whom were enjoying or anticipating a standard of living and education their parents had not even dreamed about. Selective secondary education cast 82 per cent of the nation's eleven-year-olds out into the darkness of 'modern' schools. But those who had 'passed the scholarship' were able – thanks to the expansion of higher education places and the provision of generous grants by local authorities – to become the first generation of working-class boys and girls to go on to higher education in any number. At the time of the 1955 election, the children who had sat their 11-plus examination in the year that the Health Service was inaugurated were sitting the General Certificate of Education 'A' Level and filling in their university application forms. They were too old to have benefited from the Ostermilk which strengthened the bones of post-war babies. But in general their teeth were straightened, their astigmatisms were corrected and their minor ailments were cured with a minimum amount of damage to their nervous systems. Most important of all, they had never known the insecurity of unemployment. Their fathers worked. Their mothers worked if they chose to do so. They left school at eighteen with the universities rivalling each other to find them places. They registered as undergraduates in the wholly justified confidence that, three years later, employers would compete for their services.

In Ancient Rome the slaves revolted when they began to feel the rebellious hope that came with the first improvement in their status. But in Britain, the old poor who had become the newly prosperous were not similarly encouraged to rebellion. The young were radicalised. But the middle-aged had started to become middle-class. Satisfaction set in. For ten years the prevailing feeling was a determination not to lose what had been gained since the war, and the gains were very substantial.

It was the beginning of an era in which the British people enjoyed previously unimagined levels of prosperity. All governments boast about the country being 'better off than ever before'. Sometimes they make the claim when, in truth, the country is doing no more than edge forward with the minuscule increases in gross domestic product that industrialised economies find it almost impossible to avoid even during periods of sustained depression. But in the ten years from 1948 to 1958, there was a sustained and substantial improvement in living standards. Average real personal disposable income rose by almost 50 per cent. Consumer spending increased from £173 to £258 per head – a real rise of more than 50 per cent. The improvement was not evenly distributed, however. Poverty, although not wiped out, was considerably reduced by full employment, the increase in wage-rates that full employment brings and the introduction of a comprehensive social security system. At the same time, the share of national income enjoyed by the very rich declined – with consequential increases in the proportion earned by the middle classes. There was also a significant redistribution of savings and capital. In pre-war Britain, the richest 1 per cent of the population owned 56 per cent of the wealth. By the mid-1950s the figure had fallen to 42 per cent. The share owned by the richest 10 per cent had fallen from 81 to 57 per cent.

For most British families, the war had changed the world, and the changes were most spectacular and significant for men and women who were still young enough to benefit from the revolution in educational opportunity. In 1935, less than 40 per cent of fourteen-year-olds were still at school. By the mid-1950s the figure had risen (give or take a few decimal places of truants) to 100 per cent. In 1935, there were 50,000 students in British universities. By the academic year 1954–55, the undergraduate population was 82,000, and both teacher-training and further-education numbers had doubled and the class composition of the universities had changed. Pre-war, 65 per cent of higher education spending was private. In 1954–55, 70 per cent was provided from public funds. The increased number of higher education places accounted for a substantial part of the escalation in education spending, which (although it only grew from 2 to 2.8 per cent of GDP) increased, with inflation and growth in national income, from £107 million to £410 million a year.

In 1955, despite the loss and damage sustained during the war, Britain's stock of habitable houses was two million higher than in 1939. In the year before the war 25 per cent of British houses were owner-occupied. By 1955 the total had risen to 33 per cent. Life expectancy had improved from 61 years (for men) and 66 (for women) in 1939, to 66 (for men) and 72 (for women) by 1955. And as the pattern of life changed, so did the causes of death. Tuberculosis (the affliction of the industrial poor) killed 27,000 men and women in 1939–40. Fifteen years later, it claimed only 10,000 victims. But deaths from heart disease (the health risk of the affluent) rose from 130,000 to 153,000. In housing, health and education, Britain was gradually becoming middle-class. Security and prosperity might have made the nation confident – ready to take risks, willing to accept that the world had changed and determined to find a role which was consistent with its changing circumstances. Instead, it grew complacent. It was complacency that the 'Angry Young Men' said they were angry about.

Credit for the name goes to Kenneth Allsop who, in *The Angry Decade*, described a group of young novelists and playwrights whose work was united by common characteristics – 'irreverence, stridency, impatience with tradition, vigour, vulgarity and sulky resentment against the cultivated'. The first into print was John Wain. *Hurry On Down*, published in 1953, was in many ways the least angry and the most cultivated contribution to the whole movement. Four years later, John Braine published *Room at the Top* – a statement of resentment against the established order which ended with the anti-hero exploiting rather than challenging the system. In between came Colin Wilson's *The Outsider* and then in 1959 Alan Sillitoe's *The Loneliness of the Long Distance Runner*, two descriptions of the alienation felt by sensitive souls who despised the smug standards of post-war Britain. In *Saturday Night and Sunday Morning*, Sillitoe created an authentic working-class hero, Arthur Seaton, the Nottingham lathe-operator who despised authority almost as much as he feared settling down into married respectability. All of the 'Angry Young Men' represented a reaction against middle-class morality. But it was John Osborne's play *Look Back in Anger* (first produced in 1956) which assaulted the values of suburban Britain with the most unrestrained ferocity. Jimmy Porter, the graduate of a 'white-tile' university who earns his living selling sweets from a market stall, is married to a colonel's daughter. His most pronounced characteristic is a talent for vituperation:

> *Pusillanimous*, Adjective. Wanting of firmness of mind, of small courage, having a little mind, mean spirited, cowardly, timid of mind. From the Latin, 'pusillus', very little and 'animus', the mind.

In the play, that is Jimmy Porter's description of his wife. But there is little doubt that, in the playwright's mind, it was a denunciation of the section of society which she represented. Perhaps it was Osborne's opinion of post-war Britain as a whole. Looking back, the anger seems ludicrously overdone. But in May 1956, Jimmy and John could claim that they had something to be angry about. Old England was about to rise.

Egypt had been the running sore of British foreign policy ever since 1951, when the Muslim Brotherhood declared guerrilla war on the troops who guarded the Suez Canal. By the end of the year the garrison was 80,000 strong and – to add to the drain on British resources – the 60,000 workers employed by the Canal Company went on strike. The seaway was only kept open by the employment of expensive Cypriots and Mauritians. Then, in January 1952, something approaching real war broke out. Police in the barracks of Ismailia opened fire on 'the occupying forces' and, reinforced by seven hundred armed irregulars, held out against the British Army until fifty-six of them were dead. In the days of riots which followed, Western property of every description was attacked and looted. Twenty Europeans, including eleven Britons, were killed.

The riots provided King Farouk of Egypt – the dissolute puppet of the British government – with an excuse to dismiss his Prime Minister. It was a fatal mistake. Six months later, while he was on holiday in Alexandria, the Egyptian army took control of Cairo. A young soldier, Colonel Anwar Sadat, proclaimed the revolution in a radio broadcast, and the King abdicated in favour of his infant son. The monarchy lasted another eight months. On 18 June 1953, Egypt became a republic under the leadership of General Neguib. 'I am not,' said Churchill, 'opposed to giving him a good chance to prove that he is a friend of Britain.' Imperialists on the Tory back-benches wondered if the old man was getting soft or going senile.

The Tory imperialists had endured a hard five years. On 28 April 1951 Dr Mohammed Mossadeq became Prime Minister of Iran and, within five days, the Shah announced his intention to nationalise the Anglo-Iranian Oil Company. The Attlee government – feebly, in the opinion of the Opposition – tried to negotiate an agreement with the

Persian nationalists. But the talks broke down and, on 27 September, Iranian troops occupied the refineries. Attlee referred the dispute to the United Nations, but by the time Churchill moved back into Downing Street in October all but eleven of the oil company staff had left for home. A new meaning of the word 'scuttle' passed into the English language, courtesy of the Conservative MPs who believed that the Empire should have fought back. Worse was to come.

In the following autumn, Libya, proclaiming its independence of British 'protection', began what seemed to be a pattern of annual colonial revolts. In October 1952, British troops were sent to Kenya to begin the futile campaign against the Mau Mau. Then, in July 1954, the Tory government itself negotiated its own 'scuttle'. Britain agreed that its troops would leave the Canal Zone in two years' time – retaining the right to return if free passage through Suez was endangered and promising to provide sufficient British technicians to keep the installations in working order.

The demands for freedom built and bred on each other. On 28 July 1954, four days after the agreement to leave the Canal Zone, Henry Hopkinson, a junior minister at the Colonial Office, sought to assure Conservative doubters about Britain's continued determination to maintain pressure in the east of the Mediterranean. 'There can,' he said, 'be no question of any change of sovereignty in Cyprus.' Riots immediately broke out in Nicosia. Disturbances continued through the autumn and into the winter. In December, crowds surrounded the British Embassy in Athens demanding *enosis* – Cypriot union with Greece. In the early months of 1955, British troops were sent to Cyprus to protect the RAF stations at Episkopi and Akrotiri against demands for *eoka* – freedom. It was not only the British Empire which was under siege. On 7 May 1954, the French garrison at Dien Bien Phu in northern Vietnam had surrendered to the Viet-Minh after a siege of fifty-six days. The commander of the French forces shot himself later that night. That sort of exhibitionism was inconsistent with the British character, but resentment against the apparent irresistible tide of nationalism was beginning to become a major political force in Tory politics.

According to Julian Amery – perhaps the most bellicose of the Tory imperialists – the control of the Suez Canal was essential to Britain's status as a world power. Lord Hankey, the Director of the Suez Canal Company, asked a rhetorical question which was more concerned with politics than commerce: 'If we cannot hold the Suez Canal, the trade route of world and Empire shipping communications, what *can* we hold?' Nobody in the Tory party – and very few Labour supporters – could provide a convincing answer. The only argument concerned the cost of maintaining British control. Not even Churchill thought it sensible to maintain a garrison of 80,000 men. In June 1952, the Treasury had produced a memorandum which forced the Cabinet to face the new reality. Its conclusion might have been the epitaph for the decade: 'Acceptance of the imperial obligation imposes a burden on the country's economy which is beyond the resource of the country to meet.' The ingenious solution to the dilemma of preserving power without having to pay for the privilege was described by *The Economist* as 'negotiating from American strength'. The timing was perfect. Eighteen months earlier, the Aramco Corporation had come to an agreement with the Saudi Arabian king Abdul Ibn Saud. The profits made on Saudi oil would be split equally between American company and desert king. For good or ill the United States had become a power in the Middle East.

The 1954 negotiations got off to a bad start. The Egyptians refused to allow America to take part in the discussions on the future of the Suez Canal. And, to Winston Churchill's horror, the United States reacted to the rebuff with a statement of its 'traditional dedication to political liberty', and historic hostility to 'old colonial interests'. Britain began to negotiate alone. To the astonishment of the Americans, the government which had swallowed the camel of withdrawal choked on a gnat. Britain was prepared to provide technicians to maintain the canal's efficiency, but the military personnel among them must be allowed to wear military uniform. Churchill regarded proper respect for the Queen's coat as 'a matter of cardinal importance'. The Americans were bewildered by his concern, but they agreed to withhold economic aid until the dispute was settled to Britain's satisfaction. As a result, the chance to bind Egypt to the West was lost.

After the Suez agreement was signed in October 1954, Britain attempted to reinforce its influence in the Middle East. The result was the Baghdad Pact, which brought together Turkey and Iraq – at the time led by an Anglophile government. Thanks to the pact, Anthony Eden, then Foreign Secretary, visited Cairo to emphasise Britain's continuing interest in the region. There he met the young officer who had in April 1954 replaced Neguib as Egypt's Prime Minister. His name was General Gamal Abdel Nasser, and he hated Eden at first sight. Initially their conversation was purely political. Only a 'handful of people' in Baghdad, Nasser said, supported alliance with Britain. But the animosity was personal. The Englishman, Nasser later said, 'behaved like a prince among beggars' and represented 'all that he disliked in the British'. In 1956 (when Nasser had become President and Eden Prime Minister), the world paid a terrible price for the two men's mutual animosity.

At first there was hope that Britain's new Middle East strategy had worked – in April 1955, the United Kingdom became a formal partner in the Baghdad Pact and, when Pakistan joined four months later, it seemed that a formidable alliance had been forged. Iran's membership, agreed in November that year, appeared to have secured Britain's position in Asia Minor. But two irresistible forces were coming together to make a reality of the Middle East revolution – the rise of Arab nationalism and the increasing determination of Israel to secure and defend its frontiers. Both Israel and the Arabs were, in their different ways, encouraged by the United States. America guaranteed the frontiers of the new Jewish homeland, and was prepared to provide economic assistance to Egypt. The most notable and costly project was the construction of the Aswan High Dam. But Washington was not prepared to finance military aid, and rightly or wrongly, Nasser believed that rearmament was necessary to protect his country from David Ben-Gurion's increasingly belligerent Israel.

In the early months of 1956, the British government grew increasingly apprehensive both about its position in the eastern Mediterranean and the territorial ambitions of the Soviet Union. Cyprus – the base which Britain had sworn to hold 'for ever' – was in turmoil. A general strike – called to protest against British rule – had led to a state of emergency and troops on the streets of Nicosia, enforcing an uneasy peace. Although mutually antagonistic to the colonial power, Greeks and Turks seized the opportunity to settle old scores and reiterate their conflicting territorial claims. Then, in March, Britain's oldest Arab ally turned publicly against the paternalism which had sustained the partnership between the Hashemite and British Empires.

On 2 March 1956, General Sir John Bagot Glubb ('Glubb Pasha' when he put on his red and white bedouin *keffiyeh* and mounted his camel) was dismissed from the command of the Arab Legion, the core of Jordan's army. It was a deeply symbolic act. Young King Hussein was demonstrating that the nations of the Middle East – drawn on the map with arbitrary abandon at Versailles in 1919, and governed by nominees of the Great Powers – had discovered a sort of nationalism. They were capable of running their own armed forces without European assistance and did not propose to become virtual dependencies. Eden – who reacted to the news with uncontrollable rage – took it for granted that Nasser had inspired the act of Hashemite independence. He was almost certainly right. Revolt spread from country to country. The Baghdad Pact virtually collapsed. There seemed little hope of America helping to restore British influence. John Foster Dulles, the US Secretary of State, announced his undying opposition to 'imperial pretensions in Jordan and Iraq'.

But the man who invented 'brinkmanship' was even more opposed to allowing an extension of Russian influence in the Middle East, and Nasser's behaviour might have been calculated to antagonise him. *Al-Ahram* – the government-backed newspaper – constantly attacked the West and openly courted the support of the Soviet Union. Egypt recognised Communist China. Then, expressly in defiance of Dulles' persistent advice, Nasser sent delegates to the Bundung Conference of Non-aligned Countries, which America regarded as an instrument of Russian expansion. Worst of all – and particularly offensive to the most overtly proud Secretary of State ever to represent the United States – Nasser lied about his relationship with Eastern Europe. He was negotiating an arms deal with Czechoslovakia and the Soviet Union, and Dulles knew it. But Nasser insisted that he had not even discussed military aid with the Warsaw Pact. Convinced, according to Eden's memoirs, that Nasser was infiltrating other Middle East governments, Dulles considered ways of whipping him back into line. The obvious first step was a withdrawal of American aid – most spectacularly represented by investment in the Aswan Dam.

Ironically, the Egyptian government had needed to be convinced of the dam's value. At first they were so sceptical about its advantages that Dulles abandoned his initial plan to make its completion dependent on an accommodation with Israel. Nasser, he feared, would not sacrifice an iota of his revolutionary popularity to secure the completion of a project which he believed, at best, had very little value and might, by holding back the waters of the Nile, reduce the fertility of the Delta. Eden, on the other hand, wanted to avoid driving Egyptians into the arms of the Soviet Union, and believed that he had persuaded the angry Americans to do no more than allow the project 'to wither on the vine'. But John Foster Dulles was past moderation. On 19 July 1956 the United States announced that it would not honour the loan agreement by which the Aswan Dam was to be financed.

The impending crisis distracted the British government from what it had imagined would be its brief preoccupation of the early summer. On 28 June, the Commonwealth Prime Ministers assembled for one of their regular meetings. Anthony Eden assumed that the most difficult item on the agenda would be the reconciliation of Britain's nuclear role with the leadership of a Commonwealth which included non-aligned and neutralist powers. But he also prepared to answer questions on the decision of the countries which had joined together in the Schuman Plan to build on the Coal and Steel Community and create a Common Market. The Chancellor, Harold Macmillan, proposed to reassure his colleagues with the news that Britain intended to found a rival organisation – the European Free Trade Association (Efta) – which would preserve Britain's Commonwealth links and trade.

Despite growing anxieties about the whole future of the Middle East, the British Cabinet honoured its promise to withdraw its troops from the Canal Zone, encouraged by Egypt's assurance that the canal would retain its 'international status' indefinitely. The British rear-guard sailed for home. But whatever the emollience of his formal promises, Nasser continued his vituperation against the West. On 24 July, his speech at the opening of the new Cairo pipeline denounced the United States of America in particularly violent language. Two days later, in Alexandria, he turned on Great Britain. His denunciation included a historical analysis of British imperialism and Disraeli's acquisition of canal shares. Inevitably he mentioned De Lesseps, the French engineer who had planned and built the waterway. It was the code-word by which the revolution was begun. When the message was received along the Suez Canal, Egyptian forces took control of the locks and pumping stations. The Suez Canal Company had been nationalised. Dues paid by the ships which passed through it would, Nasser announced, be used to complete the building of the Aswan Dam.

When the news of Nasser's speech (and its consequences) reached London, the Prime Minister was at dinner in Downing Street – by strange irony, in honour of the King of Iraq. Among the guests was the leader of the Labour Party. After the formalities were over, Eden and Foreign Secretary Selwyn Lloyd took Hugh Gaitskell aside and told him the news. The discussion was diffuse, and what took place was subsequently disputed by the participants. It is generally accepted that Gaitskell argued the importance of referring the crisis to the United Nations; Selwyn Lloyd talked about issuing an 'old-fashioned ultimatum', and there was agreement that American support and assistance were essential. But the informal talks began a confusion which was temporarily to convince Labour's left wing that the party had chosen the wrong leader.

The strains on an already divided Opposition were no more than a side-show. The conflict with Egypt which followed – first verbal, then diplomatic and eventually military – was a historic manifestation of Britain's changing status in the world. It was a change which public opinion did not yet recognise. Even the Labour-supporting *Daily Herald* proclaimed that, 'No British government can resign itself to Colonel Nasser being in control of a vital Commonwealth life-line.' It was the death-throes of imperial pretension, the last attempt of Britain to convince itself and the world that it was a Great Power. But it was a claim which even the old enthusiasts for Empire made without much confidence or conviction. Suez was the rearguard action of *pax Britannica*. After Nasser had challenged the might of a still imperial power, the world would have changed even if the Franco-British invasion had recaptured the canal.

The more perceptive commentators recognised that frustration was as important as anger. Nigel Nicolson, who sacrificed his political career to oppose the doomed adventure, recognised the mood at the time: 'Nobody can fully understand the Suez crisis unless he takes fully into account the growing unease that Britain's position in the world . . . was being whittled down.' R. A. Butler took longer either to recognise or to acknowledge the reality. In November 1956 – the month in which the Anglo-French Task Force invaded Egypt – he told the House of Commons that he was proud to speak for 'a united government and a united party'. Ten years later he crucially modified his position:

> There were deep-seated emotions affecting liberal-minded people, but they combined only too easily with less generous sentiments; the residues of illiberal resentment at the loss of Empire, the rise of coloured nationalism and the transfer of world leadership to the United States.

There were practical reasons to feel concern about the nationalisation of the canal. The minutes of the Cabinet which met on 27 July read as if the meeting had been wholly free from all of the chauvinistic prejudices about which Butler was to write during his retirement. The British government was, ministers agreed, 'on weak ground in basing its resistance on the narrow ground that Colonel Nasser had acted illegally'. However, the canal was 'an important international asset' which the Egyptians 'had not the technical ability to manage'. Its free navigation was essential to the British economy. Aubrey Jones, the Minister of Fuel and Power, reported that two-thirds of the oil consumed by Europe – 60 million tons a year – came through the canal. In 1955, 14,666 ships sailed its length from Alexandria to Port Said. One-third of them were British. The idea of asking the United

Nations to take action against Nasser was dismissed without discussion, since – according to Eden – it would 'only invite a Soviet veto'. Egypt's sterling balances were frozen. But, knowing that economic sanctions would have little effect, the Cabinet agreed that the canal must be kept open 'by use of force if necessary'. The Shadow Cabinet met three days later, oppressed by a fear which damaged the judgement of their successors at the outset of the Falkland and Gulf wars. Labour was determined not to be portrayed as 'unpatriotic and irresponsible'. In consequence it agreed that military preparations were justified, but it was not sure what the military should prepare to do.

Gaitskell, in part relying on the brief conversation which followed the Downing Street dinner, believed that Eden did not intend to fight for control of the canal. But he shared his colleagues' concern that the Cabinet might – for political as much as strategic reasons – become so bellicose that war might break out by mistake. The Labour leader and his deputy, Jim Griffiths, asked for a meeting with the Prime Minister. Gaitskell (rashly laying down a general rule to cover a specific situation) insisted that military intervention could only be justified in self-defence or in support of a United Nations resolution. Eden answered ambiguously that he doubted if military action against Egypt could be justified on those criteria. But he did not say that he accepted the criteria as rules which should govern the government's conduct. Gaitskell – who was predisposed to believe in the Prime Minister's good intentions – took the reply to mean that there would be no military action unless it was specifically sanctioned by the UN. In the emergency Commons debate held on 2 August, Gaitskell described Nasser's conduct as 'exactly the same as that [which] we encountered from Mussolini and Hitler in those years before the war'. His passionate denunciation was compared, not always unfavourably, with Eden's detached analysis of the choice facing the government. The misunderstanding over the United Nations' role did substantial damage to Gaitskell's standing within his party, for when war came, those who looked for a cause to complain accused him of encouraging Eden to invade. Inevitably, Gaitskell felt that 'he had been deceived and betrayed'. So when he realised that Eden was preparing to invade Egypt, the party battle became particularly bitter. Righteous anger combined with a determination to redeem his reputation among his own supporters to make Gaitskell denounce Eden in what were, at the time, extraordinary personal terms.

It is difficult to be certain whether the Prime Minister intentionally deceived the Leader of the Opposition, or if the misunderstanding was no more than the result of Eden's sloppy language compounded by Gaitskell's inclination to hear what he wanted to be true. But whatever the cause, the misunderstanding between the government and the Labour Party was a matter of little lasting consequence. Eden's failure to understand America's reaction to the crisis was fatal to his country's interests and to his own career, although he was entitled to claim that he was confused by the undoubted ambiguity of the United States' attitude. Dulles was obsessed with combating what he perceived as the communist threat. At the same time, the US regarded itself as the natural champion of nations which were oppressed by colonial rule. Unfortunately, the nations of the developing world were in the habit of turning for help to the Soviet Union. Washington's position was made even more complicated by the residual loyalty which America felt for its wartime allies, Britain and France – the two nations against which many of the anti-colonial struggles were being directed. At the heart of the Suez crisis Dulles told the President's National Security Council:

> For many years now the United States has been walking a tightrope between the effort to maintain our old and valued relations with our British and French allies on the one hand, and on the other trying to assure ourselves of the friendship and understanding of the newly independent countries who have escaped from colonialism.

Eisenhower saw life in more simple terms. He regarded America as the natural champion of independence; after all, the great republic of which he was President had been founded on a Declaration of Independence from the British Empire. And he was impatient with what he called the 'almost childlike faith' in Anglo-American co-operation as the solution to all the world's problems. But although Eisenhower was sceptical about the value or indeed existence of the 'special relationship', Eden and his Cabinet could not bring themselves to believe that the general who had led the victorious invasion of Europe had forgotten the benefits of co-operation. America, they knew, was always late in coming to the support of Europe, but in the end, as had been proved in two world wars, it supported its friends.

When Eisenhower wrote to Eden warning him of the 'unwisdom' of 'even contemplating military force at this moment', the Prime Minister chose to interpret the message as not ruling out military force for ever. Only the timing, he insisted, was in dispute. Technically his analysis of the President's syntax was impeccable, but he should have known that Eisenhower was against war in the Middle East.

Eden – whatever impression he had given to Gaitskell – was preparing for what amounted to an invasion of Egypt. A battle plan, code-named 'Musketeer', was drawn up. The landing would be at Alexandria, where 80,000 troops would go ashore. After eight days of battle, Cairo and an intact canal would have been captured. It would, the Chiefs of Staff said, take until mid-September to assemble the armada. Throughout the late summer and early autumn, troops gathered on the south coast and ships and planes moved to Cyprus. Then the plan changed. The Egyptian air force would instead be wiped out on the first day. The landing would be at Port Said rather than Alexandria. But whatever the change in tactics, the strategy was war, and Eden's continued insistence that he was not preparing to invade grew increasingly incredible.

There were signs in early September that some of Eden's ministers were beginning either to lose their nerve or re-discover their conscience. Foreign Secretary Selwyn Lloyd argued that the dispute be referred to the UN Security Council, and the Cabinet agreed. Walter Monckton – promoted from the Ministry of Labour to the Ministry of Defence – wrote to the Prime Minister what can only be described as a dissenting minute: 'If together with the French we took military measures against Egypt, our action would be condemned by a substantial body of public opinion . . . We should let no opportunity pass of securing an agreement by settlement.' Butler was characteristically opaque. The government's position would be weakened if it 'did not take all practical steps to secure settlement by peaceful means'. Eden certainly did not take Butler's advice as a reservation. The Cabinet's unanimous view was that 'the possibilities of a peaceful settlement should be explored' without 'reducing the weight of pressure on the Egyptian government'. Lest anyone should doubt what that meant, Operation Musketeer was approved with one amendment. The invasion date was postponed by seven days.

Eden wrote to Dulles hoping to secure his support by reminding him that only the Soviet Union had anything to gain from instability in the Middle East. The letter ended with one of the first signs of the Prime Minister's growing paranoia. Speaking as if he was President of Pop at Eton and Nasser was a badly-behaved fag, Eden insisted that 'we must not let him get away with it again'. The American reaction was not what the British government had expected. Eisenhower, the Cabinet was told on 6 September, had expressed 'disquiet at the prospect that the United Kingdom and France might have it in mind to take military action before all the possibilities of sealing a peaceful settlement could be exhausted'. They should begin to look for a compromise. Dulles suggested that the Suez Canal Company which Egypt had nationalised should be re-established as the Suez Canal Users' Association, and should become responsible both for the maintenance of free passage along the waterway and for the collection of dues – a proportion of which should go to the Egyptian government. Robert Menzies, the Australian Prime Minister, attempted to turn himself into a one-man peace mission and offered to conciliate between the parties. Nasser rejected both suggestions.

Eden's apologists are entitled to argue in his defence that the conduct of John Foster Dulles, the US Secretary of State, was ambivalent to the point of perversity. He veered erratically between his denunciation of Soviet infiltration into the Middle East and assaults upon Western colonialism. Perhaps, intellectually, the two positions were not incompatible. But their relationship was too subtle for Eden immediately to understand. However, by the time that the House of Commons met on 12 September for its second emergency session, the American position had been clarified in a simple sentence: 'We do not propose to shoot our way through the canal.' Convinced at last that he could expect no support from America, Eden began to search for desperate remedies to his dilemma. Christian Pineau, the French Foreign Minister, provided one.

The 1954 Anglo-Egyptian Agreement on Suez entitled – perhaps even required – Britain to reoccupy the Canal Zone if disturbance near or around the canal put free navigation at risk. All that was needed to justify an invasion of Egypt was a war. And a war, Pineau believed, was easily arranged. Israel was determined to obtain control of the west coast of the Gulf of Aqaba and the Straits of Tirana and, as a result, secure Eilat as the port to serve the hinterland of the Negev. David Ben-Gurion, the Israeli Prime Minister, had little or no interest in the row between London, Paris and Cairo. But if the prize for his co-operation was Eilat, an Egyptian assault might be arranged. The French suggestion was put to Eden at Chequers – the Prime Minister's country house – on 14 October 1956. In contradiction of his reputation and history, the hero of Munich, the opponent of appeasement, the champion of open diplomacy and the enemy of unprovoked aggression agreed to the most squalid conspiracy of twentieth-century international relations.

By mid-October, Eden was entitled to conclude that the United Nations was incapable of finding a legal solution to the crisis. At the autumn meeting, Selwyn Lloyd had argued for adoption of the Anglo-French 'Six Principles' – which included both respect for Egyptian sovereignty and international guarantees of the canal's independence from control by one country. The Egyptians studiously avoided endorsing the plan. But Eisenhower found the discussions 'most gratifying' and gave a 'prayer of thanksgiving' for the progress which had been made towards peace. Dulles apologised for the public embarrassment which Britain had been caused by the President's endorsement of stalemate. The President's public statements were, he said, the consequence of his campaign for re-election. The United Nations debate ended with support in general for the Six Principles but no decision on whether or not Egypt had an obligation to accept them. That part of the resolution was vetoed by the Soviet Union.

Selwyn Lloyd flew to Paris on 16 October for a meeting with Pineau and Guy Mollet, the French Prime Minister, which was so secret that Sir Gladwyn Jebb – Her Britannic Majesty's Ambassador to

Paris – was not allowed to attend. The three men discussed a plan which had been drawn up by General Maurice Challe, Deputy Chief of the French General Staff. Six days later, the Challe plan was put to the Israeli government. The fateful meeting took place in Sèvres, a suburb of Paris. Selwyn Lloyd (and his private secretary) arrived late after a car crash on the way from the airport. The argument had already begun. The Israeli delegation was divided, and Prime Minister Ben-Gurion was reluctant to take part in the conspiracy. Moshe Dayan, the Defence Minister, was certain that immediate action was necessary. Lloyd tipped the balance. In his judgement, the United Nations would eventually give its formal support to the Six Principles and peace would then be guaranteed on Egypt's terms. Lloyd persuaded Israel to invade in order to frustrate the solution which, a week earlier, he had proposed to the UN General Assembly.

On 25 October Anthony Eden told the Cabinet that it must 'consider the situation which was likely to arise if hostilities broke out between Israel and Egypt'. The likelihood of such a catastrophe was attributed to Israel's fear that the 'ambitions of Colonel Nasser were threatening their frontiers'. The Cabinet was asked to consider whether the invasion of Egypt would 'necessitate Anglo-French intervention in the area', advised that 'the French government were strongly of the view that intervention would be justified' and warned of the risk that Britain would 'be accused of collusion with Israel'.

We shall never know how many members of the Cabinet were told (or guessed) the full extent of the Anglo-French perfidy. Eden was certainly determined to keep the Sèvres meeting secret. When he discovered that a note had been made of the discussion, he sent two senior diplomats to Paris with the instruction to burn every copy of the record. But although the full extent of the diplomacy was probably known only to Anthony Eden and Selwyn Lloyd, none of the government's ministers could have doubted that Britain was party to Israel's invasion plans. Although some of them may not have realised the full extent of Britain's duplicity, every member of the Cabinet knew or suspected that Britain was taking part in some sort of international conspiracy. And – with varying degrees of reluctance – they became accessories to the crime.

At the beginning of the escapade – when the canal was first nation-alised – Harold Macmillan, the Chancellor of the Exchequer, had been an unrepentant hawk. But as the crisis continued, he took less and less part in Cabinet debates. Because of Britain's virtual isolation, the pound was coming under increasing pressure, and the Treasury was not sure how long the reserves would hold out. But Macmillan was reluctant to make too swift a transition from hawk to dove or, as he knew the Suez group would say, chicken.

So for more than three months, the pressure on sterling had increased without the British Cabinet seriously considering the long-term damage which was being done to the economy. There was, however – at least in private – constant speculation about the danger of Soviet intervention in the conflict. Ministers came to the invariable conclusion that since the United States would come to Britain's defence, the Soviet Union would not dare to threaten any European member of Nato. Colonel Nasser chose to believe otherwise – not least because his Ambassador to Moscow had been told that Russia was 'prepared to go all the way, including risking a third world war' in order to protect Egyptian integrity. On that point at least the Cabinet was right. The Soviet Union was lying in order to ingratiate itself with Cairo.

Certain that hostilities could be limited to the Middle East, Israel mobilised its armed forces on 28 October – encouraging fears in the United States that an attack on Jordan was imminent. Winthrop Aldrich, the American Ambassador, took advantage of the special relationship to ask Selwyn Lloyd if he knew what Jerusalem intended. The Foreign Secretary replied that he had 'no idea'. The following day, when Israeli paratroops landed at the eastern end of the Mitta Pass, Eisenhower realised that the Central Intelligence Agency had misjudged Ben-Gurion's intention and that the Foreign Secretary had lied. At least the CIA was entitled to argue that, in the late days of October 1956, it was preoccupied with other matters. There were stirrings in the Soviet empire.

In Poland, Wladyslaw Gomulka had returned to power seven years after he had been deposed by the Moscow faction in the Warsaw government for 'non-appreciation of the decisive role of the Soviet Union' in Polish affairs. Had it not been for Stalin's death in 1953, he would have been executed. But after three years in solitary confinement, he emerged into the autumn sunlight to become First Secretary of the Party and effective Prime Minister of Poland. Then a second satellite rebelled. When, on 23 October, demonstrators filled the streets of Budapest in Hungary, the world watched to see if the Soviet Union had lost its taste for domination of Eastern Europe or lost its nerve.

The Hungarian demonstrations were a classic example of a slave's revolt. Mátyás Rákosi, the hard-line pro-Soviet Prime Minister, had been replaced by Imre Nagy, who only a year earlier had been deposed for 'right-wing deviationism'. A taste of freedom always increases the appetite for liberty, and the people of Budapest went out into the streets in the hope that the return of Nagy would be the beginning, not the end, of reform. Their demand was for free elections. And for three days, the Soviet tanks – which had rolled out of their barracks on the demonstration's first day – stood still and silent while their crews watched the revolt grow. Then Nagy conceded their demands. Elections, he promised, would be held, and the Russian Army would leave the country. The promise was not kept. On the day in which the British Cabinet agreed to support the Sèvres conspiracy, Soviet tanks opened fire on the unarmed Budapest protesters. The first shooting was an isolated and perhaps unplanned incident. The protests continued and, for days, there was real hope that the Soviet Union would withdraw from Hungary as it had withdrawn from Austria and Yugoslavia. Some Western commentators claimed that the Russian conscripts who were stationed in Budapest had refused to open fire on the Magyars, whom they regarded as their friends. That slightly sentimental view gained extra credence when the garrison was reinforced by regular infantry battalions from inside the Soviet Union. For a couple of days the new troops did nothing except patrol the streets. Then, on 4 November – suddenly and without warning – they began to fire into the crowd. The streets were cleared within minutes. The fourth of November was also the day on which Anthony Eden made the radio broadcast which warned that war in the Middle East was imminent and unavoidable. The landing at Port Said took place on 5 November.

It is impossible to make a precise judgement about the extent to which the Suez adventure influenced the Soviet Union's decision to suppress the Hungarian revolt, for we still cannot be sure if Russian intelligence knew what the French and British governments were planning. Certainly, once Operation Kadesh was launched on 29 October, the West lost the moral authority which would have been necessary for either a sustained campaign within the United Nations or direct military intervention. But the likelihood is that, once the Kremlin had recovered from the shock of the popular uprising, the troops would have been ordered to face the Budapest protesters – whether or not Nato had slid into a bitter argument about the failure of two of its members to respect the rule of international law. But in the West, Britain and France were held, at least in part, responsible for allowing Russia to escape the consequences of its colonial aggression. When on 9 November a new British Ambassador presented his letter of credence to the President of the United States, Eisenhower read him a letter which Imre Nagy had sent to the White House. It claimed that had it not been for the invasion of Egypt, the Hungarian uprising would have been a triumphant success. However, there is no doubt that President Eisenhower's preoccupation with the Hungarian uprising combined with his neurotic concern about an election which he could not lose to distract him from events in Europe and the Middle East. The Israeli invasion – which made steady progress throughout 30 October – came, in consequence, as a surprise to Washington.

The Cabinet met on the morning of the 30th and, having been told of Israel's assault, agreed a note be sent to the governments of Israel and Egypt *asking* for agreement that an Anglo-French force be 'moved temporarily into key positions' at Port Said, Ismailia and Suez in order to guarantee freedom of transit through the canal. Eden's personal message to Eisenhower was intended to be an emollient description of the need to keep Suez traffic flowing and the Prime Minister's strong preference for solving the crisis in the United Nations. Unfortunately it was so emollient that it did not mention the imminent Anglo-French invasion of Suez. The offence which the omission caused provoked a letter from the President which began, 'I have just learned from the press of the twelve-hour ultimatum which you and the French government have delivered to the government of Egypt . . .'. Eisenhower published the letter within minutes of its arrival in London. From then on the Suez operation was fought on three fronts – on the banks of the canal, among public opinion in Great Britain, and by telegram across the Atlantic. It was the trans-atlantic battle that was to prove decisive.

Hugh Gaitskell, the Leader of Her Majesty's Opposition, was given fifteen minutes' notice of the Anglo-French ultimatum to Israel and Egypt. Although he did not know of the conspiracy, and still believed that Israel had mounted a surprise attack, he demanded and obtained an immediate debate in the House of Commons. It ended with Labour voting to demonstrate its suspicion that, however the war had begun, Britain and France were determined to end it by force rather than by negotiation. That suspicion was confirmed when, two days later, the resolution which America had moved in the UN Security Council – calling for Israel to withdraw within its own frontiers and the dispute to be solved by peaceful means – was vetoed by Great Britain. The veto did no more than postpone the inevitable. Before the end of the week the resolution was carried, overwhelmingly, in the General Assembly. But by then, the war had begun in earnest.

Britain's planes began bombing the Canal Zone on 31 October and the bombardment continued for almost forty-eight hours. All over Britain protest rallies – generally organised by the Labour Party and the TUC – condemned what the speakers called 'open aggression'. Inevitably the Prime Minister accused Labour of betraying 'British troops going into action' and – equally predictably – there were, within both major parties, small groups of doubters who disagreed with the position taken up by their leaders. Eleven Tory dissidents signed an open letter to Eden, asking him (rhetorically) to describe the purpose of government policy. Edward Boyle resigned from the Cabinet but agreed to keep his decision secret until the fighting was over. Walter Monckton retired 'on grounds of age and health'. Labour Party 'Friends of Israel' wondered if Gaitskell had gone too far in his demonstration against the invasion. But radical opinion – more out-raged than at any time since Munich – united in its condemnation. The *Manchester Guardian* thought Gaitskell's attack on the government was too timid. The *Observer*'s editorials expressed its outrage in language which was more intemperate than anything which David Astor had published before. It was written by Dingle Foot, a Liberal MP who later became Solicitor-General in Harold Wilson's government. At the BBC, the Overseas Service refused to broadcast government propaganda or allow its description of the preparations for war to be censored by the Foreign Office.

The bombing continued until the early hours of Monday 5 November, in the hope that the blitzkrieg would ensure an unop-posed landing and a speedy capture of the whole canal. At 7.15 A.M., the Third Battalion of the Parachute Regiment was dropped on to Gamil airfield. French paratroops – to the chagrin of their British comrades, far better prepared and equipped – landed a couple of miles away. The timing was important. At 7.00 A.M. the United Nations 'ceasefire resolution' had expired. At 7.30 the UN debate on the creation of an international peace-keeping force was due to end.

It seemed, at first, that the military operation was going slowly but well. On the morning of the Anglo-French landing, the Israelis had won a spectacular victory at Sharm el-Sheikh, and the Egyptian army – although well trained, well equipped and highly motivated – was fighting on two fronts. The Port Said garrison asked for a truce – possibly in the hope of creating an 'open city' in which neither com-batant would fight. Communications between the Anglo-French fighting troops, the tactical headquarters and the Ministry of Defence in London were pathetically bad. So the message reporting the sug-gestion of a truce became the announcement of a surrender. The General Officer Commanding the invasion did not forget his politi-cal obligation. He telephoned London, with what he believed to be the truth, just in time for Sir Anthony Eden to end his statement to the House of Commons with the news that Port Said had fallen.

The besieging British General, who thought that the offer of a truce might be the preliminary to capitulation, asked if the Egyptians would like to suggest 'terms of a negotiated surrender'. When

Colonel Nasser heard what he regarded as an impertinence, he laid down his conditions for an end to the fighting: 'Tell the British General to give himself up with all his troops.' It was a time for the British stiff upper lip to be fully deployed. The GOC telegraphed Eden with the news that the victory which Parliament had celebrated so loudly was all a mistake. His message to the Second-in-Command – on the ground outside Port Said and required to continue the battle which the Cabinet thought had been won – was a masterpiece of English understatement:

> Hard luck. Grateful if you can give me the form so that I can handle the political pressure. PM gave out in House tonight that a ceasefire had taken place so will be reluctant to agree on full-scale attack starting again.

That quintessentially Anglo-Saxon response to adversity was matched by the characteristically arcane circumstances in which the Cabinet was forced to consider the news. The sixth of November was the date set down for the State Opening of Parliament, so discussion of the Middle East war had to be curtailed in time for Her Majesty's ministers to 'attend upon the Sovereign in the House of Peers', when Black Rod so instructed them at eleven o'clock. In the time available, the fiasco of the Port Said surrender announcement was barely mentioned. There was more serious news to discuss.

Ten days earlier, Chancellor of the Exchequer Harold Macmillan had privately warned the Prime Minister that the reserves were falling so fast that there was a real risk of devaluation and a collapse of the Sterling Area. As the Cabinet – resplendent in morning dress – prepared to answer the Queen's summons, Macmillan decided that he had a duty to set out the stark facts of the impending economic collapse. He reported to the Cabinet that Great Britain no longer commanded the confidence of the international money markets and that the reserves had fallen by £20.3 million in September, £30 million in October and by £100 million during the first week of November. The figures may have been deliberately exaggerated, but the trend of international opinion was beyond dispute. In normal circumstances the United States would have provided a supporting loan, but there would be no help from America for as long as the Suez adventure continued. Indeed, the Federal Reserve was selling sterling at an unreasonably low (and, one must conclude, an intentionally punitive) rate.

There was rapid agreement that an immediate ceasefire was unavoidable. Eden telephoned Paris with the humiliating message that the Suez adventure was over, not because the British Cabinet had decided that it was foolish and wrong but because the British economy could not afford it:

> I don't think we can go on. The pressure on sterling is becoming unbearable. The English can take a lot of things, but I don't think they would be willing to accept a failure of sterling with its consequences for the Commonwealth.

The French argued that the ceasefire should be postponed until Port Said, Ismailia and Suez were captured and the operation at least appeared to be a military success. Eden insisted that it must all be finished, whatever the consequences for pride and esteem, 'within hours'. Nasser had won.

The result of Eden's folly was a combination of all the horrors which he had sought to avoid. The *casus belli* had been the need to ensure free passage from Port Said to Ismailia, but the canal was blocked for the next six months. Britain's authority in the region, far from being restored, was totally destroyed. After November 1956, the United States and the Soviet Union vied for influence in the Middle East while Great Britain vainly attempted to associate itself with America by opposing Russia's growing power. Colonel Nasser, instead of being discredited and deposed, became the undisputed leader of Arab nationalism. He was the man who had challenged the forces of Western imperialism and won. The canal become Egypt's undisputed property.

Eden himself paid the inevitable price. He had been physically frail for years, and the emotional strain of fighting – and losing – the Suez war was too great for him to endure. In late December, Iain Macleod noticed that the Prime Minister had lost interest in the Cabinet meeting over which he presided, and was staring absentmindedly out of the window. Eden resigned on 9 January 1957 and, after 'consultations', Harold Macmillan 'emerged' the next day as the new Tory leader. The former Chancellor of the Exchequer had, according to his critics, been wholly consistent throughout the crisis. He had been the first to want to go in and the first to want to come out.

Most of Great Britain reacted to the national humiliation with fury. The British people were not ready to accept that their economy – and particularly their currency – was too weak to withstand the withdrawal of international confidence. America, accused of betraying her wartime ally, was held to blame for the defeat. But other culprits were picked out for special punishment. The *Observer* and the *Manchester Guardian*, which had opposed the adventure from the start, suffered massive losses in circulation, and the Labour Party paid the price for both predicting disaster and for proposing the solution which was eventually imposed on Britain by world opinion. When, on 14 November, Gallup published its first 'post-Suez' opinion poll, the Opposition's six-point lead over the government had disappeared. The news that a United Nations peace-keeping force was supervising a withdrawal and ceasefire led to neither services of thanksgiving nor dancing in the streets.

The final irony was not disclosed for several days, and perhaps not fully realised for many years. On the morning of 6 November, when Anthony Eden had telephoned Paris to explain that an immediate ceasefire was unavoidable, Guy Mollet (the French Prime Minister) was in a meeting which he left with the greatest reluctance and only after he was told that the British Prime Minister must speak to him at once. In the Palace of Westminster, Parliament was about to take part in one of the great manifestations of faded glory. The Queen, crowned, robed and preceded by the Sword of State and Cap of Maintenance, was about to address the ermine-robed peers of the realm. In the Elysée, the leaders of France and Germany were discussing equal pay for equal work and support for French industry. Agreement on those prosaic subjects was all that was needed to enable the two countries to join together in a common market. Konrad

Adenauer had travelled to Paris to overrule the German officials whose detailed reservations were standing in the way of European unity. When he was told of the collapse of sterling he observed that America could not be trusted to defend Europe. As the old order was crumbling on one side of the Channel, a new order was being created on the other.

4

WINDS OF CHANGE
A Superpower No More

———•———

On 25 March 1957, Italy, France, Germany and the three Benelux countries signed the Treaty of Rome and began the slow progress towards economic and political integration which, almost forty years later, produced the European Union. The event was not widely reported in the British press. And even among the *cognoscenti* who knew that a continental alliance was being created, only a few polyglot eccentrics thought that Britain had anything to gain by seeking new friends across the Channel rather than maintaining the affection of Empire and Commonwealth. Both major parties believed that the Atlantic Alliance offered strategic and economic security and should not be imperilled by allying ourselves to nations with which we had little in common.

In that eventful month of March 1957, Britain seemed to be recovering the international respect which had been lost at Suez. The resignation of Anthony Eden, two months earlier, marked a new start. And in many ways it was. Harold Macmillan emerged from the usual processes of consultation to become the first Prime Minister of the television era. He chose to portray himself as a slightly raffish – though wholly respectable – Edwardian, whose patriotism, scholarship and general concern for the poor were part of an earlier, more elegant age. But his choice of image was less important than his acceptance that image had become a crucial part of modern politics. He matched his carefully cultivated reputation for patrician *insouciance* – 'unflappability', the newspapers called it – with a plebeian willingness to improve his appearance. The cut of his hair, moustache and suits were changed to meet the demands of fashion, and his teeth – which had once made him look like Bertie Wooster's elder brother – were rearranged so that he smiled like the Duke of Omnium. By the end of his premiership, it was hard to distinguish the real Macmillan from the myth that he, and his critics, had created. We know that 'Supermac' was sick with nerves before he spoke in the House of Commons and that the dismissal of his Chancellor's resignation as 'a little local difficulty' was an *ad lib* on which he had worked throughout the previous night. But counterfeit or genuine, the public persona which he acquired helped to shape the spirit of the age.

His reaction to the news that he was to become Prime Minister of the United Kingdom was carefully recorded for posterity: 'Where's the Chief Whip? We're off to the Turf to celebrate.' Once installed in his club, he observed that, if R. A. Butler had become Her Majesty's First Minister, he would have marked the occasion with 'plain living and high thinking'. Despite his much publicised (though genuine) love of the classics, Macmillan often spoke in a manner which was novel among Tory grandees. He thought that life should be 'fun' and described whatever displeased him as a 'bore'. The Whig who once rose above the petty considerations of the *bourgeoisie* became the party leader who manipulated the hopes and fears of the middle classes with ruthless brilliance. During his first year as Prime Minister, he wrote to the Director of Conservative Central Office with a request which was as significant as it was bizarre:

I am always hearing about the middle classes. What is it they really want? Will you put it down on a sheet of paper and I will see if I can give it to them.

For seven years, Harold Macmillan did his best to meet their needs. It would be wrong to suggest that he made Britain a middle-class nation. That slow transformation, beginning with changed attitudes during the war, was achieved by increasing prosperity and the expanding aspirations that prosperity encouraged. But he promoted the materialism which is the hallmark of the *bourgeoisie*. Forty years later, his nephew, the Duke of Devonshire, said that Macmillan wanted to be a Trollope grandee, but had more in common with a Galsworthy businessman. Whatever his aspiration, he presided over the years when suburbia came into its own. From 1951 (the year he returned to office as housing minister) to 1963 (the year he resigned the Tory party leadership) the number of cars on British roads rose from 2.5 to 6 million. In 1951, 5 per cent of households had refrigerators; by 1964 the figure had risen to 37 per cent. Macmillan was Prime Minister of Britain in the middle of a quarter-century of almost continuous growth – an average of 2.8 per cent a year from 1948 to 1971. During the Macmillan years, much – perhaps too much – of the new wealth was invested in consumer durables: the mark of middle-class success.

That did not mean that he was never impatient with suburban attitudes and values. Before he became Prime Minister, he had written:

> We are reaching a position in which the English people of 50 million who, in material terms, are quite unequal to the new giants, will move neither towards Europe or America.

Macmillan believed that it was his destiny to end that immobilism and determine Britain's new place in the world. The problem he faced in changing historic tack has still not been overcome. For, in the half-century which followed the war, the British people took so long to adjust to their changed status that, every time they were ready to accept the new reality, the world had moved on again and once more left them behind. The metaphor most often used to describe this constant and debilitating national syndrome was 'missing the bus'. But the image needs to be extended. Successive governments clambered on board just before the bus accelerated almost out of sight – only to find that they were too late to influence the direction of its route and that it was travelling in a direction which best suited other passengers. Macmillan himself (an enthusiast for Britain in Europe by the end of his premiership) must take some of the blame for the United

Kingdom losing its way. For his original 'Grand Design' was to make the 'special relationship' with America even more special and to create a Commonwealth which was a worthy partner for the United States.

At least Macmillan held emphatic and highly pragmatic views about Britain's proper defence capability. During his last weeks as Chancellor of the Exchequer, he sent a letter to Anthony Head, the Secretary of State for Defence, which set out an economic truth that successive governments understood but, for reasons of politics and prestige, chose to ignore: 'The true deterrent [to the outbreak of war with Russia] is the American possession, actual or potential, of these weapons. There is scarcely any question of our using deterrent weapons until the United States does so.' He concluded that Britain's defence capability should be the 'minimum necessary to convince the Americans, once they have been made aware of our economic difficulties, of our sincerity as allies'.

As soon as he became Prime Minister, Macmillan sent for Head and, having set out the cuts which he expected in the defence budget, asked him to return at four o'clock to say whether or not he thought himself capable of delivering such comprehensive economies. Head resigned and Duncan Sandys, Churchill's son-in-law, replaced him. On 4 April – barely three months after his appointment – Sandys produced a Defence White Paper. National Service was to end, reducing the strength of the armed forces from 690,000 to 375,000. The German garrison was cut from 77,000 to 64,000. The navy lost its battleships and in the original proposals (eventually abandoned) its aircraft-carriers. Transport command was to be expanded in order to give greater mobility to the forces which remained. The net result was a saving of £78 million – and an increased reliance on the United States of America. It looked as though reality had set in.

Fortunately, the United States was in a mood to co-operate. Anthony Eden's resignation had proved a great healer, and at a conference in Bermuda in March, Eisenhower had confirmed that he would provide the British government with sixty Thor guided missiles – controlled by the 'dual key' which allowed each country to veto but not to initiate their use. America's apparent generosity in sharing its nuclear know-how with its allies was to become a major obstacle to Britain accepting its role as a European rather than a global power. But no one thought of that in 1957. Britain accepted Thor and went ahead with its own independent nuclear programme.

On 15 May, the first British hydrogen bomb was detonated on Christmas Island in the Indian Ocean. And, with the autumn, there came the hope that American and British nuclear developments would progress side by side. At the Washington summit on 25 October – yet another milepost reached on St Crispin's Day – President Eisenhower proposed a Declaration of Common Purpose which, as well as confirming the Atlantic Alliance, set up two committees through which the allies pooled information on weapon production. The McMahon Act – which had so offended Attlee by its exclusion of Britain from the benefits of American nuclear research – was effectively repealed. A month later, it was formally amended out of existence.

Eisenhower's enthusiasm for pooling intellectual resources was, no doubt, primarily motivated by his wish to heal the Anglo-American breach, and Macmillan – an old friend from the days of the North African campaign – inspired a trust which Anthony Eden never enjoyed. But there was another reason for the American wish to make the best of what the Atlantic Alliance possessed. Three weeks before the Washington conference, the Soviet Union had launched Sputnik I, the world's first space satellite. Macmillan records that 'the Americans were not unnaturally alarmed by such striking proof of Russian scientific and technological progress'. No doubt the alarm increased when, on 3 November, Sputnik II was launched and a dog called Laika enjoyed the dubious distinction of being the first mammal in space. It seemed that the Soviet Union had helped to achieve Macmillan's ambition of a very special relationship between Great Britain and the USA.

At first, the fulfilment of Macmillan's other great aspiration – the creation of a united Commonwealth which was a major force in world politics – appeared also to be within his grasp. Cyprus had been a problem for years. In December 1956, shortly before Macmillan became Prime Minister, the Radcliffe Commission had proposed that the island should be partitioned. The Greeks accepted but the Turks rejected the proposal, so for more than two years the troubles rumbled on. Then, in February 1959, Greece – and, in Cyprus, Archbishop Makarios – accepted a complicated constitution which had been invented by the ingenuity of the British Civil Service. A single House of Representatives would be composed of 70 per cent Greek and 30 per cent Turkish members. The President would be Greek, the Vice-President Turkish, and Britain should retain its sovereign bases of Akrotiri and Episkopi 'in perpetuity'. The Greeks abandoned their claim to *enosis* (union with Greece) when, on 16 August 1960, Cyprus became an independent republic within the Commonwealth. Macmillan had brought to an end the problem which Disraeli had created when the island became British, to confirm that 'peace with honour' had come to the Middle East.

But in Africa the path towards reconciliation and independence remained long and hard – not least because Britain believed that honour and history required that the emergent peoples should be carefully prepared for their new responsibilities. General de Gaulle made sudden offers of self-determination to France's North African colonies. The Belgians withdrew from the Congo in June 1960, within six months of the principle of independence being agreed. But Britain always insisted on carefully preparing the ground, and the Belgian experience was taken as vindication of that cautious approach. Moise Tshombe – pro-white, anti-Communist and closely connected with the European mining companies – declared Katanga (now Shaba) independent of the new state of Zaïre. Belgium – conscious that the break-away state provided 60 per cent of the world's cobalt and 20 per cent of its copper, as well as uranium, cadmium and zinc – went to war against the forces of Patrice Lumumba, the head of the legitimate government which had followed Belgian withdrawal. He appealed for help to the United Nations. Shortly afterwards, Lumumba was deposed by Joseph Mobutu. The chaos which followed lasted thirty years. The Colonial Office might have taken pleasure in the proof that even at the twilight of Empire, the British way had proved best. But Katanga was on the northern borders of Northern Rhodesia, and Northern Rhodesia was part of the Central African Federation – already on the verge of disintegration.

The Federation – made up of Nyasaland (Malawi), Northern Rhodesia (Zambia) and Southern Rhodesia (Zimbabwe) – was doomed from the start, not least because its politicians held diametrically different views. Dr Hastings Banda of Nyasaland was bitterly opposed to federation; Roy Welensky was equally antagonistic to anything else. Federation – in the Caribbean and in the straits of Singapore and Malaysia, as well as Africa – was the Colonial Office's preferred solution. In Central Africa, all the black parties boycotted the federal elections, and in March 1959 riots broke out in Nyasaland. Order was only restored after fifty-two Africans had been killed and sixty-six members of the Congress Party (including Dr Banda) had been arrested. The Colonial Office insisted that Congress was plotting rebellion and wholesale massacre. Mr Justice Devlin was asked to conduct a public inquiry into both the allegation and the way in which the supposed insurrection had been put down. He found no evidence of incipient revolution or planned slaughter. His report added, for good measure, that Nyasaland – temporarily, no doubt – had become a police state. Even before Devlin began his examination, Macmillan decided that, 'The wider problem – can Federation continue in its present form – must be studied . . .'

The task was given to Lord (Walter) Monckton – still available, after thirty years, to stoke the boilers or clean out the bilges of the ship of state. His report of October 1960 was a model of balance and tact. Federation, he said, had great economic value and whoever had thought of the idea – at a time when Federation was the fashionable Colonial Office solution – deserved congratulation. However, the economic advantages could not make up for the political detriments. Principal among them was the fact that the black majority would not agree to such a solution. He went on to make recommendations which were not, in fact, about reforming the Federation's constitution but creating acceptable voting arrangements in its three constituent parts. Northern Rhodesia should, Monckton wrote, have an African majority in its legislature. The Southern Rhodesian franchise should be extended. Nyasaland's wish for universal suffrage should be seriously considered. The Central African Federation was dead.

The collapse of the Federation was not the only African catastrophe to prejudice Macmillan's hopes of a strong and unified Commonwealth. In the spring of 1959, Mau Mau detainees – guerrillas fighting for both independence and tribal superiority – who were being held in Kenya's Hola detention camp rioted. Eleven detainees were beaten to death by the camp guards. Outrage in the Commonwealth was compounded by the continued intransigence of the South African government. Britain, struggling to create a West Indian Federation, asked Dr Hendrik Verwoerd if a High Commission from the new Commonwealth country would be acceptable in Pretoria. The South African Prime Minister said it would not. The explanation he gave was that some of the Caribbean islands were refusing to trade with the apartheid regime. Everyone knew that the real reason was that the High Commissioner would be black.

African nationalism was on the march. And the old forces of colonial authority had, in their blundering ways, still attempted to suppress that irresistible force. It is by no means certain how closely Macmillan himself identified with the freedom movements, though history will remember him as the Prime Minister who, in a single phrase – borrowed from Stanley Baldwin – marked the end of white supremacy.

In January 1960, Harold Macmillan set off on a six-week tour of Africa – an indication, by its length, of both the leisurely life that a 1960s Prime Minister enjoyed and the importance which was then attached to the Commonwealth and Empire. Ghana (recently independent) and Nigeria (soon to become so) were both moderate successes. His visit to the Central African Federation began with a bang in Southern Rhodesia and continued with a whimper in Nyasaland, where he found the civil servants dispirited and the white settlers ready to revolt. In Cape Town, he addressed the South African parliament. His speech had been carefully prepared before he left England. So it was with premeditation that he said:

Ever since the break up of the Roman Empire, one of the constant facts of political life in Europe has been the emergence of independent nations . . . Today the same thing is happening in Africa . . . The wind of change is blowing through this continent and, whether we like it or not, this growth of national consciousness is a political fact. We must accept it as a fact and our national policies must take account of it.

Six weeks later, on 21 March 1960, troops and police in the Sharpeville township opened fire on Africans who were demonstrating against the 'pass laws' which effectively imposed restrictions on the residence and movement of every black South African. Sixty-nine demonstrators were killed and nearly two hundred wounded, and Dr Hendrik Verwoerd declared a state of national emergency which guaranteed that the riots would spread. At the Commonwealth Prime Ministers' Conference, eight weeks after the massacre, Tunku Abdul Rahman of Malaya demanded that Sharpeville be discussed. Macmillan gloomily (and rather obviously) predicted that 'once the Commonwealth begins to disintegrate, it is finished'. The break-up began on 31 May 1961, when South Africa declared itself an independent republic. In 1995, when under the leadership of Nelson Mandela it returned to the Commonwealth, the idea that so loose an alliance of disparate nations as the Commonwealth could be a cohesive force in world politics had not so much been abandoned as forgotten.

It was not only the new Commonwealth countries which had begun to believe that the old ties should no longer bind. In Britain itself there was growing impatience with the more onerous obligations of Empire – particularly the traditional right of Commonwealth citizens to enter and settle in the mother country. The Nationality Act of 1948 had confirmed the concept of Commonwealth citizens. A large number of Commonwealth citizens chose to take advantage of the right which it conferred upon them and, believing that the British Parliament really meant to create a *Civis Britannicus*, booked their passages to Southampton. Many then came to jobs for which they had been recruited at home. Companies as diverse as West Midland Foundries and London Transport sought to make up for shortages of British manpower by placing advertisements in Bridgetown and Kingston papers. In the four years before Macmillan became Prime Minister, annual immigration into Britain increased four-fold. By the end of the decade it had risen from barely forty to almost sixty thousand. A White Paper – which sought to distinguish between acceptable (white) and unacceptable (black) immigrants – was drafted but never published. Lord Salisbury suggested the idea of 'guest workers', who could remain for limited periods. There were race riots in Nottingham and Notting Hill and a Labour MP observed, 'For years, white people have been tolerant. Now their tempers are up.' Immigration controls were discussed in the press; inevitably, there was a rush to meet the anticipated ban. Demands for the repeal of the 1946 and 1952 Acts grew throughout the summer of 1961. The Tory party conference, meeting in October, insisted on immediate action. On 1 November, the Commonwealth Immigration Bill was published. It divided potential immigrants into voucher categories – work permits for primary immigrants and visas for spouses, dependent relatives and visitors – each of which could be limited by Order in Council. Macmillan said that he had not seen the House of Commons 'in so hysterical a mood since Suez'. He believed that much of the emotion was synthetic. Gaitskell described the Bill as 'a plain anti-Commonwealth measure in theory and a plain anti-colour measure in practice' – a view which he based, in part, on the exclusion of citizens of the Irish Republic from any form of control.

Gaitskell was not, however, an unequivocal opponent of immigration control. He had discussed the possibility with the Jamaican Cabinet when he had visited the Caribbean in 1960, and warned of the political problems which would be certain to arrive if West Indians, once in England, insisted in congregating in almost exclusively coloured communities. A handful of Labour MPs wanted Gaitskell to oppose the Bill but endorse the need for some sort of control. But with the slightly surprising support of *The Times*, the Opposition mounted such a fierce attack on the Committee Stage of the Bill (which was taken on the floor of the House) that it dragged on until the early summer of 1962. By the ruthless application of stick (the guillotine) and the lavish offer of carrot (concessions) the Bill became law on 1 July. Denis Healey – who made the last speech for the Opposition – was careful not to promise that the Labour government would repeal what was about to become the Commonwealth

Immigration Act. Neither the Conservatives (once the party of Commonwealth and Empire) nor Labour (still, in its own estimation, the party of brotherhood) was prepared to welcome Britannia's black children to the mother country. It took thirty years for the wheel to turn full circle. It was not until 1988 that Britain accepted the free movement of labour clause within the Treaty of Rome, and thus offered to Europe a privilege which was once limited to subjects of His or Her Britannic Majesty.

The wind of change – which gusted fitfully in the Commonwealth – blew more strongly through domestic legislation and was reflected in social attitudes of the generally more enlightened and occasionally swinging Sixties. It was the age of iconoclasm – *Private Eye* and *That Was The Week That Was*. The birth-control pill (at last available from the NHS) and the mini-skirt (*de rigueur* for most women under thirty) were an announcement of the growing demand for sexual liberation and an acknowledgement of growing teenage power. The generation, born during the post-war baby boom, had started to work. Many of them – still living at home – earned as much as their fathers and, in consequence, had more to spend. Their clothes were an expression of their individuality; a break with the dull old past. The mini-skirt was the badge of a generation which did not care. Even the Lord Chancellor's Department made a bow in the direction of liberation and equality by appointing the first woman High Court Judge.

The creation of Life Peerages was the first step towards rejecting the absurd notion that some men are born to rule, for it transformed the character of the previously hereditary House of Lords. Through the persistence of Anthony Wedgwood Benn (Lord Stansgate), the hereditary principle was further eroded in 1964 by the acceptance that a peer could turn himself into a commoner. The status of the motor car – as the future means of long-distance domestic transport – was confirmed by the opening of the Preston bypass and the beginning of Britain's motorway network, and its availability to all sections of society was increased by the development of the Mini. It was not quite the era of the common man, but the suburbs had a great deal to celebrate.

It was, perhaps, in education that the dawn of the new age was most obvious. The comprehensive idea which swept the country in the late 1950s had hardly begun to gather support. But expansion, the other feature of the new enthusiasm for genuinely universal education, was accepted as an indispensable ingredient of future prosperity. The intellectual habit of the time was to initiate a report named after the distinguished public servant who gave his or her name to the enquiry. In 1959 'Crowther' recommended that the school-leaving age should be raised to sixteen. It took eleven years to implement that recommendation. In 1960 'Anderson' proposed that every student on a first degree course should automatically receive a maintenance grant. In 1963 'Newsom' – examining the education of 'less able children' – confirmed that the leaving age should be raised by a year and suggested a longer school day. In 1963 'Robbins' recommended that the number of students in full-time education should be increased from 8 to 17 per cent of the age group by 1980 and that the national aim should be a higher-education place for everyone who wanted (and would benefit from) three years in a college or university. Spending on schools – which for ten years had not risen even enough to match the growth in pupil numbers caused by the post-war baby boom – was dramatically increased. Two thousand new schools were built between 1954 and 1963.

A hesitant start was made on the liberalisation of domestic law which was to characterise the mid- and late 1960s. Sir John Wolfenden (sometime High Master of Manchester Grammar School and Vice-Chancellor of Reading University) chaired the Royal Commission which examined the laws on homosexuality and prostitution. In these more enlightened days it seems extraordinary that two such disparate subjects should be examined simultaneously, but in the late 1950s there was much progressive rejoicing that they were examined at all. R. A. Butler – who, having failed to succeed Eden, had become Home Secretary – consulted his junior minister about how he should proceed. He felt unable to promote the legislation which would have implemented Wolfenden's proposal to decriminalise private homosexual acts between consenting adults. But he was happy to strengthen the laws against soliciting with the object of 'driving prostitution off the streets'. The Street Offences Act became law in 1959.

The Homicide Bill was already in front of the House of Commons when Macmillan became Prime Minister. It was an unhappy compromise which had been introduced as a reluctant response to a ten-year argument about capital punishment. The Labour landslide of 1945 had produced a large abolitionist majority and a resolution, suspending the death penalty, had been carried overwhelmingly in 1948. But the reform had not survived the return of the Conservatives. A renewed campaign against the gallows was prompted by two executions which – in very different ways – pricked the nation's conscience. Ruth Ellis was hanged for shooting her brutal lover, and John Christie was convicted of killings carried out in Rillington Place. It was difficult to believe that Ruth Ellis deserved to die, and impossible to accept that Timothy Evans (who had lived in the same house as Christie) committed a murder identical in every detail to those for which Christie was later hanged. But Evans, despite his protestations, had been found guilty and executed. A House of Commons debate became inevitable.

Butler (thought to be a progressive Tory) wound up for the government – according to his apologists, conscripted against his judgement in order to persuade other Conservative reformers not to split the Conservative vote. Whatever his private convictions, he defended hanging with an apparently genuine passion: 'No innocent man has been hanged within living memory. Life imprisonment is infinitely more cruel than capital punishment itself.' Certain of success, he made a rash promise. Asked how the government would proceed when the debate was over, he unhesitatingly answered, 'When we have had a free vote, we naturally expect to base our action . . . on the decision of the House.' The House decided, by a majority of thirty-one, that capital punishment should be abolished.

The government kept the Home Secretary's word and time was found for a Bill. The House of Commons gave it a Third Reading (the final vote) by a majority of nineteen. In the Lords it was defeated by a majority of 143. The result, another compromise, was the Homicide Bill which distinguished between two classes of murder – one which carried the death penalty and one which attracted the mandatory sentence of life imprisonment. The philosophical, practical and, indeed, moral justification for the idea that it is more wicked to murder a policeman than to kill a child was never adequately explained. But a small step had been taken towards civilisation and reason. And the liberal hour was about to dawn. More progress was soon to be made. Butler helped a young Labour back-bencher, Roy Jenkins, to pilot his Obscene Publications Act through the House of Commons. From then on, literary merit became a defence against the charge of obscenity. The stage was set for Penguin Books to publish *Lady Chatterley's Lover*, and be acquitted when charged with the publication of pornography.

The law was liberalised in election year. But elections are not determined by such things. They are won, and lost, according to the people's perception of their economic well-being and economic prospects. In 1957 Macmillan had come to office at a time of incipient financial crisis – the direct result of loss of confidence during the Suez crisis: 'Nearly all the available support for sterling had been mobilised.' But within a few weeks of Macmillan forming his government, American support was once again available and the new Chancellor of the Exchequer, Peter Thorneycroft, was persuaded to make £100 million tax cuts. The good times did not last for long. In the autumn of 1957 a massive deflationary package included an increase in the Bank Rate from 5 to 7 per cent. Harold Wilson, the Shadow Chancellor, claimed that change had been leaked to the City and, in consequence, friends of the Tory party had made a killing. A tribunal found the allegations totally unjustified.

Oppositions are inclined to float on the froth of the politics; governments sink or swim in the deep water. And Macmillan was beginning to become engulfed in the dilemma which broke across every government for the next twenty years – the need to balance the incompatible aims of full employment, low inflation and high levels of social spending. Often those conflicting objectives were reflected, at budget time, by arguments about increased taxes or reduced expenditure. That argument haunted the government throughout 1958. Thorneycroft was determined to cut spending by £103 million – principally by abolishing Children's Allowance for the second child.

Macmillan was prepared to increase taxes. After the usual agonised and protracted negotiations, the difference was narrowed down to £50 million. But the Chancellor – urged on by Enoch Powell, the Financial Secretary – was intransigent. All three Treasury ministers resigned from the government. The battle – fiscal prudence versus social obligation – had only just begun. R. A. Butler, speaking to his constituents, put the case for continued high levels of public spending: 'Adherence to fixed money policies could have overturned, in the course of a few days, policies on social justice to which some of us have devoted our lives.' There are members of the Labour Party who are saying exactly the same today.

The drama being over, Macmillan skipped lightly on to the next stage. At the airport on the eve of a Commonwealth tour, journalists asked him to comment on the resignations. He replied, 'I thought the best thing to do was to settle up the little local difficulties and turn to the wider vision.' Before he left he appointed Derick Heathcoat-Amory his new Chancellor, a promotion which so surprised the beneficiary that when he was called to Number Ten, he asked the Private Secretary if there had been some mistake. 'I'm the one with spectacles and a moustache,' he said.

Heathcoat-Amory arrived at the Treasury at a time when the focus of economic concern had begun to switch from unemployment to inflation. Two years earlier, a government White Paper had urged voluntary wage restraint as the best – and perhaps the only practical – way of reconciling full employment and price stability. The Radcliffe Commission, appointed to inquire into the workings of the credit and monetary system, was a concession to the view that the battle against inflation might require the tight control of the money supply, but the mood was essentially in favour of solving the country's economic problems by direct action – consensus where it could be obtained and regulation when it was necessary and possible. Macmillan's vision of the good society was a united people, adjusting its patterns of spending and borrowing on the advice of objective experts who judged what was needed to protect the national interest. Government policy was, in its simplistic way, a forerunner of the infinitely complicated systems of price control and wage restraint which were introduced by

Labour governments in the 1960s and '70s. And, like Harold Wilson and Jim Callaghan, Harold Macmillan was so firm in his belief in institutional solutions that, when they failed, he strengthened the institutions rather than abandoned the solution.

In the summer of 1957, he set up the Council on Prices, Productivity and Incomes. Its members – a judge, an economist and an accountant – were colloquially known as the 'Three Wise Men'. Their first report blandly attributed rising prices to 'an abnormally high level of demand for goods and services in general, maintained for an abnormally long stretch of time'. It advocated deflation and accepted a slower rate of growth as inevitable. The TUC – whose support was judged essential to the success of that corporatist approach – was immediately antagonised. In July 1959, eighteen months after the first report was published, the Council's third report qualified its initial judgement about the economy almost out of existence. The Council was reconstructed under a new chairman and became known as the 'Three Wiser Men'. It remained almost entirely ineffectual. But faith in progress by discussion and agreement persisted, and remained until Margaret Thatcher disbanded the National Economic Development Council in 1985.

The TUC were almost certainly right to claim that the deflation of autumn 1957 – even in the moderate form to which Macmillan had agreed – was a fundamental mistake. For 1958 was a year of recession. Throughout the year the Treasury argued with outside experts about the economic prospects. Macmillan – told by Thorneycroft that his status as the most literate Prime Minister of the century made him over-susceptible to the works of John Maynard Keynes – relied on the advice of Roy Harrod, Keynes's biographer, and Lord Mills, his slightly rusty conduit to the manufacturing industry. Their call to reflate was reinforced by the January unemployment figures – 620,000, or 2.8 per cent, the highest level since the war.

Nineteen fifty-nine was the likely election year. And, in his early thoughts about how the campaign should be managed, Macmillan had recalled that in 1955 a give-away budget before polling day had been followed by higher taxation almost immediately afterwards. But the January employment figures removed all doubts about the tactic which he should adopt. Tax cuts could be easily justified. The Treasury (as was its habit) fought on, giving Heathcoat-Amory (in the Prime Minister's opinion) 'bad advice as it has given every Chancellor', but Macmillan was determined to stimulate production by both increasing public investment and making tax cuts. Heathcoat-Amory accepted the Prime Minister's judgement as superior to the Treasury's in every way. The standard rate of income tax was reduced from 8s 6d to 7s 9d in the pound. There was also a six-pence reduction in the reduced rate. Purchase tax was reduced by £132 million, and £71 million of post-war credits were repaid. The excise duty on a pint of beer was cut by two pence. Not surprisingly, the budget was received with rapture. Macmillan decided to give what we would now call 'the feel-good factor' time to take hold. The election was postponed until the autumn, when the government increased its majority from 58 to 100. There followed a year of economic growth – balanced, as was always the case in the age of fixed exchange rates – by a reduction in the balance of payments surplus from £291 million in 1958 to £51 million in election year. But, that apart, it was possible for Supermac to argue that he had done the right thing by both his party and his country.

Critics of Macmillan's style and philosophy – Margaret Thatcher among them – have argued that the 1959 budget gave far too much away and began the years of fiscal irresponsibility that did not come to an end until Labour's IMF settlement of 1976 was reinforced and intensified by Tory 'monetarism' after the 1979 election. At the time, some critics – not just the defeated Labour Party – claimed that Macmillan knew the mistake he was making but chose to win the election rather than safeguard the economy. The evidence suggests that the cause of the error was neither political nor economic but temperamental. He worried about inflation, but he worried about unemployment even more. That was the inheritance of Stockton – the depressed Teesside borough which he had represented in Parliament before the war. He believed that it was possible to hold inflation at 'the rate of about 2.5 per cent a year, which is what Keynes always said to me was about right' and both to maintain the value of sterling and full employment. But he worried about it. Even his most famous aphorism – the catchphrase buried in a speech he made in July 1957 and destined to haunt him ever after – was meant as a warning, not as an endorsement of the Sybaritic Society:

> Let's be frank about it. Most of our people have never had it so good. Go round the country, go to the industrial towns, go to the farms and you will see a state of prosperity such as we have never had in my lifetime – nor indeed ever in the history of this country. What is beginning to worry some of us, is 'Is it too good to be true?' Or perhaps I should say, 'Is it too good to last?'

Macmillan worried, but he did not worry enough to let his concern jeopardise the Conservative party's prospects of victory at the General Election. The slogan on which it was fought and won was, 'Life's good with the Conservatives. Don't let Labour ruin it.'

When that slogan was launched, the Labour Party was genuinely convinced that it would explode in the Tory leadership's collective face. Certainly 1959 had been a boom year, but the recession, with its record levels of post-war unemployment, had ended only nine months earlier. Surely the public memory was longer than that. It seemed impossible that even the beneficiaries of the new prosperity cared so little about the welfare of their fellow citizens that they would gladly re-elect not only the party of Suez but the government of the Rent Act – legislation so repugnant to Labour that, five years later, when the party did eventually come to power, a new Bill – protecting sitting tenants and controlling rents – was its first legislative act.

In the early years of Conservative government, local councils had built so many houses, and allocated them so capriciously, that one academic expert on the subject – and undoubted sympathiser with municipal enterprise – had claimed that council houses had become 'not a social service but a public utility'. Yet although the new houses were being built, the slums, far from being cleared, were probably growing in number. The government made several half-hearted attempts to relate availability to need. The Housing Repair Act of 1954 provided better improvement grants – a carrot to encourage renovation and extension. The Housing Subsidy Act of

1956 abolished the government grant towards building for general
need rather than slum clearance or the elderly and infirm. The
Housing Ministry circular of 1956 suggested that councils introduce
'differential rents' in an attempt to drive the more affluent tenants
into owner-occupation. In 1958, the Cabinet (heirs to the government which had promised and built 300,000 houses a year) decided
that the answer to the housing crisis was private rather than public
enterprise. The pendulum was beginning to swing right. Because of
the 1958 deflation, public-sector building was about to fall to half the
level of 1954. The shortfall was to be met by 'improving the state of
rented accommodation' – and, at the same time, improving the
landlords' income.

Until the Rent Act was passed, tenants of private property enjoyed
strictly controlled rents and absolute security of tenure. The Rent Act
proposed to take 750,000 privately owned properties out of control
completely – houses with rateable values of £30 or more in England
and Wales and £40 in Scotland and London (on what was still
the pre-war valuation). In fact the government had miscalculated
and, on the specified rateable values, only 320,000 properties were
affected. Four and a half million remained under control. But their
rents were no longer frozen. The amount of increase which was
legally possible varied according to the services which the landlord
provided. Tenants who took responsibility for their own repairs and
redecoration were expected to pay less than those who expected free
maintenance.

But to Labour, rent levels – especially the rent levels in private
property – were as emotive an issue as prescription charges or means-
tested benefits. Certainly the Rent Act caused some hardship and a
great deal of anguish for tenants who no longer felt secure in their
own homes, and it spectacularly failed to achieve its three objectives – an increased supply of rented property, improvements in the
current housing stock, and a reduction of under-occupation by small
families who stayed in big houses because their rents were frozen. But
it did not generate the feeling of national outrage Labour had anticipated. Britain was already becoming middle-class, and the newly
prosperous owner-occupiers saw no reason to vote to preserve the

interests of the lower-income groups. Labour had begun to misjudge the mood of the nation.

For a party of conscience and compassion, standing out against the zeitgeist was unavoidable. And it was Labour's electoral misfortune to feel a moral obligation to identify itself with all the groups for whom the upwardly mobile and the recently affluent felt least sympathy – principal among them, the Commonwealth immigrants who had come to Britain, always with encouragement and sometimes with invitation, to meet the 1950s' shortage of labour. By 1954, the rate of entry had increased to 40,000 a year. Although in the West Indies there was restricted movement between the islands, any Barbadian or Jamaican was free to come to Britain without even applying for a visa. In August 1958, after the race riots in Nottingham and Notting Hill – both of them blamed by the popular press on the ethnic minorities rather than the National Front – Harold Macmillan announced, some observers thought gratuitously, that 'utmost strictness' would be used to ensure that there would be an impartial enquiry into their causes and the proper prosecution of those who had incited them. Labour's great test, the Commonwealth Immigration Act of 1962, described by Hugh Gaitskell as 'cruel and brutal anti-colour legislation' was still to come. But by the autumn of 1959, Labour was too often 'on the wrong side' for its own electoral good. Looking back, the astonishing aspect of the campaign was the party's genuine belief that it was going to win.

Less than two months after the 1959 General Election, the Labour Party met in Blackpool to lick its wounds. In those days, three consecutive election defeats seemed to be symptoms of a political condition which might easily turn out to be terminal. Barbara Castle, who chaired the special conference, tried to dispel the gloom with her own variation on Oscar Wilde's judgement on the first night of *The Importance of Being Earnest*: the election campaign, she said, had been a complete success, but the electorate had been an absolute failure. Hugh Gaitskell himself took a more introspective view. The Labour Party, he told delegates, no longer represented the hopes and aspirations of modern Britain. The attachment to the trade unions was too close, the commitment to public ownership was too total, and the party's name was an anachronism which suggested that Labour's politics were rooted in the interests of a single class. It was a speech which some of his closest associates had urged him not to make, and was deeply resented by much of his audience. The following day, the dying Aneurin Bevan addressed the conference for the last time. It was a bravura performance which contained very little of substance but sent the delegates home happy. Gaitskell dropped his plans for major reform. Thirty-six years later, Tony Blair succeeded where Hugh Gaitskell had failed. Clause IV of the Labour Party's constitution – the commitment to the public ownership of the means of production and distribution – was re-written to give Labour a quite different primary aim. Trade union power within the party was finally reduced, and the informal influence that trade union leaders had enjoyed for a hundred years was diminished almost out of existence. New Labour was not born when Tony Blair was elected leader in the summer of 1994; the idea came to life when Hugh Gaitskell spoke to the 1959 Special Conference in Blackpool. But the aims of the two men were widely different. Gaitskell hoped to improve democratic socialism. Blair aimed to put something different in its place.

Nineteen fifty-nine was the year in which, for the only time in history, an American President intervened in a British General Election. The United States' concern about the Soviet Union's nuclear superiority had forced Eisenhower to work more and more closely with Great Britain. Macmillan exploited the anxiety by demanding tangible demonstrations of the harmony in which they worked. The President, determined that the West should preserve complete unity of purpose and action, agreed (during a visit to London) to appear on television with the Prime Minister. Thirty years later, a more cynical and sophisticated electorate would have laughed at the spectacle of two elderly gentlemen in dinner jackets pretending to have a serious discussion about the future of the world. In 1959, the people were impressed.

To his credit, Eisenhower was dubious about the propriety of action as an agent of the Conservative party. But John Foster Dulles, his Secretary of State, wrote that the President explained and excused his intervention in British domestic politics with the comment that he was 'not unsympathetic to this since we don't want Bevan to win the election'. Not for the first time, Eisenhower had misjudged his man.

At the Labour party conference in 1957, the old unilateralist had urged dismayed delegates to oppose a resolution which called on the next Labour government to renounce nuclear weapons immediately upon its election, and added a stern and much resented warning: 'If you carry this resolution . . . you will send a Foreign Secretary naked into the conference chamber.' For some months the unilateralists and pacifists within the party were in disarray. They had lost the support of the man who had once been their undisputed leader. The Cabinet minister who had resigned because NHS charges were being imposed in order to finance a bigger defence budget had suddenly begun to talk about the strategic balance. And the Member of Parliament who had almost been expelled from the Labour Party because of his opposition to what he described as 'American militarism' had suddenly announced that a nuclear capability was essential to Britain's world standing. It was a savage blow to the anti-nuclear cause. But by early 1958, the most passionate adherents had regained their nerve, and in February of that year the Campaign for Nuclear Disarmament was created 'to demand a British initiative to reduce the nuclear peril and to stop the arms race, if necessary led by unilateral action by Great Britain'. CND collected a distinguished list of patrons and sponsors – Bertrand Russell, Henry Moore, Doris Lessing, A. J. P. Taylor, J. B. Priestley, Michael Foot and John Braine.

That Easter, CND organised the first march to the Atomic Weapons Research Establishment at Aldermaston. The claim 'that those who detest war – which includes nearly every man and woman in these islands – can best avoid it by divesting themselves of the means of fighting it' was almost as naïve as it was prolix. The reference to 'every man and woman' was intended to emphasise the 'non-sectarian and non-party' nature of the organisation. But, inevitably, it drew most of the members from the Labour Party and the radical left. In consequence, although its formal purpose was a change in government policy, its only real influence was on the Opposition. For the next twenty-five years CND had an almost entirely adverse influence on Labour's prospects of election.

It was not until the end of the Cold War – and the unilateralists' belated discovery that it is wrong to equate the possession of arms with their use – that it ceased to be a political liability. Some of its members were unable or unwilling to understand that the purpose of a deterrent (as the name implies) was to prevent a war, not win one. For more than two decades, Labour leaders were plagued with the intellectually meaningless question, 'Would you push the button?' Until the early 1960s – when it became clear that Nato's nuclear capability might well destroy the Labour Party while it saved Europe – the reaction of the party leadership was almost invariably craven and confused.

Immediately after CND was founded, sixty-five Labour Members of Parliament signed a statement which called for a new defence policy. Their ardour and self-confidence was increased by the knowledge that, one by one, the big trade unions were changing their policies from support for collective security to demands for unilateral disarmament. For twenty years those unions had been described as the Labour leader's Praetorian Guard – often by commentators who did not know that, every twenty years in Ancient Rome, the Praetorian Guard turned on the emperor. On Good Friday 1958, Frank Cousins – the General Secretary of the massive Transport and General Workers' Union – had marched with CND to Aldermaston. In June of that year, the Municipal and General Workers' Union (normally the Labour establishment's most loyal supporters) voted for a non-nuclear defence policy by 150 votes to 120, with 75 abstentions. The union leadership discovered that the missing votes were not conscious neutrals but delegates who, not realising that the voting had begun, were 'out at tea'. An emergency conference was convened to reconsider the issue. Unilateralism was defeated by 194 votes to 138. Tea not being served at the time, there were only three abstentions. But it was too late to save Labour's commitment to the nuclear alliance. The progress towards unilateralism was gradual but irresistible.

Throughout the year which followed – with brief lulls during the

General Election campaign and after the death of Aneurin Bevan –
supporters of unilateralism campaigned assiduously within the
Labour movement. One by one, the unions were converted. First
the shop workers changed their policy. Then, to the dismay and the
near disbelief of the leadership, the National Committee of the
Amalgamated Engineering Union abandoned its traditionally robust
support for the deterrent. By the time the Labour Party was in
Scarborough for its 1960 conference, it was taken for granted that
the unilateralist resolution would be carried by an overwhelming
majority. On the Sunday before the conference began, five thousand
CND supporters gathered outside the headquarters hotel and
chanted not slogans of peace and brotherhood but 'Gaitskell must
go'.

Hugh Gaitskell's speech, winding up the defence debate, was one of
the turning points in Britain's post-war history. It was not, by conventional standards, an oratorical triumph. For Gaitskell's style did not
encompass the rolling cadence and the carefully constructed aphorism. The best and most important passages in his speech were very
near to being spontaneous. And they made a compromise with unilateralism utterly impossible. At the moment when he sat down, the
Labour Party knew that it either had to return to its support for the
nuclear deterrent or find a new leader:

> Do you think that we can become overnight the pacifists, unilateral-
> ists and fellow travellers that other people are? There are some of us,
> Mr Chairman, who will fight and fight again to save the party we
> love. We will fight and fight and fight again to bring back sanity and
> honesty and dignity so that our party with its great past may retain its
> glory and greatness.

After that speech, Labour could prevaricate and dissemble no
more. For almost three years the party had attempted to maintain a
show of unity by initiating parliamentary defence debates on anything except the main issue – unilateral nuclear disarmament itself.
The attempts to paper over the party's cracks had never succeeded in
finding the deep divisions. Discussions of motions which demanded

a non-proliferation treaty, the end to testing and a commitment against first use, were invariably enlivened by back-bench demands for the complete repudiation of nuclear weapons. The Opposition's problems were complicated by the incompatibility – on defence and most other subjects – of Hugh Gaitskell and his new deputy, George Brown.

Both men were passionate opponents of unilateral nuclear disarmament. But their views of defence sharply differed, not least because Gaitskell was, by instinct, an Atlanticist while Brown saw Britain's future in closer ties with continental Europe. Their conflicting views reflected a debate which was to split the British political parties, and Britain itself, for the rest of the century. The partnership which they built, and their mutual belief in collective security, was described by Gaitskell's biographer as 'a spurious unity between two men whose views were fundamentally irreconcilable'. Even that was shattered during the spring of 1960. Gaitskell was in Israel for a meeting of the Socialist International when the House of Commons held its annual defence debate. George Brown (deputising for his leader) allowed himself to speculate – rashly – about how Britain should react if either the cost or the withdrawal of American co-operation meant that the British missile programme was either emasculated or cancelled: 'The argument for maintaining an independent British deterrent for political reasons is one thing when we have one. The argument about going back when we are out of it is different altogether.'

Gaitskell – who believed that Brown had blundered another step down the road to unilateralism – was furious. He should have realised that his deputy was doing no more than facing the dilemma which, for thirty years, most politicians were not even willing to admit existed. The 'independent' deterrent – which could not be fired at any designated target without the assistance of the USA – had a primarily political purpose. A nation, with a bigger spending programme than it could afford, ought to have at least considered whether the existence of a 'British' nuclear weapon provided a protection which was in any way superior to that which the American nuclear capability guaranteed. The reason why that question was so rarely asked was that the answer was unacceptable. Much of the defence budget was spent on doing nothing more worth-while than pretending that Britain was still a superpower.

Britain had struggled since the early 1950s to produce its own delivery system which would complement the Thor missile – the American rocket which had been installed in Britain and was controlled by the 'dual-key system'. Blue Steel, a surface-to-surface missile, was planned and developed but abandoned before it was put into production. It was replaced by Blue Streak, which – after a development cost of £50 million – was, in turn, discarded when it was discovered that another £600 million was needed to complete the programme. Gallantly, with Anglo-American relations fully recovered from the bitter aftermath of Suez, the United States offered to fill the gap in the British arsenal with one of their own rockets – Skybolt. Indeed, the President went even further than the offer of an off-the-shelf stop-gap. The Pentagon was developing a new submarine-launched missile, Polaris, and was prepared at least to consider making the new weapon available to Britain. Macmillan's first reaction was that Polaris was 'ill thought-out and dangerous'. But within six months of the offer being made, the Prime Minister had agreed to station Polaris nuclear submarines in Holy Loch, a few miles outside Glasgow.

As a result of the Polaris agreement, CND doubled both its membership and its programme of protest. And the Labour Party's internal disagreements escalated to the point of near civil war. But, paradoxically, the 'fight again' speech – which had caused such bitterness at the party's conference that Hugh Gaitskell felt obliged to apologise for its passion the following day – marked a turning-point in the party's fortunes. The leader who refused to accept the unilateralist policy which had been imposed upon him became a hero – a shining beacon of courage and consistency. Gaitskell's personal popularity was, during the next year, to become part of the foundation on which Labour's low climb up the opinion poll was built, and it helped to create the myth that Labour leaders who make war on their own rank-and-file had found the secret of electoral success. But in the weeks which followed the promise to fight again, it seemed that

Labour was near to self-destruction. Gaitskell himself accepted that if the conference disowned him the following year, he would have to resign the leadership.

Macmillan, contemptuous of Gaitskell's 'inability to rise to the level of events', pursued his dream of a new world role for Britain. But during the first three years of his premiership, his vision of what that design should be radically altered. He still believed in a united Commonwealth playing a major part in bridging the gap between the developed and developing world and exercising a global influence which was consistent with its size. He remained absolutely convinced that Britain and America, in the unique partnership which sentimentalists call a 'special relationship', held the key to the preservation of the freedom, and the civilised values, of the free world. But he had begun to believe that Britain also had a potentially special place in the Common Market. Ironically, it was nuclear policy – thought in the early 1960s to be the nemesis of Labour hopes – that prevented Harold Macmillan from achieving his dream of making Britain the keystone of the arch which joined Europe to America.

Charles de Gaulle was opposed to what he regarded as Britain's pretensions. On 30 May 1958, the general left Colombey-les-Deux-Eglises, where he had lived as a recluse since the end of the war, and agreed to form a government. The following November he sponsored a new constitution which gave the President of the Republic executive powers. Four weeks after it was accepted by the Assembly, the Fifth Republic was created. Its first President was Charles de Gaulle. His immediate concern was Algeria, where the Arab majority had rebelled against French rule. He brushed aside both the *colons* (who had once believed that he would save France's North African empire) and the Americans, who advised that the French and British should withdraw from their imperial obligations in careful unison. The withdrawal was total and almost immediate. But the new President's real concern was less with peace and prosperity than with the respect in which France was held in the world. Opponents claimed that he was preoccupied with a commodity which they called *la gloire*.

It was President de Gaulle's firm conviction that France was, by its nature, a superpower. So, since superpowers possessed a nuclear weapon, logic dictated that France should possess something which made a big bang. It was a difficult concept for the British to dispute. For a succession of Prime Ministers – Attlee, Churchill, Eden and Macmillan himself – had come to the same conclusion about the United Kingdom. Macmillan, realising the President's sensitivity, decided to flatter his ego before they met at the summit which had been arranged to take place in Paris on 16 May 1960. General de Gaulle was invited to make a state visit to London during the preceding month. The President's behaviour – condescending, aloof and superior – scandalised the Prime Minister. But he hoped that the guards of honour, the Buckingham Palace banquets and the trumpeters of the Household Cavalry had done their work and smoothed the path towards greater co-operation in Paris. Unfortunately, the summit was cancelled before the 'discussions in the margin', for which Macmillan hoped, could even have been arranged. On 1 May a U-2 American reconnaissance aircraft was shot down over the Soviet Union. The Paris meeting, said Nikita Khrushchev, First Secretary of the Soviet Communist Party and head of both state and government, could only go ahead if the United States apologised for its intrusion into Soviet air space, promised never again to spy on the Warsaw Pact and to punish the individuals within the military establishment who were responsible for the assault on peace. Eisenhower refused to meet Khrushchev's terms and the summit was postponed for six to eight months. Macmillan – who had hoped that the meeting would establish his reputation as a world statesman – was devastated, and told the Queen, 'We have fallen from the summit into a deep crevasse.'

Before the world leaders had an opportunity to reassemble, a new young President had been elected to office in the United States. John F. Kennedy inherited Dwight D. Eisenhower's commitment to supply Skybolt to Britain and at least consider arming its old ally with the new, submarine-launched, Polaris missile. But unlike his predecessor, Kennedy possessed firm views on Britain's role in Europe. For reasons generally concerned with the liberalisation of trade, he believed that the United Kingdom's future should lie in the Common Market. He made that view clear when, within weeks of taking office, he visited France – describing himself after reading press accounts of his visit as 'the man who went to Paris with Jackie Kennedy'. While he was there, he refused absolutely to share America's nuclear secrets with the French. So in De Gaulle's proud mind the two attitudes – advocacy of British Common Market membership and refusal to accept France as a nuclear equal – were related parts of an Anglo-Saxon conspiracy to rule the world. All that could stand against it was France – supported by that part of her old enemy which was now known as the Federal Republic of Germany.

Macmillan, undoubtedly distressed by what he saw as a breach between America and Europe, turned his energies to a more limited version of his grand design. Perhaps he could not unite the old world and the new. But he could work for British membership of the Common Market. Then, when British leadership of Europe was established, he could initiate a reconciliation with the USA. It took almost a year before he was prepared to invite the Cabinet to consider joining the six original signatories of the Rome Treaty. Even then, Macmillan asked to do no more than discuss entry terms. Anxious to do all that he could to avoid a French veto, he tried his best to reassure De Gaulle that Britain was completely converted to the creation of a European customs union. At the same time he had to balance the application against Britain's membership of two other international alliances to which Britain already offered tariff-free trade – the Commonwealth and the European Free Trade Association.

Thoughts of Efta should have been enough to awaken Macmillan's fears about the response he would receive from De Gaulle. The European Free Trade Association was the idea of The Six themselves, a proposal made in the spring of 1956 in an attempt – as Macmillan later wrote – 'to prevent antagonism as well as economic rivalries springing up'. The Common Market – a customs union in which genuine competition was encouraged by harmonisation of commercial law and practices – would exist inside the free trade area. The idea was enthusiastically received by the British Tories. Indeed they claimed parentage and called it (after the President of the Board of

Trade) the Maudling Plan. A free trade area – as distinct from an integrated community – was, and to a great extent remains, the Conservative dream of European co-operation. Within such a loose arrangement, free trade is promoted and competition is encouraged while government intervention in the economy is kept to a minimum. A 'community' seeks to harmonise and integrate and, in consequence, becomes a vehicle for regulation by the governments of the states of which it is composed, or – in the worst hypothesis – the government of the superstate which intervention creates. What the Tory party of 1956 did not realise – and what some of that party's members have not realised yet – is that a free trade area is likely to become a customs union, a customs union is likely to become a community, and a community is likely to become a federated state. Bismarck understood. That is why he created his *Zollverein* as a first step towards a united Germany.

Innocent of such ideas, the British government built its hopes of a partnership in which The Six worked within The Thirteen. But De Gaulle, on the point of assuming supreme power within the Fifth Republic, began to hint that France's economic interests could not allow British and Scandinavian goods to enter the country tariff-free. At the beginning of November 1958 he had won Chancellor Adenauer's support for the idea that Efta and the EEC were incompatible. Despite a last-minute plea from Macmillan, he announced his formal opposition to The Six relaxing their common external tariffs. The following month he was elected President of France.

For the next three years, Britain made do with membership of Efta. Then Macmillan realised the folly of being outside what he at last understood would be a European union. He was not a man to borrow second-hand images about missing either boat or bus, but his speech in the House of Commons was devoted to that theme:

> Unless we are in the negotiation, unless we can bring our influence to bear, we shall not be able to play a part in deciding the future structure of Europe. In a changing world, if we are not able to be left behind and to drop out of the main stream of the world's life, we must be prepared to change and adapt our methods.

The official application was made, and Edward Heath was sent to Brussels to negotiate the details of British membership. Labour – the party of international brotherhood – contemplated the prospect of European unity in a mood of heroic uncertainty. The New Commonwealth had been created in its modern form by the Attlee government. But there was as much concern, on the Opposition benches, for the white sheep-farmers of New Zealand as for the black sugar-cane farm-workers of the Caribbean. Labour had given cautious approval (with one absenting voice) to the creation of a European Free Trade Association but majority opinion within the party was clearly against the creation of a Common Market. Some of the objections were at least the product of genuine socialist prejudices – the Treaty of Rome's commitment to the market economy in particular – while some were little more than chauvinism. Replying to a Prime Ministerial television broadcast, Hugh Gaitskell asked, 'Could federation be avoided?' For federation meant 'an end to Britain as an independent nation'. At the conference itself, he expressed his doubts in less measured language:

> For although, of course, Europe has had a great and glorious civilisation, although Europe can claim Goethe and Leonardo, Voltaire and Picasso, there have been evil features in European history too – Hitler and Mussolini . . . You cannot say what this Europe will be: it has its two faces and we do not know as yet which is the one which will dominate . . . When people say, 'What did we get out of New Zealand; what did we get out of Australia; what did we get out of Canada?', I remember that they came to our aid at once in two world wars. We, at least, do not intend to forget Vimy Ridge and Gallipoli; we, at least, do not intend to forget the help they gave us after this last war.

The party conference speech ended in tumultuous applause. Harold Wilson – who had challenged Gaitskell for the Labour leadership after the unilateralist vote of 1960 – suggested that it be printed as a leaflet. Frank Cousins, who had led the unilateralist revolt, immediately offered to pay the bill.

There is an infinity of explanations of why Gaitskell opposed Common Market membership with such passion and, in doing so, was rewarded with the acclaim of delegates whom his wife described as 'all the wrong people'. One old friend attributed his antagonism to Dora Gaitskell herself, a refugee from Nazi Germany. Another suggested that he was more influenced by Commonwealth Labour Party leaders who believed that 'if Britain entered on the basis of what had been agreed' by the autumn of 1962, 'great damage would inevitably be done to many countries in the Commonwealth and therefore to the unity of the Commonwealth itself'. That view was subsequently endorsed by the meeting of Commonwealth Prime Ministers of every party. Since his death, it has been suggested that Gaitskell thought it right (or at least politically necessary) to reject the Common Market because he understood with remarkable prescience that the Common Market would soon reject us. And Roy Jenkins – his friend and disciple, who has never disguised the distress which that speech caused him – has recently suggested that the Labour leader had grown weary of confrontation with his own party and, having reversed the unilateralist vote the previous year, chose to express (in uncharacteristically extreme language) a point of view which he held in moderation and could be exploited to unite the party behind him. Whatever the reason, it is hard to describe it as either his, or the Labour Party's, finest hour.

The British application – the result of Edward Heath's careful negotiation about target prices and external tariff – was due for formal examination after Macmillan visited De Gaulle at Rambouillet. President Kennedy – still glowing from his success in facing down Nikita Khrushchev in the Cuban Missile Crisis – had invited the Prime Minister to meet at Nassau. Macmillan accepted but – anxious not to offend De Gaulle's *amour propre* – insisted on seeing the French President first. No doubt De Gaulle appreciated the courtesy. But the meeting still ended in double disaster. The President was sceptical about Britain's ability, or at least willingness, to accept the obligations of Common Market membership, and absolutely frank about the changes in the balance of power which British entry would bring. Within The Six, 'France could say "no" against even the Germans.

Once Britain and all the rest joined the organisation, things would be different.' But the real catastrophe was the result of what the two men believed to be their agreement over defence policy. Macmillan had begun to fear that America would not fulfil its promise to supply Britain with Skybolt missiles and he told, or thought he told, De Gaulle that if his fears were realised he would insist on Polaris being provided in its place. The President thought, or claimed that he thought, that Macmillan had made him a conditional, but highly attractive, offer. If America broke its word, Britain and France would co-operate in the development of a European nuclear weapon.

The Rambouillet meeting ended on 16 December. On 19 December, Macmillan landed at Nassau in the Bahamas – where he was told that America no longer intended to develop a Skybolt missile for its own use. As a compromise, President Kennedy suggested that it should be produced as a purely British weapon with the two countries sharing the cost. That proposal Macmillan turned down with a complicated joke about shotgun marriages and lost virginity. He had set his heart on getting Polaris and – thanks to a personal decision of Kennedy – that is what he got, despite the bitter opposition of American officials from the Defence and State Departments. George Ball, the passionately 'Europeanist' Under-Secretary of State, actually warned that De Gaulle might be so offended that he would block Britain's Common Market application. But whatever his reason, Macmillan persisted in his demands and Kennedy, over-ruling his advisers, agreed.

On Boxing Day 1962, Macmillan wrote to Heath in Brussels that he feared the French would cause insuperable difficulties. Kennedy tried to assuage De Gaulle's wrath by offering him Polaris on 'similar' terms. At first, the French confused 'similar' with 'the same' and were about to accept. When they realised that since France, unlike Britain, did not possess its own warhead, Polaris would only be of value if America provided them with warheads as well as a delivery system, they asked if 'similar' meant more than the offer of a rocket which carried no payload. The United States was adamant in its refusal to share nuclear information. The telegram from Paris read, 'The General is no longer interested.'

The General – slapped in the face by the 'special relationship' – waited until the middle of January for his revenge. Then, at an Elysée press conference, he repeated to the world what he had said in private to Macmillan at Rambouillet – though the public version was composed in more offensive language:

> England is insular . . . In short, the nature and structure and economic context of England differ profoundly from those of the other states of the Continent . . . In the end, there would appear a colossal Atlantic Community under American dependence and leadership which would soon swallow up the European Community . . . It was a great honour for my friend, Harold Macmillan, to have perceived so early the need to join Europe.

The statement ended with an attack on what he called the Anglo-American Nassau Agreement. But although it was obvious enough that Britain's European adventure was temporarily over, Heath spent another two weeks in Brussels attempting to rally support from other members. On 28 January 1963, Maurice Couve de Murville, the French Foreign Minister, told France's five European partners that British membership was not acceptable to the President. On the following day, Britain's application was formally vetoed.

It had been agreed that Britain's reunion with continental Europe should be marked by the Prime Minister visiting the Vatican and having an audience with the Pope. That was, in itself, a strange way to mark accession to what British adherents had always claimed was not a reincarnation of the Holy Roman Empire. At first, Macmillan – who had never been enthusiastic about the idea – argued that to continue with the visit after the rebuff had been delivered would be an intolerable humiliation. But he was persuaded that it was too late to change his plans. In those days even Prime Ministers travelled on scheduled flights, and Macmillan and Heath were ushered into the two front first-class seats before the rest of the passengers boarded the plane. Ted Heath recalls that a large air-hostess offered Harold Macmillan a drink. She was black. Suddenly the Prime Minister realised that he was travelling on an airline which was owned by one of the new African Commonwealth members. Heath was required to visit the cockpit and discover the colour of the pilot. Reassured that he was being piloted to Rome by an Australian, the Prime Minister completed his journey reassured, if not relaxed.

The French veto – by any standards indefensible – was not the result of the Nassau summit and the Polaris deal. It was, as De Gaulle made clear at his press conference, the product of an objection, *in principle*, to British membership, and Macmillan was perfectly entitled to complain that the French should have made their position clear long before the detailed negotiations began. But – marking as it did, the final collapse of Macmillan's Grand Design – it emphasised the folly of a British Prime Minister believing that his place in history could be guaranteed by grandiose schemes to make Britain a world power. Macmillan had first hoped that a strengthened Commonwealth would guarantee the international status of the mother country. That Edwardian dream had been shattered by independence movements all over Africa and Asia, the obduracy of the Boer government in Pretoria and the final concession – through the Immigration Bill of 1962 – that Britain could no longer afford to fulfil its imperial obligation.

The second dream was a 'special relationship' with the United States, made even more special by nuclear partnership that linked Europe to America. Little that had happened during the decade which followed the war should have led Macmillan to believe that it would be a partnership of equals. And his wise decision – taken immediately on coming to office – to cut back the defence budget only underlined what the Americans regarded as reluctance or inability to play a superpower's part in the defence of the free world. At Nassau, for all the hauteur and old-world charm, Macmillan was a beggar. Britain had become, for a while, wholly dependent on American favours. But it was Nassau, not Rambouillet, which encouraged France to stand in the way of Britain's true destiny. France's defeat – and its liberation by the Anglo-American Allies – had made standing out against the English-speaking partnership essential to French pride. The paradox of Harold Macmillan's premiership is that although he was the first Prime Minister to apply for British membership of the Common Market, much of what he had come to represent postponed the date at which Great Britain was admitted. De Gaulle was not in a mood to do business with Old England.

5

WHITE HEAT
Wilson's Liberating Zeal

———•———

Rejection by the French produced the anticipated wave of national resentment. The Common Market – never an object of British veneration – grew increasingly unpopular for the simple reason that the people of a proud but uncertain nation took the opposite view from Groucho Marx's first rule of social conduct: they did not wish to belong to a club which would not allow them to join. Briefly, the Prime Minister became a tragic hero. Macmillan himself – who had seriously considered the possibility that De Gaulle had gone mad – regarded the French veto as a national tragedy but not a personal humiliation. No doubt Hugh Gaitskell regarded his autumn opposition to the enterprise as wholly vindicated, for he had told friends of his belief that General de Gaulle would not let Britain in. But at a time when he might have taken political advantage of his prescience, he was in hospital suffering from a 'mystery illness' with symptoms that the official bulletin described as both pleurisy and peritonitis. On 18 January, four days after De Gaulle's Elysée press conference, he died.

Hugh Gaitskell's death was one of the great ironies of modern politics. For fifteen years – ever since he had replaced Emmanuel Shinwell as Minister of Fuel and Power – he had been a controversial figure, some of his enemies would say a major divisive force, in the

Labour Party. Two years before his death, thanks first to his support for 'revisionism' and then because of his opposition to unilateral nuclear disarmament, he had become as hated on the left as he was admired on the right, but the 'fight, fight and fight again' speech had changed his status in the country. His 'personal rating', more than 20 per cent behind Macmillan in 1959, was almost 10 per cent ahead by the end of 1962. Then his assault of the idea of British Common Market membership transformed his standing with the party. The old left paradoxically applauded his emotional attachment to a 'thousand years of British history'. It seemed that he was certain to lead a united Opposition to victory. However, within days of fate and General de Gaulle playing into his hands, he was dead.

Three candidates fought for the succession and the hope of Downing Street – Harold Wilson, Jim Callaghan and George Brown, who, in a predominantly moderate and trade union-dominated party, should have been the favourite. But Brother Brown drank. Harold Wilson had not been entirely forgiven by the left for taking Aneurin Bevan's seat on the Shadow Cabinet when the Great Tribune of the People had resigned. And the right recalled that he had left the Attlee government – when it was deep in crisis – because of a disagreement over defence expenditure. But nobody doubted his intellect or his industry. Jim Callaghan – who later rejoiced at the quality of his small vote – was eliminated on the first ballot. Wilson won on the second by 144 votes to 103. And although it was not recognised at the time, a new era in Labour history had begun: the meritocrats were about to take over from the radicals. Pragmatism was on the point of becoming a major socialist virtue.

The 1959 Parliament still had eighteen months to run and Harold Macmillan was still to face the final tribulation of his premiership. It concerned an issue infinitely less important than the United Kingdom's exclusion from the Common Market – the relationship between John Profumo, Minister for War, and Christine Keeler. We know now – indeed most senior politicians knew then – that the relationship between the politician and the call-girl created not the slightest risk to security, even though Ms Keeler was carrying on a simultaneous affair with the Russian Defence Attaché. But on such occasions it is necessary to justify prurient vote-grabbing by claiming that it is all being done in the national interest. George Wigg – a self-proclaimed defence expert and Harold Wilson's nark in the House of Commons – brought the whole issue to a head and public notice with a parliamentary question. Barbara Castle supported him, at one moment darkly suggesting that the young lady had been abducted and might soon be smuggled out of the country. It was not a situation with which Harold Macmillan was temperamentally equipped to deal. He was 'not much in the company of young people'.

There had been plenty of opportunities for the Prime Minister to practise his skills in dealing with genuine security crises. In January 1961, the 'Portland Spy Ring' at the Underwater Warfare Establishment had been exposed. Its members had been prosecuted, convicted and sentenced to long periods in prison. A Committee of Enquiry was set up to find out how such large-scale (if low-level) treason could go unnoticed for so long. Before it could report, George Blake – a senior MI6 officer – was convicted of working as a double agent for the KGB. He was sent to prison for forty-two years – an exemplary sentence awarded after the discovery that he had betrayed scores of British agents. A second enquiry, conducted by Lord Radcliffe, examined all aspects of national security, not just the performance of the professional counter-espionage service but also and equally the government's role in protecting vital national interests. The Radcliffe Commission suggested nothing very radical, so the government was able to accept its recommendations and trumpet its determination to set its own house in order. Then, in October 1962, an Admiralty executive officer, W. John Vassall, was found to be supplying classified information to the Soviet Union. The evidence suggested that his treason stretched back over four years. Vassall, a homosexual, had been assistant private secretary to Tam Galbraith, a junior (and unmarried) defence minister. Inevitably newspapers began to speculate about their relationship. Two journalists – one from the *Daily Mail*, the other from the now defunct *Sketch* – wrote that Vassall had connections with the Portland Spy Ring. Summoned before the Radcliffe Tribunal to explain the evidence on which they based that view, they 'refused to reveal their sources'. The journalists were convicted of contempt and sentenced to six months' imprisonment. The newspapers feared – some perhaps actually believed – that the prison sentences were retaliation or even revenge for the damage that the newspapers had done to his government. Macmillan's relationship with the press never recovered. He was Supermac no more.

The security dramas – part tragedy, part farce – dragged on. Kim Philby, a suspect when Burgess and Maclean defected to the Soviet Union, announced, in a London press conference, that he was, indeed, the third man. Ms Barbara Tell – an elderly, comparatively junior and entirely uninfluential employee at the Central Office of Information – gave her young Yugoslav lover classified information of no importance. Each new incident whetted the press's appetite for more. By the time that the Profumo scandal broke, combining the irresistible ingredients of sex and security, the newspapers were insatiable and the details – some purely imaginary – were reported with loving care. The ministers who interrogated John Profumo – tragically reproducing John Morley's cross-examination of Charles Stewart Parnell – found him innocent of all impropriety. Foolishly he made a statement in the House of Commons insisting that the insinuations were lies and the allegations all invented. When it became certain, beyond all argument, that the stories were (in general) true, the sanctimonious charge against him was lying to Parliament – which Members on both sides of the House agreed was a virtually unknown as well as an unforgivable offence. Profumo resigned both his office of state and his seat in Parliament. Harold Macmillan suddenly looked not so much an elegant survivor of a more serene and certain age as an anachronism.

It was not, however, the Profumo scandal that brought the reign of Supermac to its end. It was something much more like hypochondria – or valetudinarianism, as the man who read Jane Austen during the Suez Crisis would probably have called it. R. A. Butler had noticed that Macmillan treated a common cold with 'enormous swigs of cough linctus every half-hour at the risk of poisoning himself'. When, just before the 1963 Tory party conference, he suddenly felt excruciating bladder pain, he bravely continued with his duties but began to fear for his future. The idea of retirement was already in his mind. For, quite independently of the unexpected illness, he had arranged for the Cabinet in his absence to consider whether or not he should lead the government into the election which he took for granted the Tories would win. Only one minister – the predictably unpredictable Enoch Powell – thought that he should go. While the Cabinet considered his future, the Prime Minister had treatment to relieve his agony.

After another sleepless night and more pain, two specialists were consulted. Both diagnosed a prostate tumour which, they believed, was most likely benign. A complete recovery was certainly probable and probably certain. But Macmillan had made up his mind that the growth was malign and that, after weeks of debilitating treatment, he would die. The Tory party conference had already assembled when he announced his resignation. Lord Hailsham – who had lost his temper on television when asked about the Profumo affair – made an ass of himself again by announcing that he was a candidate for the leadership of his party at one of the black-tie social events which were the high-light of the Conservatives' four days by the sea. The delegates went wild with delight. But the unseemly spectacle probably ended what chance he had of being the choice of 'The Magic Circle' which, in those days, chose the Tory leader. Hailsham's career had been marked by a vulgar awareness of press photographers. There had been pictures of him bathing in the sea, embracing his infant daughter and preparing for a visit to the north-east by buying a flat cap. Macmillan manipulated the media in an altogether more gentlemanly way. In the autumn of 1963, old Conservatism made its last stand. At first it seemed that Rab Butler, so often the bridesmaid, would at last be the bride. But after 'the usual consultations', Alec Douglas-Home 'emerged' as leader and Prime Minister of the United Kingdom. He renounced his peerage, won a by-election and held office for barely a year. It was the bridging passage between the old Conservatism of inherited wealth and accustomed privilege and the new Toryism of self-made success. The meritocrats, already in command of the Labour Party, were about to take over the Conservatives as well, and the middle classes who had made such social advances in the Macmillan years were on the brink of capturing his once-patrician party.

In the year before the 1964 election, it was Harold Wilson who campaigned on behalf of the upwardly mobile society of which he was such a distinguished member. The son of a chemist from Huddersfield, he made his brilliant academic way by scholarship. Years at Oxford – as undergraduate and assistant to Sir William Beveridge during the preparation of the historic report on the future of social security – had blunted, but not eliminated, his West Riding accent. Unlike so many other scholar-politicians, he was neither a philosopher nor an economist but a statistician, whose academic discipline equipped him to live in the hard world of industry and commerce. He sounded (and in his space-age Gannex raincoat looked) like the politician to lead Great Britain into the bewildering world of valve-driven computers. It was a reputation which he worked hard to develop. In the autumn after his election he promised to harness 'the white heat of technological revolution' to the cause of economic growth and industrial revival. The 'emergence' of the 14th Earl of Home had, he claimed, confirmed the Tories' unsuitability to lead Great Britain into the modern world: 'At a time when even the MCC has decided to abolish the distinction between amateurs and professionals, the Tory party has chosen to be led by a gentleman rather than by a player.' The references to 'the 14th Earl' were so frequent that the new Prime Minister retaliated with the suggestion that the Labour leader was probably the '14th Mr Wilson'. The joke only added to the impression of unworldly gentility. For what was important about the Wilson jibe was not the length of the line but the extent of the pedigree. The new Prime Minister did nothing to improve his reputation by making a self-deprecatory joke about needing a box of matches to help him understand economics.

When the government chose to postpone the election to what Harold Wilson called 'the last humiliating moment', it looked as though Labour would win by a landslide to be compared with 1945. But Labour's opinion-poll lead, 12 per cent in April 1964, had been reduced to 6 per cent by August. Three polls published during the campaign put the government ahead. In retrospect it seems probable that, if Harold Macmillan had not retired, the Conservatives would have hung on. Indeed, if the events of the following week – the fall of

Khrushchev and the explosion of the Chinese Republic's first nuclear bomb – had occurred seven days earlier, uncertainty might have saved the Home government. But on Thursday 15 October 1964, Labour won 317 seats, the Tories 304 and the Liberals 9. The Speaker – who had been Churchill's Solicitor-General – was re-elected. But his deputies had to come from the new government's side of the House. As a result, Labour's effective majority was three – easily workable by modern standards. But the Prime Minister was certainly oppressed by the fear that another General Election would be forced upon him within months. Over the next decade Harold Wilson was to acquire a reputation for what *The Times* described as 'counting the minutes and forgetting the hours'. His undoubted natural inclination to live for the moment was encouraged by the narrowness of the victory which carried him to power. What Labour needed at that crucial moment in the autumn of 1964 was time to take the long-term view. Time was denied them from the start.

Throughout the campaign, it had been taken for granted that, whichever party was elected, its first duty would be to eliminate the balance of payments deficit and the lethal effect it was having on sterling. But when, in Harold Wilson's phrase, Labour 'opened the books', the crisis was far greater than the new government had anticipated. The balance of payments had shown a deficit of only £35 million in 1963 and actually recorded a £14 million surplus in 1962. But as was their usual habit, the Tories had prepared for the election by allowing consumption – in those days regulated by a variable purchase tax and borrowing regulations – to boom to a level which the domestic economy could not accommodate. The published estimate for the 1964 trade balance deteriorated from a £300 million deficit in May to a £500 million deficit in August. On 16 October, the Treasury told the new Prime Minister that the figure was more likely to be £800 million. Instant action was necessary to combat the threat to sterling which was the unavoidable result of the catastrophic imbalance of exports and imports and the international market's inevitable lack of confidence in a Labour government.

There was a Saturday morning meeting with Treasury officials. Late in the evening, Wilson, Jim Callaghan (his Chancellor) and

George Brown (First Secretary of State and head of the newly created Department of Economic Affairs) assembled at Downing Street, without civil servants present. Inevitably Wilson – not only Prime Minister but the only man present with any experience of government – dominated the discussion. He ruled out devaluation – the one effective remedy. There was no great disagreement with his decision, even though the Oxford economists who had thought up the idea of the DEA as a counterweight to the Treasury had tried to persuade George Brown that it was essential. Jim Callaghan had actually attempted to persuade Reggie Maudling, the Tory Chancellor, to sign a joint statement which would have asserted before the election campaign that whoever won would maintain the value of sterling somewhere between $2.78 and $2.84. The decision to fight for an overvalued pound was unanimous.

Nobody can be certain about the balance of political and economic consideration which prompted the three men's decision. Certainly they were all determined that Labour (perhaps only months away from another election) should not acquire the reputation of 'the devaluation party'. But there was also Labour's social programme to protect. And devaluation only works when it is backed up by deflation. Perhaps the crucial consideration, at least in Harold Wilson's mind, was the 'sterling balances' which were held in London – in those days the centre of what was called 'The Rest of the Sterling Area'. When, late in November, the Prime Minister met the new Labour Members of Parliament, one tyro had the effrontery to suggest that devaluation was both necessary and inevitable. The Prime Minister replied with real passion. He was not prepared to 'lop off' 5 per cent from the savings which underdeveloped members of the Commonwealth had left in London for safekeeping. By delaying what he should have accepted as unavoidable, he 'lopped off' almost three times as much.

So, within forty-eight hours of the Labour government's election, the pattern of palliatives was established. Believing that the balance of payments deficit could be permanently eliminated by a short-term reduction in imports and the long-term promotion of growth, the three ministers narrowed the options for action to either the physical control provided by import quotas or the financial constraint imposed by a surcharge on physical imports. A surcharge was illegal under the General Agreement on Tariffs and Trade and contrary to the rules of the European Free Trade Association. It was, nevertheless, the remedy which they chose, believing it would protect the government from the accusation of denying consumers a free choice. The full range of imports would still be available to the reduced number of families who could afford to pay for them after the surcharge had increased their price by 15 per cent. Labour governments, often lacking self-confidence in their own ideas, almost always worry too much about the opinions of their enemies. Back in the autumn of 1964, Harold Wilson made the crucial mistake of attempting to assuage opinion that would never be reconciled to his government. There is little doubt that most of the blame must lie with him. For his two inexperienced colleagues were, in effect, accessories after the fact. Incredible though it now seems, the Cabinet as a whole did not discuss devaluation until July 1966, almost two years after the first crucial mistake had been made.

The events of those first few fateful days provides another moral for all new governments. A White Paper was produced, admittedly in something of a hurry, setting out the 'emergency measures' which would accompany the import surcharge. Defence and overseas spending were to be cut. As part of the eventual package, two embryo aircraft projects (the P-1154 and the H-S681) were cancelled and the TSR II fighter-bomber (at a much more advanced stage of development) was abandoned in favour of buying the American F1-11. But the major and explicit economy proposal of the draft White Paper was the cancellation of Concorde. Roy Jenkins – Minister of Aviation but outside the Cabinet – heard of the decision by chance. He regarded it as possibly justified but certainly precipitous and argued successfully for further consideration. Meetings were held in Paris with the French government, who insisted that the collaborative project should continue. There were hints that if Britain abrogated the treaty unilaterally, the breach of contract might be taken to the Court of International Justice. The Law Officers advised the Prime Minister that if Britain lost, the French might be awarded £200 million compensation. The argument went on from October to January. Callaghan and Brown still wanted to take the risk of cancellation. But protracted consideration always breeds caution. Concorde, at a cost of £100 million a plane (a billion at today's prices) went ahead. The moral – which every new government must learn – is the folly of waiting.

The import surcharge staunched the haemorrhage for a month. Then, in early November, the 'emergency budget' was introduced. Despite the economic crisis, Labour kept its promise to increase pensions and national assistance, abolish prescription charges and end the earnings rule by which widows lost a shilling from their pension for every shilling, over eight pounds, which they earned in a week. The Chancellor was particularly enthusiastic for the last of these reforms. His mother, the sole earner in the family after his father died from war wounds, had been forced to scrape and struggle to provide her family with a decent life. One of the benefits of Labour government is – or ought to be – that its ministers remember.

Income tax was increased by 2½d in the pound (6p in today's coinage) and petrol duty by 6d a gallon. National insurance contributions were raised. The Conservative Opposition, like the government, nevertheless judged the impact of the budget to be broadly neutral. The Chancellor also announced that, the following April, he would introduce a capital gains tax and replace the complicated system of company taxation with a single corporation tax. He did not, however, set out the rate at which the new taxes would initially be applied; the Inland Revenue needed time to work out the details. Once again failure – or in this case inability – to come to a quick decision proved crucially damaging.

The pound immediately came under renewed pressure. It was intensified when an anticipated increase in the Bank Rate did not materialise and Efta was reassured that the import surcharge would not last for long. But the City's claim that the damage had been done by uncertainty about the fiscal stand was only an excuse. The real problem was political. The British manager's concern for his own disposable income always outweighs his support for an economic strategy which benefits the whole nation. Ten days after the budget, speculation against the pound had risen to such a level that the government was forced to sell $180 million in one day in order to prevent total collapse. A couple of days later $70 million was recovered. But on 24 November the pound was under such pressure that literally four times as much ($281 million) had to be spent to save the pound. The Prime Minister sent for Lord Cromer, Governor of the Bank of England, to discuss how a rescue package might be arranged with other central banks. The governor's response was an object lesson in the institutional obstacles which a Labour government has to overcome. Lord Cromer's prescription for restoring confidence had very little to do with the fiscal stance. The foreign bankers required the Labour government to stop being Labour. It had, he said, been a fatal mistake to improve welfare benefits before the balance of payments deficit was eliminated – notwithstanding the compensating increases in the revenue. A severe deflation was essential. Trade union restrictive practices must be made illegal and the plan to nationalise steel dropped.

Harold Wilson, to his eternal credit, told Lord Cromer that the City of London was not so much arguing with the government's economic policy as challenging its democratic mandate. Having been elected on the promise of expansion, there could be no question of buying support by contracting the economy. If international finance made it impossible for Labour to keep its promises there would have to be an immediate General Election and, in consequence, chaos in the world's financial markets. Cromer shrank from the prospect of financial Armageddon and began to organise an international rescue. The Federal Reserve and the Bundesbank responded with a $3,000 million guarantee. There was much talk of speculators' fingers being burned when it was clear that Britain would go on buying sterling until the exchange rate, if not the reserves, were stabilised.

The credits were repaid on schedule, initially by drawing £500 million from the International Monetary Fund. By the middle of 1965, debts to the IMF and Federal Reserve had risen to £1,000 million – almost the sum total of the guarantee. For the rest of its life, the government was forced to look nervously over its shoulder to make sure that predators were not stalking its wounded currency. Confronted with its first crisis, it had chosen to respond with traditional and discredited remedies. It was a strange beginning for a government which had been elected to find new cures for old ills.

There is no way of knowing if the conventional remedies would have worked for a conventional government. Labour believed in redemption by assuaging the international opinion which regarded deflation as essential to the British economic disease. But the people on whom the pound was dependent believed that it was vulnerable because a Labour government was in office. So when, during the winter of 1964–65, the economy expanded at the annual rate of 6 per cent, although there was rejoicing in George Brown's Department of Economic Affairs, there was consternation on the money markets. The Labour government was, they believed, overstretching itself and the economy. The Chancellor had no choice but to check the expansion. Monetary policy was tightened and military expenditure cut. Beer and tobacco duties, like the motor vehicle licence, were increased as part of a fiscal package which raised an extra £200 million of revenue in a full year – the amount which the OECD said was necessary to satisfy Britain's international creditors. They were not satisfied. Labour was beginning to learn that it was judged against different criteria from those by which the success and failure of Tory governments are measured. Labour cuts are never quite deep enough. There are always demands for more.

Certainly the 1965 April budget failed to stop the run on the pound. By July new measures – in effect a second budget – were judged to be necessary. The 'July Measures' included another £200 million reduction in public expenditure, a licensing system to hold back new building and the promise to introduce a statutory incomes policy. Initially, the currency speculators smelled panic and believed that devaluation could not long be avoided. But the United States led another successful rescue operation. The government had survived two sterling crises in a year.

The third came in July 1966, after a hopeful winter. It was triggered off by a seamen's strike and the international conviction that reduction in unemployment confirmed that the economy was overheating. Another package of July Measures was put together. Domestic demand was to be reduced by £500 million and overseas spending by £150 million. Unemployment would, as a result of the deflation, rise to 2 per cent. There would be cuts in the public investment programme and travel allowance was to be limited to £50. The Cabinet, whether they knew it or not, accepted cutbacks which they had rejected in November 1964. To the general public, Labour government seemed to be a succession of economic crises followed by mini-budgets which never quite solved the problem.

Once again the government had bought time, although the Prime Minister's reputation had been badly damaged. Public criticism led to the paranoid belief that, while he was away in Moscow, a plot to replace him had been hatched. But by the spring of 1967, the Chancellor felt so confident about the new stability that he felt able to write his own budget headlines. Always proud of his naval past, he chose 'Steady As She Goes'. Two days later, the Six-Day War between Egypt and Israel closed the Suez Canal and tilted the terms of trade against a trading nation which was still dependent on imported oil. Then an unofficial dock strike – against 'decasualisation', once the dream of every docker – again convinced foreign bankers that Britain was in a state of industrial anarchy. The final blow was a report from the Common Market Commission. It predicted, and therefore helped to bring about, an immediate devaluation. George Brown, who displayed all the zeal of a convert, had wanted it for two years, but Jim Callaghan – who knew that 'sterling had turned into a symbol of national pride' – had stubbornly resisted. Then, on 2 November 1967, Sir Alec Cairncross, the Head of the Government Economic Service, left a hand-written letter on the Chancellor's desk. It was marked 'Top Secret'.

The letter told the Chancellor that his principal economic adviser had also become a convert to devaluation. Unlike George Brown, he was 'reluctant' to change his mind. Resistance was no longer possible. On 18 November sterling was devalued by 14.3 per cent and the pound's value reduced from $2.80 to $2.40. Harold Wilson, broadcasting to the nation, struggled to reassure a worried public that prices would not increase the following day: 'It does not mean that the pound in your pocket is worth 14 per cent less to us than it is now.' The sentence was the product of much careful drafting by the Prime Minister and his advisers. In a way it was true. But it did incalculable damage to the government's reputation. There had been too many recoveries, too many false dawns and too many victories that turned into defeat. From that moment on, Labour was destined to lose the next election.

It is possible to argue – and it was argued with great passion at the time – that Labour's first three years were prejudiced by unpredictable misfortunes. The phrase 'blown off course' was constructed to make clear that it was the elements, not helmsman, that stopped the government from sailing safely into port. Certainly the British economy was assailed by every sort of misfortune. The Six-Day War was the least predictable and the most spectacular. But the real damage was done by the irrationality of international opinion – the bankers who regarded every strike as proof of Britain's incipient Bolshevism and rejected as inadequate Labour policies to stabilise the pound which, had they been introduced by a Conservative government, would have been regarded as draconian. But true and understandable though the claims against malign fate may be, Harold Wilson and his senior colleagues made too much of their own bad luck. Locked into conventional economics, they refused even to consider early devaluation. Perhaps even more important, they lacked faith in their own remedy.

Labour's pre-election plan was to invest in industry and solve the balance of payments crisis by exporting more. That would have been possible if early devaluation had been accompanied by an immediate deflation to drive goods abroad and, in the longer term, investment-led growth that provided gradual prosperity and permanent stability. The new government pursued only half that policy – trying to reform and revitalise industry while, crisis by crisis, imposing extended fiscal and monetary restraints which made the reinvigoration impossible. At the same time, the savings which should have been made were neglected. For far too long the government was unwilling to reduce commitments as well as capabilities, so the defence reviewers never cut deep enough. Not even all the reductions which were agreed were implemented. The Head of the Government's Economic Service at the time has since wryly observed, 'There is no evidence in the historical record of the promised saving of £100 million on military expenditure abroad.' For three years the government attempted to construct a compromise between the growth it had promised and the economic contraction that the bankers demanded. Of course it failed. Labour governments are not at their best when they adopt Tory policies.

It says much for the ingenuity of the 1964 government that, despite the constant and recurring economic crises, it managed to at least divert the course of welfare policy. The bold beginning – pensions increased and prescription charges abolished – was intended as no more than first-aid for a sick system. Real surgery had been promised in the manifesto. Discretionary payments – based on need as determined by an Assistance Board Officer making a home visit – had been introduced to inject some much-needed flexibility into a system which, being bureaucratic and rigid, often neglected real want. They had come to be regarded as a humiliating means test. Labour promised to replace the variable and inconsistent individual grants with an 'income guarantee'. The slogan was 'receive as you need and pay as you earn'. The idea foundered on the rocks of the 1965 July package. Even without that emergency, it would almost certainly have gone the way of the Tory 'tax credits' five years later. A single system could not meet the variable needs of disparate categories of claimants. With pensioners the problem was widely different housing costs. As social patterns changed – the growth in one-parent families and the increase in unemployment – the difficulties of a single rate of benefit grew increasingly impractical. But at least the idea of *rights* had been established.

But although the 'income guarantee' was soon abandoned, two small administrative steps helped to end the humiliation of the public means test and, in consequence, reduced a major cause of pensioner poverty. National Assistance became Supplementary Benefits. Both the supplement (paid after a proof of need) and the pension (an entitlement based on contributions) were paid after the presentation of a single benefit book at the post-office counter. 'One book', an achievement about which the government boasted for years, produced remarkable results. Relieved of the embarrassing necessity to demonstrate their poverty, 365,000 pensioners who had not previously applied for supplementary help chose to claim what was theirs by right.

Means testing was, however, to enjoy a new lease of life. The government committed to ever-increasing house-building targets – which were never hit but acted as an important stimulus to the industry – subsidised owner-occupiers through mortgage tax relief and council tenants with both building subsidies and rent rebate schemes. The subsidies, designed to promote the best use of land, often encouraged height rather than high density. So there was another decade of multi-storey developments. The tower-blocks of the 1960s were, in a sense, the trademark of the age – architecturally part of the new brutalism that was so popular in public buildings. They also represented the state's belief in its capacity to solve a housing (or any other) crisis. However, the tenants of private landlords, among them the poorest families in the country, received no help until rate rebates were introduced. The repeal of the Rent Act guaranteed them security, but rate rebates – like differential rents – were means tested. Having got rid of one complicated humiliation, the government introduced another.

By then, the country had begun to realise that homelessness – which had been graphically brought to public attention by the television drama *Cathy Come Home* – possessed more complex causes than successive governments had recognised. The problem was not just shortage of houses, and could not therefore be rectified by indiscriminate new building. There were empty houses in some areas and waiting lists in others. Nothing could be done about that. But the thousands of unfit houses could be repaired and renovated. 'Old Houses, New Homes' launched the rehabilitation programme. It marked the merciful end of the 'comprehensive redevelopment' policy which had ripped the heart out of so many towns and cities.

Much has been made of the influence that John F. Kennedy's inaugural speech had on the conduct of his presidency. The promise to 'pay any price, bear any burden, meet any hardship, support any friend, oppose any foe to assure the survival and success of liberty' has been blamed for the tragedy of Vietnam which followed. Kennedy, it has been argued, felt an obligation to live up to his own rhetoric, and his staff believed that they had a duty to make his extravagant dream come true. In a more modest way, Harold Wilson's commitment to the 'white heat of technological revolution' and his contempt for 'Tory amateurs in the boardrooms of Britain who are unable to think or speak in the language of our scientific age' made an indelible mark both on Labour's manifesto and the character of the government which he led. The manifesto contained paragraphs which were no more than extended versions of the purple passages from his Scarborough speech. Like the policy statements of New Labour more than thirty years later, it was strangely deficient in verbs:

A New Britain – mobilising the resources of technology under a national plan; harnessing our national wealth and exploiting our genius for scientific invention and medical discovery; reversing the decline of the thirteen wasted years and affording new opportunities to equal and, if possible, surpass the roaring progress of other Western powers.

Nobody who watched Wilson at work during the early years of his Labour government can doubt the sincerity with which he personally believed in the ultimate triumph of technology. When, in the late 1960s, he set up a committee of junior ministers to review government statistics, he addressed the first meeting for forty minutes – explaining that computers (then barely more than the machine which Joe Lyon lent to the government to choose the Premium Bond winners) were, wonder of wonders, increasing their capabilities as they grew smaller. One day, he predicted, a single terminal at London Airport would be able to display the name of every passenger on every scheduled flight in the world. The Parliamentary Secretaries present marvelled but felt unsure how this remarkable achievement was going to help the balance of payments.

The key elements in the new strategy were industrial expansion combined with more restraint. And the new morality of investment rather than consumption was to be mapped out on a national plan and implemented by a whole series of new institutions which would look upon economic management in a way which the Treasury could not understand. Frank Cousins – the old unilateralist warrior from the

Transport and General Workers' Union – was brought in to the Cabinet to head a Department of Technology, partly as a gesture to the unions but mostly to demonstrate a dirty fingernail approach to the regeneration of manufacturing industry. But the real powerhouse of innovation and expansion was to be the Department of Economic Affairs, headed by George Brown and intended, because it rivalled the Treasury and openly questioned fiscal orthodoxy, to bring 'creative tension' to the government. Cousins, though industrious, was not a natural minister. George Brown was passionate, energetic, impressionable and intolerant – a prescription for tension without creativity. Because he possessed all those virtues, he was able to get the new policy off to a flying start with a Declaration of Intent – signed with a fanfare by both the CBI and TUC – to moderate wage claims and settlements. A Prices and Incomes Board, under the chairmanship of Aubrey Jones – the Tory Minister of Fuel and Power at the time of Suez – was set up to monitor progress and recommend good practice. By the time that the Chancellor of the Exchequer introduced his budget in April 1965, he felt sufficiently confident of George Brown's success to predicate his plans on wage rises of no more than 3 to 3.5 per cent.

The ultimate manifestation of the new approach was the National Plan – built around thirty-nine action points, none of which could have been implemented without co-operation from what was then called 'both sides of industry', and some of which could not have been operated under any circumstances at all. The government itself promised a ceiling on domestic expenditure and a reduction in overseas aid and defence spending, two commitments so close to the heart of the CBI that it is difficult to understand why they refused to support the Plan until George Brown, in his turn, threatened an election if they, in theirs, made Britain ungovernable. The only possible explanation is that the CBI, like the foreign creditors, judged the National Plan less on its contents than on their own nightmares about how the Labour government would behave. Obsessed by fears of direction and regulation, they forgot that Harold Wilson had made his ministerial reputation twenty years before as the President of the Board of Trade who promised, and actually ignited, a 'bonfire of controls'.

The National Plan was published in the autumn of 1965. It set a target of 25 per cent increase in national output over the next six years – an annual growth rate of 3.8 per cent. It was an ambitious aim, but Labour could not afford to promise less. The OECD had predicted that European production would rise by 50 per cent within the 1960s. And between the slump of 1958 and the boom of 1964, the British economy had grown by 24 per cent. The party of growth had to improve on the Tory record and match the OECD's aspiration. Unfortunately, expansion was certain to increase the importation of raw materials before it promoted the export of manufactured goods – with disastrous consequences for the balance of payments and therefore for sterling. To ensure the policy's success, devaluation or domestic deflation (and ideally both simultaneously) was necessary to drive consumption from home to abroad. The government would not or could not deliver the whole policy until it was too late.

A succession of budgets depressed domestic demand as much as it was thought the political situation would allow. But the one consistent attempt to slow down domestic consumption was a physical rather than fiscal restraint. All that was needed, the government at least convinced itself, was proper respect for the 3–3.5 per cent 'pay norm'. During 1966, hourly wage rates rose by 7.3 per cent and average hourly earnings by 10.1 per cent. The failure of the National Plan to achieve the earnings target set by the declaration of intent – or indeed many of the other 'norms' it proposed to industry – is now often regarded as proof that the whole exercise was futile. Some ministers and officials were privately sceptical at the time and, after a suitable period of mourning, expressed rejoicing rather than regret that the idea was dead. But the National Plan did focus attention on the real causes of British industry's chronic decline. Much of it was no more than sketches of the future drawn up by industry itself. Each sector outlined as much of its manpower needs, investment plans, output forecasts and export potential as its constituent companies were prepared to reveal. The illusion of central planning certainly helped the leaders of the TUC to argue for income restraint: 'You can't plan everything except wages.' But the aggregated information itself had a crucial influence on economic policy. The Plan was prepared when almost every major British industry was suffering from a shortage of skilled labour and the demand for workers so exceeded supply that it was impossible for managers to make a successful assault on restrictive practices. The Labour government was learning that the trade unions themselves could be an inhibition on the improved living standards that their members demanded and that 'full employment' – either by Keynes's or Beveridge's definition – was sometimes the enemy rather than the ally of growth. Visiting the Midlands – where the motor industry was simultaneously short of labour, attracting skilled engineers to well-paid non-skilled jobs and wrestling with mindlessly militant trade unions – the Prime Minister was astonished to discover that the local employment exchanges recorded fourteen unfilled vacancies for every man or woman who was looking for a job.

The 'shake-out' – Wilson's euphemism for higher unemployment – was perversely necessary to achieve the National Plan's hopes of expansion. The Plan, now generally derided, can take credit for a whole series of initiatives which, at least at the time, were universally admired. There was a major acceleration in the creation of the Industrial Training Boards – charging each company a training levy and repaying it to those who did the job themselves rather than poached skilled manpower from their more enlightened competitors. Regional Employment Premiums (which subsidised jobs in Development Areas), Selective Employment Tax (that raised revenue but actually repaid more to manufacturing industry than it collected), and the Redundancy Payments Scheme (which, in effect, compensated workers for the inconvenience of changing job) were all innovations which sprang, if not directly from the National Plan, at least from the idea of government intervention in the economy on which the Plan itself was based. In effect, the government was – in a crude and primitive way – working on the supply side of the economy, manipulating its structure rather than attempting to secure growth simply by managing effective demand. Increases in demand stimulate consumption before they increase investment, and demand increases when wages rise. That is why the government began not only to think the unthinkable but work out ways of putting the forbidden ideas into practice. Wage increases would have to be limited by law.

The decision of a Labour government to intrude into the process of 'free collective bargaining' was an intellectual and ideological leap which, five years before, most people would have thought inconceivable. Even against the background of recurring economic crisis, it was only possible to overcome the atavistic opposition by approaching the idea of legal restraint with formal reluctance. Statutory wages policy had to be a last resort. And it had to be temporary. In fact, even as the government insisted on always influencing and sometimes determining pay rates, it conceded that the whole process was fundamentally undesirable. It was not the ideal way of ensuring the initiative's success.

It was, however, one way of guaranteeing re-election. The trade unions were plunging down a spiral of unpopularity – blamed both for inflation (for which they were certainly in part responsible) and low productivity, which was chiefly the responsibility of their employers. Limiting their powers was a vote-winner. So was the constitutional dispute with the illegal Rhodesian regime. The British electorate does not turn on a government which is locked in international combat. Conflict with the unions and Ian Smith combined with the feeling that the new government 'should be given a chance' to reinforce the principal reason for Harold Wilson's renewed and increased success. That, ironically, was the increase in personal disposable income which the government had tried, unsuccessfully, to prevent. The result of the election of 31 March 1966 was a Labour majority of ninety-six.

The power to impose statutory wage control (lying dormant but ready to be activated by an Order in Council) was included in a Bill which Parliament was discussing when the General Election was called. In consequence, it never reached the statute book. The new Bill which replaced it was easier to justify in traditional labour terms. On 16 May, the National Union of Seamen called an official strike – with obvious consequences for a trading nation. Clearly there were circumstances in which voluntary restraint was not enough. The law was needed to make sure that a selfish minority did not take advantage of the generally public-spirited trade union movement. Wilson chose – probably out of frustration rather than calculation – to

denounce the strike leaders as a 'tightly-knit group of politically motivated men'. Everybody knew that the coded message really meant
that the Communist Party was behind the dispute and the *cognoscenti*
suspected that the Prime Minister knew about it because their tele-
phones had been tapped. Labour and liberal opinion were scandalised,
but Wilson himself insisted that it was the 'feeling of public revulsion'
stimulated by his speech which forced the NUS to end the dispute
without winning any of their demands. The stoppage did, however,
precipitate the third sterling crisis and convince the hawks in the
government that a statutory incomes policy must be introduced on
the classic terms – temporarily and to prevent the selfish few exploiting the responsible many.

Even when the decision was taken – and the urgency of convincing foreign bankers that Britain meant business confirmed – discussion
about the content and timing of the wages legislation dragged on,
mostly in the hope of avoiding the resignation of Frank Cousins who,
although Minister of Technology by name, was still, in his heart, the
General Secretary of the Transport and General Workers' Union.
Cousins resigned on 3 July. The legislation to give statutory powers to
the National Board for Prices and Incomes was published the next
day. The government's decision to impose a six-month wage freeze,
followed by another six months of 'severe restraint', was announced
together with the second austerity package in two years – by the
Prime Minister himself, to what he later described as 'the roughest
House since Suez'. The TUC was more understanding and endorsed
the government's policy. Parliament was kept in session until the
Glorious Twelfth of August in order to pass the Prices and Incomes
Bill into law, but its powers were not invoked until October. Then, on
the eve of the Labour party conference, the managers' and foremen's
union took an employee to court for failure to honour a wage agreement. The court ruled that the voluntary wage freeze had no standing
in law and the new act was used, for the first time, in order to prohibit
the wage increase and relieve the management of the duty of enforcing government policy. It was rarely used thereafter. Only 50,000
workers out of a total labour force were ever subject to statutory
control. But the knowledge that the controls were there had an

undoubted effect – at least in the short term. Between July and December 1966, there were no reported increases in weekly wages and, for the next six months, average earnings rose by 2 per cent. The government believed that it could relax. But the Six-Day War and the closing of the Suez Canal had, once again, proved that Britain was vulnerable to economic pressures which it could neither anticipate nor avoid.

After he had supervised the devaluation which he had struggled against for so long, Jim Callaghan resigned from the Treasury and became Home Secretary. His new appointment was announced on the day that Milton Obote decreed that Europeans and Asians – no matter how long they had lived in the country – could only be employed in Kenya if they possessed a work permit.

At the time of Kenyan independence in 1963, Iain Macleod – speaking on behalf of Her Britannic Majesty's Government – had explicitly promised that, if the new rulers of Kenya introduced an 'Africanisation' policy, the local Asians (many of them Kenyan by birth) could find refuge in the mother country. When they began, in numbers, to redeem that pledge – 70,000 landed in Britain within three months – the Cabinet decided that the promise must be broken. A new Commonwealth Immigration Act was passed in a single day. British Commonwealth citizens (already a special class of passport-holder) were excluded from Britain unless they had 'special connections' with what was once the centre of the Commonwealth – that is to say, unless they were white.

The 1960s were the liberal hour of modern British politics – but the liberating zeal was almost all directed towards middle-class causes. The *bourgeoisie*, who had done so well both in terms of income and influence during Macmillan's premiership, had developed a radical tendency. But the policy for which they argued with such lucid zeal rarely involved any inconvenience to themselves or their neighbours. They had been, and would become again, the backbone of the CND, and they were to lead the fight against both the war in Vietnam and co-operation with the apartheid regime in South Africa. In the early days of the Labour government, they lobbied for social reform. They were not so progressive about race and immigration. Neither was the government.

Four months after it was elected, the party which had once opposed immigration controls completely tightened the entry regulations – claiming, as is always claimed on such occasions, that the problem was caused by illegal entrants. According to the Home Office, 10,000 had slipped into the country in three years. In August 1965, a White Paper – abandoning all face-saving arguments about the evasion of passport control – simply announced that primary immigration must be reduced from 28,000 to 8,500 a year, with stringent limitations on the entry of dependent relatives. Despite its support for – indeed its initiation of – policies far worse than those which it had denounced with such righteous anger less than a year before, Labour remained, in the perception of the public, 'the immigration party' – more concerned with the welfare of black and Asian intruders than with the legitimate grievances of 'its own people'. For the next thirty years, in government and opposition, Labour struggled to lose that electorally lethal reputation. Sometimes it succeeded in limiting the damage, but in general it remained so closely identified with the ethnic minorities that its vote would not have substantially changed had it chosen to do what it knew to be right rather than what it hoped would be popular.

For there had developed in parts of Britain an antipathy to blacks and Asians which was both vicious and pathetic. It was also highly irrational. Uncertain of their country's place in the world – and resentful of the increasing prosperity of competitor nations – a segment of British society needed a clearly visible underclass which could, at once, be blamed for the immediate social problems of the inner cities and be treated, by people who lacked confidence in their own social standing, as obvious inferiors. When Enoch Powell told a Birmingham audience in April 1968 that he had, 'like the ancient Roman, seen the Tiber foaming with much blood', his view that 'we must be mad, literally mad, as a nation to be permitting the annual inflow of some 50,000 dependants' of black and Asian citizens already settled in this country, was supported (at least according to Gallup) by

74 per cent of the population. Perhaps more significant, London dockers – who, only a year before, had heeded the strike call of the group of politically motivated men – marched on the House of Commons to give Powell their moral support. Interviewed on television, one of the demonstration's leaders said that London's East-enders would 'tolerate anything except threats to their women'. He could not describe the threat which he would not tolerate. In its sad way, it revealed all the ingredients of modern British racialism – ignorance, fear, and the feeling that, by some mistake of destiny, the lesser breeds without the law were beginning to elbow the British aside.

Despite – perhaps because of – its increasingly illiberal attitude towards immigration, the Labour government showed real concern for the immigrants who were already in Britain and for their children who, whatever they might be called, were not immigrants at all. Despite the good intentions of the two Race Relations Acts – the first outlawed discrimination in public places, the second in housing and employment – the idea that strict limitation of numbers was essential to harmonious race relations was diametrically wrong. When politicians spoke as if the entry of another dozen Kenyan Asians would do deep damage to British society, it was not surprising that resentment was encouraged against the Kenyan Asians who had lived next door for five years. The Race Relations Board – a typical Wilson creation – did its best to speak up for reason. But race relations, a subject of genuine concern to the Prime Minister, did not begin to improve until the typical British family came to terms both with Britain's diminished world status and changed society. In the worst days of inner-city unemployment in the 1990s, black and white (much to their mutual credit) chose not to blame each other but accept that they were partners in adversity.

Society was changing in attitude as well as in composition. 'Permissiveness', now said to be a malign legacy of the 1960s, has many different definitions. To Mary Whitehouse, who formed her Viewers' and Listeners' Organisation in November 1965, its worst manifestation was the portrayal of explicit sex on television. The campaign to legalise cannabis attracted one or two fashionable recruits. But although the Beatles – not altogether the models of propriety – were awarded MBEs, the Establishment was suitably scandalised when Mick Jagger and Keith Richards were convicted of drug offences. In truth, Britain only 'swung' for most of its citizens through the columns of their tabloid newspaper. Topless models, open marriages and drunken orgies were what they read about. But it is doubtful if a majority of adult voters even supported the state's gradual withdrawal from the private lives of its citizens.

Certainly, there was no popular majority in favour of the abolition of capital punishment – a decision carried in principle by the over-whelming majority of 355 to 170 in the House of Commons within three months of the Labour government's election. Feeling against the other liberalisations of the law was not so strong; usually it took the form of surprise that Parliament wasted its time on such issues. Special interest groups complained and campaigned. But most of the reforms were accepted with bored detachment. The mid-1960s were not the British people's liberal hour, but the liberal hour of the British Parliament. The Medical Termination of Pregnancy Bill legalised abortion during the first twenty-eight weeks when it was recom-mended by two doctors. The Matrimonial Causes Bill made 'the irretrievable breakdown of marriage' the only grounds for divorce, thus ending the notion of 'matrimonial offices' and the idea of a 'guilty party'. The Sexual Offences Act belatedly implemented the Wolfenden Committee's recommendation that homosexual acts between consenting adult males in private should no longer be an offence. If the Wilson government had done nothing else, its exis-tence would have been justified by the opportunity it provided for Parliament to create a more enlightened society.

But it did far more – particularly to change the ethos of English education from a preoccupation with the talented and fortunate minority to concern about the generality of children. The Labour government – elected in 1964 and confirmed in office two years later – did not have much good luck. But it was fortunate in one par-ticular. It came to power at a time when national opinion had begun to focus on the inadequacy of the English schools system. Three cru-cial education reports – Newsom, Robbins and Crowther – had been published in the years immediately before its election. But more and better was to come. The Plowden Committee was set up 'to consider primary education in all its aspects and the transition to secondary education'. In the counter-revolution of the 1990s – when the return to 11-plus selection was being promoted in the disguise of 'concern about falling standards' – Lady Plowden became one of the hated figures of the unreconstructed right. The wife of the man who thirty years before had reorganised budget procedures and Treasury accounting was an unlikely revolutionary, but her report did contain one recommendation – the prohibition of corporal punishment – which was anathema to the educational old guard. And, by describing some of the new practices which were gaining increased professional approval, she appeared to be the advocate of 'child-centred' teaching, 'finding out rather than being told' and 'topic work' rather than whole classes focusing on a single subject.

In one particular, the Plowden Report was certainly guilty of what, to educational elitists, was an unforgivable sin. It proposed the creation of Education Priority Areas – defined by the educational and social disadvantages within these boundaries and the recipients of government grants with which to finance compensatory education. The extra resources, Plowden proposed, should be used to reduce class sizes, attract more teachers (by means of special EPA allowances) and increase the number of nursery places. Its other proposals – middle schools for pupils to attend from eleven to sixteen before moving on to sixth-form colleges, a single starting date at the beginning of the autumn term and in-service training for teachers – were of immense technical importance. But it was the invention of EPAs – proclaiming, as that recommendation did, the importance of meeting the consequences of education deprivation head-on – that gave the Plowden Report its historical significance. It did more than emphasise the relationship between background and performance (a denial of the absurd Tory notion that only personal effort is necessary for success). By demanding extra resources to compensate for the damage done by poverty, it also asserted the importance of creating an education system which met the needs of the whole nation.

The national mood had begun to change long before Labour's

election victory. The inadequacies of the 11-plus 'scholarship' had been plain for years. The test was intrinsically unreliable and, as well as having a 10 per cent margin of error, was unavoidably biased in favour of pupils with middle-class upbringings. And the propensity of the selective system to select the wrong pupils – even according to its own criteria – was not its only weakness. Academically, the records of many grammar schools were a disgrace. Having selected what they believed to be the most talented eleven-year-olds in their area, they often sent only a small minority of them on to higher education six or seven years later. One problem was the alienation of the working classes. The report 'Early Learning' showed that a third of grammar school pupils from lower-income homes left before they took 'O'-levels. England and Wales – Scotland always being more progressive – were in urgent need of an education system which met the needs of the whole school population.

But the comprehensive revolution did not come about because of a sudden realisation that the whole needed to be educated and that a selective system often failed many of the young people it claimed to favour. It was destroyed by the knowledge that, even when the grammar schools system worked, it worked for too few people. Selection at 11-plus ended because the emerging middle classes refused to have their sons and daughters selected – or at least they refused to have them publicly branded as failures. The 1944 Education Act had promised 'parity of esteem' for all types of school. But every family who had waited anxiously in May for the letter that announced 'pass' or 'fail' knew that the pious hope could not be fulfilled. As early as 1955, David Eccles – the anti-comprehensive Tory education minister – had told his officials that 'parity of esteem has not been and cannot be achieved'. By the early 1960s, the suburbs had worked out that if 15 per cent of children went to grammar schools and 85 per cent to secondary moderns, it would not be just the sons and daughters of the inner cities and rural backwaters who were assigned to the visibly inferior institutions.

Edward Boyle – Macmillan's last education minister – certainly accepted the inevitability and probably the benefit of the comprehensive revolution. By the end of his period of office, 96 of the 140 local education authorities had applied to end selection. The Labour government promised to accelerate that process. Within a few months of taking office, the sudden necessity to reshuffle the government brought to the Department of Education and Science (as it had been renamed) the ideal Secretary of State to force the pace. Anthony Crosland's strength – tragically, almost unique in the Labour Party after the defeat of the Attlee government – was absolute and total confidence in the superiority of egalitarian socialism over all other philosophies. In *The Future of Socialism* he had written that 'the school system of Britain remains the most divisive, unjust and wasteful of all aspects of social equality'. At the DES he determined to do what he could to right that wrong. Circular 10/65 – which *requested* local education authorities to end 11-plus selection – had been drafted before his arrival. He decided not to replace 'request' with 'require' in the hope that the reform, being voluntary, would survive a change of government. And so it turned out. Between 1970 and 1974, far from reversing the Crosland policy, Margaret Thatcher enthusiastically carried it on. But Crosland did introduce an element of coercion. After 1966, permission for new secondary school building was only granted to authorities which were, in the jargon of the day, 'going comprehensive'.

In August 1967, Crosland was 'promoted' to President of the Board of Trade. His successor, under pressure from the Treasury, abandoned plans to increase the school leaving age to sixteen – though the retreat was only carried in the Cabinet by a single vote. Crosland himself voted with the minority. But before his move from Curzon Street to Victoria, he introduced the 'binary system' – the creation of a two-tier higher-education sector in which polytechnics (under the control of local authorities and awarding their own degrees) existed side by side with independent universities. The intention was to create institutions which took technological education seriously and 'to move away from the snobbish caste-ridden hierarchical obsession with university status'. If Crosland hoped for parity of esteem in higher education, he was disappointed, and Lord Robbins, speaking in the House of Lords, was entitled to express his surprise that the man who had wanted to unify secondary education should want to divide the higher-education sector. But he might well have added that Crosland had come very near to making the central aspiration of his report a practical reality. The expansion of the universities, the creation of degree-awarding polytechnics and the easier availability of maintenance grants meant that there were more students in higher education than ever before.

Ironically the 'achievement' for which Crosland's time at the Department of Education will be remembered is the Open University, an innovation for which he had no great enthusiasm and would have gladly sacrificed if the money it cost could have been switched to preschool education. The idea – pioneered by Michael Young, one of Crosland's many occasional gurus – was built on a combination of the British correspondence course and the American experiment in education by television. Harold Wilson was so enthusiastic for a 'University of the Air' that the Treasury was never able to cut the infant institution's budget. The paternal interest was maintained in good times and in bad. A civil servant with him aboard HMS *Fearless*, when he made his last despairing attempt to end Rhodesia's secession from the Commonwealth, recalls that, over dinner at the end of a desperate day, the Prime Minister talked happily about the Open University.

Wilson's wish to relax with discussion of an unequivocal success was understandable. Rhodesia, another of the Labour government's inherited troubles, was part of the price Britain paid for its imperial inheritance. Nyasaland and Northern Rhodesia had passed to successful, if not wholly democratic, independence. But in Southern Rhodesia (as it was at the time of Central African Federation) the white minority was implacably opposed to African rule. Winston Field, by Rhodesian standards a moderate, lost office in April 1964 and was replaced as Prime Minister by Ian Smith – at once a more able and more extreme proponent of the white settlers' cause. On 14 October (the day before polling day in Britain) he announced his intention of calling an *indaba*, the historic gathering of tribal chiefs, in order to discuss Rhodesia becoming independent on the basis of the 1961 Constitution, which guaranteed power to the white minority.

The Conservative government, on the eve of its defeat, informed Ian Smith that independence on such terms was unacceptable and, if declared without agreement, illegal. Britain faced the classic dilemma of withdrawal from Empire – how to deal with a colony which, at the point of independence, announces its intention of behaving in a way of which the imperial power disapproves. The British government had enjoyed no practical influence over Rhodesia's internal policy since the 1920s, and there was general agreement that the time had come for it to go its own way. The question that Britain had to decide was whether or not it was right – and whether or not it was practical – to predicate the transfer of legal power on the assumption of a democratic constitution. Other European empires had been dissolved without concern for what was left behind. The Belgians had abandoned the Congo within weeks of taking the decision to go – and the result had been civil war. But Britain had the Commonwealth to consider. For when the break came it would not be total; Rhodesia would want to remain members of the club. And the club had rules.

Harold Wilson – genuinely concerned about the welfare of black Rhodesia and conscious of his status as Prime Minister of the country at the centre, if no longer the head, of the Commonwealth – warned Ian Smith that a unilateral declaration of independence would be treason. The initials 'UDI' became common currency of political debate. Smith's response was a referendum among Rhodesia's white voters. Not surprisingly, it endorsed his policy.

There followed a year of pointless manoeuvring. Smith came to London in January 1965 to attend Winston Churchill's funeral and agreed that two senior British ministers should visit Rhodesia. They made no progress towards a settlement, and the Commonwealth Prime Ministers – impatient with the stalemate – called on Britain to take military action against the rebel regime. In October, Smith was back in London at his own request for a meeting which he intended should fail. Unavoidably, Wilson contributed to his cynical tactic when he, in turn, visited Rhodesia two weeks later. He laid down the Five Principles on which a settlement must be based. They included progress towards majority rule, a demand which he knew

Smith would never accept. Smith dismissed the suggestion as dangerous and impractical, but it was not Rhodesian intransigence that most angered the British Prime Minister. He was moved to righteous fury by the sight of the African leaders – Joshua Nkomo and Ndabaningi Sithole – cold and hungry in prison. But he still confirmed the impression that he had given in London. Rhodesia might be punished with economic sanctions, but there would be no military action. It was a crucial error. The invasion of Rhodesia was not possible. The general staff was not certain that the army would fight its 'kith and kin', and there were insurmountable logistical difficulties in arranging so distant an operation. But Smith did not know that; military action was all that Smith feared. While it seemed at least a possibility, there was a faint hope of a negotiated settlement. On 30 October 1965, the Prime Minister compounded his error in a television broadcast:

> If there are those in this country who are thinking in terms of a
> thunderbolt hurtling through the sky and destroying their enemy,
> a thunderbolt in the shape of the Royal Air Force, let me say
> that this thunderbolt will not be coming.

Reinforced by the public announcement that he need not fear invasion, Ian Smith declared independence on 11 November. The United Nations Security Council immediately condemned the 'unilateral declaration of a racist minority' and called 'on all member states not to recognise the regime'. In London, Parliament passed the Southern Rhodesia Act, asserting Britain's continuing responsibility for the government of the colony, invalidating legislation passed in Salisbury and authorising the imposition of economic sanctions. The following week, the Security Council called for an oil embargo. It seemed that the whole world, with the single exception of South Africa, was against Rhodesia. Few people believed that the sanctions would have much effect. A Royal Navy patrol prevented oil from being landed at Beira and transported across land by pipe-line from Mozambique to Umtali. But the oil came in by tanker from South Africa and from the neighbouring Black African States – particularly

Zambia – which wanted to see the end of the Smith regime but felt that poverty prevented them from making the economic sacrifice which might have brought it about.

However, the Prime Minister remained, or claimed to remain, optimistic about Rhodesia being brought to heel. If the optimism had any justification at all it was the support that British policy in general – and sanctions in particular – was receiving from the United States administration. Harold Wilson had, from the day that illegal independence was declared, consulted – he liked to call it notified – President Lyndon Johnson about every move. While in Salisbury he sent Washington daily messages which described the progress of his negotiations. Johnson was certainly sympathetic, sometimes even supportive. But there was a price to be paid for American endorsement of the sanctions policy. It was at least tacit endorsement of the United States' increasingly unsuccessful military action in Vietnam.

Johnson wanted a British unit in South-east Asia fighting side by side with the Americans. Its size was not important. The fashionable phrase was 'a military band would do'. For it was moral, rather than material, support that the President needed. But despite the Prime Minister's desperate need for American help with both sterling and Rhodesia, the best he could do by way of reciprocation was avoid openly criticising the continuing war in Vietnam. There is little doubt that Wilson, with his historic concern for colonial independence, was a critic of State Department policy. But even if he had been as enthusiastic as Lyndon Johnson himself, he could not have sent British soldiers to fight side by side with Americans as – the President never ceased to remind him – the Australian government had done. The Parliamentary Labour Party – its loyalty already stretched taut by doubts over economic policy – would not have allowed it. Back-benchers rarely revolt to the point at which their government is destroyed, particularly when their party has just returned to power after thirteen years of frustrating opposition. But the feeling against the war in Vietnam was so strong that Labour would rather have destroyed itself than become an accomplice to what it regarded as the most immoral act since the Holocaust.

Somehow, Wilson managed to convince the President that he was doing his best for America, and the parliamentary party helped by constantly attacking the government's refusal to condemn the bombing, the napalm and the burning of villages. But Lyndon Johnson was, at least in this particular, not easily satisfied – particularly in the light of Britain's own belated decision to abandon its own commitments 'East of Suez' – which seemed to leave half a continent exposed to subversion. The treaty commitments in the Gulf, Malaysia and Singapore – which Britain could not afford and should have been brought to an end as soon as Labour was elected – were hardly comparable with the American operations in Vietnam. Certainly the British presence provided stability for less than democratic governments. But they were not fighting and killing the local population. They were there to defend what had been colonies and protectorates from external aggression. Nevertheless, the announcement that Britain would no longer be involved in South-east Asia was a rebuke of sorts. However, Johnson continued to help sterling when help was needed and endorse the imposition of sanctions on Rhodesia. Wilson was immensely grateful. Sometimes his gratitude was so great that he convinced himself that American support guaranteed a speedy solution.

Wilson certainly believed that a 'quick kill' was necessary. The Commonwealth – scheduled to meet in Lagos for the Prime Ministers' conference in January 1966 – was growing increasingly critical of Britain's failure 'to crush the rebellion and restore law and order to Southern Rhodesia [thus] preparing the way for majority government'. And the Prime Minister knew that a General Election could not be long postponed. A success of sorts was therefore necessary. Natural optimism, fuelled by American support, encouraged him to make up for the absence of a real triumph by declaring a bogus victory. Reminding his colleagues that petrol rationing had been introduced in South Africa and that Treasury restrictions had cut off the flow of current-account funds between Salisbury and London, Wilson told his colleagues that 'the cumulative effects of the economic and financial sanctions might well bring the rebellion to an end within a matter of weeks rather than months'. There were two flaws in his logic – legal as well as psychological. The sanction legislation did not prohibit the foreign subsidiaries of British companies from trading with Rhodesia. Petrol was carried over land in·sufficient quantities to avoid disruption, if not inconvenience. And the inconvenience stiffened Rhodesia's resolve. Fortunately for the prospects of the Labour government, the British people took some time to realize how hollow the Prime Minister's boast was. Wilson increased expectation of a quick and happy outcome by describing to Parliament his plans for a brief period of direct rule between the collapse of the rebellion and the elections which would mark the birth of a new democracy. In March, Wilson's 'mastery' of the Rhodesia situation was a major factor in Labour's landslide victory.

It is still unclear how much, in his more contemplative moments, Harold Wilson believed his own forecasts of imminent success. But it is certain that, in the calm that followed the General Election, he certainly realised that he did not possess the power to topple Ian Smith. The summer Commonwealth conference again demanded the use of force to restore constitutional government to Rhodesia. Once again, the Prime Minister rejected their demands. Kapwepwe of Zambia – the country which, more than any other, had frustrated the 'quick kill' by refusing to pay the economic penalty which it involved – walked out 'disgusted' by what he regarded as the British abandonment of NIBMAR – no independence before majority rule. 'This conference,' he said, 'makes us know that Mr Wilson is coming to be a racist.'

Wilson was coming to be a realist. The Avenging Angel who in 1964 and 1965 had laid down the terms of surrender, had gradually turned into the Spirit of Compromise, in search of a solution which was acceptable to all parties. Twice – at meetings aboard British battleships – he attempted to provide one. On HMS *Tiger* in June 1968 he warned that there would be no more concessions and then offered the greatest concession of all, the abandonment of NIBMAR. Aboard HMS *Fearless*, in October, he proposed independence on the basis of what amounted to the 1961 Constitutional formula rejected by the Conservative government on election day in

1964. The result would have guaranteed white minority rule for the rest of this century. Fortunately for Harold Wilson's reputation, Smith – guided by personal animosity rather than cool judgement – turned him down.

It was Britain's duty to confront the white Rhodesian settlers and do all in its power to set the country on the path to independent democracy. The social and political composition of the colony was what the imperial power had made it. Historically and legally, the United Kingdom was responsible for what Rhodesia had become and therefore had a moral duty to prevent it from becoming the replica of South Africa which Ian Smith and the Rhodesian front hoped to create. But no one can doubt that the burden of that responsibility was an immense detriment to a government which had, already, too many simultaneous problems to solve. Once again, the Empire – which had done so much for the mother country in the nineteenth century – proved an enormous liability in the twentieth.

Among those detriments was the almost unique vulnerability to changes in the exchange rate which put sterling under constant threat. That, combined with the neglect of manufacturing industry which the reliance on invisible earnings had encouraged, was the historic cause of the economic traumas which the Labour government had to face and survive. Inevitably, the more imaginative politicians looked for new and more radical solutions. In the autumn of 1965, Edward Heath, who had succeeded Douglas-Home in July of that year, told his party conference that a Conservative government would renew Britain's application to join the European Economic Community. In the Labour Party, the long-time Common Marketeers were joined by previous agnostics who had come to believe that Britain should not try to stand alone. Rhodesia had confirmed the view that the Commonwealth, whatever its past advantages, had been a liability. Within two months, Shell reported a major oil find off the coast of East Anglia, and Philips Petroleum announced the richest North Sea gas strike to date. But thinking people knew that whether or not Britain became a net energy exporter, it still needed friends. The obvious place to look was Brussels.

Some of his critics claimed that Harold Wilson's renewed interest in

the Common Market was no more than an attempt to deflect attention from the Rhodesian failure. But a much more plausible
explanation is the rational conclusion that a drifting Britain had no
other positive direction in which to steer. As early as October 1966,
the Prime Minister and George Brown, his Foreign Secretary, set off
on a Grand Tour. Wilson's enthusiasm increased with every stage of
the journey. After he met De Gaulle he was unequivocal in his determination to join – dismissing the suggestion of Associate Membership
out of hand, although he had proposed it two years earlier. But, back
in London, he was warned that not all the Parliamentary Labour
Party had experienced the same conversion. The row broke out at the
weekly PLP Thursday night meeting. Believing that the Cabinet anti-
Common Market minority was behind the trouble, he issued one of
his frequently expressed (but rarely heeded) formal warnings.
Ministers who did not respect the rules of collective responsibility
would be sacked. The warning was a preparation. On 2 May 1967,
Harold Wilson announced that Britain would once more apply for
membership of the European Economic Community.

Nine days later, the House of Commons approved the Prime
Minister's proposals and, the same night, the formal application to the
EEC, the European Coal and Steel Community and Euratom. There
was little talk of preconditions – a complete, though not uncharacteristic, change of position from the man who, a year earlier, had
promised, 'Given a fair wind, we will negotiate our way into the
Common Market, head held high, not crawl,' and replied to accusa-
tions that he was 'anti-European' with the allegation that Ted Heath
was 'rolling on his back like a spaniel'. Once again, President de
Gaulle spoke *ex cathedra*:

Was it possible for Britain at present – and was Britain willing – to
follow any policy that was really distinct from that of the United
States whether in Asia, the Middle East or Europe? This was what
France did not know. The whole situation would be different if
France were genuinely convinced that Britain really was disengaging
from the US in all major matters such as defence policy and in areas
such as Asia, the Middle East, Africa and Europe.

Those 'formidable obstacles' prompted the President to veto Britain's application for the second time. Once again De Gaulle had behaved intolerably and once again, instead of becoming a bridge between Europe and America, Britain had fallen into the gulf which divided old world from new.

6

A PLACE OF STRIFE
Who Governs Britain?

———•———

Labour had come back to power in 1964 as the unashamed and unequivocal trade union party. The party leader was no longer protected from conference rebellions by the block vote. But there was still much talk of the 'industrial wing of the movement', and within twenty-four hours of victory Frank Cousins of the TGWU was made a Cabinet minister. It was during the early years of Harold Wilson's first government that tea and sandwiches in 10 Downing Street became a regular finale to industrial disputes. But, although few people realised it at the time, the 1960s was also the decade in which trade union power began to wane.

Trade unions were the by-product of the Industrial Revolution. The men who combined to match the power of their employers, laboured in the factories and mines side by side with hundreds of other workers whose interests were identical to their own. For them the virtues of solidarity and the advantages of collective action were obvious. But the white heat of technology which Wilson hoped to harness had begun to change the pattern of employment. The old industries – in which men worked together – began to shrink. And what remained relied more and more on machines and less and less on men. With labour no longer in a seller's market, the unions lost the lever of the full employment years. Gradually the balance of membership was to switch from manufacturing to public services — and the striking hospital porter does not attract the sympathy that was once enjoyed by the shipyard welder in dispute with the ship-building millionaire. And, as the government staggered from crisis to crisis it — after the brief gratitude it felt for the wage freeze and 'period of severe restraint' — was growing impatient with the way the unions pursued their members' interests.

The Royal Commission on Trade Unions and Employers' Assoc-iations was set up on 2 February 1965. Its chairman was Lord Donovan, a Lord Justice of Appeal and former Labour MP. It was the first formal examination of trade union rights and responsibilities since the Liberal government, in 1903, had prepared to repeal the Taff Vale Judgement which had made unions collectively responsible for the damage done to trade by the actions (that is to say, strike actions) of their members. Believing that the government was on the unions' side, the TUC — led by George Woodcock, at once a visionary and an intellectual — gave the Commission a guarded welcome. They took it for granted that there would be no retreat from the sacred historic belief that 'the law must be kept out of industrial relations'.

It took the Donovan Commission almost three years to report. In the early summer of 1968 it confirmed what everybody knew, and drew attention to the problems which were so well-known that they had resulted in the Royal Commission being set up in the first place. There were, Donovan said, too many independent trade unions which overlapped and competed with each other, both for members and during wage negotiations. The result was pay settlements which leap-frogged each other and negotiation disputes that disrupted pro-duction in companies which were no more than observers of the argument about who represented whom. Paradoxically, Donovan was also critical of the great general unions' failure adequately to represent the interests of the many groups for which they negotiated. The feel-ing that national officers were remote and only sensitive to the needs of the biggest and most powerful trade groups was, Donovan believed, a major cause of unofficial disputes and stoppages. But it rejected calls for legal constraints and prohibitions. Its solution was the volun-tary extension of local bargaining. It did, however, recommend that unofficial strikes should not enjoy legal immunity from the consequences of their disruptive action.

In anticipation of the report's publication, Ray Gunter – the old right-wing trade union boss – had been replaced by Barbara Castle, complete with a new and grander title. The Secretary of State for Employment and Productivity (also First Secretary of State, after George Brown forfeited the title) was by temperament an activist. She was also an empire-builder. The new department assumed responsibility for the administration of the statutory wages policy and the supervision of the National Board for Prices and Income. Battling Barbara took absolute control of the policy which the Prime Minister believed would demonstrate that Labour had, after the hard financial pounding, regained its verve and vigour. It was also a policy – and Barbara Castle never doubted it – which could have an immense influence on the progress of the British economy. Not only were the network of restrictive practices stifling whole sections of the economy; competitive wage bargaining, unrelated either to the profitability of the company or the performance of its employees, was pushing up inflation. And, as Harold Wilson had learned during his hard first three years, the belief that the unions are out of control undermines international confidence, whether it is true or not. The stage was set for major reform.

Barbara Castle – reinforced by civil servants from other departments and industrial relations academies – began the long process of discussion and consultation. She was determined to do something, but not sure what to do. The TUC – by then led by the down-to-earth Vic Feather – was unyielding in its opposition to government interference. The allegation that the unions were above the law was, Feather insisted, a lie. Unions were subject to the common law, but were not governed by any specific statutes designed to regulate their conduct. Nor should they be. Some of the most sensible – and traditionally most moderate – Labour MPs shared that view. Barbara Castle did not agree.

The idiosyncratic way in which she worked is illustrated by the method she used to determine the name of the White Paper in which her policy was eventually set out. Numerous discussions in the

Department – and days of reference to dictionaries of quotations – ended with the collective view that the solemnity of the document demanded that it be known by a plain statement of its serious contents, not a fancy title. 'The Government's Plans for the Reform of Industrial Relations', or 'Proposals for Industrial Relations Reform' were the favoured alternatives. Barbara Castle seemed to agree. Then one morning she arrived in her office excited by her own (and her husband's) ingenuity. The Secretary of State had, in her time, been a passionate Bevanite, and like other politicians of that persuasion was blinded to the intellectual inadequacies of their hero's testament, 'In Place of Fear'. The White Paper would be named, part in tribute to Bevan and part because the title was so apt, 'In Place of Strife'.

The White Paper did more than involve the law in industrial relations. It involved the government. True to Barbara Castle's belief in the state's duty to influence the lives of its citizens, 'In Place of Strife' proposed that the Employment Secretary – that is to say Barbara Castle – should be given the power to instruct a trade union to hold a pre-strike ballot and observe a twenty-eight-day 'conciliation pause', known in the vernacular as 'a cooling-off period'. The Minister would also be entitled to impose a settlement when an unofficial strike followed an inter-union dispute. A Commission on Industrial Relations was to be given the semi-judicial right to levy fines from unions which broke or ignored the rules. Other recommendations ranged from the provision of funds to finance the training of trade union officials to the Donovan proposal that legal immunity should be withdrawn from unions whose members took unofficial strike action. It was the fear that the government would be given the power to control trade unions which caused so much resentment, fear and anger. Typically, the TUC mounted an oblique attack on the idea and directed their fire towards the Commission on Industrial Relations which, they claimed in equally characteristic nineteenth-century language, would 'introduce the taint of criminality into industrial relations'. There followed a period of political mayhem which combined with the government's mishandling of the sterling crisis to guarantee defeat at the General Election. Even now, no one can be sure if the political opponents of the Bill were motivated by principled disagreement, calculation that it was doomed to fail or the desire to ingratiate themselves with the trade unions.

The whole debate was confused by two conflicting certainties. Something had to be done to improve industrial relations. But 'In Place of Strife' did not provide an adequate solution. Only Barbara Castle, driven on by an energy which left no time to spare for judgement, could have believed that the Labour Party of 1968 would support such a scheme. And only a politician with ideological roots buried deep in the 1940s and '50s would have thought it right for the state to adjudicate on the behaviour of individual trade unions. The degree to which a woman of undoubted brilliance can be out of touch is illustrated by a proposal that she made to Len Murray, then deputy but soon to become General Secretary of the TUC. It was meant to be conciliatory:

> At one point she threw out the extraordinary idea that any money taken in fines from trade unions because of transgressions against the new law would not benefit the government financially and that an equivalent sum would be given to the TUC for educational purposes. We could hardly believe our ears.

The idea that the TUC should benefit from the penalties imposed on its constituent members having been rejected with disbelief, Barbara Castle appealed to the General Council's solidarity with the aims of her sort of socialism: 'Comrades, this government has got to control forces in this society. It has to control the City, industry and the trade unions.' Murray told her that she 'was not within a million miles of making it a saleable commodity'.

But Barbara Castle pressed on. In early March 1969, the House of Commons approved 'In Place of Strife' as the basis for legislation – but only because the Conservative Opposition abstained. Fifty-five Labour MPs voted against the motion and forty abstained with the Tories. So, almost a third of the Parliamentary Labour Party had registered its disapproval of what the White Paper recommended. But the Employment Secretary believed that she had acquired an ally whose firm support would guarantee eventual legislation. Roy

Jenkins – who had succeeded Jim Callaghan as Chancellor after devaluation – reluctantly accepted that an incomes policy, supervised and implemented by the government, was no longer practical politics. But foreign bankers had to be convinced that Labour had not gone soft on the trade unions. Implementing 'In Place of Strife' was, in the Chancellor's opinion, the way to provide the essential reassurance. The budget statement included the promise of industrial relations law.

The TUC responded with their own proposals – all of them wholly inadequate. 'Industrial Relations: A Programme for Action' amounted to little more than the rejection of legal constraints and the promise to use the General Council's best endeavours to reduce unofficial strikes and inter-union disputes. But the opponents of statutory powers had an alternative for which to argue. Jim Callaghan, at a meeting of Labour's National Executive, voted for the motion that criticised the government in which he was Home Secretary. Then, addressing a trade union conference, he criticised the basic principle on which 'In Place of Strife' was based and the practicality of using the law to influence trade union behaviour. On the same night, Douglas Houghton – ex-Cabinet minister, Chairman of the Parliamentary Labour Party and sometime General Secretary of the Inland Revenue Staffs Association, the union for which Callaghan once worked – addressed the assembled MPs. He told them what every Labour Party member, with the possible exception of Barbara Castle, already knew. Legislation, based on the White Paper, was unacceptable and could not be carried by the House of Commons unless the government appealed, over the heads of its own back-benchers, for the support of Tory MPs. On 18 June, the Prime Minister announced that the publication of an Industrial Relations Bill would have to be postponed until the next session – and that, when it was presented to Parliament, it would not be based on 'In Place of Strife'.

There are two crucial conclusions to be drawn from the whole tragic farce. Barbara Castle's error could, in part, be blamed on the advice which she received. The civil servants failed her not by attempting to frustrate her plans but telling her what she wanted to hear – even when they knew it to be bad advice. The Secretary of

State paid the penalty of a forceful personality. Roy Jenkins suffered the fate of impetuous honour. Warned not to endorse 'In Place of Strife', he ignored the appeals for caution. When the policy – the new foundations on which the Prime Minister had hoped to build Labour's recovery – foundered, the idea that the party might need a new leader was transformed from a by-product of Harold Wilson's paranoia into an increasingly popular opinion among back-benchers. The favourite to take his place was undoubtedly Roy Jenkins – remembered as a radical Home Secretary, regarded as a successful Chancellor and the only one of the Prime Minister's rivals to have cultivated a cadre of devoted supporters. But Jenkins's hopes of the succession depended on his disavowal of 'In Place of Strife'. He had first privately encouraged Barbara Castle to press ahead with her reforms and then publicly supported her in his budget statement. Honour obliged him to stay on board the sinking ship.

A couple of days after Roy Jenkins introduced his 1969 budget, a by-election in Mid-Ulster returned to Westminster the candidate of the Ulster Unity Party. Her name was Bernadette Devlin and she was twenty-one years old. She made her maiden speech on the day on which she took her seat and created an immediate sensation – partly because she spoke with such confidence and conviction and partly because the House of Commons, being a sentimental institution, was pre-disposed to be moved by one so young. It was a bitter, resentful speech and, because so many members crowded into the chamber to listen, Parliament heard – for the first time – the authentic, bitter and resentful voice of Catholic Ulster.

The resentment which Bernadette Devlin expressed had its roots in the partition of 1922, and Protestant domination of the Six Counties during the forty years which followed. For much of that time, the Catholics had suffered in silence – denied jobs in the shipyards, houses on the 'loyalist' estates and influence on the Unionist town councils. But in the mid-1960s the militant Protestants began to complain that the Unionist hegemony in the province was becoming soft on Catholicism. In June 1960, the then unknown Ian Paisley led a demonstration which protested against the 'Rome-ward trend' of the Presbyterian Church. After a year of 'loyalist' harassment, and at least one sectarian murder, Ulster Catholics formed the Northern Ireland Civil Rights Association (NICRA) – an essentially legalistic institution modelled on the London National Council for Civil Liberties.

In June 1969 a Catholic family was evicted from a house in the Dungannon Rural District and a single nineteen-year-old Protestant (and secretary to a Unionist politician) was given the tenancy. The protest march (organised by the NICRA) approached – 4,000 demonstrators strong – the police barriers outside Dungannon council offices. When the police asked the organisers to call halt, they immediately agreed to stop. The Civil Rights movement had become a peaceful force in Ulster politics.

Critics insisted that the NICRA was a front for the previously dormant Irish Republican Army, and there is little doubt that IRA members and sympathisers played an important part in its development. But it is impossible to argue against its aim – one man one vote in local elections, the redrawing of gerrymandered boundaries, laws against discrimination in local government, council houses to be allocated on a points scheme, a repeal of the Special Powers Act (which allowed arbitrary arrest) and the disbanding of the B-Specials, the police auxiliary which had always (rightly) been regarded as the instrument of Protestant supremacy. The Civil Rights Association announced that it would march in support of its demands on 5 October.

A week before the march took place, the Apprentice Boys of Derry told the Ulster Constabulary of their intention to hold their initiation parade on the same day and over some of the same route. It now seems that confrontation was not their intention. But that is not how it seemed at the time. The Ulster Constabulary banned both march and parade. The Civil Rights Association refused to capitulate. Sometime during the afternoon, the police lost either their patience or their nerve and attacked the demonstration. Seventy-five marchers – including Gerry Fitt, member of both the Stormont and Westminster parliaments – were injured. The brutal confrontation was shown on every United Kingdom news bulletin. British public opinion, shocked by the scenes of violence, began to exert its influence on both James Callaghan, the Home Secretary, and Terence

O'Neill, the Prime Minister of Northern Ireland. Six weeks after the march, the Stormont government proposed five reforms – local authority housing allocated on the basis of need; the appointment of an Ombudsman to investigate allegations of partiality by city and county councils; the replacement of the Londonderry City Council (elected on gerrymandered boundaries) by a Development Commission; universal local government franchise by 1971 and the abandonment of those parts of the Special Powers Act which conflicted with the European Convention on Human Rights. The Civil Rights movement had, for the moment, won.

The loyalist reaction was violent and immediate. When a third Civil Rights march was announced for 30 November in Armagh – the seat of both the Cardinal Archbishop and the Archbishop of All Ireland – the Paisleyite 'loyalists' took armed control of the town centre. The police, fearing that the unarmed marchers would be annihilated again, asked them to stop and disband. Again they agreed. After that, Civil Rights marches were organised all over the province and Orangemen who believed marching – admittedly of another sort – to be their speciality began to resent it. When the People's Democracy – an umbrella organisation embracing all the civil rights groups – arranged a seventy-five-mile march across Ulster from Belfast to Londonderry, the Paisleyites decided to ambush it. In their defence it must be said that militant elements in the People's Democracy chose to cross Protestant territory with the calculated intention of provoking the ancient enemy. The attack took place at Burntollet. Among the men who carried it out were a score of off-duty Special Constables. The B-Specials had seen action at last. Burntollet passed into Irish Catholic folklore.

It was only the beginning. In April, a march scheduled to start symbolically at Burntollet Bridge and end in Londonderry was banned by the Stormont government. Yet again the leaders acquiesced. But the rank and file, when they heard of what they regarded as capitulation, staged a demonstration of their own. It was broken up by the police who, in the course of their action, burst into the house of the Devenney family – who were wholly unconnected with the Civil Rights movement. Samuel Devenney, a consumptive with a weak heart, was beaten so badly that he had to be taken to hospital. A few weeks later he died. Although his death could not be directly attributed to the police action, the People's Democracy had a martyr and the IRA, which had been sleeping for ten years, began to stir. Old republicans, still dreaming of the Plough and the Stars, returned to the colours. They were joined by civil rights activists who despaired of the police ever protecting the Catholic community, men for whom any sort of violence was attractive and a criminal element which rightly believed that there was money to be made out of what amounted to a protection racket hiding behind the honourable cause of Irish unity. Throughout the early summer there were amateurish bombings and one, more carefully planned, explosion which cut off half of the province's water supply for a full day. Catholic Ulster was not yet ready for revolt. But the 'marching season' was only weeks away. On 2 August, an organisation called the Junior Orangemen paraded provocatively down Belfast's Shankill Road. When they reached the Unity Flats – the scene of the July troubles – the residents turned out in protest. News bulletins reported that the flats were under siege. Catholics from all over the city rallied to defend their co-religionists and Protestants rushed to rescue the marchers. The police, who claimed to be keeping the belligerents apart, were thought by the residents to be leading the 'loyalist' attack. The battle raged all night. General Sir Ian Freeland, General Officer Commanding Northern Ireland, was warned by the Inspector General of Ulster Constabulary that the army would soon be needed 'to assist the civil power' in restoring order.

In London, Harold Wilson and James Callaghan (who, as Home Secretary, was then responsible to Westminster for the affairs of Northern Ireland) were determined not to intervene until and unless the involvement of British troops was unavoidable. The GOC and James Chichester-Clark, the Northern Ireland Prime Minister who had replaced O'Neill, were told that there was no question of the army being deployed until Stormont's own resources had all been employed. In effect, Chichester-Clark was being told to mobilise the hated B-Specials. A request for helicopters and CS smoke was refused – until it was discovered that the Ulster Constabulary already had the far more lethal CN gas.

During the week that followed, Derry City Defence Association prepared for 12 August and the historic march of the Apprentice Boys around the walls of the old town. In 1969 a novel addition was made to the ritual. Pennies were thrown into the Catholic streets below – where one man in four was unemployed. Certainly the Bogside was provoked, but the Bogside was also spoiling for a fight, and the Bogside was prepared. A leaflet was distributed explaining how to withstand CS smoke. The Irish tricolour and the Plough and the Stars flew from house windows. People began to talk of 'Free Derry'. Fire-bombs – made from petrol stolen from the local GPO Sorting Office – were used, for the first time, in calculated assaults upon the police. Catholic Derry was in open revolt. Belfast followed suit next day. The violence was too great for the exhausted police to contain; in London, the Cabinet agreed that it could not maintain its refusal to deploy troops on the streets of Northern Ireland while the Stormont, rather than the Westminster, Parliament was responsible for security in the province and help was requested from the legitimate civil government. On 14 August the First Battalion of the Prince of Wales' Own crossed the Craigavon Bridge. The Ulster Unionist Party was still the titular government of the Six Counties. But from then on, the government of Northern Ireland moved in fact (though not for some time in constitutional theory) to Downing Street.

Four days after the riots spread to Belfast, Chichester–Clark flew to London. The result of his meeting with Wilson, Callaghan and Denis Healey (the Defence Secretary) was the Downing Street Declaration – the first of many Northern Ireland policy statements to glory in that sonorous name. The parties

> reaffirmed that in all legislation and executive decisions of government, every citizen of Northern Ireland is entitled to the same equality of treatment and freedom from discrimination as obtains in the rest of the United Kingdom, irrespective of political views or religion.

That was, by any standards, an implied rebuke to the Unionist hegemony at Stormont and by becoming parties to it, the Belfast

politicians were making an apology of sorts. But they were less concerned with self-respect than with what they know to be the
consequences of the statement. The sectarian B-Specials – generally
recruited from the Orange Lodges – would be disbanded. Their fears
and the Westminster government's determination to act were both
increased by the conclusion of the Cameron Commission, which had
been set up to enquire into the causes of violence in the province
during the early part of the year. Although it claimed that extremists
were behind the individual outbreaks of violence – a judgement
seized on by the ruling Unionist Party – its main conclusion was a
damning indictment of sectarian rule. The contention that civil rights
were constantly denied had 'a substantial foundation in fact and were,
in a very real sense, an immediate and operative cause of the disorders'. The future of the Ulster Constabulary was examined by Lord
Hunt – a cross-bench peer and leader of the Everest expedition which
had reached the summit just before Coronation Day. His report recommended that the B-Specials be disbanded and that the RUC give
up its weapons and, like the police forces of Great Britain, come
under the statutory control of a Police Authority and the operational
direction of a Chief Constable.

There were immediate riots, aimed – according to the rioters – at
'saving the police'. One Orangeman was so passionate in his defence
of the RUC that he shot Constable Victor Arbuckle dead. The insurrection was put down with what the army regarded as 'all necessary
force'. The army was later to claim that the rioters had fired more
than a thousands rounds of ammunition, some of them from machine
guns. Twenty-two soldiers and police officers were injured. The army
fired sixty-six rounds. Two rioters were killed. The number of
Protestant wounded is unknown. Ireland grew bloodier with every
incident.

Jim Callaghan – for whom the Northern Irish crisis provided the
opportunity for political regeneration – had, throughout the weeks of
rioting, attempted to reduce the risks of major slaughter by talking, in
his inimitably emollient way, to the leaders of both factions. He had
told a delegation from the Central Citizens' Defence Committee that
if they removed the barricades, which blocked the road into and out

of the Catholic ghettos, he would have British soldiers stationed at every street corner as a guarantee against a pogrom by the Protestant paramilitaries. The CCDC was infiltrated by the IRA – whose part in the riots had previously been reduced by disagreements over its tactics. One faction wanted to use the arms (supplied by supporters in the Republic) to mount assaults against the Imperial Parliament and as part of the historic struggle for a united and independent Ireland. The other believed it was its duty to act as a militia which defended the lives and property of the beleaguered Catholics. There was much legalistic wrangling about how the high command should be formed – nominations from all Ireland or simply from the Six Counties – and whether or not various constitutions amounted to the *de facto* recognition of partition. The real argument was between violence and protest. The IRA formally split in November 1969, with the formation of a Provisional Army Council. Inevitably, the statement on which the Army Council based its whole existence looked to the past rather than the future. Ireland's continuing tragedy has always been compounded by a morbid obsession with history:

> We declare our allegiance to the thirty-two county Irish Republic – proclaimed, Easter 1916, established by the first Dáil Eireann in 1919, overthrown by force of arms in 1922 and suppressed to this day.

The Provisional IRA had been created. Sinn Féin, the IRA's political wing, split into 'official' and provisional factions soon afterwards. The only question to be decided was how much support the terrorists would receive from the local population. The military handbooks always make it clear that guerrillas need hinterland into which to escape when their raids were over – forests, mountains or the dilapidated houses of the Bogside and the Shankill Road. In the months which followed the August 1969 riots, law-abiding Catholics were increasingly driven into support for the IRA.

It was a year for inquiries and reports. Sir Leslie (later Lord) Scarman – a High Court Judge – investigated the cause and the consequences of the summer riots in which 8 civilians were killed and 740 men and women injured. His conclusions left no doubt about the extent to which the minority community was alienated. Scarman and the two businessmen (one Catholic and one Protestant) who assisted him exonerated the RUC of the political charge which had been made against it. It was not a partisan force which colluded with the Protestant paramilitaries in their attack upon Catholicism. Indeed, the regular police had often 'struggled manfully to do their duty in a situation which they could not control' and their courage 'had been beyond praise'.

However, the professional conduct of the Royal Ulster Constabulary was the subject of serious criticism. The RUC was 'seriously at fault' on six occasions. There was a 'lack of firm direction' in the handling of the Derry disturbances on 12 August. The use of a Browning machine-gun in Belfast in August was a tragic mistake, and the firing of them into the Falls Road Divis Flats – killing nine-year-old Patrick Rooney – was 'wholly unjustifiable'. On the next day, the error had been compounded when the Belfast RUC failed to prevent Protestant mobs from burning Catholic houses. The incidents in West Belfast on 14 August had 'resulted in a complete loss of confidence by the Catholic community in the police force as it was then constituted'. The phrase 'then constituted' was a euphemism. The RUC was a sectarian force which did not welcome Catholic recruits and which very few Catholics were prepared to join. In consequence, it was always under suspicion. Even honest mistakes were attributed to tribal loyalties. The auxiliaries were included in the criticism.

The Ulster Special Constabulary had neither the training nor the equipment for riot duty. In consequence, when cornered, it had thought it necessary to act in a way which Scarman described as 'lack of discipline with firearms'. The B-Specials should not have been used for riot control in Dungannon and Armagh before they were disarmed.

Because of the suspicion, the IRA were able to portray themselves as the only certain protection that the Catholic community possessed. Genuine errors made by seriously overstretched forces were invariably interpreted as the result of the army's indifference and the police's Orange prejudice. Invariably the story ended with heroic republican gunmen defending innocent women and children from the brutal attacks of loyalist mobs. Sometimes the stories were true.

In the Short Strand – then an outpost of 600 Catholics which nestled, among 60,000 Protestants, on the east bank of the Lagan – the Gertrude Street Orange Lodge, marching home from a carnival, noticed the Irish tricolour flying in one of the houses behind St Matthew's Church. A few bricks and slates were thrown and half a dozen shots were fired. But, by early evening, the district was quiet. At ten o'clock, assuming that the Catholics had dropped their guard, the Protestants began to take revenge for the insult to the Union flag. Petrol bombs were thrown at the church, but did not set it alight. The nearby sexton's house was, however, burned down. The local Stormont MP ran to the Mountpottinger police station, half a mile away, and asked for help. He was told that the army was already overstretched and that there was no hope of rescue for hours. An infantry patrol and the driver of a police armoured car gave terrified residents the same answer. The forces of the law could no longer guarantee order.

It was at about that time that the families of Short Strand heard that the army had blocked the bridges across the Lagan. The GOC's intention was to prevent a Protestant invasion of West Belfast. But malice exploited panic to encourage the belief that the occupying forces were cutting off the escape route from St Matthew's parish. A Belfast Brigade Commander of the IRA, who lived in the area, a couple of his comrades-in-arms and two or three 'freelance' republican gunmen, took up positions in the churchyard and waited for the next assault. It came an hour before midnight. The battle went on until five o'clock next morning. When the army eventually arrived, two Protestants had been killed and two mortally wounded. Another legend had been added to Northern Ireland mythology. The Catholics believed that only the IRA would defend them from their ancient enemy.

For six months the army and the RUC did their best to prevent the outbursts of sporadic violence from turning into civil war. Some real attempts were made to remedy old grievances. A new Housing Executive guaranteed that at least some council houses were allocated according to need rather than religion. The B-Specials were disbanded and replaced by the Ulster Defence Regiment – a militia, under the control of Whitehall not Stormont. But there was no real peace in the Bogside and the Ardoyne or along the Shankill and Falls roads. A lasting settlement depended on a major constitutional initiative which Jim Callaghan looked forward to promoting after the Labour government was re-elected – a prospect which most commentators took for granted during the early months of 1970. The new Labour government would rewrite the Northern Ireland constitution.

According to the opinion polls, Britain was swinging back to Labour because the country believed that the ailing economy had been cured by unpleasant medicine. The government's opinion-poll lead increased after Roy Jenkins introduced an austere budget. And on 18 May 1970 – in a broadcast recorded in his Downing Street garden with the St James's Park birds singing audibly in the background – the Prime Minister announced that he had asked the Queen to dissolve Parliament. Even when, during the last week of the campaign, the polls recorded a Tory revival, only Edward Heath believed them. Robert Carvel, the *Evening Standard*'s distinguished commentator, told listeners to the BBC's *World at One* to disregard the opinion survey published in his own paper. Despite its predictions, the Tory party was, he insisted, doomed. He had just attended the press conference at which Ted Heath began the fight for the soul of his party in defeat. They won the election on 18 June with an overall majority of thirty. The natural party of government was in opposition again.

As soon as Labour recovered enough composure to consider the reasons for its unexpected defeat, it began to attribute its comprehensive rejection to factors outside its control. The most popular excuse was a freak entry in the balance of payments statistics – the cost of a couple of jumbo jets – which should have been spread over several months but added £18.5 million to the deficit which was published immediately before the election. The least convincing explanation was that England's defeat by Germany in the quarter-final of the 1970 World Cup had sparked off a mood of national despondency which had swung marginal voters away from the party of hope to the party of fear. Wilson's critics were divided. Some blamed the undoubtedly complacent campaign. Others – more plausibly – said that defeat had been inevitable since the forced devaluation of 1967 was compounded by the surrender to the unions in 1969. What nobody seemed to realise was that the nation was in a mood to punish Labour's errors because it was beginning to lose patience with the ideas on which Labour's two great victories – in 1945 and 1966 – were built.

After Mr Attlee's post-war landslide, the Tory party – under the intellectual direction of R. A. Butler – had seemed to adopt the idea of government which was crudely described as 'the welfare state'. But as soon as the Conservatives were re-elected on the promise of providing more and better social services than Labour could deliver, thinkers on the fringe of the party had begun to question the accepted wisdom that 'more and better' should be distributed by universal benefits. The 'One Nation' group – now either praised or excoriated as the embodiment of Conservative compassion and moderation, proclaimed in its inaugural pamphlet:

> Socialists believe that the state should provide an average. We believe that it should provide a minimum standard above which people should be free to rise as far as their industry, their thrift, their ability will take them.

Two years later, Enoch Powell – anticipating the fraudulent theories of 'Trickle Down' and 'Echelon Advance' – wrote in the *Political Quarterly*, 'The machinery of the welfare state was not helping the weak by its repression of the opportunities and independence of the strong.'

Hayek's *The Road to Serfdom* was gradually becoming a standard text for right-wing intellectuals who, increasingly denying the ideas of Harold Macmillan's 'Middle Way', insisted that individual liberty, no less than economic efficiency, depended on the state playing a minimal role in the lives of its citizens. In Chicago, Milton Friedman was developing the economic analysis which complemented Hayek's philosophy. Competition would make us free as well as prosperous. Choice was all. Taxes were theft. The market must be employed to determine the distribution of social services no less than consumer durables. Tories who shied away from the harness of the Friedman–Hayek extremes, interpreted their view as proof that means-testing was right and necessary. Friedman's idea of 'vouchers' – by which parents bought their children's education in a free market and paid a little more out of their own income when they wanted to buy a place in a 'better' school – was of immediate attraction to the competition zealots who conveniently discovered that non-selective education was resulting in the deterioration of academic standards. At the same time, devotees to the welfare state as a universal provider had begun to fear that Beveridge's assumptions about the way in which it would be financed were proving woefully mistaken.

All that Beveridge hoped to achieve was based on the principle that became the title of his work's 'popular edition', *Full Employment in a Free Society*. Full employment was, in itself, the best guarantee against poverty. And once unemployment began to rise, the balance of contributions to receipts was radically disturbed. Fewer men and women paid national insurance and tax, while more received benefit and supplementary payments. Beveridge also assumed that the cost of the NHS would remain more or less constant, and hoped that it would actually fall as pre-, peri- and post-natal care created a more healthy society. Beveridge actually predicted that the £175 million that was forecast as the cost of a Health Service for 1945 (the year he expected the national service to be inaugurated) would be higher than the cost twenty years on in 1965. At the end of the 1960s, the health budget was £1,400 million – when corrected for inflation, an increase of 74 per cent of the cost at the end of the 1940s.

State spending on education and housing – totals which Beveridge had not predicted – rose just as fast. In the decade which ended with Labour's 1970 defeat, the total budget for all of the public services rose by 137 per cent. Inevitably, taxation was increased to meet the bills. When the Attlee government lost office in 1951, a married man with a wife and two children to support paid tax when his wage rose to three-quarters of average earnings. When Harold Wilson's first government was defeated, a man with the same size family started paying tax when he earned half the average wage. And in the years of that government consumption patterns, like expectations, radically changed. Dick Crossman – Secretary of State for Health and Social Security – set out in a 1969 lecture how great the changes had been. During the previous four years, the number of families owning a washing machine had risen from 54 to 63 per cent of the total. Car ownership had increased from 38 to 49 per cent. Central heating was enjoyed by 23 rather than 13 per cent of families and 53 rather than 35 per cent of all households owned a refrigerator. The equations could hardly have been more daunting. The social services were costing more each year. In consequence, there was a virtually inevitable increase in public expenditure. It was financed by levying ever higher taxes from a population which – thanks to television and glossy magazines – wanted more disposable income to spend on what, more and more, were regarded as the necessities rather than the luxuries of life. And what was more, despite the extra bills and the extra taxes, the social services were failing to meet the needs of the people who depended upon them.

Twenty years before, at least politicians had believed that poverty had been banished for ever. But as the 1960s came to an end, poverty was back at the top of the political agenda. To be fair to the Labour government and its predecessors, the claims that the poor were still with us were based on new definitions. Poverty, said Richard Titmuss, may be a relative rather than an absolute condition – the result of a sudden drop in standards of living that follows unemployment, retirement or illness. Then – together with Brian Abel-Smith and Peter Townsend – he attempted to construct an absolute definition. He concluded, reasonably enough, that anyone who qualified for supplementary benefit – the government's own criterion of poverty – was, by definition, below the subsistence line. He went on to argue that anyone who lived on 140 per cent of the minimum supplementary level must live 'at the margins of poverty'. The acceptance of the Titmuss benchmarks led to an inescapable conclusion. Five per cent of the population lived below the poverty line, while another 10 per cent lived in poverty's shadow.

The discovery – or at least the assertion – that one in seven families remained what once was called 'the poor' could hardly have come at a worse moment for the future of socialism. For almost twenty years, the right of the Tory party had edged nervously towards the idea that the market economy – supported by the selective use of limited public expenditure – would improve the welfare services as well as reinvigorate the economy. The work done by Titmuss, Townsend and Abel-Smith seemed to confirm – albeit from the other end of the ideological spectrum – that the hopes of 1945 had not been realised. Nobody can be sure if the combination of sudden disillusion with the old theory and the offer of a new one encouraged a significant number of voters to swing from government to opposition. But it had a devastating effect on Labour morale. In the half-dozen years which followed, the consequences of the revelation were catastrophic. Nothing contributed more to the general disillusion with politics and the increasing popular conviction that the party system could solve none of the nation's problems. One by-product of the growing dissatisfaction was the development of single-subject interest groups.

The Child Poverty Action Group had been the first to be formed – the direct product of anger and astonishment that the Labour government did not adequately increase Family Allowance during its first year in office. In 1966, the year of *Cathy Come Home*, Shelter came into existence. Then came CHAR (campaigning for single person's accommodation), SHAC (arguing for affordable rented property), Gingerbread (promoting pre-school education, particularly for children of one-parent families), the Low Pay Unit and the Disablement Income Group. The one-issue pressure groups moved members in and out of the Labour Party, damaging it as activists moved out to pursue single causes and single-cause enthusiasts moved in to demand special help for the sector of the welfare system which they believed deserved special treatment. The inevitable result was both a confusion of aims and the promise to pay for more welfare than the country could afford.

The country – consciously or without much thought – hoped for a new solution. And, for the first few months of the Heath government, it seemed that the Conservatives were going to provide one. It was a myth for which Labour was more responsible than the Tories. During January 1970, the then Shadow Cabinet met in the Selsdon

Park Hotel in order to discuss economic policy. Ted Heath wanted the meeting to be private, for he was not sure that it would come to any conclusion which it was worth the press reporting. But the newspapers found out and reporters arrived uninvited and demanded to be told something original.

Nothing original had happened. The only remotely radical idea that the meeting even discussed was dismissed out of hand by Iain Macleod, the Shadow Chancellor. Maurice Macmillan, son of Harold, suggested a reform of the Health Service which would not have been acceptable to the author of *The Middle Way*. The NHS, Macmillan suggested, should meet only 80 per cent of treatment costs. The other 20 per cent should be met by personal insurance, in private schemes which the state regulated and underwrote. Macleod asked what weekly premiums a family man on average wages would have to pay. Macmillan told him fifteen shillings – seventy-five pence in decimalised money. The scheme, the Shadow Chancellor said, was impossibly expensive. The discussion instantly ended and the one truly radical idea was forgotten.

However, something had to be said to the eager journalists. Macleod suggested that law and order was always a popular theme. Heath said that trade union reform would certainly be on the new government's agenda – though he was not sure what form it would take. Somebody else thought that a mention of tougher immigration control would be welcome to party members. And a higher pension for the over-eighties was added to provide a dash of compassion. Macleod ad-libbed a statement and the grateful journalists wrote it down in their notebooks.

Next day, the newspapers announced that the Tory party had swung to the right and Harold Wilson chose – either out of conviction or hope of tactical advantage – to repeat their views. He, or his advisers, hit on the idea of Selsdon Man – a name which actually sounded like a description given to one of the prehistorical skulls which are unearthed from time to time. 'Selsdon Man,' said Wilson, 'is not just a lurch to the right. It is an atavistic desire to reverse the course of twenty-five years of social revolution. What they are planning is a wanton, calculated and deliberate return to greater inequality.' It was no such thing. Indeed it was nothing much at all. But Wilson elevated an inconclusive meeting into the birth of a new political philosophy. As the Parliament of 1970 progressed, the fiction that he had promised a radical revision of welfare policy – cutting both taxes and welfare spending – became an enormous liability to the new Prime Minister. For he was said to have lost his nerve, gone back on his word and broken promises which he had never made. But in 1970 it made him look as though he was offering something new. And something new was what the people wanted.

In one sense Heath was the personification of the new Tory party, but it was his social background and personal characteristics, not his ideology, which was novel. His three predecessors were Old Etonians with aristocrats for kinsmen. Before them the Conservatives had been led by three Old Harrovians. Heath was a grammar-school boy, the son of a jobbing carpenter and ladies' maid. His scholarship to Balliol was won from a county grammar school and he retained – despite Oxford, a 'good war' and almost ten years of continuous government service – the accents of the Kent coast. Perhaps more significant, he showed a wish to become an amateur gentleman. In the year when he became Leader of the Opposition, one commentator predicted that he would become the first Tory Prime Minister to have wall-to-wall carpet – thought at the time to be a symbol of suburbia. In 1963, Harold Wilson had proclaimed the advance of the technological revolution. In 1970, Ted Heath symbolised the triumph of the suburban middle classes. *Private Eye* immortalised both the man and his mannerisms with the *soubriquet* 'Grocer'. But the shopkeeper was no Poujadist.

So, fewer policies changed than the idea of 'Selsdon Man' had led the hopeful right wing of the Tory party to believe. In the two years before the election, a group of New Libertarian writers and academics had launched a campaign against non-selective secondary education with the publication of the 'Black Papers' – intellectually dubious polemics which claimed that 'more means worse' and demanded the return of a system designed to meet the needs of an elite. Ten days after her appointment as Secretary of State for Education and Science, Margaret Thatcher issued Circular 10/70. It told local education authorities that they were no longer under an obligation to develop the comprehensive system. The hope that the grammar schools would be re-created by the edict of the new government was reinforced by Margaret Thatcher's rough treatment of a delegation from the National Union of Teachers which, in the great tradition of lost causes, urged her to change her mind and, after withdrawing Circular 10/70, reaffirm her support for Tony Crosland's Circular 10/65. But it was all window-dressing. By 1970, local education authorities of every political persuasion wanted non-selective secondary education. When they asked to create comprehensive schools, the Secretary of State agreed. Margaret Thatcher endorsed more proposals for comprehensive reorganisation than were approved in the lifetime of a six-year Labour government by four education ministers.

Margaret Thatcher's behaviour – behaving in a way which was at diametric variance with her stated policy – was characteristic of the whole government. John Davies – Director-General of the CBI turned Secretary of State for Industry – told the Tory party conference, 'I will not bolster up or bail out companies.' Four months later, when Rolls-Royce faced both bankruptcy and extinction, the government chose to buy a controlling interest. Although great care was taken never to use the word, Rolls-Royce Ltd was nationalised. After a year of Conservative government, both main parties chose to exaggerate the differences.

The approach to the ever-deepening Ulster crisis was genuinely bipartisan. Certainly, after the spring of 1970 the level of violence escalated and the British Army reacted with increased ferocity, but that was probably a natural and unavoidable progress of events that no government could avoid. In July no fewer than 2,000 British troops raided the Lower Falls Road in Belfast and, although they found fifty revolvers, twenty-five rifles and five machine-guns, they were accused of malicious assault on the 3,000 houses which they searched. The army's reaction to stones was tear-gas, and the IRA's reaction to tear-gas was sniper fire. At the beginning of August 1970, 'baton rounds' – rubber bullets, in the vernacular – were used for the first time. By the end of the month they were a regular feature of the recurring street battles. It was February 1971 before the first British soldier was killed.

From then on, the level of violence escalated week by week until it climaxed in the summer's 'marching season'. August was bad enough. Internment without trial was re-introduced, a deaf-mute was shot dead because he appeared to ignore a soldier's order to halt, and a bomb destroyed the front gate of the Crumlin Road Prison – allegedly in protest against the brutal regime inside the gaol. But September was worse. The IRA, with what became its customary combination of brutality and incompetence, murdered two innocent civilians in a public-house bombing, and an eighteen-month-old baby was killed by a sniper while playing in the street. Despite – or perhaps because of – the arrest and detention of 980 Republican suspects, the violence became more indiscriminate. An explosion in the Post Office Tower closed it to tourists for ever, and a bomb in a Belfast department store injured forty-five women and children.

On 30 January 1972 in Londonderry, British paratroopers – believing themselves to be under attack – opened fire on a peaceful demonstration. Thirteen Catholics were shot dead and sixteen seriously wounded. 'Bloody Sunday' took its place in Irish history as another cause of resentment and bitterness to be remembered and avenged. In retaliation a Dublin mob burned down the British Embassy and on 22 February a bomb, planted in an Aldershot barracks, killed seven people. It was, the government decided, time for desperate action. On 30 March, the parliament at Stormont was dissolved. From then on, Northern Ireland was formally ruled from Whitehall and Westminster. In itself, 'direct rule' solved nothing, but it did concentrate the British mind on the real problem. There was nobody else to take the credit for success or, more likely, the blame for failure. Nobly, the Labour Party chose not to take advantage of the government's new vulnerability, so the 'bi-partisan' policy endured. Both parties co-operated in staunching the flow of blood rather than attempting to heal the wounds. And a succession of ambitious ministers believed – wrongly, as it turned out – that they could make their reputations in that most distressful country.

If the Labour Party is to be given credit for 'keeping Ireland out of politics', it must take much of the responsibility for engineering an initially bogus and then positively fraudulent political division over industrial relations legislation. The Tory party had been elected on the promise of 'trade union reform'. Nothing that happened during the Conservatives' first months in office undermined the government's belief in the urgent need for legislative action. The dockers went on strike in July – requiring, in the government's opinion, the first of the five States of Emergency which were declared during Heath's four years in Downing Street. The TUC reaffirmed its undying hostility to interference in the free collective bargaining process. The number of days lost by stoppages and disputes was higher than at any time since 1926, the year of the General Strike. It was only to be expected that, since the basic pattern of industrial relations remained much the same after the General Election as it was before the government changed, Edward Heath's solution in many ways mirrored and in some ways matched the proposals which Wilson had endorsed in Barbara Castle's 'In Place of Strife'. Sadly, it was equally predictable that Labour would do a sudden about-turn and become again the party of free collective bargaining. Labour's *volte-face* was an early example of the disease which was increasingly to afflict Labour in the 1970s and early '80s – the passion for unity defined as agreement with what the Tribunite left demanded. It was an attitude which simultaneously ignored both the national and the party interest, for it edged Labour out of the mainstream of politics and, simultaneously, drew attention to the disunity it attempted to hide.

On 3 December 1970 the government published the Industrial Relations Bill, which promised to establish 'a new legal framework' within which orderly industrial relations could be conducted with an emphasis on individual rather than collective rights. Collective agreements, once negotiated, were to become legally binding unless mutually abrogated by both parties. Unions which were guilty of 'unfair practices' (including sympathy strikes in support of disputes in which the strikers were not involved) forfeited their legal immunity and could, in consequence, be sued for damage done by their members. A National Industrial Relations Court was established, with which unions were required to register if they wished to enjoy the protection and benefits – the right to strike when strike action was properly determined – which the Bill proposed. Two of the key

proposals from 'In Place of Strife' were disinterred and brought back
to life – the duty to ballot members before a union took strike action
and a sixty-day 'cooling-off period' which could postpone industrial
action if and when its consequences might lead to a national emergency. Perhaps Labour's ideas were incorporated in the hope of
causing embarrassment, or improving the chances of an easy parliamentary run. Or it may be that the civil servants who had advised
Labour ministers, advised their Tory successors in the same way. It is
even possible that both parties came independently to the same
apparently sensible conclusion. What is undoubtedly true is that the
similarities with Labour policy did nothing to smooth the Bill's passage through the House of Commons. Barbara Castle promised to
fight the Bill 'tooth and nail, line by line'. It would be difficult to
argue that her approach to industrial relations reform was wholly
consistent, but at least she did not deviate from her intention to
wage guerrilla warfare. It was a long Bill of 150 clauses, so there were
immense opportunities for obstruction. The debate went on for so
long that the government's business managers introduced a 'timetable
motion' which limited debate. Labour retaliated by voting even
when the 'guillotine' prevented discussion. The demonstration
reached its climax during the session in which the Opposition called
sixty-three successive divisions. The House of Commons voted,
without interruption, for eleven and a half hours. The Bill was only
passed into law when the government saved time by scrapping forty-
two amendments. So Labour declared a great victory and Barbara
Castle went some way towards re-establishing her reputation as
'Battling Barbara', the heroine of the left.

Seven years later, Labour was to pay a terrible price for becoming
again 'the trade union party'. In 1978, the unions turned on Jim
Callaghan's government. As strike after strike paralysed the public
services, the general public blamed the Prime Minister for the behaviour of the militants who were determined to destroy him without
much sign of gratitude for the battle fought on their behalf against
'Tory laws'.

The resistance to the Bill outside Parliament was even more fero-
cious than the House of Commons battle. A TUC-sponsored Day of

Protest was intended to be – though did not quite become – a twenty-four-hour general strike. There were giant protest marches, lightning stoppages in the engineering industry and mass rallies – at one of which a wholly shameless Harold Wilson defended 'free collective bargaining'. But paradoxically, it was legal resistance to restraint that virtually emasculated the Act after it came into force in August 1971. One by one – and in some cases with considerable reluctance – the unions refused to register as the Act required. In consequence they were excluded from the benefits that the Act provided, including tax concessions and some legal immunities, without absolving themselves from the obligations and penalties. But they made the Act – and its author – appear ridiculous.

However, the Act had some initial success. The National Industrial Relations Court ruled that Liverpool dockers had acted 'unfairly' by preventing container lorries from entering their port. The Transport and General Workers' Union was fined £5,000. When it refused to pay, indeed refused to recognise the Court's authority, the fine was increased to £50,000 and accompanied by a threat to sequestrate the union's entire assets – estimated at £22 million. The Union had no choice but to pay the fine. The dockers, having challenged the law head-on, lost. The railwaymen, behaving with more subtlety, won. When their leaders were told that a 'cooling-off period' must precede a proposed strike, they accepted the ruling and resumed the strike as soon as the cooling-off period was over. Told to ballot their members, they agreed and won a five-to-one majority for the withdrawal of labour. Then the dockers struck back.

First the TGWU appealed against the Industrial Court's ruling that it was responsible for the actions of its members. Lord Denning, in fine disregard for what the Act laid down, quashed the fine. Sir John Donaldson, the Chairman of the Industrial Court, then solemnly warned the London dockers that if their union was not responsible for their 'unfair conduct', they must take personal responsibility. Three dockers who persisted in 'blacking' a Hackney cold store were threatened with immediate arrest. Every docker in the country went on strike. Calamity was averted by a spectacular climb-down. The Official Solicitor (with Donaldson's agreement) asked the Court of

Appeal to cancel the warrants on the grounds that they had been issued on insufficient evidence.

A month later five dockers – including two of the original Hackney pickets – blocked the container depot again. They ignored the injunction to allow free passage, were arrested and committed to Pentonville Prison. The dock strike was augmented by stoppages in other industries – including a print union walk-out which prevented the publication of national newspapers for almost a week. The TUC threatened a general strike in support of the 'Pentonville Five' – activists whom most of the General Council detested. The government was rescued by the Judicial Committee of the House of Lords which overturned Denning's Appeal Court ruling. The men were not (at least legally) responsible for their actions. The law clearly laid the responsibility – even for the effect of unofficial disputes – on the parent union. The Industrial Relations Court met within minutes of the ruling and ordered the men's release.

The degeneration into farce was – like the government's lack of resolution – only one of the reasons for the Industrial Relations Act's failure. The national mood was against criminalising what was regarded, often with exasperation, as normal trade union conduct. The national attitude towards trade unions was changing. But it had not changed fast enough to provide general support for court rulings, arrests and imprisonment. In the view of most British voters, prison was the appropriate penalty for burglary, rape and assault, not for standing in the road outside a container depot and shouting at lorry-drivers. Ten years later, Margaret Thatcher succeeded where Harold Wilson and Edward Heath failed because her Industrial Relations Act did not make martyrs and because, after the 1978–79 'Winter of Discontent', the public perception of trade unions and trade unionists had radically altered. They were no longer heroic industrial workers struggling, in hard and often dangerous jobs, to earn a living wage to keep their families; they had become instead public-sector parasites who lived off other people's taxes. Wilson and Heath were ahead of their time. Margaret Thatcher caught the tide of new resentment which, unfortunately for Edward Heath, had not become a flood of hostility by the time at which he, foolishly, decided to square up to the miners.

In the summer of 1971, the National Union of Mineworkers submitted pay claims that ranged from £5 a week increases for coal-face workers to £9 for the badly-paid underground labourers who did not actually cut coal. The Coal Board was sympathetic to the claim, but the government was struggling to rescue its bizarre pay policy – each settlement a little lower than the last – and told the NCB to stand firm on its counter-offer, which averaged less than £2 a man. A couple of weeks before Christmas – normally a bad time of year for union militancy – 56 per cent of the union voted in favour of strike action. The strike began on 9 January. Not a single miner reported for work.

The government certainly underestimated both the strength and the determination of the NUM. But even if the Cabinet had realised how hard the miners would fight, surrender (at least at that stage) would have been impossible. For Heath was battling for acceptance of a new Industrial Relations Bill, by which he thought that the conduct of trade unions could be regulated. The NUM had balloted its members – an essential feature of the Heath proposals. But if the government had capitulated to a wage demand which far exceeded the national guidelines, an unmistakable message would have been sent to the TUC and to the country: 'The government has no stomach for a fight.' Unemployment had risen to over a million for the first time – with the brief exception of the 1947 fuel crisis – since the war. Ministers felt guilty as well as vulnerable. For there remained in the Tory party a strain of 'Middle Way Conservatives' who shared Harold Macmillan's belief that full employment should be the central objective of economic policy. They were convinced that unsustainable wage increases made the achievement of their aim impossible. They added intellectual, and moral, justification to the 'get-tough policy'. Nobody realised that the miners could get tougher still.

The 'flying picket' was not a novel development. Yorkshire miners had tried to pick off pits, one by one, during their unofficial dispute in 1966. Then miners from all over the country had concentrated on a single pit until the management, and the few 'blacklegs' who remained at work, were intimidated by sheer weight of numbers. But what had been no more than a battle six years before was escalated in

1972 into full-scale war. Arthur Scargill, in charge of armies of militants which were sometimes ten thousand strong, had no doubt what they were fighting for:

> We took the view that we were in a class war . . . We had to declare war on them and the only way to declare war was to attack the vulnerable points . . . the power stations, the coke depots, the coal depots, the points of supply . . . We wished to paralyse the nation's economy.

Most of the striking miners – and certainly their President, Joe Gormley – hoped for no more than a big wage increase. They achieved their object because the flying pickets managed to paralyse the economy without alienating public opinion.

The flying pickets' greatest victory was at Saltley coke depot where, before the strike began, there was said to be 100,000 tons of coke ready for use in the Midland Power Station. At the start of the dispute seven hundred lorries went in and out each day. At its height, only forty-three ran the jeering pickets' gauntlet. There was very little violence, but the Chief Constable of the West Midlands Police – acting under the established rules of policing rather than according to government instruction – thought that the numbers alone (ten thousand pushing and chanting trade unionists) were a threat to life and safety. So he closed the depot. On its second day, 'The Battle of Saltley' was won by twenty-four miners who stood outside the locked gates as a token force which reminded the police of the previous day's big battalions. The Home Secretary tried to stiffen the police's resistance and, believing that he had succeeded, told the Cabinet that the depot would be opened even as he spoke. Before he had finished, a message was passed into the meeting. The depot was closed again. In the Chief Constable's opinion, it could only have been kept open if the police had employed tactics which were both out of keeping with a civilian force and highly offensive to public opinion that, by a substantial majority, supported the miners' cause.

The miners' victory at Saltley had a crucial effect on the confidence of a government which knew that, at the beginning of the dispute, it had failed to take the threat to the economy as seriously as the prospects of industrial disruption warranted. The appointment of a Court of Enquiry was, in itself, a surrender. Naming Lord Wilberforce – distinguished lawyer and Vice-Warden of All Souls – as its chairman made the surrender unconditional. Only a year before, his arbitration of the power workers' pay claim had ended with an award which was so extravagant that the government had publicly criticised its generosity. By inviting him to adjudicate in the dispute between the NUM and NCB, ministers were announcing that the miners would be paid whatever was necessary to persuade them to end the strike.

Knowing that they had won, the miners refused the government's offer of a £4 a week interim payment in return for an immediate resumption of work. As it turned out, it was hardly necessary. Wilberforce finished his work in three days. It proposed increases of between £4.50 and £6 – all backdated by three and a half months. The union asked for an extra pound without expecting to get it, and (for good measure) added a 'shopping list' of minor claims that ranged from longer holidays to full pay for eighteen-year-olds. The extra pound was refused, but the shopping list was conceded. When the strike ended, Ted Heath made a Prime Ministerial broadcast insisting that the government had not been humiliated – which proved that it had.

The humiliation was so grave that the wounds it caused had not healed when, in early 1974, the miners challenged the government again. Heath knew that his reputation would not survive a second defeat, but he was equally certain that, even with ministers to stiffen its spine, the National Coal Board – the Cabinet's surrogate in the conflict – would concede the NUM's demands. So the Prime Minister decided to wage total war. Power stations were required to implement nationwide power cuts, and factories were forced to work a three-day week. Heath hoped that the inconvenience which the emergency measures caused – take-home pay cut by two-fifths and darkened houses from early evening to the small hours of the morning – would unite the country in their opposition to the strike. But the miners remained more popular than the government. Then the

Prime Minister played what he believed to be his trump card. An election was called to answer the question, 'Who Governs Britain?'. The voters decided that, whoever had governed Britain during the first four years of the decade, they did not wish for the Conservative party to govern it any longer.

After the election on 28 February 1974 Labour, with 301 members, had the largest number of seats. But the Tories won only four fewer. For a desperate few days Heath attempted to form a coalition with the Liberals. But on Monday 4 March 1974, Harold Wilson was summoned to the Palace and asked to form a government. He accepted the Queen's commission but chose not to move back into Downing Street.

So Ted Heath left office – as it turned out, for ever – with only one major success to his credit. But it was an achievement of such abiding importance that, in itself, it guaranteed him a place in the pantheon of Prime Ministers who have changed British history. Heath took the United Kingdom into the Common Market, which became the European Economic Community which, in turn, became the European Union and will, one day, become the United States of Europe.

It is fashionable, at least among Heath's critics, to argue that he succeeded where Harold Macmillan and Harold Wilson failed purely because he had the luck to negotiate at the right time. In one particular, he was undoubtedly fortunate. The great obstacle to British entry into Europe – General Charles de Gaulle – resigned the French Presidency on 28 April 1969 and died eighteen months later. Georges Pompidou, his successor, was less irrational in his doubts about Britain's capacity to become a European, as distinct from an Atlantic, power. Heath, whose belief in Britain in Europe had never wavered, acted as a personal guarantee of Anglo-Saxon good faith. And because he believed in the Common Market, he took the trouble to understand how it worked. In previous negotiations Britain had tried to mobilise the sympathetic five against the antagonistic one. Heath realised that attempts to isolate France only made the French President more determined to include his opponents. So Heath made the approach directly – setting up a personal line of communication between Downing Street and the Elysée by appointing Christopher Soames – ex-Cabinet minister, Francophile and (most importantly) Winston Churchill's son-in-law – as Ambassador to Paris. In retrospect, it is tempting to argue that sooner or later – Heath or no Heath – the European Community would have wanted and accepted Britain. But that is not how it seemed at the time. Public opinion, soured by two vetoes, had turned violently against membership. Had Britain not joined in 1973, entry into Europe would certainly have been postponed for a decade. Another ten years of uncertain identity would have severely compounded the political and economic errors of the post-war years.

The consequence of those errors was dramatically illustrated by President Pompidou, who chose to complete the implementation of the Common Agricultural Policy before he considered the possibility of extending the Community. Because of French enthusiasm for CAP it is often assumed that it was designed purely in France's interest. In fact the tightly managed market – output limited to keep prices artificially high, surplus bought by a central fund and subsidies to selective activities – favoured all the extensive farming industries of Europe, German no less than French. But Britain, with intensive and efficient farming and high levels of agricultural imports, was always destined to do badly out of the system. Unfortunately, Britain was not a member when the Common Agricultural Policy was decided. The result provided a classic example of missing the bus and then running after it, despite the fact that it was travelling in the wrong direction.

When informal talks began in June 1970, Heath took it for granted that British entry into Europe was not a party issue. The subject had hardly been mentioned during the previous month's election campaign, and the Foreign Office assured Alec Douglas-Home – reincarnated as Foreign Secretary – that the government's negotiating brief was identical to that which Labour would have used in the new attempt at membership it had planned for immediately after its anticipated victory. When the formal negotiations began, there was even agreement about the most important, as well as the most emotive issues: the newspapers were filled with demands to preserve the

Commonwealth connection by safeguarding the interests of New Zealand sheep and dairy farmers, while civil servants worried most about the size of the British contribution to the Community budget and the future of sterling as an international reserve currency. There was also much concern about the speed at which Britain would be expected to adopt the common external tariff. Once the negotiations got seriously under way a tariff compromise was quickly agreed. Britain wanted a three-year transition for industry and six for agriculture. The Community offered five for both. Assuming the offer to be a sign of enthusiasm for enlargement, the British negotiators accepted without argument.

The negotiations formally opened on 29 October 1970, and did not make progress at the speed for which the British had hoped; they were still going on in the spring of the following year. The French – notoriously over-sensitive about such matters – had been offended by what they regarded as the British petty obsession with the size of its net budgetary contribution. A true believer in European union would, they insisted, rise above such mundane considerations. In retaliation, President Pompidou demanded an immediate end to sterling's role as a reserve currency.

While the negotiations rumbled on, British public opinion – never enthusiastic about the Common Market – grew increasingly sceptical about the advantages of membership. A proud people had been deeply offended by the double rejection of the 1960s. The fear of a third veto encouraged the view that Britain should rebuff France before France rebuffed Britain yet again. The polls showed that opposition to British membership had risen to 70 per cent. Then, in one of these inexplicable sea-changes which often alter the direction of protracted negotiations, there was a sudden breakthrough. Caribbean sugar was to be allowed into the Common Market without the burden of the full external tariff. Britain's budget contribution was to begin at 8.6 per cent and rise to 19 per cent over five years – an equitable compromise between the 3 per cent that the British had offered and the French counter-proposal of 21 per cent, made after the suggestion that the smaller figure was an example of the famous English sense of humour. It was even agreed that Britain's sterling holdings should be run down gradually – even though Heath knew that Britain would do well to lose the liability of acting as banker to the Commonwealth. The time had come to confirm the agreement at an Anglo-French summit. It was held in Paris on 20–21 May 1971.

Even though a handful of details were still to be resolved, Edward Heath's report to the House of Commons described the result of the summit in unequivocally triumphant language. And – impelled by either adrenaline or concern that Parliament and people might still deny his place in history – he answered one critical question which was to haunt him, and other enthusiasts for European union, for the next twenty years: 'Joining that Community does not entail a loss of national identity or an erosion of essential national sovereignty.' Even allowing for the qualifying adjective 'essential', that answer was disingenuous. It enabled Eurosceptics to claim that Britain had been taken into the Community under false pretences. And it prevented the honest examination of sovereignty that the situation required – its nature, its purpose, its meaning and the way in which it is both protected and extended in the age of the global economy.

A White Paper was published within days:

> Either we choose to enter the Community and join in building a strong Europe on the foundations which the Six have laid, or we choose to stand aside from this great enterprise and seek to maximise our interests from the narrow – and narrowing – base we have known in recent years.

Undoubtedly, Heath had hoped that the House of Commons – with the exception of a handful of dissidents on both extremes – would sanctify his achievement with an all but unanimous vote. But the Opposition was in a mood to oppose. Harold Wilson almost certainly supported membership and knew that, given the chance, he would have followed the same path to Brussels as the one which Edward Heath had trod. But, as always, his great concern was preserving the unity of the Labour Party. A special one-day party conference had concluded without a vote on British entry, but the mood had been clearly antagonistic. When Parliament debated the White Paper in

July 1971, Heath thought it prudent to ask for no more than agreement to 'take note' of its contents.

In September the TUC recorded its official opposition. And Harold Wilson began to fear that he would be outflanked by Jim Callaghan, who had begun to make speeches about Shakespeare and food prices. Tony Benn renewed his call for a referendum – a proposal which had not been discussed by the Shadow Cabinet three months earlier because no one was prepared to second it. But, by the autumn of 1971, Callaghan believed that 'Tony has launched a rubber dinghy into which we all may have to climb one day'. As opposition to Common Market membership (in all its bizarre forms) grew within the Labour Party, Harold Wilson hit on a formula which he believed would satisfy the anti's without irrevocably alienating the pro's. He would oppose entry – but not in principle, only on 'Tory terms'. The party followed his lead – the annual conference by a vote of five to one and the Parliamentary Labour Party by two to one.

The formal vote on membership came in the House of Commons on 28 October 1971. Both parties considered allowing their members a free vote, and both party leaders initially insisted that a decision on Britain's future world role could hardly be treated like a Private Members' Bill on Sunday licensing. Then, on cooler reflection, both Heath and Wilson realised the tactical advantage of not whipping their supporters into Division Lobbies. Party pressure prevented Harold Wilson from following the wiser course, but Heath relaxed party discipline with the conscious intention of attracting Labour support for his Common Market motion. Even if the battle lines had been drawn along rigid party lines, there would have been a major Labour rebellion. The size of the revolt was probably increased by the comforting knowledge that the pro-marketeers were not responding to the government whip. Sixty-nine Labour MPs voted in favour of accepting the negotiated terms and, in consequence, the resolution was carried by a majority of 112. Britain, it seemed, was at last secure within the Community.

In the months that followed, Labour maintained its opposition to membership on 'Tory terms'. As a result, Roy Jenkins resigned the deputy leadership of the party and although he returned to the

Shadow Cabinet before the election and, after it was won, again became Home Secretary, the wounds never healed. His resignation was one of the milestones along the road to the realignment of British politics. When, almost ten years later, the Social Democratic Party was formed, three of the Labour dissidents who were its founding fathers were men who had left the Opposition front-bench rather than continually vote against the Bill that took Great Britain into the European Community. The fourth was Shirley Williams, the most emotional European of all.

Even at the moment of his resignation, Jenkins had suspected that Wilson was less antagonistic to the European Community than determined to produce a formula on British membership that kept the Labour Party sufficiently united to make a serious challenge at the next election. Tony Benn, writing in his diary on the last day of the House of Commons debate, recorded the view that, 'Wilson hedged so clearly that it was clear that if a Labour government was elected when he was Prime Minister, it would simply accept the Common Market.' Denis Healey took a similar view, but believed that holding the party together without counterfeiting out-and-out opposition to Community membership was a great achievement. But whatever the motives of its leader, the Labour Party's inconsistent antagonism had an important constitutional importance. The British people remained basically antagonistic to the Community. Sadly, the Labour Party reflected the confused insularity of the island race.

JOINING THE CLUB

Trade Unions and a Trading Union

———•———

It is the practice of the Conservative party to prepare for a General Election by promoting a credit-financed and consumer-led boom that the country cannot afford. And it is the habit of the Labour Party to come to power at a time when the economy is about to collapse under the consequent weight of inflation and over-spending. In 1974, by challenging the country to decide 'who governs Britain', when the Parliament still had more than a year to run, Edward Heath destroyed all possibility of a brief (but carefully manufactured) increase in disposable income boosting the Tory government's prospects. The Barber Boom – called after the Chancellor of the Exchequer – was the product not of electoral cynicism, but economic incompetence.

In the first couple of years after his unexpected victory in 1970, Edward Heath had maintained the stringent fiscal and monetary policy which had been Roy Jenkins's recipe for recovery (if not electoral success) during the dying days of the Labour government. Then he and Anthony Barber lost their nerve and, desperate for a quick stimulus to growth, crashed the economic gears from reverse into forward overdrive. For a year the expansionist policies were mitigated by the introduction of a formal incomes policy and the decision to float the pound on the world currency markets. The end of fixed exchange rates liberated the government from the obligation to spend vast amounts of the reserves in order to keep the pound at a predetermined and arbitrary level which bore no relationship to the strength of the economy. It also produced an immediate effective devaluation of 7 per cent and months of further depreciation, which the Chancellor had the sense to shrug off as the unavoidable price of adjusting to reality. Roy Jenkins – who clearly wished that he could have got away with something similar – called Barber 'a dainty devaluer'.

Unfortunately, the benefits that might have flowed from that great leap of a floating exchange rate were more than counter-balanced by an economic catastrophe which was wholly outside the government's control. Claiming that it was retaliating against Western support for Israel during the Yom Kippur War of October 1973, the Organisation of Petroleum-Exporting Countries (OPEC) increased oil prices by 400 per cent. That was just the start of a continual escalation which made the American State Department at least speculate about the propriety of invading the 'economic aggressor'.

The oil-price increase was more than the product of Arab resentment. Massive increases in demand had created a sellers' market, and OPEC transformed itself from a pressure group into a cartel in order to exploit the strength of its combined position. For Britain – at the time almost entirely dependant on imported oil – the result could only be 'stagflation': the disease which Edward Heath had hoped to drive out of the national system for ever. As prices rose, production slumped. In 1970 the retail inflation rate was barely 5 per cent. By 1975 it was over 10 per cent. As always, the Labour Party inherited an economy in chaos.

Ironically, at the time when oil imports were incapacitating the British economy, the government knew, or at least hoped, that within the lifetime of the new Parliament, Britain would become a net oil exporter. Harold Wilson made jokes about his hope of joining OPEC. On 19 October 1970 – almost four years before his return to Downing Street – British Petroleum made its first significant discovery in the British sector of the North Sea oil-fields. And – as if to remind the miners that coal would not always be king – another major BP find was announced on the day after the NUM decided to ask its members to support the strike which brought the

Heath government down. But oil (which first trickled down the pipeline in June 1975) did not make a significant contribution to the British economy until three years after the 1974 General Election. And, even in 1977, it accounted for only 1.5 per cent of gross domestic product and contributed nothing to government revenue.

Forced to deal with the economy as it was, rather than how the forecasters believed it would become, Labour chose to deal with the crisis not by a fiscal monetary adjustment that cut back demand but by what it believed was a unique package of remedies – statutory price control, voluntary wage restraint and the subsidy of essential food stuffs. At first, public expenditure – particularly the social programme – was protected and preserved. For the second time in ten years, Labour had to think of tomorrow rather than next year. The government's resolution was undermined by the certainty that, since it did not enjoy an overall House of Commons majority, a second election could not be long delayed. And, while it wrestled with inflation that rose to 26 per cent during its first year in office, the government had to decide how to fulfil its promise to renegotiate the 'Tory terms' on which the country had become part of the European Community.

During the campaign, Jim Callaghan had been the Common Market's fiercest critic – pioneering what became the most hackneyed visual assault on the consequences of membership: two baskets of shopping in which the prices of European and British groceries were compared. Joseph Chamberlain had done much the same with the 'imperial' and 'foreign' loaf, eighty years earlier. Callaghan's appointment as Foreign Secretary, although not unexpected, convinced many Community politicians that, whatever the cynics had hoped, Harold Wilson's anti-Market speeches really did represent his anti-Market attitude. Jim Callaghan's conduct reinforced that view. He had barely settled in the Foreign Office when he called to London Her Britannic Majesty's Ambassadors to the other Common Market capitals. Copies of Labour's election manifesto were distributed among them, and the beginning of the meeting was delayed to give Their Excellencies time to read the section on 'renegotiation'. The most arrogant of the assembled mandarins asked if he had to pay for his copy, and was told that all he need to do was implement the policy which it set out.

That meeting was accepted by the Foreign Office (and by the European governments to whom it was very properly reported by the ambassadors) as no more than *joie de vivre* brought on by unexpected office. But the Foreign Secretary's address to his first Council of Ministers was taken more seriously. After waiting several hours while ministers discussed an Italian application for emergency tariffs to protect its livestock industry, Jim Callaghan addressed his colleagues in terms which he must have known, and intended, to be unfriendly. They were particularly offended by his constant references to the manifesto which – although taken by the ambassadors as a joke – were regarded by the foreign ministers of the Community as proof that the new British government put its party commitments above the aim of achieving European unity. They were, of course, right.

The renegotiation dragged on for a momentous year, in which the French President died and the German Chancellor was forced out of office. Both changes, ironically, helped the new British cause. Valéry Giscard d'Estaing, Pompidou's successor, inaugurated meetings of the European Council – gatherings of heads of state and government. By their nature, they were able to respond to Britain's demands more quickly than was possible for meetings of foreign ministers. And Harold Wilson – under constant pressure from anti-Europeans in his Cabinet – often needed a quick answer more than he needed an agreement. Willy Brandt was no less an Anglophile than Helmut Schmidt, his successor. But Schmidt's more aggressive support of Britain's renegotiated membership was – after he was convinced of Harold Wilson's personal good intentions – crucial in providing a deal which could be recommended to party and people. In fact, the Labour government was a good deal less antagonistic to the European Community than it had appeared during the first 1974 General Election. Callaghan, converted by his experience of the informal 'political co-operation machinery', decided that Europe had a great potential as a force for good in the world – even if it could not guarantee the prosperity which Macmillan and Heath had promised. No one tried to pretend that the original objectives of the renegotiation had been achieved; indeed, Harold Wilson was remarkably frank in his report to the House of Commons:

> The government cannot claim to have achieved in full all the objectives that were set out in the manifesto on which Labour fought. It is thus for the judgement now of government, shortly of Parliament and in due course of the British people, whether or not we should stay in the European Community on the basis of the terms which have now been negotiated.

With six unrelenting anti-Europeans in the Cabinet, it would have been difficult for the Prime Minister to pretend anything different. For the check-list that the Foreign Secretary drew up showed more failure than success. Certainly Britain had succeeded in establishing a regional policy which would provide special help for Wales, Scotland, Southern Italy and Ireland. Germany – contemplating the monetarist deflation that later infected all of Europe – agreed to stimulate investment in a way which would increase trade (and therefore jobs) across the Community. Caribbean sugar would continue to enter into Europe under the tariff barrier. The initiative to provide more aid to the developing world (which ended with the Lomé Convention of February 1975) was only obliquely related to the renegotiation. But, sensibly, the British government claimed credit. It was the sort of thing that was popular with the Labour Party.

But the Common Agricultural Policy – keeping farm prices high by destroying the so-called 'surpluses' which might have been used to feed starving Africa – remained unchanged while Wilson and Callaghan consoled themselves with the thought that one day it would collapse under the weight of its own contradictions. Attempts at immediate reform were frustrated by the discovery that Common Market wheat cost less in world markets than the alternative. New Zealand dairy farmers – every one regarded by imperial sentimentalists as a veteran of the Anzac battalions in both world wars – were left to find alternative markets in other continents. And Britain's budget contribution – a proportion of Common Market expenditure which bore little relationship either to the United Kingdom receipts or to its share of total Community income – was left for revision at some future (and indeterminate) date when a new, and fairer, formula was to be applied to all the member countries. It was the failure to negotiate a new budget deal which particularly excited Labour's anti-Europeans. The pattern of Nato finances was to be reproduced. Britain would, once again, subsidise its richer partners. The system of budget payments was to be revised so as to reflect more closely gross domestic product, but the more equitable formula would not be introduced at once.

By one of the ironies which make history interesting, the agreement eventually to relate budget contribution to national income worked immensely to Britain's advantage – but not in time for Wilson, Callaghan and Labour to take the credit. When, in 1983 – almost a full decade after the 'renegotiation' – Margaret Thatcher argued for a reduction in Britain's contribution, she was able to remind her 'colleagues' that the principle of relating payments to gross domestic product had been agreed almost ten years earlier after Labour's 'renegotiation'. But the irony of the renegotiation did not end with what seemed to be the chimera of a reduced payment. Wilson and Callaghan came home from the Dublin Summit at which the dubious deal was struck absolutely convinced that they had solved one problem for at least the rest of this century. There would be no more argument about political union. Although Giscard d'Estaing had insisted on talking about economic and monetary union, Helmut Schmidt had assured them that it was a fantasy only kept alive by politicians who did not know how international finance worked. There would be no pressure, in the immediate future, to sacrifice essential British fiscal sovereignty or to create a single currency within a monetary union.

The formula by which Harold Wilson kept his party in one piece was to hold the referendum about which he had been so contemptuous only months before. A special party conference in April 1975 judged, by a huge majority, that the new terms were not sufficiently different from the old to justify continued membership. But the slogan above the platform was 'the party recommends, and the nation decides' – allowing scope for individual members to campaign for the result which Labour officially deplored. That was the concession made by the anti-Market majority, conscious that a refusal to allow ministers to campaign for continued membership would certainly destroy the government and possibly the party. In reciprocation, the Prime Minister agreed that, although the Cabinet had agreed to recommend acceptance of the terms, the dissentient minority of ministers should be allowed to campaign for a 'No' vote – though not to speak in favour of withdrawal in the Commons debate.

The outcome of the June 1975 referendum – support for continuing membership by 17,378,581 votes to 8,470,073 – was not the result of a conscientious electorate carefully considering the momentous alternatives. Undoubtedly the massive two-to-one majority was a divisive endorsement of something. And the decision, which was thought to put British membership beyond all possible future doubt, was essential to the nation's welfare and prospects. But the suggestion that twenty-five million voters had studied the terms and carefully considered the alternatives was palpable nonsense. What really happened illustrates the futility – indeed the constitutional impropriety – of referendums.

The governing party decided to 'consult the people' not in a sudden excess of democratic zeal but as part of a stratagem to preserve its unity and protect its reputation. The ballots were cast not on the strength of the case for European unity – and even less in response to the precise and limited question on the ballot paper. It was a choice of men, not measures, which decided the result. Harold Wilson, Margaret Thatcher, Ted Heath, James Callaghan and David Steel campaigned to remain in the European Economic Community on the renegotiation terms. Barbara Castle, Enoch Powell, Jack Jones and Tony Benn advocated withdrawal. It was an unequal contest. If there were to be another referendum in the future on an equally complicated issue, the outcome would be decided in exactly the same way. Party convenience would be dressed up to look like respect for the general will and the result would be decided according to the public esteem of the protagonists, not the merits of the issue. And it would certainly not end the argument about the question on the ballot paper. The notion that 'once the people have spoken' politicians respect their decision is sentimental nonsense, as the history of the story to European unity has demonstrated, time after time, since 1975.

The 'Great Common Market Referendum' was, perhaps, necessary for the survival of the Wilson government and essential to the unity of the Labour Party. But it was a distraction from what should have been the government's principal concern – the revival of an economy which was close to collapse. Import prices (partly, but not wholly, as a result of the oil price hike) were rising by 60 per cent per annum. The terms of trade had deteriorated by 20 per cent during the previous year. Consumer prices were escalating by an annual rate of 19.2 per cent – compared with an average of 14.2 per cent in other OECD countries. The cumulative result, inherited by Labour, was a balance of payments deficit of £3,000 million and a public-sector deficit which, by gloomy coincidence, was the same size. The forecast was deterioration rather than improvement.

One of the wounds, still bleeding when Harold Wilson returned to office, was self-inflicted. In his eagerness to negotiate an incomes policy – a mere palliative at best in an economy which needed radical surgery – Ted Heath had agreed to 'Threshold Agreements', wage deals which could be re-opened when the Retail Price Index rose by more than 7 per cent during the period of their operation. Between May 1973 and January 1974, eleven major settlements were renegotiated under the threshold clause. As a result, wage costs rose by 16 per cent during the second half of the year. In 1975, hourly wages rose by 33 per cent and retail prices by 20 per cent.

The new Labour government attempted to remedy the crisis by policies which, had they been adopted throughout the industrialised West, might well have avoided the world slump which followed. Indeed, the International Monetary Fund initially believed that the proper response to the OPEC price increase was expansion, not contraction. Only Labour Britain – and that for reasons of political necessity rather than economic judgement – accepted the IMF's advice. It was an agreement for which a substantial price had to be paid two years later. It was impossible for one country to sustain growth in a shrinking global economy. By trying to achieve the impossible, between 1974 and 1976 Britain spent five pounds for every four that it earned. When the crisis came in the summer of 1976, the IMF was insistent that Great Britain abandon every vestige of the policy which the Fund had recommended in the spring of 1974.

Labour came back into office promising that a 'Social Contract' with the unions would end wage inflation. Initially, the new policy undoubtedly achieved that limited, though crucial, aim. Talks between the government, the TUC and the CBI ended, in July 1975, with a voluntary agreement that annual incomes of more than £8,500 should be frozen and that wages and salaries below that figure should not increase by more than £6 a week. The matching clause in the 'contract' was the protection, indeed the improvement, of the 'social wage' – the benefits provided for the community by the NHS, retirement pensions and low-cost housing. There were also to be measures to provide employment – the Temporary Employment Subsidy, a Job Release Scheme and a Youth Opportunities Scheme. In all, they kept about 400,000 men and women off the unemployment register. Food subsidies – one of them reducing the price of butter, and therefore helping the rich more than the poor – were introduced as an added incentive to moderation. In terms of wage costs the deal was immensely beneficial to the national interest. The increase in hourly wage cost fell from 33 per cent to an annual rate of 18 per cent in the first half of 1976 and 10 per cent during the second half of the year. The government's contribution to the bargain was an unsustainable increase in public expenditure – an 18 per cent rise in the first two years of its reckless existence.

It would be wrong to suggest that the price was reluctantly paid. Labour came back into office in 1974 genuinely committed to 'a fundamental and irrevocable shift in the balance of power and wealth in favour of working people and their families'. It was sustained in that belief by the new public-sector trade unions, whose members increasingly dominated the local parties. So during 1974, the government's first year, the Houghton Report awarded teachers a wage increase which averaged 30 per cent. The Halsbury Report did almost as well for the nurses. At the same time, private industry was being persuaded to operate a strict, though voluntary, wages policy – even though its employers were paying higher taxes to finance public sector expansion. In the 1974 Parliamentary Report, Denis Healey – Chancellor of the Exchequer – confirmed the new government's enthusiasm for 'tough measures to redistribute income'. He was as good as his word. The liabilities of the rich tax-payers substantially increased. A single man earning £20,000 per annum paid £595 more after Healey's first budget. The initial increase in benefits, housing and food subsidies, pensions and other benefits cost something approaching £2 billion. The rich were subsidising the poor.

Education policy remained unchanged for two full years. But there was immense activity in the Departments of the Environment and Health and Social Security: council rents were frozen; the annual local authority rent subsidy rose to £1.35 billion; owner-occupiers received £1.1 billion in mortgage tax relief. Increases in the Health Service budget were institutionalised by a formula which convincingly demonstrated that an additional 2 per cent was needed each year simply to maintain existing provision – 0.5 per cent to finance medical advance, 0.5 per cent to meet the needs of the increasingly over-stretched 'Cinderella' sectors of mental health and domiciliary care, and 0.5 to 1 per cent to meet the needs of an ever-ageing population.

The largest spending increases – immediate and proposed – financed changes in the social security system. The take-up of supplementary benefit – intended by Beveridge as a last resort for the few recipients who did not qualify for other help – had already begun the massive increase which was to heap an ever-growing burden on the Treasury for the next twenty years. Retirement pensions were to be upgraded each year in line with either the increase in earnings or inflation, whichever was the greater. Had the scheme survived, the pensioners' share of national income would have increased with the years as the annual upgrading either equalled the rise in earnings or exceeded them at times of high inflation. When the package of proposals was presented to Parliament, the Tory Opposition's only complaint was that the upgrading was calculated only once a year rather than every six months. By 1976 – thanks to rising unemployment, the growing number of single parents, the reduction in the value of student grants and the more liberal definition of disability – 10 per cent of the population received assistance supplements of one sort or another. And, for the first time since the modern welfare state was created, the existence of 'scroungers' – real and imaginary – became a political issue.

Paradoxically, the change in the nation's social composition which made 'scrounging' an issue was reflected in the most radical revision of the social security system – the introduction of SERPS, the State Earnings Related Pension Scheme. For more than a decade, both major parties had supported the idea of 'national superannuation' – a pension, related to retirement income, which offered working men and women the security in old age which was, before the 1970s, available only to the middle classes. The idea had first been examined in Macmillan's time; the first Wilson administration had made a real effort to devise a workable scheme, and Heath's government made the third attempt to resolve the apparently intractable problems. Each attempt foundered on the same questions: should the scheme be 'funded' by future recipients investing in their own retirement, or should the working population pay, year by year, the current pension bill? Should the graduated payment be separated from or grafted on to the basic pension? Should the new scheme accommodate, or even encourage, the private pension schemes which – by the time that Harold Wilson was re-elected in 1974 – boasted eleven million members?

The 1975 proposals claimed to include the best features of all the previous failures – earnings-related contributions, a flat-rate basic pension which rose with earnings as well as SERPS, and the positive endorsement of private schemes. There was a three-year gap between the Bill becoming law and the scheme being implemented. But nobody doubted that – because it could not be completely funded – it would impose an immense burden on public expenditure. It was accepted nevertheless, because the mood of the time allowed nothing else. The country as a whole had begun to demand the privileges of the prosperous. A nation which felt middle-class expected the advantages of that status.

For thirty years the idea of industrial action in the NHS had been regarded as morally indefensible – not least by the underpaid nurses and auxiliary workers. Then, in 1972, Keith Joseph – the Conservative Secretary of State – cut the pay link between local government hourly-paid grades and Health Service ancillaries. Seven hundred and fifty hospitals were disrupted by strike action. The taboo was broken. And the most senior members of the Health Service – it would be wrong to call them employees – followed the example of the lowest paid. Consultants – who had argued about the right to increase their incomes by private practice since the Health Service had been created – believed that their job was getting more difficult and that the differentials, which reflected the gulf which divided them from 'juniors' and general practitioners, were being eroded. When Barbara Castle arrived at the Department of Health and Social Security, they were already squaring up for a fight.

True to character, Barbara Castle – far from compromising with the doctors as her hero, Aneurin Bevan, had done when the Health Service was created – increased the antagonism by announcing her intention of fulfilling Labour's manifesto commitment to 'phase out pay beds'. She had little other choice. The National Union of Public Employees – the Health Service ancillaries' unions – began to 'black' private patients. The two issues – private patients and consultants' salaries – were intimately connected. The most senior members of the medical profession (who had, only months before, expressed their horror at porters, cooks and cleaners disrupting the NHS) cancelled outpatients' clinics and allowed waiting lists to grow as they 'worked to contract' – or 'to rule' as manual trade unionists would have said.

The previously unknown militant virus spread the industrial disruption disease throughout the NHS. Junior doctors, on the point of taking action, were placated by the promise that their working week would be cut from eighty to forty hours. Family doctors, who had negotiated a new pay deal to come into force during the spring of 1975, threatened to resign from the service *en masse* if the increased salaries were not paid on time.

In the end, a compromise of sorts was agreed – although a third of the consultants voted to reject the package. The terms of the agreement confirmed that the battle – although theoretically fought over pay beds – was really a contest to decide who controlled the Health Service: the politicians on behalf of the people who elected them or the consultants themselves. There were only 4,500 pay beds in the whole NHS, and the 120,000 patients who occupied them each year were less than 1 per cent of the total number of men, women and children who received hospital treatment. So the Labour activists who fought against private medicine in Health Service hospitals were far more concerned with principle than with practice. Barbara Castle, who shared their conviction, persuaded her colleagues to insist on a deal that went some way to satisfying their demands by repeating the warning that the alternative was chaos in the wards. In the end, after all the anxiety and suffering, the consultants agreed to one thousand pay beds, almost a quarter of the total, being removed from public wards within six months of the necessary legislation becoming law. For their objection was based less on principle than the right to be paid for private work. The rest were to be phased out according to a timetable agreed by an independent committee. The consultants were not fighting for the ideal of a health service in which private and public patients were treated side by side. If that had been the object of their action, they would have lost the fight. But the biggest loser was undoubtedly the NHS itself. The country began to fear that it could no longer guarantee swift and adequate treatment. The notion of the saintly doctor, sacrificing health and leisure in the service of the sick, was destroyed for ever. So was the belief that 'the British health service is the best in the world'. Doubts about the quality and reliability of public medical care were to grow throughout the 1970s, but the worm began to eat deep into the bud during the first two profligate years of the 1974 government. The nation was not in the mood for Barbara Castle's bravura defence of a free, comprehensive health service which did not provide special favours for paying customers. It wanted a health service which was not disrupted by political and industrial controversy. The pay beds dispute increased dissatisfaction with what, in the mid-1970s, the service was able to provide.

That dissatisfaction had grown with the years. It was exemplified, for diametrically different reasons, by the increased popularity of private medicine. In 1950, three years after the Health Service's creation, 100,000 citizens invested in private medical insurance. By 1955, the total had increased to half a million. In 1974, the year in which Harold Wilson was re-elected for his third term, the figure had risen to two million. That was still only 4 per cent of the population, and private spending on hospital care was only 2 per cent of the Health Service budget – a small figure in itself but a 400 per cent increase in twenty years. During the first two years of the new Labour government, the number of potential patients actually fell by 80,000 – unfortunately less because of renewed faith in the Health Service than because a reduction in insurance premiums was one of the ways in which the middle classes economised. Between 1977 and 1980, there was an increase of more than 60 per cent, taking the total to three and a half million. By 1980, 6.4 per cent of the population was covered by private medical insurance. For thirty years, as increasingly sophisticated treatment increased the cost of medical care, patients who once would have simply paid for private treatment took the precaution of insuring against accident and injury. And, during the years of Harold Wilson's second administration, two short-term factors accelerated the long-term trend. Because of pay policy, perks were often increased instead of wages. Health insurance was the most popular. Paradoxically, the party which had founded the Health Service seemed to be tearing it apart.

Barbara Castle left the government within forty-eight hours of Jim Callaghan succeeding Harold Wilson as Prime Minister. Wilson's departure was entirely unexpected by press and general public and was, in consequence, regarded as a mystery which might have sinister origins. In fact, Wilson had at least considered the possibility of early retirement ever since the defeat of 1970 had been redeemed by re-election in 1974. He had certainly told friends that he planned to stand down on his sixtieth birthday – though none of them believed him. But he did. On 16 March 1976 – possibly influenced by deteriorating health – Harold Wilson told the Cabinet that his remarkable political career was over. Only Jim Callaghan had been given early warning. He was Wilson's natural, as well as chosen, successor and it was assured that he would govern in the Wilson style, choosing compromise rather than confrontation and initiating very little that was new or daring. Circumstances were to prevent him leading the quiet life which it was thought he would prefer. But 'steady as she goes', his rallying cry as Chancellor, a few weeks before a sterling crisis, was not always his natural instinct. In the year during which he became Prime Minister he began the great education debate which rumbled on with increasing intensity for the rest of the century. Arguments about the core curriculum and the publication of examination results – in effect criticisms of, and demands for improvement in, state education – began with Jim Callaghan's Ruskin Speech.

Jim Callaghan was a highly educated though generally self-taught man. During a Foreign Office discussion on continued membership of the European Community, he startled the diplomatic advisers by criticising their convoluted position papers with a quotation from Roy Campbell's judgement on a fellow South African novelist:

> I'm with you there, of course;
> They use the snaffle and the bit all right,
> But where's the bloody horse?

Like so many autodidacts, Callaghan was obsessed by the organisation of formal education. When, in 1967, devaluation had forced him to resign from the Treasury, his first choice of alternative ministry was the Department of Education and Science. When he became Prime Minister, with licence to roam through all the departments of state, he immediately turned his attention to the performance of British schools and school teachers. His concerns were set out as questions to the Secretary of State in the classic third person of a Civil Service memorandum:

> Is he satisfied with the basic teaching of the three Rs; is the curriculum sufficiently relevant and penetrating for older children in

comprehensive schools, especially the teaching of science and math-
ematics; how does the examination system shape up as a test of
achievement; and what is available for the further education of six-
teen- to nineteen-year-olds?

The questions might well have been answered in the civil servants'
slow and discreet fashion had the Prime Minister not been asked to lay
the foundation stone for a new hall of residence at Ruskin College,
Oxford. Jim Callaghan – who did not need much encouraging – was
encouraged by his policy staff to use the occasion to make his concerns public.

Until the Ruskin Speech, the education establishment had assumed
that teachers – like lawyers and doctors – would be left to regulate
their own professional lives, if not their own entry requirements and
discipline. Teachers would continue to decide what they would teach
and how they would teach it. The *Times Educational Supplement* came
very near to telling the Prime Minister to mind his own business, and
the purists regarded his definition of education's purpose – 'to equip
children to the best of their ability for a lively and constructive place
in society and also to fit them to do a job of work' – as heresy. But it
was too late. For good or ill, concern about the relevance of the syl-
labus, the competence of teachers and the success of modern teaching
methods was on the political agenda.

Although the achievements of the system were questioned, the
way in which it was organised was accepted, with varying degrees of
enthusiasm, by all three major parties. That was because the people
supported non-selective secondary education. The suburbs had at last
grasped the arithmetic. When under a selective system, one in five
children 'passed' for 'superior' grammar schools, four out of five were
allocated to 'inferior' secondary modern schools. Unable to pay for
high-quality private education and unwilling to risk their sons and
daughters joining the disadvantaged 80 per cent, they developed an
enthusiasm for comprehensive education. Although there were token
Tory demands for the reintroduction of selective education, the 1977
Conservative conference was told that non-selective schools were
'here to stay', and the following year delegates were warned about the

catastrophic effects of 'another educational earthquake'. The arguments of the 'Black Papers' – 'all equal and all stupid' – which had sought to undermine the comprehensive idea in the 1960s, were largely forgotten. When the Labour government fell in the spring of 1979, 85 per cent of state pupils were in non-selective schools. Even 54 of the 154 direct-grant schools chose – when they were forced to decide between total independence and comprehensive reorganisation – to welcome children of all abilities. The argument about selection seemed to be over. But the debate about teaching methods and standards of performance had begun.

Labour's economic policy was undoubtedly prejudiced by a whole series of initiatives which, although not damaging in themselves, undoubtedly created the impression that the government, although serious about its recovery programme, was not serious enough to give it absolute and overwhelming priority. The education reforms – perceived by the prejudiced as an assault on 'excellence' – was only a small part of the process. Callaghan's defence of 'traditional teaching methods' reassured some of the government's domestic critics. But foreign doubters – the arbiters of 'international confidence' – were profoundly alienated by Labour's insistence on maintaining its social programme and the consequent increases in the health and welfare budgets. Those commitments could not have been broken without a conscious betrayal of both the election manifesto and the basic beliefs of the party. The government intensified the antagonism by its wilful pursuit of peripheral industrial policies which were, at best, irrelevant to its economic difficulties and, at worst, positively injurious because they appeared ignorant, doctrinaire and (worst of all) frivolous. Radical governments always need to balance the obligation to pursue their basic principles against the need to avoid unnecessarily offending the vested interests on which, in part, they depend. That requires the ruthless culling of intellectually unsustainable items in their published programme. Regrettably, the Labour governments of 1974 and 1976 flinched from the necessary killing.

It was, however (with much reluctance and even more apprehension), prepared to offend one more important pressure group – men. Child Benefit – which replaced both child tax allowance and family allowance with a single cash payment made to the mother – respected a different adjustment in social attitudes. That provided two measures of distribution – marginally from rich to poor and absolutely from men to women in what the jargon of the time called 'from wallet to purse'. The government, apprehensive about alienating working men by reducing their take-home pay, wanted to postpone the introduction of the full scheme and proposed to phase it in gradually. But, lacking a majority and uncertain of its own back-benchers' loyalty, it was forced by the Opposition to promise the complete implementation of its own legislation. Child Benefit was to be paid in full during 1979. The Cabinet – highly nervous at the time – probably overestimated male opposition to paying the extra taxes which were required to finance their wives' weekly cash payment. But the concern was understandable. The Labour Party feared that it was losing the support of the (predominantly male) trade unions.

The unions had grown convinced that pay restraint was not being matched by reductions in inflation, so policies were invented that provided the TUC with circuses to compensate for the loss of bread. The statutory limitation on retail price increases continued long after the government recognised its limitations because it did a little good, no great harm and provided something for the government to say to the unions about 'counter-inflation policy'. The nationalisation of the ship-building, steel, the ports and aerospace industries seemed, on the other hand, a conscious decision to operate on the fringes of economic reality. The National Enterprise Board – picking 'winners' and investing in them in return for the government receiving a share of the equity and exercising the influence which part-control provided – was a doomed attempt to usurp the function of both the market and the professional managers which operated within it. Planning Agreements – arrangements by which companies agreed to provide business information to their employees and discuss their long-term objectives with the trade unions – were regarded by the world outside the Labour Party first with fear and then with ridicule. An idea which was thought to confirm the government's wish to set up workers' communes became proof of ministerial ineptitude. Only one Planning Agreement was signed in four years, and that was with the Chrysler company – whose British operation was entirely dependent on government help.

The National Economic Development Council – meetings at which the leaders of industry and the trade unions discussed the economic prospects with the Cabinet – was accepted as part of the proper framework of democratic government. But it had been set up by Selwyn Lloyd in 1961, and therefore enjoyed the respectability that comes from antiquity as well as all-party support. The 'Little Nedys' – replicas of the NEDC, itself composed of representatives from individual industries – were regarded as particularly useful, not least because they provided opportunities for business and commerce to tell the government what it wanted rather than a chance for the government to tell business and commerce what it should do. But the innovations – which were thought to be socialist and were, in fact, chimeras of an alternative policy – were regarded by much of industry as a distraction.

The last Wilson government should have been more than satisfied with the distractions which it could not avoid. Chief was the need, if not to find a solution to the Northern Ireland problem, at least to work out a constitutional formula and a package of economic initiatives to drive a wedge between the gunmen and the civilian population which supported them out of sentiment and desperation.

Bloody Sunday, 30 January 1972, had been a turning-point in the turbulent history of the Six Counties. The reaction to the death of thirteen Catholic demonstrators had been predictably, perhaps even understandably, violent. The IRA vow 'to kill as many British soldiers as possible' had been followed by rioting in Belfast and a bombing in Aldershot. Four weeks later, 6 pedestrians were killed and 146 injured in a Belfast city blast. Edward Heath had disbanded the Stormont Parliament and imposed direct rule from Whitehall. The Ulster Unionist politicians accused the Prime Minister of capitulating to the IRA, and a hundred thousand Protestants marched in protest against the decision. The British Cabinet had no friends left in Northern Ireland.

For the next two years the violence ebbed and flowed. From time to time doomed attempts to find a solution were made – including a secret meeting between the Secretary of State for Northern Ireland and the IRA leadership. Unionist leaders stepped up their campaign, openly confronting the armed forces of the crown to which they claimed allegiance and calling crippling strikes in the public utilities which, traditionally, only employed 'loyalists'. In a referendum – a 'border poll', as it was known – the majority for the Six Counties staying in the Union was overwhelming. But Catholics boycotted the plebiscite. The government's reaction was proposals for a new constitution – devolved government which, because the legislature was elected by proportional representation, guaranteed 'power-sharing' between Republicans and Unionists. It took Willie Whitelaw – the Tories' Irish Secretary – more than a year to persuade both Protestants and Catholics to participate. But despite continued bombings – and the new horror of sectarian killings – direct rule was ended on 1 January 1974. Less than two months later, Harold Wilson was once again Prime Minister.

If the Labour Party believed that the warring Northern Ireland factions would give the new government a fair wind, it was badly mistaken. The death toll in Ireland since 1969 rose to a total of one thousand two months after the General Election, and four weeks later a car-bomb in Dublin killed twenty-three innocent civilians during the evening rush hour. The bombing campaign moved to the mainland. In June it was Westminster itself, in July Birmingham, Manchester and Heathrow airport and London again. Yet as the violence escalated and came ever closer to home it was clear that what was described as a 'bi-partisan' approach to the crisis amounted to neither of the parties having a long-term strategy. Perhaps a long-term strategy was impossible. For politicians of every sort provided persuasive arguments against anything that might be called a 'solution'. Ceding the Catholic counties to the Republic would satisfy no one. The Republic did not want to incorporate any of the Six Counties within its national boundaries, and it would be intolerable to 'give away' any of the million United Kingdom citizens who passionately wanted to remain the Queen's subjects. The only possible result of a pull-out would be civil war in Ulster and Protestant terrorism in Britain. Although there was growing agreement that 'a military solution cannot be imposed on Northern Ireland', changes in policy were usually the reaction to events rather than attempts to change the future.

In May 1974, the power-sharing executive collapsed and direct rule was re-imposed. In the following October – the day after the date which Harold Wilson had chosen for the General Election which would provide him with a working majority – IRA bombs exploded in Pall Mall and Marble Arch. Five days before the election, explosions in two Guildford public houses had killed five young people and injured sixty-five. The Guildford bombings, and the way in which the police pursued the suspects, were to haunt successive governments for almost twenty years. But worse was to come. On 21 November, two Birmingham city-centre public houses were demolished by IRA bombs. Many of the victims – 19 dead and 182 injured – were Irish. That night, an Irish piper who had been at the Birmingham airport to play a lament for the body of a dead terrorist was thrown through the glass door of the Birmingham Irish Club by Irishmen. Their anger was increased by the knowledge that the city would suspect everyone with an Irish accent.

Six men were arrested as they travelled by train to catch the Holyhead ferry. At their trial in July, the police conceded – they could hardly have done anything else – that the suspects had been badly beaten shortly after their arrest. Their wrongful conviction, quashed in 1990, was very largely the result of the police responding to mindless demands for immediate arrests and swift retribution. Perhaps the frustrated anger of the British people was understandable. The reaction of government and Parliament was less excusable. The Prevention of Terrorism (Temporary Provision) Bill passed through both Houses of Parliament in eighteen hours. It empowered the police to hold designated terrorist suspects for up to seven days without either charging them with an offence or allowing them to see a lawyer. Exclusion Orders – described by a troubled Attorney General as providing for 'internal exile' – enabled the arbitrary expulsion of Northern Ireland citizens from other parts of the United Kingdom. Few people believed that the Bill would do much either to prevent terrorism or to apprehend terrorists. It was a response to the anxieties of the British people – whose traditional lack of concern for civil liberties the government chose to endorse.

For the next four years, the government vacillated between conciliation and what at least the Catholic minority regarded as repression. The residual affection for the British Army – a remnant of the gratitude republicans still felt for their rescue in 1969 – was extinguished on Bloody Sunday. And there was little sympathy from either extremist wing for the government's doomed attempts to balance justice with security. Detainees who had been held without trial were released, but convicted terrorists lost the 'special status' which they believed made them 'political prisoners'. A Northern Ireland Convention was elected to discuss how 'power-sharing' could be implemented. Two-thirds of its members opposed power-sharing altogether and it was dissolved after ten months – not least because 'loyalist' workers in Belfast demonstrated their opposition to partnership with republicans by calling a strike which crippled the province. In the meantime the cycle of violence – in which assassination had been added to indiscriminate bombing – continued. The Labour Party's failure to please any of the Northern Ireland warring factions – perhaps a mark of its impartiality – was vividly illustrated by the voting record on 28 March 1979, when the Callaghan administration became the first government to lose a vote of confidence in over half a century. The Opposition won, and forced a General Election, by one vote. Two Ulster Unionists supported the government. The rest would have done so if the Prime Minister had been prepared to make policy changes which Jim Callaghan had rejected not on their merits (which had not been discussed) but on the principle that a government should not buy votes. And the SDLP – Labour's sister-party in Northern Ireland – cast its two votes for Margaret Thatcher and the end of the Labour government. Ireland, for Labour in 1979, was again the most distressful country.

It was, though, the politics of Scotland and Wales – Labour's heartland – which eventually brought the Callaghan government down. For the two years which followed 23 March 1977, the Labour government was sustained in office by what came to be called the Lib–Lab Pact. It was a loose arrangement which prevented the administration from doing many things which it had wished to do, but obliged it to do nothing with which it disagreed. Liberal support was usually augmented by an agreement thanks to the grudging endorsement of the Scottish and Welsh nationalists who – whatever they thought about Labour's programme in general – were enthusiastic for the devolution of power from Whitehall and Westminster to Edinburgh and Cardiff. And Labour's devolution bill was making its slow way through the House of Commons. Unfortunately, the people of Scotland and Wales were not.

The debates dragged on through long days and nights of the sustained opposition of the Conservative party and a group of Labour rebels and, by the time that it became law, it contained a new clause which was to change the course of history in a way which few of its supporters intended. The government had, as a concession to the opponents of devolution, announced that it would hold a 'consultative referendum' before the proposals were put into effect. The amendment proposed that unless 40 per cent of the total Scottish electorate voted in favour of a Scottish Assembly with devolved powers, the whole plan should be abandoned. The devolution poll in both countries (59 per cent in Wales and 64 per cent in Scotland) was, in Jim Callaghan's view, a reflection of the government's unpopularity, not opposition to devolution. But, whatever the reason, it made the 40 per cent target impossible to achieve. In Scotland there was only a bare majority (33 per cent to 31 per cent) in favour. Wales voted against the creation of Welsh parliament by 47 per cent to 12 per cent. Devolution was finished, and so was the government. But everybody knew that it was not constitutional reform which brought it down; the failure to deliver devolution was merely the occasion of the government's defeat. The cause was its failure to manage the economy in a way which provided painless growth – the illusion which successive governments had pursued since the war. The pursuit of that aim during the two years between re-election and resignation had been so wilfully irresponsible that, when the inevitable change in direction was made, it looked like – and eventually became – a repudiation of the ideas on which all socialist economic and welfare policies are based. The old ideas were abandoned in the autumn of

1976. But it was clear that Labour had begun to lose faith in its own prescription long before alien remedies were forced upon the government by its international creditors.

At his first party conference as leader – just before the IMF crisis broke – Jim Callaghan, having made a ritual assault on 'stop–go' economics and brief consumer booms financed by borrowing, attempted to inflict grievous bodily harm on John Maynard Keynes's General Theory of Employment:

> The cosy world which we were told would go on for ever – where full employment could be guaranteed at the stroke of a pen, cutting taxes and deficit spending – that world has gone for ever . . . We used to think that we could spend our way out of recession . . . I tell you in all candour, that opinion no longer exists.

He then went a stage further in his analysis. It was not that the global economy had made Keynes's one-nation demand management out of date. The General Theory had always been wrong. The thirty-year Keynesian experiment had failed.

> In so far as it ever did exist, it only worked on each occasion since the war by injecting a bigger dose of inflation into the economy, followed by a higher level of unemployment as the next step.

There followed an attack on British labour costs and the low level of productivity in many British industries. A side-swipe at the growth in public expenditure was rounded off with a frontal assault on 'what Denis Healey calls confetti money – the result of a willingness to pay ourselves more than we earn'.

The climax to the conference at which Jim Callaghan changed the government's economic philosophy was Denis Healey's return from London airport after deciding – as he was about to board his plane – that, rather than attend the meeting of the International Monetary Fund, he would begin the reorganisation of economic policy which led to an application to the IMF for a standing loan. The continuing deficit on the balance of payments was undermining illusive 'international confidence'. As a result, countries which held sterling began to exchange it for other currencies. British reserves – used to buy pounds in the hope of holding up the exchange rate – fell by £800 billion during the last nine months of 1975. Inevitably the floating pound's value continued to fall – not least because of unconfirmed rumours that the government was considering a formal devaluation. Export prices became more competitive but pressure on the reserves increased. Unfortunately, the rumour was unfounded. But the pound continued to lose value. It was worth $2 in January 1976 and $1.80 in June. By the time that the Labour party conference assembled in late September it had fallen to $1.64, and the Bank of England privately forecast that it would lose a cent a day until it bottomed out at $1.50 by the end of the year.

The summer's deterioration had continued despite genuine attempts to prevent it. In July, public expenditure was cut by more than £1 billion and Jim Callaghan – Prime Minister for barely three months hoped that, reinforced by a new wage agreement with the TUC (which limited increases to between £2.50 and £4), the reduction in spending would be enough to stem the tide of disappearing sterling. It was not. And Callaghan had almost certainly decided – weeks before Healey's spectacular return from Heathrow – that the government must do everything that was necessary to liquidate the anticipated £3 billion balance of payments deficit and stabilise sterling at an acceptable exchange rate. In a sense, only a holding operation was needed. For oil revenues would soon both increase government income and reverse the adverse movement in the terms of trade which had contributed to the deficit. But even that required a stand-by credit which would only be available if it were underwritten by the IMF.

The weeks which followed Healey's spectacular *volte-face* – both at London airport and in the Treasury – are now called the 'IMF crisis'. The description is a misnomer: it certainly seemed like a crisis at the time, but it is now clear enough that the government was always destined to accept whatever terms guaranteed the stand-by credit and, once that credit was in place, the economy was certain to make at least the convalescent's progress towards the complete recovery which

North Sea oil guaranteed. What is more, the central economic indicator – on which the IMF's demands for fiscal retrenchment were based – was wrong. The IMF believed that Britain's Public Sector Borrowing Requirement for the financial year 1976–77 would be almost £12 billion. Indeed, the Treasury had conceded as much. The IMF insisted that the PSBR be reduced to £9 billion. In fact the out-turn – before the effect of the crisis cuts was felt – was only £8.82 billion. It is reasonable to assume that, if the IMF had known the true figure, far from being gratified by the government's prudence, they would have demanded a reduction to £6 billion or less. For what they wanted was a demonstration that the government was willing to run the British economy their way. A sacrifice had to be made to prove the sincerity of Labour's conversion. Public expenditure – particularly the welfare budget – had to be cut.

It is fair to say – in the Treasury's defence – that the PSBR is a notoriously difficult figure to calculate. It amounts to no more than the comparison of two aggregates, total government income and total government expenditure. Many of the items which made up the two cumulative figures were either estimates or approximations. Indeed, it was traditionally assumed that the errors would be sufficiently numerous to cancel each other out. When expenditure was larger than income, the balance was the borrowing requirement, and when income was the larger of the two figures, everyone was surprised. Only once since the war – Roy Jenkins's 1970 budget – has it actually happened. Usually Chancellors expect a deficit, and normally it is bigger than they publicly admit.

That was certainly the case during the early years of the 1974 Labour government. Healey's first budget forecast a PSBR of £2.73 billion. It turned out to be £7.6 billion. The 1975 forecast was £9.06 billion and the out-turn £10.77 billion. So it was reasonable for the IMF to suppose that the following year's estimate of £11.2 billion would also be exceeded. Their scepticism was reinforced by the July estimates which – despite large cuts in major programmes – were revised to show substantial increases in expenditure. However, thanks to galloping inflation, the real rise in public expenditure over the first three years of the government's life was far less than the estimates suggested – £27.3 billion in cash terms, but only £7 billion in constant prices. Almost as important, cash limits – Healey's innovation – had done their work. As the Chancellor's left-wing critics predicted, they did not so much hold public expenditure to the forecast figure as reduce it below the planning estimate. Even as the Cabinet was agonising about reducing government spending it was being reduced to below the IMF target.

For the next three years, the Opposition taunted the government with the accusation that its monetary and fiscal stance had been dictated by the foreign creditors who guaranteed the loan. In fact the terms which the IMF 'imposed' were obligations which Callaghan and Healey were anxious to accept. The need to implement the bankers' instructions became the lever with which they moved the government into the path that they wanted it to take – a route which they would have followed, without IMF pressure, as soon as the Labour Party allowed.

The IMF would not endorse any rescue package which did not include the two changes in domestic economic policy which the international bankers regarded as essential – a tightening of credit and a reduction in public expenditure. Initially they asked for cuts of £4 billion in two years, followed by stricter control of the money supply and a reduction in the exchange rate. The Chancellor, believing cuts of that size to be unacceptable to the Cabinet, agreed to recommend that the PSBR be cut by £3 billion by a combination of higher taxes, lower expenditure and the sale of BP shares. Ironically it was, therefore, a Labour government which first began to auction 'the family silver' – though there was a clear determination to retain control of the company. The share sale was the least controversial of the Chancellor's proposals. The real fight was over the reduction in public services which the public expenditure cuts made unavoidable. After three weeks of Cabinet meetings, agreement of a sort was reached around a compromise cut of £2 billion and a further £500 million reduction in the PSBR, effected by the BP sales. Thus the IMF was convinced that the PSBR would fall to a figure between £8 and £8.7 billion – a higher figure than that for which they had originally asked and about the total which would have been achieved without the cuts. And the Labour Party began to wonder, for the first time, if the level of public services to which it had aspired was sustainable. More damaging to its traditional ideological commitment was the sudden sneaking suspicion that private affluence and public squalor was not so politically unattractive as socialists had once supposed. The new middle classes were more interested in tax levels and inflation rates (which affected disposable income) and interest rates (which influenced the size of their mortgage repayments) than they were in the extent and quantity of public services which they increasingly aspired not to use.

And it seemed that the drastic remedy was working – economically and, therefore, politically. Traditional Keynesians assumed that reductions in the government deficit – consequent upon the cuts in the PSBR – would actually increase unemployment levels. In fact unemployment rose faster in 1975 (when the PSBR was rising fast) than in 1976 when the PSBR and unemployment both rose far more slowly. For a couple of years, public expenditure in Britain – at 44 per cent of GDP – was lower than in Germany and the United States, where GDP expanded more slowly than in the United Kingdom. By March 1977, the Chancellor of the Exchequer introduced a generally expansionary budget which, although it further reduced public expenditure, also cut taxes. The exchange rate improved at such a speed that it had to be 'capped' to avoid an over-valued pound pricing British exports out of foreign markets. At the turn of the year, the pound was worth almost $2. Inflation still in double figures remained the one economic enemy to be defeated. And the retail price index could, the government felt confident, be held down with the help of the trade unions. Having abandoned its traditional approach to macro-economic management, the Labour government relied on its traditional partnership with the TUC to deal with the outstanding liability.

The Opposition under Margaret Thatcher, Conservative leader since she had replaced Heath in February 1975, had sloughed off all Heath's enthusiasm for the corporate economic management which embraced (and when necessary coerced) trade unions and employers. New

Conservatism believed that economic success came from deregulation and the liberation of the market. Inflation was best held down by tight control of the money supply and interest rates kept acceptably low by holding down public investment. In consequence it applauded the policies which it claimed had been imposed on the government by the IMF. But it opposed – and did its best to sabotage – the wage agreements which were negotiated with the TUC. It was particularly, and perhaps understandably, antagonistic to the way in which incomes policy was to be monitored. Fearful of imposing sanctions on unions which demanded higher wages, the Labour government legislated to punish companies which conceded the demands. So, in the battles over wage control, Thatcherites (convinced that 'abrasion' should replace 'consensus') combined with the traditional trade unionists who believed in 'free collective bargaining', uninhibited by government interference. The important change in the political scene was not the brief co-operation of opposites. It was the mutual acceptance (overt in the Conservative leadership, implied and barely conceded by Labour) that the time had come for the new form of economic management which, in its most extreme form, was called 'monetarism'.

But monetarism and planned earnings do not fit easily together. During the first two (extravagant) years of Denis Healey's Chancellorship, the trade unions (certainly the leadership and probably the led) were gradually convinced that they had a vested interest in moderating their wage claims. The domestic programme – improved health service, universal superannuation and a whole raft of employment protection measures – was presented as the government's half of a bargain which it could only fulfil if the economy was strong enough to pay the consequent bills. Trade unions (or trade unionists), the other party to the agreement, helped to create the essential economic growth by limiting pay increases to the figure which the government judged held back, rather than promoted, inflation. For a while 'the social contract' – a not wholly inappropriate name – worked remarkably well. But such arrangements, although formalised by declarations and signatures, are essentially dependent on mood and instinct rather than careful calculation of gains and losses. The mood began to change after the IMF agreement.

In July, four months before the Cabinet accepted the £2.5 billion reduction in the PSBR, the unions had agreed a new pay formula – despite the expenditure cuts which were announced in the same month. They were assured that restraint was justified because of its effect on prices. A small pay increase would actually buy more than a large one, for it would not be eroded by inflation. So the complicated formula – intended to allow the lowest paid the biggest pay rises – was endorsed by the TUC. The promised benefit did not materialise. In the following year, hourly wages rose by 53 per cent, retail prices by 17 per cent.

The following July the government suggested and the TUC accepted the far more generous ceiling of 10 per cent. Because the economy had begun to expand, the formula provided the deserved answer. Hourly wages rose by 14 per cent and retail prices by 8.3 per cent. To the government – largely, though not completely, composed of reasonable men and women – the advantages of restraint seemed self-evident. In the summer of 1975, the TUC was asked to endorse a pay-rise ceiling of 5 per cent. It refused.

It refused not because members of the General Council disagreed with the government's economic analysis. Most of them accepted it without reservation – even though the leader of the Transport and General Workers' Union sternly told one Cabinet minister that it was the policy of his union, confirmed at that year's biannual conference, that wage costs were not related to inflation. It was the rank and file members – encouraged and often provoked by local activists – who refused 'to give another year for Britain'. That patriotic description of a further year's restraint encapsulates the reason why pay policy broke down. Ministers – and General Secretaries – asked for sacrifice. Often that was the short-term consequence. But the long-term result – rarely mentioned – would have been greater prosperity. Opposition was intensified by the increasing belief that the government was not keeping its side of the bargain. As early as March 1977, the government's Public Expenditure White Paper had, because of abstention by left-wing Labour MPs, been rejected in the House of Commons. From then on the idea that the government had abandoned its commitment to high-quality public services gained ground with every militant assault on Treasury policy.

In fact, the pay policy which the government hoped to 'impose' on the unions would have been of immense benefit to many low-paid NHS and local government manual employees. Few of them had ever received a pay increase of 5 per cent, the government's new pay-rise ceiling. And many of the most militant opponents of 'another year for Britain' would have qualified for the additional payments which were allowed (and therefore encouraged) in low-wage industries. It was because rational self-interest demanded co-operation with the government that the most senior trade union leaders – the six men who sat on the National Economic Development Council – unhesitatingly advised ministers to 'blind it through'. Conference decisions prevented them from officially endorsing an extension of incomes policy, but they believed that, if the government went ahead alone, it would succeed in imposing its policy on industry. Neither the union leaders nor the ministers had realised how much trade union members had changed.

Nineteen seventy-nine marked the emergence   as both a political and industrial force – of the public service unions. The decline of British manufacturing capacity had coincided with a massive escalation in the number of men and women employed by local authorities, government agencies and the NHS. Many of them lived on little more than subsistence wages. But they also enjoyed something which approached absolute job security. For in private industry – where wages were almost always higher – demand for labour was determined by the market. In the public service sector, the size of the work-force was decided by a political process which the employees themselves could often influence and sometimes control. Delegates from the public service unions sat on the committees which determined municipal policy and trade unionists (who were also individual Labour Party members) helped to select or deselect the candidates who – when elected as councillors – would eventually implement those policies. Indeed, many full-time trade unionists were themselves senior figures in local government.

In the new world of continental holidays, consumer durables and television advertisements which linked status directly to the acquisition of 'positional goods', what mattered was disposable income. And the younger generation of public service employees – bored by their grandfathers' stories of inter-war unemployment – were certainly prepared to sacrifice the certainty of a job for the hope of a higher wage. For they too were part of the ideological coalition which instinctively supported Thatcherism. What they expected from Labour was not pious talk about 'service' and 'community', but the decent wage which they had been denied for so long. The belief that the level of net pay was all that mattered permeated the whole of society. Militant 'socialist' shop stewards – made impotent by an incomes policy which determined the level of pay increases without their intervention – told the 'hourly paid' workers that they had waited long enough and helped them to dress up their wage demands in the rhetoric of common concern: protecting the public service, fighting for the patients and speaking up for the welfare state.

Even as the 1978 Labour party conference was recklessly repudiating its own government's income policy, Zbigniev Brzezinski – President Jimmy Carter's National Security Adviser – made a secret visit to the party conference in Blackpool. The President feared that the Federal Republic of Germany would not support his plans for comprehensive arms control. The second round of Strategic Arms Limitation Talks (SALT II) was about to end, and the United States hoped that SALT III would begin as soon as the Senate had ratified the treaty which guaranteed a ceiling on Soviet and American strategic weapons. But Helmut Schmidt, the German Chancellor, had already spoken publicly about the 'destabilising effect' of SALT II if the massive disparity in tactical and conventional weapons was not negotiated away. President Carter hoped that Jim Callaghan would join him at an informal meeting in which Germany, Britain, America, and possibly France, ironed out their difficulties.

So, while the British Prime Minister was fighting for the survival of his government and sterling, he was invited to help solve the problems of the Western world. Britain's 'independent' nuclear weapons, and the 'special relationship', qualified him to attend any meeting which determined the future of the Atlantic Alliance. But the invitation emphasised the schizophrenia which every British Prime Minister was, and to some extent still is, expected to accommodate. Certainly during the Cold War years, Britain's influence abroad was wholly out of line with its impotence at home. It can help to decide between peace and nuclear war, but it could not get its balance of payments into surplus or stabilise its exchange rate. And its status as a semi-superpower did not encourage the real giant which was its partner to rush, unconditionally, to its economic aid – even though the partnership involved the United Kingdom spending more on defence than it could afford.

Twice, during the autumn crisis of 1976, Jim Callaghan had attempted to use his undoubted personal influence with Gerald Ford (President Carter's predecessor) to persuade him to help provide a safety net which guaranteed the value of sterling – before the IMF insisted on politically unsustainable and economically unnecessary cuts in public expenditure. On the first occasion Arthur Burns, Governor of the Federal Reserve Bank, refused point-blank even to consider guaranteed support until the cuts in the PSBR, which the IMF demanded, had been made. A month or so later, Helmut Schmidt joined with Jim Callaghan in again suggesting that the dollar should underwrite the pound. It was then the turn of William Simon, Secretary of the Treasury, to veto the idea.

There is no doubt that important business was done at the meeting which President Carter proposed. When the four leaders met in Guadeloupe – France having been elevated from possible guest to host – they examined the whole world scene. As well as disarmament, the primary purpose of the summit, they discussed Ayatollah Khomeini's malign influence on the Middle East, relations with the apartheid regime in South Africa and the prospect of a Rhodesian settlement. Not surprisingly, when Jim Callaghan returned home, his mind was on matters of great international consequence. So when, at the airport, he was asked about the black plastic bags of uncollected refuse which were piling up all over the country, he tried to put the 5 per cent dispute into proper perspective. The *Sun* translated his answer into 'Crisis? What Crisis?'. It was a cruel, indeed dishonest, interpretation of what he had said. But it was profoundly damaging to the government's reputation. Once again a British Prime Minister had paid an awful price for leading a country which had still not adjusted to its status as a medium-sized power – and did not, therefore, concentrate its energy on the need for economic survival.

Trade union reaction against the 5 per cent pay limit was not confined to the public sector. Indeed, the government's greatest humiliation was the result of its unsuccessful attempt to prevent the Ford Motor Company paying its workers a 17 per cent increase. The company – having announced record profits – was easily able to meet the TGWU's claim and the union believed that its members should be rewarded for the success which they had created. Had it not been for the intervention of ministers, new pay rates would have been easily and quickly negotiated. But the Ford management agreed that, as the pace-setter in what was then the annual pay round, they had a duty to set an example. The strike which followed lasted nine weeks. Then the company – complaining that the shut-down cost more than the pay increase – capitulated. The government, desperate lest other companies should follow suit, 'blacklisted' Fords. But it transpired that the power to punish a company by the calculated refusal to buy its product was only legal if the sanction had been explicitly endorsed by the House of Commons. The motion to penalise Ford was lost by 285 votes to 283. And although the government easily survived the vote of confidence which followed, its prestige had been cruelly damaged. The disruption of public services permanently changed the climate of opinion – against the Labour government and everything for which it stood.

It was the public service unions which guaranteed that the 1978 Trades Union Congress rejected the 5 per cent pay limit. And when, a month later, the Labour Party condemned 'any wage restraint by whatever means including cash limits and specifically the government's 5 per cent', the initiative came from Liverpool – the city under the firm municipal control of the Trotskyites. From then on the Labour government had to contain a guerrilla war fought by school caretakers, hospital porters and dustmen. That conflict undoubtedly guaranteed a Conservative victory in the General Election which followed six months later. It also contributed towards – and perhaps even brought about – a change in political attitude which survived long after Margaret Thatcher left Downing Street in 1990.

The British middle classes' traditional ambivalence towards the trade unions – a sentimental admiration for defence of the disadvantaged and the dispossessed, matched by intense irritation whenever fulfilling that duty inconvenienced more prosperous members of the community – turned into outright and unequivocal antagonism. And the disruption of that bitter winter changed more than the public perception of trade unions. It undermined the country's faith in public provision. The great claim of the NHS – universal and free at the point of use – could not be sustained if pickets were closing hospital out-patients' departments. Faith in state education was hard to sustain when schools were closed because the heating had not been switched on. The growing enthusiasm for private provision was boosted by the belief – wholly in tune with the spirit of the time – that payment guaranteed service. And a country which had lost patience with the public service unions and confidence in the public services grew increasingly reluctant to finance either the irresponsible employees or the inadequate provision out of its taxes. Six months of sporadic mayhem – never as widespread or damaging as it was represented in the tabloid press – did simultaneous and irreversible damage to the reputation of trade unions, public services and government spending. Even the low-paid public sector workers, and the extremists who encouraged the disruption which they caused, contributed to the spirit of the age – the belief that individual and private initiative always provided a better result than collective action. Middle-class ideas, if not the middle classes themselves, were taking over.

The saga ended on a note of farce. The TUC – desperate to rescue its authority and the government – produced a new policy statement which urged its constituent unions to moderate their wage claims and declared that 'adherence to its guidelines within the system of free collective bargaining would result in settlements consistent with bringing down inflation'. The government regarded the statement as just better than nothing. The General Council was not so complimentary. Its discussion ended in a tied vote – 14 for and 14 against. So the chairman – acting properly on precedent – announced that the statement was rejected. On 14 February 1979, James Callaghan announced that the government's new counter-inflation policy would not include a ceiling figure for pay increases. Margaret Thatcher called it (or him) a 'boneless wonder' – Winston Churchill's famous description of Ramsay MacDonald. But one element in the new arrangement was to stick in her throat. As part of the reversion to comparability – the determination of pay by committee after comparisons with wage levels in private industry – Professor Hugh Clegg of Warwick University examined public sector earnings. He recommended increases as high as 25 per cent. During the 1979 General Election campaign, the Tories felt it necessary to promise the full implementation of the Clegg Report.

History is often made by vague impressions rather than hard evidence. And the impression left by what came to be called the 'Winter of Discontent' was the collapse of both the public services and the spirit which should have sustained them. The images of the time, which have yet to be obliterated from the national memory, are of patients being turned away from hospital out-patients' departments, rat-infested garbage accumulating in the streets and, most desperate of all, funerals postponed because the grave-diggers were on strike. In a bitterly cold winter, snow was not cleared from the streets and frost-damaged water pipes were left cracked and leaking. The case against collective provision – the ethos of democratic socialism – could not have been argued more eloquently.

The Winter of Discontent did not change the nation's judgement about what was wrong with British society. It merely confirmed it. The national mood had already swung against consensus and co-operation and in favour of competition and confrontation. Even before the breakdown of incomes policy and the disruption which followed, New Conservatism – based on a bar-room version of Hayek and Friedman – was articulating the country's dissatisfaction of collective bargaining and corporate planning. In the autumn of 1977 – over a year before the refuse was left in the streets and the dead were left unburied – John Hoskyns, recently appointed policy adviser to the Leader of the Opposition, drafted a new policy statement for her. Its title, 'Stepping Stones', suggests that it described no more than the opening of the revolution. In fact, at least in one particular, it recommended a change so fundamental that even the radical Tory leadership thought it wise to accept the paper's ideas but suppress its publication:

> The one precondition for success will be a complete change in the role of the trade union movement . . . Even with a radical new union role, to find a way out of our problems will be like finding a needle in a haystack. But if the unions' role and political objectives remain unchanged, then all parties would in effect be agreeing to restrict their search to those haystacks which they know do not contain the needle . . . We cannot say, 'Win the election first with a low profile on the union problem, then implement a high-profile strategy when in power.' The countdown for both has already begun.

The trade unions had become the symbol of an old and discredited view of society, and the Tory party had in 1975 elected a leader who was determined – as a matter of deeply-held personal belief – to inaugurate the era of individualism which the nation believed would bring the long-delayed prosperity.

8

WHERE THERE IS DISCORD
The Tory Decade

——•——

M argaret Thatcher, whatever her more excitable supporters may
have once claimed, was not the first 'conviction politician' to
lead the Tories. Her predecessors – from Peel at the dawn of modern
Conservatism to Heath in the twilight of the 'One Nation' party –
were all men of profound belief. But their convictions were different
from those which motivated Britain's first woman Prime Minister.
They believed in maintaining the established order – adjusting it to
the needs of the time and according to their personal judgements
about the advantages of free trade or the desirability of a closer partnership with continental Europe, rather than aspiring to fundamental
change. They felt neither the psychological compulsion nor the ideological obligation to stand British society on its head. Their instinct
was for compromise. Margaret Thatcher – whose passion for individual action once led her to assert that society does not exist – had
only contempt for the conventional wisdom that united both major
parties in the struggle for consensus. She was a radical in the
American sense of the word who wanted and intended to alter the
course of British history. Before Margaret Thatcher's time, Conservatism was based on the importance of continuity. She made it the
gospel of change.

It was because she promised a new beginning that she was elected leader of the Conservative party in 1975, and much of her Conservatism's popular support, which brought her a landslide victory in 1979, was the result of the promise to govern Britain in a way in which it had never been governed before. When she replaced Edward Heath, Margaret Thatcher was neither a very senior nor a very successful politician. She had been Secretary of State for Education in the Heath government — most notable for ending free milk in secondary schools and promoting comprehensive education — and was no more than deputy to the Shadow Chancellor on the Opposition frontbench. Certainly Heath's demeanour, after his two successive General Election defeats, made his replacement inevitable. But the obvious successors were Willie Whitelaw (from the patrician left) and Geoffrey Howe (from the intellectual right). Margaret Thatcher was nominated and chosen because her views made her the apostle of the abrasive new philosophy which attracted the self-made businessmen and small-town entrepreneurs who had begun to dominate the Conservative party of the 1970s.

The real prophet of New Conservatism — by Hayek out of Friedman, as the old bloodstock Tories might have described it — was Keith Joseph. But he (and the rest of his party) rightly judged that a man of his temperament could never become Prime Minister. So the adaptation into Tory policy of *The Road to Serfdom* (not to mention the prejudice of provincial shopkeepers) was left to Margaret Thatcher — the candidate who, before the contest began, was assumed, at least by her critics, to have no hope of victory. The House of Commons joke concerned Airey Neave, her campaign manager and wartime Colditz escaper. 'Absurd,' they said in the smoking room, 'for a woman who wants to get in pinning her hopes on an expert in getting out.' On the first ballot of the 1975 leadership battle, 130 Tory MPs voted for Margaret Thatcher, 119 for Edward Heath and 16 for Hugh Fraser, the real outsider. A second round was, therefore, necessary. According to the arcane rules which governed Conservative leadership contests, new candidates were allowed to enter the second ballot. The final victory on 11 February was overwhelming — Margaret Thatcher, 146; William Whitelaw, 79; Geoffrey Howe, 19; Jim Prior, 19; and John Peyton, 11.

The Tory party won the General Election of 1979 with a majority of forty-three, a victory which Margaret Thatcher's Tory critics – numerous and vocal from the moment she was elected leader – attributed solely to the unpopularity of the Labour government. That was only part of the reason. Her success had more positive and more significant causes. Margaret Thatcher personified the mood of angry resentment which characterised much of the nation. While the economics of the defeated Axis powers had exploded into ever-increasing prosperity, Britain struggled on from sterling crisis to balance of payments deficit and from inflation to recession. Factories closed and the products which they once made were imported instead from Germany, Italy and Japan. Japan's gross domestic product per head was $7,489, Germany's $7,632 and France's $8,593. Even Italy – derided for the sudden surrender during the war and regarded as a nation of gigolos and ice-cream sellers – was about to overtake the United Kingdom in the league tables of comparative prosperity. An increasingly insecure people needed someone or something to blame. Margaret Thatcher provided the essential villains. Immigrants, work-shy layabouts and perfidious foreigners were all, in turn, accused of (and excoriated for) undermining the national interest. But the real enemy was an idea – the sentimental notion that progress was best made by uniting the country round a common purpose. Redemption, Margaret Thatcher told Britain, depends on abandoning the tender virtues and replacing them with a belief in competition and confrontation. The new Tory leader promised policies as abrasive as her personality. Under her leadership, Britain would not waste time and energy on the failures and misfits who had held the country back for so long.

Margaret Thatcher began as she meant to go on. The budget (introduced six weeks after the election) cut the standard rate of income tax from 33 per cent to 30 per cent and reduced the top rate from 83 per cent to 60 per cent. Petrol duty was increased, public expenditure cut by 3 per cent (£1.5 billion) and an extra £1 billion was raised by selling more BP shares. But the Chancellor still had £4.5 billion to find in order to keep the budget 'neutral'. He raised the balance by increasing VAT from its variable rate of between 8 per cent and 12.5 per cent to a standard 15 per cent. The switch from direct to indirect taxation benefited the rich and disadvantaged the poor. It also produced simultaneous inflation and stagnation.

The government accepted the deflation as part of the price which had to be paid for long-term recovery. That was just as well. The 1979 Autumn (economic) Statement forecast a 3 per cent fall in output over the next year. The prediction proved optimistic. Manufacturing production fell by 16 per cent – a greater reduction than during the Great Slump of 1926–31. A record number of bankruptcies and liquidations was recorded. Giant companies – ICI among them – reported a loss on the year's work. The effect on the labour market was immediate and dramatic. Wage rates, which had risen by 17 per cent in 1979, increased by only 6 per cent three years later. Although the Autumn Statement prophesied that these events – terrible, by the normal political criteria – would come about, the government pressed on. Public expenditure was slashed again in July and November, and the autumn package included both increased prescription charges and the Bank Rate raised to a record 17 per cent.

There was barely less concern about the Retail Price Index, which recorded a 20 per cent increase between May 1979 and May 1980 – almost twice the rate which the government had inherited. Holding down inflation was the government's first priority. But Margaret Thatcher had no doubt that it could only be achieved by reducing the money supply. So the consequences of the VAT increase, the effect on prices of ending all nationalised-industry subsidies, and the insistence that local government pass on the cost of wage awards to the local rate-payers, was regarded not so much as a short-term necessity as an essential ingredient in the war against inflation. According to the theory, on which the least pragmatic of Tory leaders based her economic policy, inflation would be held down by forcing up prices.

To complete the enterprise package – and as a necessary part of the squeeze on the money supply – exchange control was first relaxed and then abandoned. As oil prices increased, sterling appreciated – helping to hold down the cost of living by reducing the price of imports and making British goods too expensive to penetrate new export markets. Although the unemployed and owner-occupiers (who were paying record interest on their mortgages) complained bitterly, Thatcher pronounced herself delighted. After a year, a theory was invented to justify the practice. The Medium Term Financial Strategy (MTFS), set out in a White Paper, committed the government to floating exchange rates, high rates of interest and a continually contracting money supply, come what may. The certain result would be inflation down and unemployment up. It would be a good bargain.

Unfortunately – more for the country than for the government – the MTFS did not quite work in the way that the government hoped it would. Targets were missed and output fell more rapidly than the Treasury expected. By the time of the 1980 budget, the recession was beginning to get out of hand. Unemployment was rising by 100,000 a month. Manufacturing industry had lost 10 per cent of its workforce. The exchange rate at $2.46 to the pound was ruinous for exporters. The Public Sector Borrowing Requirement, instead of falling as predicted, rose by £2 billion – largely as a result of the need to finance unemployment pay for the recently redundant. The government – momentarily and uncharacteristically apprehensive about public opinion – launched an armada of 'special measures': Temporary Employment Subsidy, Temporary Short Time Working Compensation, the Job Release Scheme and the Youth Opportunity Programme. Sometimes even the canons of the new free-enterprise economies were disregarded. Tax relief on stock appreciation was introduced for no better reason than slowing down the rate of bankruptcies. At the same time, government spokesmen insisted that bankruptcies were essential to genuine competition.

Margaret Thatcher had time on her side. She could afford to struggle through an unpopular couple of years and then win back her support well in time for the next election. But she never gave the impression of counting off the days until the economy, and public opinion, turned. She honestly believed that she was leading a crusade for national regeneration. And in the holy war which was to make Britain strong and free, there was no time to weep for the inevitable casualties. Indeed, there were times when she expected the victims to rejoice that they had been selected for the honour of sacrifice. Ten years earlier, her certainty would have been rejected as fanaticism. In the early 1980s, a country longing to be told that change would bring success was infected by her self-confidence. So politics was reduced to cavalry charge after cavalry charge, and because she galloped towards the enemy with such mindless élan, men and women who were not her natural allies trotted along behind her. Paradoxically, had Margaret Thatcher not been so comprehensively unreasonable, fewer reasonable people would have tolerated her government for so long.

The 'welfare state' – for so long regarded by both main parties as the bedrock of civilised stability – was regarded by the new Prime Minister as little more than a drain on public expenditure. In the early years she said little about the 'dependency culture' and the consequent damage to the will to work and self-respect. One of her closest advisers recalled that social policy rarely featured on the Downing Street agenda. The Prime Minister was concerned with the economy, the unions and the nationalised industries. All that was required of health, housing and pension policies was that they did not conflict with pursuit of the central objective. In short, spending on each of the three social services had to be reduced.

Before the election, the Conservative party had promised to cut public expenditure by £8 billion. In fact, far from achieving a reduction, the new government presided over continual increases. Between Margaret Thatcher's first and third election victories, government spending rose by 16 per cent in real terms. The impression of cuts was given by the constant reduction on small items in the national budget. But, in truth, the increase was constant and remorseless. Part of the problem was the added cost of social security brought about by accelerating unemployment. But revenue expenditure on housing, health and social security rose from £36 billion in 1978–79 to £93 billion in 1987–88 – an increase of 30 per cent when national income only rose by 20 per cent. Investment expenditure fell as it had fallen during the years of Labour government. But it was not until 1988–89 – almost the end of Margaret Thatcher's long reign – that the aim of reducing public expenditure (even as a percentage of gross domestic product) was achieved. By 1989, GDP had only risen to the point at which public expenditure, still expanding, was a reduced proportion of total national wealth.

Election rhetoric had made the promised cuts more difficult to deliver. In a television debate, the Conservative party spokesman had undertaken that a Tory government would match Labour's health spending plans. And Margaret Thatcher herself had announced, 'We will maintain the purchasing power of the pension.' But even within the limits set by such rash undertakings, some savings were possible. Prescription and dental charges were raised, and charges for eye tests were announced and then abandoned after opticians stimulated national outrage. The Treasury actually proposed a pension freeze that went back on the Prime Minister's word. But, unwilling to risk the damage to her reputation, Margaret Thatcher agreed only to break the link with earnings. Pensions continued to rise with the cost of living, but not with the average increase in working income. Over the twelve years 1980–92, that one change of policy produced a public expenditure saving of £43 billion – and pensions were reduced from 20 per cent to 15 per cent of national earnings. But that was only the beginning of the policy which economised at the expense of the most vulnerable citizens. The Social Security (No. 2) Bill switched most of the cost of sick pay from government to employers, ended the earnings–related supplement to sickness and unemployment benefit and cut the basic value of invalidity benefit by 5 per cent. The Prime Minister hardly needed to tell her party conference that 'the lady was not for turning'.

Education, an inevitable candidate for early economising, was the area chosen for one of the few items of social engineering that Margaret Thatcher had time to bother with during the 1979 Parliament. The Assisted Places Scheme was introduced. But £280 million was saved by the reorganisation of school meals and milk, and more might have been cut from the education budget had the Duke of Norfolk and Lord (R. A.) Butler not combined in the House of Lords to defeat a proposal to abandon school transport. It was the universities that suffered worst, losing 10,000 academic staff in three years as the result of a 13 per cent reduction in funding. The education budget was allowed to wither slowly with inflation. In the year after Margaret Thatcher was first elected, it absorbed 55 per cent of gross domestic product. In the year before her third successive victory it was down to 48 per cent.

It was in housing that the greatest financial and social success was achieved. The sale of council houses to sitting tenants – an obligation placed on local authorities within weeks of the 1979 victory – raised £28 billion in thirteen years. Councils were not allowed to use the receipts for new building. So taking the money out of circulation made a real contribution to the government's policy of damping down domestic demand. Foolishly, the Labour Party initially opposed a scheme which was so popular among prospective owner-occupiers that 500,000 municipal properties were sold in three years. By the time Margaret Thatcher was deposed, one and a half million council houses had been sold and, as she would have put it herself, a major step had been taken towards the creation of the property-owning democracy. Whether or not the new status encouraged tenants-turned-home-owners to switch from supporting Labour will never be known. For there were many other good reasons for abandoning the Labour Party in the early 1980s. What is clear is that the emphasis on sitting tenants buying their houses diverted attention from the need to build new houses to accommodate the homeless. Council building fell to less than 50,000 properties a year.

Much has been written about the change in the intellectual climate which either stimulated or accompanied 'Thatcherism'. The early 1980s was the age of the 'think-tank'. And very many of them, financed by private industry, struggled to give a spurious respectability to industry's call for a deregulation economy in which the government rarely, if ever, intervened. There were plenty of fashionable academics who were prepared to advance the case for less government and lower public expenditure, although 365 distinguished economists wrote to *The Times* to warn that Treasury policy could only end in disaster. But although *soi-disant* intellectuals announced a victory for the idea of unrestrained markets, the evidence suggested that there was still much work to be done by a government which was even vaguely committed to social justice.

The Black Report – commissioned by the Labour government in 1977 – was published in 1980. It reported that although death rates in Social Groups I and II had improved between 1950 and 1970, in Social Groups IV and V they had either remained the same or deteriorated.

The health gap between the rich and poor was certainly growing in relative terms and, for the very poorest members of society, the prospects of a long and healthy life were actually deteriorating. The causes, Black said, were the nature of lower-income work (or long periods without employment), inadequate housing, inferior education, debilitating environment and a lifestyle which (mostly because of the diet which it encouraged) was itself a threat to health. The Black recommendations were, to say the least, comprehensive. They included an increase in child benefit, a maternity grant quadrupled from £25 to £100, a new infant care allowance, free school meals and a massive drive to improve the nation's stock of houses.

It was not the sort of report that the government felt an instinctive desire to implement. More to its liking was the Royal Commission on the National Health Service. Its terms of reference were limited to an examination of the NHS's structure and organisation, and its conclusions contained the sort of criticism which Margaret Thatcher was always happy to hear when it applied to public services. Too many administrators, operating in too many layers of bureaucracy, were wasting too much money. The government's reforms were expected to result in 435 retirements at a cost of £9 million. The eventual number was almost 3,000, and the final cost of compensation £54 million. But another, and more serious, price had to be paid. National confidence in the Health Service was further eroded. During the next five years the percentage of the population covered by private medical insurance doubled from 13 to 26 per cent.

Socially, politically, and perhaps even psychologically, Britain was living through a period of unprecedented upheaval. But the government − or at least its head − was still not satisfied with the degree of change it had brought about. Yet even the new revolutionaries shrank from the proposals for further public expenditure cuts which were proposed by the Central Policy Review Staff − the end of price protection for social security benefits and state funding for higher education, payments for each visit to hospital and doctor's surgery and vouchers for primary and secondary education. There is no doubt that Margaret Thatcher was sympathetic to the ideas, but her colleagues convinced her that she could not get away with implementing them.

They were mistaken. If the government could survive its unemployment record – 1,288,000 and falling when it was elected, 2,000,000 in November 1980, 2,500,000 in July 1981 and 3,000,000 in June 1982 – it could survive anything. Its survival was assisted by a piece of almost unique good fortune. Labour, the government's principal opponent, was doing its best to destroy itself.

At the 1980 Labour party conference, the savagery which was directed towards the recently defeated government was very largely the product of disappointment. Callaghan and his colleagues had, the delegates believed, failed not because the idea of socialism was flawed but because it had not been pursued with sufficient enthusiasm. And it was not only the Cabinet of the late 1980s that the rank and file indicted. From Ramsay MacDonald, who deserted the party, to Harold Wilson, who often ignored conference decisions, party leaders had a fatal weakness for betrayal. Even the venerated Clement Attlee had done less than justice to the undoubtedly saintly Aneurin Bevan. It seems that election to office automatically transformed honest socialists into cowards who flinch and traitors who sneer. Doubtful of ever finding leaders who could be trusted, the party rank and file determined to force honesty and honour upon them by changing the party's constitution in such a way that betrayal was impossible. The leaders must be controlled by the led. Three major reforms were proposed to achieve that essential objective. The party leader (that is to say the prospective Prime Minister) should be elected by the whole movement, not just by Members of Parliament; and members themselves should be subject to 'mandatory reselection' – the right of local activists to choose a new candidate to fight each election. Furthermore, the manifesto – the party's political prospectus – should be written by the party conference not a cabal of past and prospective ministers. The rank and file attitude was brilliantly, if bitterly, expressed by the delegate from St Pancras North:

> There is nobody in this conference who is not angry about the
> way in which the Tory government is attacking the people of this

country. But many of us in this conference are also angry about what the last Labour government did and a great deal of what the last Labour government failed to do. And we have the right to be angry . . . What we need and what we have a right to demand is a guarantee that the next Labour government will implement the policies on which we fight the election.

Tony Benn – although not the leader of the campaign for Labour Party democracy – was flattered into becoming its spokesman. Replying to the 'constitutional debate' on behalf of the national executive, he made a speech which might have led an uninformed observer to believe that he had not been a member of the defeated government. The leader, he claimed, was able to veto the inclusion in the manifesto of any item of which he disapproved. Having accused the Labour leadership of breaking promises that it had never made, Benn turned to the Labour Cabinet's almost final act – the refusal to make promises which it could not keep. The example he gave made red blood course through the veins of radical delegates, since the 1979 manifesto had not contained a promise to abolish the House of Lords:

My resentment about the exclusion of the House of Lords was not just that it was vetoed, but when conference discussed it and decided by an overwhelming majority, no voice was raised from the platform to persuade us to drop it. They let conference pass it and it was vetoed secretly, late, quietly, before the party could discover what had happened. That is wrong and it is out of that that mistrust in our party grows.

The promise to abolish the House of Lords had been left out of the manifesto because Jim Callaghan had set out the consequences of its inclusion. If it went in, Labour would need a new leader for the General Election campaign. There were two possible interpretations of Callaghan's conduct – strong leadership, or insufferable arrogance. The conference – despite the frantic applause which followed every attack on the defeated government – was in a mood to consider both possibilities. The demand that the whole conference – two thousand delegates in all – should write the manifesto was rejected by a small majority more out of horror at the thought of how the drafting session would be organised than because of constitutional concern that election promises should be made by the people who have the duty to keep them. The resolution which required MPs to face regular re-selection was, however, carried; so was the motion to set up an electoral college which would assume the right to choose the Labour leader. Unfortunately, all the proposals for how the electoral college should be composed were defeated, so it was agreed that the agony should continue. A special conference, to tidy up the loose ends, would be held in London later in the year. When the conference closed on the Friday, with the ritual singing of 'Auld Lang Syne', the next election was already lost.

With the passionate arguments long laid to rest, it is easy to argue that the call for 'constitutional reform' and 'democratic accountability' was reasonable, if prolix. United States Senators and Congressmen are required to win party primaries before they contest the real elections. And the idea of 'reselecting Members of Parliament' has become part of Labour's democratic routine. The party leader is now elected by 'one member, one vote', and a suggestion that the privilege of choosing the next Prime Minister should be left to Members of Parliament would be dismissed as dangerous eccentricity. In 1996, Tony Blair was openly critical of the traditional way in which the manifesto was written, and asking individual members to vote for a draft version of the programme was at least a concession to the idea of wider democracy – even though it offered party members no more than the chance to endorse what had already been decided. But back in 1980, the 'Campaign for Labour Party Democracy' seemed – and was – a threat to the ideal which it claimed to support. For its object was not so much the end of the old autocracy as the creation of a new despotism which imposed its will on powerless Members of Parliament. The party wanted policies which, whatever their real ideological location, were believed to be 'left-wing'. The desire, although exploited by a hard-core of full-time agitators and professional activists, was common to thousands of decent party members who believed that the failures of the 1970s had to be redeemed by change.

One great change came fourteen days after the Labour Party decided, at least in principle, to change the way in which it elected its leader. On 15 October 1980, James Callaghan announced that he was stepping down. According to his memoirs he had only soldiered on for a year 'in order to take the shine off the ball' before Denis Healey, the natural successor, began his innings. But Callaghan's decision to lead the Opposition for a year proved fatal to Healey's chances. By the time that the leadership election was held, the party in the country was in a frenzy of recrimination, and many Labour Members of Parliament (who made up the electorate) were hysterically pessimistic about the chances of remaining in the House of Commons.

For Healey, the timing of the reforms could not have been worse. Members of Parliament were required to face, for the first time, 're-selection' by local activists who were, or were believed to be, deeply antagonistic to anyone who had supported (or even expressed sympathy for) the Callaghan government. And, at the same time, those same beleaguered MPs were required to elect a successor to the leader who, according to recently established folk-lore, had betrayed the party and its principles. And Denis Healey had been an accessory to the act of betrayal.

After a couple of weeks it was clear that, although there were five contenders, the contest was between two candidates – Denis Healey and Michael Foot, a nominee who (until his nomination had been formally lodged) was assumed to be too modest even to aspire to the party leadership. According to the opinion polls, Healey was the most popular politician in Britain – comfortably outscoring Margaret Thatcher – while Michael Foot did not attract enough support to appear in the ratings. Yet Foot beat Healey by 139 votes to 129 in what was the most bizarre election ever to be held by a democratic political party. Foot was the candidate of despair. He won because Labour Members of Parliament thought that the certainty of the party losing the next General Election was preferable to the risk of them not being allowed to fight their own seats.

Foot – although no longer regarded as a genuine left-winger – was rightly accepted as a man of honour and integrity who could be expected to keep his political promises. And it was taken for granted that he would promise to carry out whatever instructions the Labour party conference gave him. He was, therefore, the activists' choice. And it was assumed that his election would cement a bond between the constituency parties and the Members of Parliament who had loyally respected grass-roots opinion. Some members actually showed their ballot papers (duly marked for Foot) to their constituency party officers before they dropped them in the ballot box. Others – who shrank from that ultimate humiliation – simply announced that they were recent converts to Foot's cause. And they meant it. For it was assumed, among the more timorous MPs, that personal support for the constituencies' favourite was not enough. If the Parliamentary Labour Party rejected the rank and file's choice, the resentment which its arrogance aroused would not discriminate between MPs who had respected the will of 'ordinary members' and those who thought, in their elitist way, that they knew best. A victory for Healey would be followed by continuous and indiscriminate 'deselection' of sitting MPs. In November 1980, newspapers reported Foot's triumph with undisguised astonishment. In retrospect it is only surprising that, with so many Labour MPs neurotically anxious about their personal future, the result was so close.

After November 1980, there was no way that Margaret Thatcher could have failed to be re-elected. The British people were never going to make Michael Foot Prime Minister. But, for the Labour Party, worse was to come. In January 1981, the party began to fall apart. Perhaps the disintegration was inevitable after Roy Jenkins resigned the deputy leadership in 1972, rather than continue to vote against the legislation which took Britain into the European Community. It was certainly unavoidable once he had delivered the BBC's 1979 Dimbleby Lecture and gave the natural social democrats within the Labour Party an intellectual justification for finding a more congenial home.

The lecture did not so much call for the creation of a new party as condemn the old party system, 'which had remained virtually unchanged since 1868'. Jenkins argued that the British public had grown weary of the ritual political battle and, in a reckless leap of logic, somehow equated their dissatisfaction with Britain's economic decline. He praised the virtues of coalition and advocated the change in the electoral system which would make coalition inevitable – proportional representation. By rejecting the 'rigidity' of the old party system, he also turned his back on the doctrine of the manifesto and the mandate – the duty of each party to publish (before an election) a statement of the policies which the parties hope to implement when the election is over. That notion – allowing the electorate to choose directly between rival programmes – had been the cornerstone of British democracy for a hundred years. Jenkins's Dimbleby Lecture, at least by implication, proposed a return to the system which prevailed before Gladstone's first administration – shifting alliances within the House of Commons which decided, *after the election*, both the composition of the government and its legislative proposals. Jenkins defended the idea of letting Parliament, rather than the people, make those choices by insisting that the outcome would be more rational government presiding over a more prosperous and more contented nation. For some unaccountable reason, he expressed his hopes in the second person:

> You want the nation to be self-confident and outward-looking, rather than insular, xenophobic and suspicious. You want the class system to fade without being replaced either by an aggressive and intolerant proletarianism or by the brash and selfish values of a 'get rich quick' society. You want the nation, without unnecessary controversy, to achieve a renewed sense of cohesion and common purpose.

Having set out the case for multi-party politics – mainly unpopular in Jenkins's view because of the single Disraeli aphorism, 'England does not love a coalition' – he made the indisputable assertion that the creation of the new democracy which he proposed 'could be assisted by a strengthening of the radical centre'. He went on:

> I believe that such a development could bring into political commitment the energies of many people of talent and goodwill who, although perhaps active in many other voluntary ways, are at present

alienated from the business of government (whether national or local) by the sterility and formalism of much of the political game.

Thus, in his heavily intellectual way, did Roy Jenkins set out a case which in essence is repeated in public houses and golf-club bars on every night of the week. The government of Great Britain would be much improved if we took the politics out of politics.

If Roy Jenkins's Dimbleby Lecture was the anvil on which a new political party was forged, the hammer which beat it into shape was the constant attacks – by Labour's self-styled left wing – on both the moderates within the party and the constitution which protected their right to be moderate in government. And the blow was struck time after time. On 24 January 1981, the Labour Party held a special conference to complete the business which had been left half-finished at Blackpool the previous autumn. The theoretical object of the gathering was to decide how to 'widen the franchise' by which the party leader was elected, but the real purpose was to ensure that the election was taken out of the hands of Members of Parliament. Minutes before the delegates were called to order, there was still no clear recommendation about the form which the electoral college should take. A trade union delegate suggested that it should have three sections, each of which cast a percentage of the total votes – trade unions 40 per cent, constituencies 30 per cent and the Parliamentary Labour Party 30 per cent. The idea seemed as good as anything else that had been suggested, and after the usual acrimony – MPs who spoke were booed and opponents of the proposal shouted down – the 'reform' was carried. Michael Foot – the last Labour leader to be elected by the old method – was opposed to the new formula. But he chose to speak emolliently after the vote was taken, rather than decisively before the decision was made.

The next day, David Owen, Bill Rodgers, Shirley Williams and Roy Jenkins published the Limehouse Declaration – denouncing Labour's drift towards intolerance and extremism and promising to set up a Council for Social Democracy. The grandiose title – council rather than party – was intended to postpone the final break with Labour, or at least make it appear reluctant. The purpose of the

Council – 'to rally all those who are committed to the values, principles and policies of social democracy' – made it clear enough that a new party was intended. The claim that the initiative had been prompted by the Wembley conference, and the constitutional change which would allow 'a handful of trade union leaders to dictate the choice of a future Prime Minister', was clearly bogus. The launch of the SDP had been planned for months, and even heralded in newspaper articles which the authors of the Limehouse Declaration had written to warn that if the Labour Party continued its drift out of mainstream politics – particularly the rejection of Common Market membership – they would feel unable to continue their membership. The Wembley decision to set up a trade union-dominated electoral college to choose party leaders was an ideal opportunity for the righteous announcement. From then on the creation of a new party gained pace. Nine sitting Members of Parliament gave their formal support to 'the Council'. One by one they withdrew from whatever positions they held in the party, announced their decision not to stand as Labour candidates in the next election and resigned the Labour whip in Parliament. From then on, the announcement of new adherents in both the Commons and House of Lords were made with carefully calculated regularity. On 26 March 1981 the Council became a Party, supported by fourteen Members of Parliament and twenty peers. Its object was to 'make Britain successful and tolerant at home, self-confident and far-sighted abroad'.

That was the sort of pledge that almost every politician would be happy to endorse. Even Margaret Thatcher – in other contexts, particularly concerning dissidents within the Cabinet, openly sceptical about the advantages of tolerance – supported a self-confident and far-sighted foreign policy. As always with such anodyne statements of intent, the problems only arose when the platitude was given precise meaning. There is no doubt how the new Tory government – or at least its leader – interpreted that universally acceptable pledge. Being all of a piece, she applied just as much ideological zeal, and exactly the same philosophical principles, to domestic and foreign policy. The deregulated free market, combined with a dramatic reduction in government spending, ownership and intervention, was the guarantee of freedom and prosperity abroad as well as at home. In August 1980, she was encouraged in that belief when the employees at the Lenin Shipyard in Gdansk, Poland, began the only strike of which she approved in the whole eleven years of her premiership.

The dispute began when the workers struck in sympathy for a dismissed colleague. Three days later, the dispute dramatically escalated from the defence of a single victimised welder into the demand for industrial freedom. A sixteen-point manifesto demanded a fundamental change in the way in which the shipyard – and therefore the whole economy – was run. To challenge the principle of economic centralism – the determination of prices, output, investment and wages by diktat rather than supply and demand – was also to challenge the core philosophy of Marxist communism. Yet, within a week, the Warsaw government had agreed to negotiate with the shipyard workers – a capitulation unique in the history of the Soviet Union and its satellites. By the end of the month a concordat had been agreed between the Polish Deputy Prime Minister and the electrician who led the strikers, Lech Walesa. The government conceded the right to strike and accepted the existence of free trade unions and a relaxation in the censorship laws. The capitulation was not absolute, however, and Solidarity, as the shipyard workers called themselves, still had many bitter battles to fight. And after more than a decade, Lech Walesa – who had risen from dockyard electrician to President of Poland – was replaced, in a democratic election, by a reformed Communist. But Margaret Thatcher had been given a sign. She regarded Walesa's triumph as proof of her belief that 'socialism' – her generic description of everything from the teaching of Mao Zedong to the Bad Godesberg Declaration of the German Social Democrats – was in a world-wide humiliating retreat. Swept by what she believed to be the tide of history, she sought to impose her idiosyncratic philosophy of political interference and economic *laissez faire* on British foreign policy.

Once again there was no concession to the doubts of her timid friends or the complaints of her ideological enemies. The arms embargo imposed on Chile during the early weeks of the 1974 Labour government was lifted, with the unconvincing explanation that the government of that country had begun to respect human rights. It later transpired that Claire Wilson, a British citizen, had been arrested and tortured by the Chilean police six days before the British decision was taken. Margaret Thatcher was less sympathetic to dictators who caused her personal inconvenience. Rhodesia – whose illegal status the Labour government had struggled so unsuccessfully to regularise – was a problem which she was determined to solve. Guiding the colony to legitimate majority rule was more than a matter of principle. It was a political necessity. Democracy was the only way to get Rhodesia off the government's agenda, so democracy would have to do. Margaret Thatcher did not propose to allow a handful of white settlers to distract her from her life's work of making Britain a country fit for the middle classes to live in.

For that reason – and to general surprise, since it was totally out of character – Margaret Thatcher told the 1979 Commonwealth Prime Ministers' Conference that the leaders of the Rhodesian (or Zimbabwean) independence struggle – rebels and terrorists, according to some of her most passionate supporters – must take part in the discussions which produced a new constitution and secured the country's international recognition. In December, Zimbabwe became a British colony again, with Lord Soames (the Tory leader of the House of Lords) its titular governor. United Nations sanctions were immediately lifted. An amnesty was declared for both white rebels and black guerrillas. In the following month, Robert Mugabe (the leader of ZANU) returned to Salisbury after five years in exile. On 4 March 1980 he was elected Prime Minister. Where a succession of governments, sympathetic to the African's cause, had failed, Margaret Thatcher (who was instinctively on the side of the tobacco farmers and mine-owners) succeeded.

Margaret Thatcher's attitude towards collective security and nuclear defence was the predictable response of a Prime Minister who saw herself as a partner (first junior, then equal and, in the end at least, morally senior) in the Atlantic Alliance. In June 1980, the government announced that American Cruise missiles – accepted by its Labour predecessors – would be stationed in Berkshire and Cambridgeshire. The Campaign for Nuclear Disarmament – dormant for years – came back to life and in October 60,000 protesters took part in the biggest anti-nuclear demonstration for two decades. Ronald Reagan, elected President of the United States in the following month, gave CND an argument which almost justified its existence. By mistake, he spoke of winning rather than preventing a nuclear war and, for some still unexplained reason, the Supreme Allied Commander in Europe made a strategic assessment of what life would be like after Armageddon. All over Britain, banners were taken out of dusty cupboards and half-forgotten badges pinned back on to lapels. It seemed that the greater the protest, the stronger Margaret Thatcher became. She stood, unyielding and triumphantly unreasonable, like an island of immovable reaction in a sea of turbulent dissent. The nation felt safe and reassured.

Had Labour won the 1979 General Election, American Cruise missiles would have undoubtedly come to Great Britain. They were the natural and rational extension of collective security, and the United States could not have sustained the alliance if its then closest ally had refused to station the latest nuclear technology within its boundaries. In 1980, officials in the American State Department were still echoing Henry Kissinger's view that whatever the gross domestic product of the Federal Republic of Germany, the ties of language, history and culture kept the English-speaking peoples particularly close together. And for Margaret Thatcher, what she still believed to be the 'special relationship' had a special significance. She was vociferously in favour of Cruise because it was American, a bastion against Soviet aggression, the proof of her status as warrior-queen and likely to expose the Labour Party as pinko-pacifists. But her most important ingredient of the compulsion to be NATO's most enthusiastic member came from the emotional need to be visibly allied with the United States.

The instinctive belief in the innate superiority of the English-speaking peoples had been suppressed during the referendum campaign which confirmed British membership of the European Community. But once Margaret Thatcher became Prime Minister she barely attempted to hide her reservations about what she regarded as an incompatible alternative to a close Atlantic partnership. Perversely, she began to exhibit all the prejudices which Charles de Gaulle believed characterised every British political leader. The new Prime Minister was temperamentally incapable of accepting the idea of 'Twin Pillars' – the United States working in happy partnership with a more integrated Europe which included the United Kingdom. She wanted the relationship to be not so much special as unique. Her entire approach to life was all or nothing. America was all, and Europe very little. Even in the early days of her premiership, her scale of values was clear enough.

Britain's contribution to the European Community budget was, Margaret Thatcher believed, too large – an argument which she was able to advance at European Council meetings because of one of the few real achievements of Labour's generally bogus 'renegotiation'. The argument went on for months. Britain demanded a rebate of £1,000 million. The Community offered £350 million. Margaret Thatcher imperiously rejected 'a third of a loaf' and threatened to withhold the proportion of British VAT revenue which the Treaty of Rome required the Treasury to transfer to Brussels. The Community replied with an offer of £750 million. The offer was rejected not because it was too little but because it applied to only one year's payments. After much agonised discussion, Britain's European partners – anxious to conciliate – agreed that the £750 million annual rebate should be paid for two consecutive years. Margaret Thatcher announced that she was happy with the extension in time, but it must be accompanied by a revision of the amount for the second year to insure that the rebate increased at the same speed as the basic British contribution. Community heads of state and government began to suspect that their new colleague was looking for trouble. But they still struggled to find an agreement.

Largely by chance – but partly because the other European leaders began to fear that their exasperation could not be disguised much longer – discussion of the rebate was transferred to the Foreign Affairs Council, the meeting of foreign ministers and their deputies, not heads of state and government. When a new offer was made – three years of guaranteed rebates and a formula that insured an annual revision to reflect the increasing size of Britain's payments – the UK representatives were jubilant and accepted the deal on the spot. The

Prime Minister was horrified. She wanted to fight on because she believed that fighting would win her greater popularity than could possibly be achieved by coming to an agreement. But for once she could not carry her Cabinet. So she declared a personal victory and scoffed at the Opposition suggestion that the rebate should have been larger and guaranteed for longer.

Britain's European course had been set. Brussels and its bureaucrats, the Commission and the Council of Ministers were Britain's enemies. The Prime Minister's task, and the duty of all who served her, was to pursue Britain's short-term interests without regard for the longer-term interests of the Community as a whole. Further integration must be resisted. A Europe of the States would enable Britain to pick and choose – supporting (and participating in) those items which were of benefit, but boycotting or vetoing measures of which the Prime Minister disapproved. And until the aberration of the 1987 Single European Act – a measure which she endorsed, promoted, disowned and denounced in turn – Margaret Thatcher disapproved of almost everything that the European Community did.

There was no doubt that 'standing up for Britain' and 'putting Britain first' was immensely popular in a country which was insecure about its place in the world and resentful of the success enjoyed by countries for which it traditionally felt only contempt. Margaret Thatcher had been elected, not least, to recover British pride and to reawaken the innate virtues which had been sleeping for so long. Principal among them was an enthusiasm for disposing of foreigners who got in Britain's way – particularly when they attempted to bar the path towards British prosperity. At a time when inflation and unemployment rose to record heights, the distraction of fighting and winning a European war was immensely beneficial to a Prime Minister who, had she been capable of such an emotion, would have felt beleaguered. The lesson was well learned. Margaret Thatcher had discovered that having the right sort of enemies was even more important than having the right sort of friends.

Margaret Thatcher was a lucky Prime Minister. On 19 March 1982 the fortune that favoured her for so long provided an ideal dragon for the Prime Minister to slay. It breathed fire and smoke in the South

Atlantic. In December of the previous year, General Leopoldo Galtieri had seized control of the military Junta that governed Argentina. In order to bolster up his dubious authority he first made bellicose claims about the imminent expulsion of the British from the Malvinas and then, as a token of his serious intent, landed a party of scrap merchants on South Georgia – an isolated outpost of the Empire – where they scavenged for metal and ran up the Argentine flag. The Falklands War had begun in farce. It was to end with over 650 Argentine and 255 British servicemen and women killed in the battle for those inhospitable islands.

The irony was the cost. For General Galtieri might never have begun his mad escapade had the British Defence Review, of June 1981, not unwittingly sent a signal which the Argentine Junta thought confirmed Margaret Thatcher's infirmity of purpose. The survey ship *Endeavour* – guns, helicopters and twenty Royal Marines as well as hydrographic equipment – cost the navy £3 million a year to keep at sea. The Secretary of State for Defence – a devout believer in the overriding need to reduce public expenditure – brushed aside Foreign Office warnings about how the Argentinian Junta would interpret British withdrawal from the South Atlantic and insisted that the saving be made. It was a false economy. The Falklands War, for which the £3 million cheese paring was, in part, responsible, cost £1.6 billion.

It was some time before the British government decided how to respond to the 'occupation' of South Georgia. The island was 800 miles east of the Falklands, and the invasion force was not of a size or character which suggested that they were the advance guard of a real assault. The British Embassy in Buenos Aires continued to warn of the Junta's aggressive intentions. But it was not until the last day in March that troop movements in the River Plate prompted action. HMS *Spartan*, a nuclear submarine, set sail for the South Atlantic. The next day, on 2 April 1982, Argentine forces invaded and captured the Falkland Islands. It took twenty-four hours for the United Nations to condemn their action and forty-eight for the Argentine troops to complete their occupation.

The House of Commons met on a Saturday for the first time since the war. Margaret Thatcher was unusually subdued, but almost every member who spoke called for swift and decisive action. Michael Foot, Leader of the Opposition and the least bellicose of men, said that Britain had 'a moral duty, a political duty and every other sort of duty' to win back the islands. The aircraft-carriers *Hermes* and *Invincible* left for the South Atlantic three days after the debate, and Lord Carrington, the Foreign Secretary (together with two of his junior ministers) resigned after accepting 'responsibility for a very great national humiliation'. But the real task force – troops and the equipment necessary to recapture the island – took a month to prepare. Thanks to the earlier despatch of *Endeavour*, a naval war of sorts could begin. Margaret Thatcher announced a 200-mile 'exclusion zone' around the Falkland Islands and Argentine ships evacuated the area.

Enoch Powell, who asked rhetorically in the House of Commons why the Marines on South Georgia had not died rather than surrender it to Argentina, no doubt agreed with Margaret Thatcher when it was recaptured on 25 April. The Prime Minister stood on the steps of 10 Downing Street in her warrior-queen mode and told the nation, 'Rejoice. Just Rejoice.' But until the end of April Britain seemed to be engaged in just a phoney war. On the last day of the month, President Reagan announced that the United States would supply war materials to Britain, 'its closest ally' and, identifying Argentina as the aggressor, imposed economic sanctions and a trade embargo on the Galtieri regime. It was assumed that the respite from real war was being used to search for a negotiated settlement. General Alexander Haig, the American Secretary of State, acted as the honest broker for fear that – because of either weakness or intransigence – General Galtieri would not choose to negotiate. He was soon to discover that Margaret Thatcher would not negotiate either. She wanted a victory, not a settlement.

The Prime Minister's enthusiasm for preserving the Falklands' imperial connection – undoubtedly the wish of the islanders – was a comparatively recent development of her policies. In the late autumn of 1979, six months after taking office, she had allowed – with what enthusiasm we cannot now know – the Foreign Office to promote a 'solution' to the 200-year-old dispute. Formal sovereignty over the islands would be ceded to Argentina, but effective government of the islands would be leased back to Britain for a period to be determined after consultation with the Falklands' people. The Falklanders rejected the idea, the Argentine government dismissed it with contempt, and the House of Commons was outraged that such a scheme should even be contemplated. The idea was abandoned in embarrassed confusion. But while a negotiated settlement was tolerable to Margaret Thatcher when it was initiated by her government, there was no question of her accepting any sort of compromise after the Argentine Junta had invaded British territory.

The Americans suggested five versions of a peace plan, all of which were variants of the idea that the Argentine troops should withdraw from the island, the task force should halt (about 1,000 miles north of the Falklands) and a constitutional conference, chaired by the United States, should consider the future status of the islands. Both Argentina and Britain dismissed the idea out of hand. With the task force – including the commandeered liners *Canberra* and *QE2* acting as troop ships – at its staging post in the Ascension Islands, General Haig began to suspect that he had been wrong to assume that the British invasion plans were just a stratagem to frighten the Argentines into a swift and reasonable settlement. When, on 1 May, Vulcan bombers strafed the airport at Port Stanley, he realised that Margaret Thatcher was determined to go to war.

The next day nobody could have been left in any doubt. The Argentine cruiser *General Belgrano* – outside the exclusion zone and steaming due west, away from the action – was torpedoed by the British submarine HMS *Conqueror*. It was a calculated, if not a very carefully considered, decision. The Chief of the Defence Staff asked the Prime Minister to change the 'rules of engagement', so that the ship, safe under the old guidelines, could be sunk. She agreed at once. Three hundred and sixty-eight Argentinian sailors died. Two days later, HMS *Sheffield* was hit by an Exocet missile and sunk with the loss of twenty-one lives. It was not retaliation. Given the chance, the Argentine air force would have put the British destroyer out of action whether or not the Royal Navy had made the first kill. But the two sinkings made all thought of negotiation impossible. General Galtieri was too weak to talk and Margaret Thatcher was too bitter to negotiate. In Washington, the British Ambassador told General Haig that the British Prime Minister 'would not mind sinking the whole Argentine fleet'. In London she confirmed the message by telling the visiting American Secretary of State, in the Cabinet Room, that they were sitting at the table around which Neville Chamberlain's appeasement Cabinet had sat. The result had been the Second World War and forty-five million dead. To compromise with Galtieri would 'send a signal round the world with devastating consequences'.

In truth, Margaret Thatcher was enjoying herself. On 14 May, the week before British troops landed at San Carlos Bay, the Prime Minister confided in Scottish Conservatives, 'When you've spent your whole life dealing with humdrum issues like the environment, it's exciting to have a real crisis on your hands.' At the time, she could not have been aware how great the crisis might have become, had all the Argentine Exocet air-to-ground missiles exploded.

International arms sales, combined with modern weapon technology, became a great leveller. High-explosive bombs   not unlike those used in 1945 – sank HMS *Coventry*, *Ardent* and *Antelope*, and *Sir Galahad*, a landing ship, was damaged beyond salvage. But it was the Exocet, bought by Argentina from France, which might have swung the war against a country whose lines of communication were stretched over eight thousand miles. Exocets sank HMS *Sheffield* and the SS *Atlantic Conveyor*, and HMS *Glamorgan* was hit (but not sunk) by an Exocet launched from a crudely improvised land platform. If the same missile had sunk one of the carriers, the British task force would have lost half of its air cover. A hit on either of the commandeered liners turned troopers would have reduced the task force's size beyond acceptable limits. But, thanks partly to the skill of the navy's helicopter pilots and partly because some of the missiles which found their targets did not explode, the casualties were comparatively light. There were heroic passages of arms at Tumbledown Mountain and Goose Green. Then, on 14 June, the Argentine forces surrendered.

The euphoria which followed was carefully cultivated. Margaret Thatcher told the House of Commons that the victory in the South Atlantic had been 'boldly planned, bravely executed and brilliantly accomplished'. When the troops came home, a victory parade (at

which the Prime Minister, not the Queen, took the salute) was followed by a service of national thanksgiving in St Paul's Cathedral. And
the heroine of the hour wrote her own valediction on the campaign:

> We fought to show that aggression does not pay and that the robber
> cannot be allowed to get away with the swag. We fought with the
> support of so many throughout the world . . . Yet we fought alone.

In the emotion of the hour, the shameless identification with 1940 –
when civilisation itself might have been destroyed – was forgiven. And
there was a more general message and more important moral to be
drawn from Britain's victory. The lion had roared again and her sons
had travelled half-way round the world to redeem the nation's honour.
It was the re-creation of Victorian glory – 'Gentlemen in khaki,
going South'. For this was Margaret Thatcher made. Vindication was
at hand. Her popularity rating rose to 44 per cent. For she convinced
them that their dearest political wish had been granted.

> We have ceased to be a nation in retreat. We have, instead, a new-
> found confidence born in the economic battles at home and tested,
> and found true, 8,000 miles away.

★ ★ ★

The national amnesia which followed the Falklands War did not last
for long. But for a week or two the nation downgraded, if it did not
altogether dismiss, events which in other circumstances might have
remained in their bitter memory for years. The ten weeks between 2
April and 14 June 1982 became not so much a turning-point in the
life of the first Thatcher government as a dramatic break in its normal
activities, which separated it into two distinct parts. All that had happened before – the riots in Brixton and Toxteth, the ten Northern
Ireland prisoners who died on hunger strike, the constant assaults on
trade union power and local government – had been the responsibil-

ity of a government which seemed different from the administration that followed the Falklands War. It was not, as the vulgar theory has it, that Margaret Thatcher 'wrapped herself in the union flag' – although she certainly did assume the character of Britannia. It simply seemed that her way of governing succeeded. And success is what, above all other things, the British people wanted.

However, it would be quite wrong to pretend that the 'Falklands factor' won the Conservatives the General Election of 1983. That was the excuse of those Labour Members of Parliament who could not face the truth. But there were stronger influences at work on the electorate; one of them was incipient economic recovery.

The headline figures continued to deteriorate. In January 1983 the pound fell to the lowest exchange rate in history, $1.52, and the February unemployment figure – 3,224,715 – was the highest since the war. But output had begun to rise – only by 1.5 per cent between the last quarter of 1980 and the last quarter of 1981, and about the same figure a year later – but a rise nevertheless. The rate of growth in election year was much greater, almost 4 per cent. Consumer spending was rising – imperceptibly in 1980 and 1981, rather more a year later, and strongly by 1983. The increase in public spending, which continued despite all the protestations during each year of Margaret Thatcher's first government, helped to moderate the recession in the private sector. But the biggest single cause of the eventual economic upturn was the return to stock-building. Companies which had chosen not to replace raw materials and primary products had suddenly to decide to buy or go out of business. They chose to buy. And the first ripple of recovery ran through the economy. The moment when manufacturing companies and retailers decide to buy rather than run down stocks is, in classic trade-cycle theory, known as 'bottoming out'. Unfortunately, an emasculated and impotent Labour Party – the government's principal guarantee against defeat – did not bottom out until the General Election was over.

The election of Michael Foot as Leader of the Opposition was not Labour's final act of self-destruction. As soon as the new rules for Labour leadership election were in place, Tony Benn challenged Denis Healey for the deputy leadership. Benn lost by the narrowest of margins – 49.574 per cent of the electoral college to 50.426 per cent. But the damage to the party's reputation was not the extent of the left-wing vote. It was the way that, during the campaign, Healey (still the most popular politician in the country) was howled down at public meetings by mobs which newspapers and television always described as being made up of Labour Party supporters – even though most of them were members of Marxist and Trotskyite fringe groups. Michael Foot – who thought that the party leader had a duty to remain neutral in the contest between Benn and Healey – found that some of the most passionate supporters turned against him when he failed to follow the extreme course they demanded. He was not the first radical politician to be disowned by old supporters for being reasonable over Ireland.

The situation in Northern Ireland had, a couple of weeks after Foot's elevation, appeared to improve dramatically. In December 1980 a hunger strike, organised by republican prisoners in the Maze prison, was abandoned after the government promised to review the status and treatment of special category prisoners. But the lull in hostilities did not last. On 1 March 1981, Bobby Sands, serving a fourteen-year sentence for terrorist offences, went on hunger strike again to reinforce his demand for 'prisoner of war' status and segregation from 'loyalist' prisoners in the Maze. When his fast was a fortnight old, the IRA – or Sinn Féin, its political wing – decided on a brilliant *coup de théâtre*. Sands would be nominated as candidate in the Fermanagh and South Tyrone by-election. He won.

Sands died on 5 May. During the inevitable riots which followed, Margaret Thatcher told the House of Commons that to give political status to men and women convicted of terrorist crimes would only lead to more violence and more deaths. Rightly and reasonably, Michael Foot supported her. And although, in private, he urged a softening of her position, he regarded it as his duty – at least in public – to hold the bi-partisan line. The violence escalated. British soldiers were killed by bombs and Irish demonstrators by plastic bullets. Before the hunger strike ended, ten prisoners died. A few days before the tenth death, Owen Carron, 'Anti-H Block Proxy Political Prisoner' and Sinn Féin supporter, was elected to be Member of

Parliament for Fermanagh and South Tyrone to fill the vacancy caused by the death of Bobby Sands. In the atmosphere surrounding such emotive events, Michael Foot attempted to preserve both the peace and his own impeccable libertarian reputation. But Labour's far left – almost certainly looking for a reason to turn against him – argued that his failure to support the hunger strikers was unforgivable. His reputation among his original supporters was damaged still further by his endorsement of the Falklands War and his (undoubtedly half-hearted) agreement to investigate Trotskyite infiltration of the Labour Party. By the time that the General Election was held on 9 June 1983, it was difficult to find anyone who regarded him as a credible candidate for the office of Prime Minister.

The campaign was probably the most one-sided contest in modern political history, and the worst result for Labour since 1931, when Ramsay MacDonald split the party and formed the National Government. The tally of seats was bad enough: Conservatives, 397; Labour, 209; and the Liberal–SDP Alliance, 23. Judged by the percentage of votes cast, the result was even more catastrophic. Labour, with 27.6 per cent, won its smallest percentage of the poll for fifty years, and barely beat the Alliance on 25.4 per cent. There had been times, during the campaign, when it actually seemed that Labour would receive less overall support than the new centre party. Had that happened – as a result of a swing of 1.5 percentage points – the mould of British politics would (as the SDP promised) have been broken and the aircraft (which Roy Jenkins warned might crash at the end of the political runway) would have soared into the stratosphere. Not surprisingly, with its popular vote so close and the disparity of seats so great, David Steel (Liberal leader since 1976) demanded an enquiry into the 'unfair voting system'. Labour seemed suddenly to recognise how close it had come to extinction.

For Labour, the problem had been policies as well as personalities, the prospect as well as the inheritance. The manifesto – 'The New Hope for Britain' – was more absurd than extreme. Having promised 'to ensure that all animals are slaughtered as near as possible to the point of production', Labour's prospectus for government moved immediately on the European Economic Community:

The next Labour government, committed to radical, socialist policy
for reviving the British economy, is bound to find continued mem-
bership a most serious obstacle to the fulfilment of those policies . . .
Britain's withdrawal from the Community is the right policy for
Britain to be completed well within the lifetime of a Parliament.
That is our commitment.

Defence policy was more moderate. The nuclear arsenal was not to
be immediately abandoned but run down during the lifetime of a
Parliament, and continued membership of Nato was confirmed. The
spending commitments – to be paid for out of growth and borrowing – were vast, and the planning was prescribed as the stimulant to a
healthy economy. The overall effect was wilful incompetence.

When the election was over and thoroughly lost, Labour, suddenly
uncertain about its traditional commitment to community solutions
administered by governments and paid for out of public revenue,
stepped one pace back from the brink of destruction. In October
1983 it elected as leader, in succession to Michael Foot, his protégé
Neil Kinnock. The party was not yet ready to repudiate its five-year
madness. And Kinnock – a passionate unilateralist, vocal opponent of
the European Economic Community and unequivocal advocate of
public ownership – provided, members hoped, improvement without
change. He was also untarred by the brush of the Callaghan and
Wilson governments, in which he had refused to serve. Yet he was
clearly ministerial material – eloquent, industrious and determined.
He was almost certainly more anxious to win than most of the delegates who elected him realised. Despite his background in the
romantic left, he was committed to modernise the party which he
led – to bring its organisation up to date, and to improve its increasingly important public relations.

On policy, Kinnock was initially immovable – at least in public. And
we shall never know when the long march – which ended as his
appointment as a European Commissioner, devotee of competitive
markets and supporter of the nuclear deterrent – began. We can, however, be sure that, from the very start, it was his intention to purge the
Labour Party of what he regarded as the 'illegitimate left' – the

Trotskyites and Stalinists and Maoists who organised their own cells within the local organisations. He was not ready to push his supporters towards policies which might endear them to potential Labour voters. Indeed he was not, at that stage, even prepared to attempt a reconciliation between the typical party activist and the traditional Labour supporter. But he was determined to remove what he regarded as parasites, cuckooing in Labour's nest – as much because of the electoral damage that they did as because of his undoubted opposition to their philosophy. His plan – confided to colleagues in the week of his election – was to draw breath until the New Year and then, after three or four months of personal consolidation, take the dangerous but essential first step back into the mainstream of politics. Unfortunately for the Labour Party, on 12 March 1984, miners in Yorkshire and Scotland went on strike.

The miners have always had a special place in Labour Party folklore and Tory demonology. They were the enemy who carried on the battle for a full year after the rest of the unions had abandoned the General Strike in 1926. They had brought down the Heath government nearly half a century later and, in February 1981 – with Thatcherism, if not at its high water-mark, at least in full flood – the South Wales miners had gone on unofficial strike against the threat of pit closures. On the following day, the government had changed its mind and announced that it would increase the coal subsidy. Margaret Thatcher did not forget old wounds. And between 1981 and 1983, she had acquired a taste for the right sort of enemies. Arthur Scargill – President of the National Union of Mineworkers – was exactly the adversary she would have chosen. His unpopularity among the general public was so great that it more than offset the nation's traditional sympathy for the miners. From the start of the conflict, his tactics were certain to damage his cause. And he had a love of publicity which, combined with an extraordinary verbal facility, was guaranteed to keep his unpopular persona in public view.

Arthur Scargill was almost certainly right to argue that Margaret Thatcher set out first to break the NUM and then to destroy the coal industry. His claims – brushed aside at the time – that she had 'hit-lists' of pits which she was planning to close, proved accurate in almost every particular. But it was not just antagonism to coal and coal miners – or the obsessive need to win – which made Margaret Thatcher's victory over Arthur Scargill essential to the future success of her government. Back in 1979, 'curbing the trade unions' had been a central plank of the Tories' election manifesto. Had she not beaten the miners – always the shock troops of the TUC – the reputation for constancy as well as courage would have been damaged beyond repair.

It had taken the new Conservative government of 1979 more than a year to enact its first major industrial relations Bill. The 1981 Employment Act restricted both the number and permissible activities of legal pickets, outlawed the closed shop and provided government funds to finance the ballots which, it was said (if not actually believed), would result in the election of fewer militant trade union officers. A second Employment Bill became law in October 1982. In January 1983, the government published a green paper, theoretically canvassing the possibility of compulsory ballots not only to elect officials but also to confirm the members' wish to strike. Few people thought that its purpose was consultation. The government had already decided to go ahead with the proposals it contained – including a members' vote of the desirability of affiliation to the Labour Party – before it was published. A Bill, giving legislative effect to its proposals, was published the following July. The pressure exerted on organised labour was, because of the virtually annual legislation, enormous. The claims that Margaret Thatcher was determined to destroy the unions were almost certainly justified – though their emasculation came as a result of the changes in the economy, not what the demonstrators called 'Tory laws'. The unions' massive influence could not have survived both the changes in industrial organisation that reduced the number of workers huddled together in mass production and class solidarity and the reduction in employment which reduced the number of workers in any job at all.

The zeal with which the government pursued its campaign against the unions was illustrated by its decision to deny the rights of membership to workers at the Cheltenham Government Communications Headquarters (GCHQ). There was no evidence that union members had been anything other than loyal employees of the government's interception and monitoring service. The decision to offer £1,000 to every employee who repudiated his or her trade union carried two distinct (though related) offensive implications: trade union members could not be trusted to keep the state's secrets, and they were easily bought. Having implied on 25 January that trade unionists were potential subversives, it could not retreat and regroup on 12 March in the face of the miners' onslaught.

The National Union of Mineworkers talked about calling a national strike every time that a new pit closure programme was announced or rumoured. A ballot – called in March 1983, against Arthur Scargill's wishes – had failed to secure the majority necessary to legitimise a strike. In July 1984 a more subtle approach was tested. A conference resolution instructed the executive to hold a second ballot 'at the time deemed to be appropriate' if the Coal Board continued to close collieries and sack miners. On 1 March 1984, Ian MacGregor – the American 'downsizing' expert who had been appointed as NCB Chairman with the explicit instruction of ending all but the most profitable production – announced the closure of Cortonwood Colliery in South Yorkshire.

It was probably not his intention to provoke the conflict which followed. But, if he had chosen to look for trouble, he would not have behaved very differently. The NUM claimed that Cortonwood was, or could be made, profitable and the insistence that the colliery could be made economically viable (slightly undervalued by the repetition of the same assurance every time a closure was contemplated) was, for once, backed up by strong evidence. Miners from other 'uneconomic pits' had been transferred to Cortonwood with the promise of long-term employment. South Yorkshire was not only a 'militant' coal-field, it was also the home and power-base of Arthur Scargill. There was no doubt that the Cortonwood colliers would fight, and that the NUM President would lead them into battle.

The Cortonwood miners walked out within minutes of the closure announcement being made. Within an hour their colleagues all over the Yorkshire coal-fields had done the same. The strike was made 'official' by the regional executive when it met five days later. The

Scottish miners, with fellow feeling for their Yorkshire comrades and fearing imminent closures in their own region, called for a national strike. On 8 March, the miners' National Executive declared official 'proposed strike action in Yorkshire, Scotland and any other area which takes similar action'. It was not a national strike; that would have required a national ballot. But it was the next best (or worst) thing.

By the end of the month, 123 out of 174 pits were either on strike or closed by pickets from other collieries. Durham and Northumberland in the north-east and Kent in the south were the first regions to follow Yorkshire and Scotland. South Wales voted against industrial action, but pickets made sure that no coal was cut. In Nottingham – the coal-field which anticipated fewest closures – the vote was three to one in favour of working on. The regional executive was split over how best to respond to the clear will of its members. Flying pickets from outside the region descended on the Nottingham pits. But most of them continued in production. Nottingham – both the coal it cut and the damage it did to morale in a normally 'solid' union – played a crucial part in the miners' final defeat.

So did the new industrial relations laws. 'Flying pickets' – attempting to close pits outside their own region – were illegal under the 1980 industrial relations legislation. That did not prevent the militant miners driving from pit to pit. On 14 March, the National Coal Board won a High Court injunction which forbade further 'secondary picketing'. The flying pickets continued to dash from colliery to colliery – particularly in Wales, where there were fears that the majority view might prevail. In June the Welsh NUM was fined £50,000 for contempt of court. It refused to pay. In August its funds were sequestrated by the courts.

The sporadic violence that accompanied the strike undoubtedly did harm to the miners' cause – even though the first man to die was a 'flying picket' outside the Ollerton pit in Nottingham. The television pictures of jeering colliers, apparently attempting to intimidate the 'scabs' and 'blacklegs', offended the new middle classes far more than the newsreels and documentaries which revealed mounted police charging peaceful demonstrators. Arthur Scargill was photographed getting himself arrested and a striker was convicted of dropping a slab of concrete from a motorway bridge on to the passing car of a working miner. On one day in April, the police who were on duty in the Nottingham and Derbyshire coal-field – many of them drafted in from the south of England – arrested one hundred protesters, most of them miners and their wives. During a single May morning, forty-one police officers and twenty-eight picketing miners were injured during clashes outside the Orgreave coking plant in South Yorkshire.

There were negotiations of a sort. They almost always ended in greater bitterness than before they began. In May, Scargill walked out of his first talks with MacGregor, calling him 'a butcher sent to destroy the industry'. There were two more rounds of unsuccessful discussion in June and July. Just as it seemed some progress might be made, the meeting broke up over a disagreement about the definition of an exhausted pit. Neither side ever intended to compromise. In a fight to the death the result was always going to depend on which side could hold out the longest – the miners and their families, living on starvation strike pay, or the Coal Board and its customers, denied the coal they needed to stay in business.

The miners' union probably had no choice but to fight when the Cortonwood closure was announced. But it was a bad moment to begin a war of attrition. In April, Arthur Scargill had claimed that the Central Electricity Generating Board had only nine or ten weeks of coal supplies in stock and that British Steel had less than fourteen days. That was certainly a wild underestimate. More important, it gave no indication of the true strength – in reality, weakness – of the miners' position. For it assumed that new fuel supplies would not get through. Power stations switched from coal to oil, lorry-drivers – many of them freelance 'cowboys' specially recruited for the task – ran the pickets' blockade and, crucially, production continued in Nottingham from which the NUM was virtually expelled and replaced by the Union of Democratic Mineworkers.

Scargill himself must take much of the blame for allowing his enemies to open up a second front in Nottingham. On 12 April he had vetoed proposals for a national strike ballot on the disingenuous grounds that it was unnecessary. His private explanation was more convincing. He could see no reason why Nottinghamshire miners – where wages were high and pit closures were unlikely – should be given the chance 'to vote away other men's jobs'. The NUM rules had been changed so that a national strike became official if the ballot result showed 55 per cent of the votes in favour of industrial action. But, even so, a strike call might not have been endorsed. Wales was against – albeit by a small majority. A massive 'no' vote in Nottingham could have resulted in the whole union lamely watching pit closures in Yorkshire, Scotland and the north-east. A nationwide ballot was, however, the miners' only hope. The denial of a democratic decision was the excuse on which Nottingham built its refusal to support the other regions. The hope that their pits could be closed by moral (and sometimes physical) pressure from the striking coal-fields was always vain.

There were moments when it seemed that victory for the miners might be possible. The TUC was never willing to give the NUM the support for which Scargill asked, but in August NACODS (the pit deputies' union) voted by a massive 82 per cent for an all-out strike in protest of their members' pay being docked when they refused to cross picket-lines. A strike of deputies would have closed the whole industry. For without them at work, the safety regulations – enshrined in law for a hundred years – could not be observed. But despite the massive vote, the strike was half-hearted – not least because on the day when it was called 34,000 miners were back at work. The Nottingham numbers had been swollen by disillusioned and virtually starving strikers.

By November the number of working miners had virtually doubled. After a Christmas which was bitter for the strikers but not cold enough to increase the usual demand for coal, the NUM agreed to talks about holding talks. They broke down on the NCB's insistence that there must be a written undertaking to discuss pit closures. The collapse of the peace initiative, instead of provoking the anger that Arthur Scargill predicted, resulted in two thousand despairing strikers returning to work in a single day. From then on the government knew that it could dictate its own terms. By the end of February more than half the nation's miners were back down the pits. On 3 March 1985 a NUM delegate conference agreed, by 98 votes to 91, to return to work the following Tuesday – without asking the Coal Board for concessions, assurances or even promises of goodwill towards the returning strikers. At Cortonwood they marched back to work behind the colliery band to prove that they were beaten but not broken.

The pit strike had lasted for a year and cost the country at least £2.5 billion – much of the money spent on importing oil to replace the depleted coal stocks. The balance of payments deteriorated by an even larger figure, perhaps £3 billion, and the extra borrowing required to raise the increased public expenditure certainly contributed to the rise in the interest rates from 9.5 to 14 per cent. The Chancellor of the Exchequer told the House of Commons that winning the strike had been worth every penny of the extra cost.

Politically speaking, he was certainly right. The government – whatever was said about its ruthless brutality by its natural enemies – consolidated its reputation for the single-minded pursuit of its chosen goals. The public admires decisive politicians, even when it disagrees with their aims. The warrior-queen had won another spectacular victory, and there was little general sympathy for her defeated foe. It was only seven years since the Winter of Discontent, and the desire to see union power diminished was almost universal. And proof that a resolute government – reinforced by its own labour laws – could resist the demands of militant strikers, seemed like evidence that the nation was recovering its nerve as well as its prosperity. Once again Margaret Thatcher had made a wise choice of enemies. For once, sympathy for men who earned their living in the danger and dust of the coal-face was transcended by dislike for their leader and his bully-boys. The defeat of the miners was as much a triumph for the government's idea as for the government itself. Meanwhile, the unhappy Leader of the Opposition, who eighteen months before had been so eager to make a new start, was left bewildered and prematurely shop-soiled. He had neither condemned the largely imaginary picket-line violence nor denounced the very real denial of democracy. His silence was the product of sentimentality, not cowardice. Labour leaders do not (or did not in those days) criticise striking miners. So he was abused by the left for his failure to give the NUM his full support and held in contempt by the right for not attacking Arthur Scargill head-on. It seemed that fate was on the side of the Conservative party and that it was destined to rule Britain for ever.

9

THE FAMILY SILVER
Selling Out, Selling Off

———◆———

The miners' strike – with its televised confrontations between police and picket lines – was represented in those papers which stood for law and order as a terrible symptom of the way in which society was slowly descending into brutal anarchy. In fact, the previous four years had been marked by outbreaks of communal violence of a sort that Britain had never endured before. Most of the incidents were described as 'race riots', and were taken by the government as irrefutable justification for tightening the immigration regulations which had been drastically changed back in spring of 1980 – less than a year after the Thatcher government was elected. The husbands and wives of British citizens had never enjoyed an automatic right to enter the United Kingdom. But the new rules made their admission subject to a test which few of them passed. The 'primary purpose' rule was redefined to allow an immigration officer to decide whether an applicant's principal intention was reunion with a spouse or settlement in the UK. The law thus depended on the mind-reading abilities of a junior official who knew that the government did not expect the regulation to be applied with sentimental laxity. Dependent relatives were subject to a more rigorous test of dependency, and visitors were not allowed to convert short stays into permanent residence, even if they qualified for settlement. In January 1984, the government had decided that further limitations might well be needed.

The more restrictive policy was based on a new Nationality Act, which redefined British citizenship. Two of the categories – Citizens of British Dependent Territories and British Overseas Citizens – enjoyed virtually no rights except the privilege of a passport which bore the Royal Cipher on its cover. The definition of full British citizenship was, in one crucial particular, different from that which was laid down in the 1948 Act in response to the creation of an independent India and Pakistan. British citizenship was no longer the automatic and inalienable right of everyone who was born on British soil. The government insisted that the new definition was no threat to families lawfully resident in the United Kingdom. But its adverse effects on race relations were undeniable. Black and Asian Britons knew that it was they – visibly different from the majority of other nationals – who would face questions about the validity of their passports and whether or not their parents were 'normally and properly resident' in Britain at the time of their birth. And the idea that 'illegal immigration' was a serious problem was placed firmly both in the public's mind and on the political agenda. The temptation to attribute the problems of the inner cities to race rather than deprivation became almost irresistible. The best of the Tory Home Secretaries were benign and understanding about the 'problems' which the ethnic minorities caused; the worst were bellicose to the point of racialism. But good or bad, they all represented the multi-racial society as 'a problem'.

In the spring of 1980, nineteen police officers were injured in a disturbance which followed a raid on a drinking club in the St Paul's district of Bristol. The Home Secretary insisted that 'all the evidence suggests that it was not in any sense a race riot'. When, in April 1981, violence on a scale previously unknown in Britain broke out on the streets of Brixton, it seemed that the trouble had been caused by police action against the sale of drugs and alcohol. A total of 779 crimes were reported during the three days of mayhem. A hundred and fifty police officers were injured and more than two hundred arrests made. The local black community claimed that the police had been heavy-handed. Suggestions that poverty had bred alienation and despair were dismissed out of hand by the Prime Minister. When asked, in the House of Commons, if social conditions had ignited the Brixton explosion, she replied, 'If the Honourable Gentleman considers that unemployment was the only cause of the riots, I disagree with him. If he considers that it was the main cause of the riots, I disagree with him. Nothing which has happened with regards to unemployment would justify those riots.' The Home Secretary was, however, less certain of their origins. Lord Justice Scarman was invited to discover why they had happened and how a repetition could be avoided.

While Scarman deliberated, the riots spread. In June, five hundred youths rampaged through Peckham. In July, there was a battle on the streets of Southall between three hundred 'skinheads' and four hundred Asian youths. Forty police officers were injured. During the two weeks which followed there was rioting in Toxteth, Liverpool and Moss Side, Manchester. In thirty other towns – Birmingham, Leeds, Derby and Bradford among them – there was minor violence. Then it was Brixton again. When it was revealed that Merseyside police had dispersed the Toxteth crowd with CS gas, the Home Secretary supported them with the view that 'there was no alternative'. At the end of the month, when they changed their tactics and charged the crowd, a disabled man was hit by a police van and killed.

Despite the Prime Minister's tough talk, at least some gestures were made in the direction of the inner-city poor. Ministers descended on Liverpool with platitudes and promises, and £10 million was provided to redevelop the city's derelict dockland. When the Scarman Report was eventually published, it was openly critical of inner-city neglect and of the police's attitude towards both the decaying central areas and the black and Asian Britons who lived there. At least by implication he recommended 'affirmative action' (more robustly described as 'positive discrimination') to remedy the 'racial disadvantage' which had bred the resentment from which the riots grew. The immediate cause of the riots was, Lord Scarman wrote, 'a wholesale breakdown of trust between the authorities and the people' of Brixton. Community leaders and the police were, he believed, equally to blame. His proposals for improving life in the inner cities were largely ignored.

But his recommendations for efficiency – and accountability – of the police were implemented. Included among them were new, and more draconian, powers to stop and search anyone suspected of carrying an offensive weapon.

The extension of the police's powers to arrest, interrogate and obtain evidence – combined with increases in the severity of sentences – became the basis of the government's policy on 'law and order'. Crime prevention was largely ignored. The social causes of criminal behaviour were at best discounted and usually denied. To accept that poverty breeds despair and that despair encourages alienation from the laws that regulate a civilised society would have been a denial of the doctrine of individual responsibility which was at the heart of the government's philosophy. Deterrence was regarded as the only protection that society needed. And, as the crime rate inexorably increased year by year – instead of accepting that deterrence does not work – the Tory party (particularly at its annual autumn conference) bayed for more savage punishment. Right from the start of the Thatcher government – when a 'short sharp shock' was promised as the punishment for youth offenders – Conservative Home Secretaries, with varying degrees of reluctance, indulged the atavistic inclinations of the party activists. Gradually, the rejection of the claim that crime has social causes became an article of New Conservative faith – as important to the doctrine of individualism as the market economy and the extension of private property. Margaret Thatcher never lost faith in either notion. Indeed, the longer the government lasted, the more fervently she attempted to put them into practice.

The tough approach did not work. Occasional violence – regarded in the spring of 1984 as serious enough to require some Metropolitan police officers to be armed with automatic weapons permanently – became a feature of British life. What initially had been regarded as a purely urban problem gradually spread to the suburbs and the countryside. Then, in the late autumn of 1985, another outbreak of rioting spread across the country in a depressing reproduction of the contagious outbreaks of 1981.

The trouble began in Birmingham, where it was rightly attributed to drug-dealers trying to protect their patches from predatory competitors and a new Chief Constable. In Brixton, a month later, the rampage followed the injury of a black woman during a police raid on the house in which she lived. Shops were set on fire and looted. The police made more than two hundred arrests. Within a week, the trouble had spread first to Toxteth and Peckham and then to Tottenham's Broadwater Estate, where PC Keith Blakelock was brutally murdered and more than two hundred of his colleagues injured.

The hard truth was that a sub-stratum of violence had begun to undermine the historic tranquillity of British life. For the rest of the century, Britain was destined to agonise about its causes. Powellites, recalling the 'rivers of blood' speech of 1968, attributed the trouble to racial tension. A more plausible explanation was provided by the Church of England's report, *Faith in the City*, 'a call for action by Church and Nation' to hold back the 'social disintegration of many inner-city areas as the successful move out to middle Britain'. But one vein of violence had no obvious social cause. A new (or at least previously dormant) section of society – usually male and most often young – appeared to enjoy violence for violence's sake. Some blamed their conduct on original sin. Others said that American television had taught them that it was glamorous to murder and maim, and that the breakdown of the traditional family unit had left them without moral roots. Whatever their motivation, these young men insinuated themselves into occasions and activities which, without them, might well have been peaceful protests and pleasures. They erupted at the football match between Birmingham City and Leeds United in May 1985 and killed a man during their tribal wars. They went with Liverpool supporters to the 1985 European Cup Final in Brussels' Heysel Stadium and instigated a pitched battle which left thirty-nine Italian and Belgian football fans dead and three hundred and fifty injured. It is still not clear if it was mindless violence, police incompetence or simply fate which combined to cause the death of ninety-six Liverpool supporters at the Hillsborough FA Cup semi-final in 1989. But it prompted immediate and urgent action. Lord Justice Taylor – soon to become Lord Chief Justice – enquired into football ground safety. His report recommended all matches in the

First Division (soon to become the Premiership) should be played in all-seater stadiums. The Prime Minister who promised small government and less public intrusion into private lives legislated to make football spectators sit down during matches. Lord Taylor's proposals rescued the government from the idea that attendance at matches should be limited to 'members' of the club, but it did achieve Margaret Thatcher's ambition of 'changing the culture of football'. New stadiums combined with higher prices to make it a middle-class game.

It will never be possible accurately to explain why a wave of violence swept across Britain in the 1970s and '80s and why it subsided as mysteriously as it arose. But one thing is certain. In some terrifying way it was the product – perhaps the excrescence – of the new creed which was thought to guarantee economic success. The men who went out looking for trouble rejoiced in their self-reliant individualism. They were part of a society which had turned its back on community values.

By 1984, the drive towards New Conservatism – glorifying individualism and repudiating the politics of consensus as well as the economics of state intervention – had begun to pick up speed. The principles on which it had been founded – small government and low taxes – had been set out in the Tory party's 1979 election manifesto and tentatively implemented in the Thatcher government's first budget. It achieved its apotheosis during the 1987 General Election campaign, when Margaret Thatcher proclaimed, with absolute confidence, the doctrine of self-help and competitive efficiency which she had almost convinced the country was the real path to salvation. There was, in the middle of the campaign, one electrifying moment which crystallised the strength with which she held her convictions and the degree to which her certainty had suffused the nation. It was discovered that the Prime Minister had suffered from Dupuytren's syndrome: a hardening of the tendons which results in the little finger being pulled into the palm of the hand. The necessary surgery had been performed, not by a Health Service doctor, but by a private consultant. Ironically, she had once told the Tory conference that the Health Service was safe in her hands; the question for the General

Election press conference was why were her hands not safe in the Health Service. Instead of prevaricating, blustering or temporising, as the assembled journalists hoped she would, she replied in the language of free market capitalism. Private medical insurance 'enables me to go into hospital on the day that I want, at the time I want and with the doctor I want'. The implication that since she was spending her own money she had every right to make those choices was clear even to the political correspondents. Margaret Thatcher had become conviction politics made flesh.

During the 1979 Parliament, the government had chosen to attack soft targets. It had chosen to privatise those industries which were obviously part of the commercial economies: companies which were (before government help) on the point of extinction or subsidiaries of the public utilities which were nationalised as part of a package. Among them were British Aerospace, Ferranti, Cable & Wireless, Rolls-Royce and British Rail Hotels. British Leyland (which had been 'rescued' by the Industrial Development Corporation) was prepared for denationalisation by the injection of the million pounds of taxpayers' money which was needed to make it attractive to potential investors. The payment was justified, effectively if not entirely logically, by comparing it with the annual subsidy of half a million pounds that was paid to British Coal and the £900,000 that was received by British Steel. During Mrs Thatcher's first Parliament, only the introduction, in 1982, of the legislation which prepared the way for the sale of the British National Oil Corporation was the sort of privatisation of which the free market devotees dreamed. Until then, the private sector had reclaimed its lost ground by management buy-outs and straight commercial sales. The real privatisation programme was built on the flotation of new public companies and the consequent creation of a property-owning democracy.

When, back in 1976, a Labour Chancellor had first hit upon the notion of selling BP shares to help meet the borrowing target set by the IMF, he had introduced the idea to his Cabinet colleagues as a 'ripping wheeze'. His Tory successor described the continuation of the policy in different language. Privatisation was 'an essential part of the long-term programme for promoting the widest possible participation of the people in British industry'. When the major sales were made, the government attempted to ensure that 'the people' (as distinct from the financial institutions) would acquire the new equity. Some of the shares were sold off in small blocks and prospective purchasers were limited by law to the acquisition of a single tranche. A Tory MP, who had bought several blocks of shares under an assumed name, was convicted of fraud and sent to prison. The hope of creating a property-owning democracy was not entirely fulfilled. Much of the new equity was transferred to the ownership of pension funds and insurance companies when the 'small investors' sold their holdings at a substantial profit.

As each new item of privatisation was either initiated or implemented, the party battle took on the same depressing ritualistic form. Labour accused the Conservatives of feathering their friends' nests. Tories then claimed that socialists have a doctrinaire antagonism to free enterprise and a pathological aversion to the commercial and industrial success that the market guarantees. What was more, and worse, because they were in the pockets of the trade unions Labour supported the interests of the producers, not the consumers who ought to guide the market. When, as was invariably the case, the flotation was oversubscribed, the Opposition insisted that a precious national asset had been sold at a price which was well below its real value. The government countered with the claim that the demand for shares confirmed the success of the operation. The continuous crossfire of allegations and counter-allegations left no time or energy for serious discussion of public ownership – its benefits, detriments and the sectors of the economy in which it was appropriate or wholly unsuitable. The Conservatives had a single idea – the market. They repeated their mantra with the unquestioning faith of a primitive religion. Labour, on the other hand, had no ideas at all.

So the privatisation programme surged on at an accelerating pace, with little or no intellectual challenge to the view that the utilities should, as a matter of self-evident principle, be privately owned – even when, because of their nature, they could not be subject to the rigours of true competition. In July 1984, Sealink (the cross-Channel ferry company) was sold to a Bermuda-registered shipping line. Four months later, 51 per cent of British Telecom was sold with the promise that the rest would soon be on the market. The year ended with the announcement that the Trustee Savings Bank would be on sale during early 1985.

From then on, the drive to privatise was unremitting – or at least it seemed to be so as, week after week, there was another announcement of future intentions, the introduction of another enabling Bill, the television advertisements which promoted each flotation and the eventual sale itself. Within a single week in April 1985, the government gave notice that it would sell its remaining 48.8 per cent holding in Britoil and that it intended to introduce the legislation necessary for the sale of the British Gas Corporation. Labour naturally claimed that the rush to sell was the product of panic, the reaction of a near-bankrupt government which, in the words of Harold Macmillan, was forced 'to sell the family silver' in order to pay its mounting debts – principal among them the cost of social security, which continued to escalate as a direct result of unremitting increases in unemployment. In truth, the Conservatives bounded helter-skelter onward because of their childish belief that it was impossible to have too much of a good thing – acting with such ill-considered haste in the case of British Leyland that the first initiative was found to be illegal. As always in politics, conviction was contagious. Because the government believed so passionately in privatisation, the public came to believe in it as well.

The number of shareholders in the United Kingdom rose from three million in 1979 to nine million in 1987 – an immense increase, but not quite the distribution of equity of which the government boasted. A million applicants for shares in British Telecom had never owned shares before. But, three years after the flotation, only 40 per cent of the original shareholders still owned a stake in the new company. The pattern of British Airways ownership changed even more quickly. After only six months, 35 per cent of the original shareholders had sold out.

That, the government insisted, was all part of the free market process by which the economy would be stimulated into greater efficiency. Overall regulation was to be left to control of the money

supply – a remedy in which the government believed with such conviction that whenever it proved not to work, they changed the way in
which the money supply was defined. The City was to be 'deregulated' – stockbrokers allowed to become underwriters, building
societies encouraged to become banks, and banks persuaded to turn
themselves into estate agents and building societies – in one 'Big
Bang'. The 'welfare state' was, for the first time, denounced as morally
debilitating as well as insatiably expensive. Competition – which
Harold Macmillan had not even regarded as the appropriate economic model for the public utilities – was exalted as a sure remedy for
inefficiency in education and the Health Service. The privatisation
programme was a crucial element in the liberation of the economy.
The speed with which it accelerated as the 1980s came to an end was
illustrated by Margaret Thatcher in the House of Commons on 10
February 1986: she boasted that, since 1979, twelve major companies
(20 per cent of the state commercial sector) had been sold into private
ownership – and another 20 per cent would be added to the total
before the 1987 General Election. The Prime Minister was as good as
her word: receipts from privatisation increased from £500,000 in
1983–84 to £7 billion in 1988–89. The BP sale alone (spread over
four years) raised £8 billion. By 1987, total receipts were £25 billion.
A million jobs had moved from the public to the private sector.

The pressure was kept up. The Bill which abolished the Airports
Authority (and vested its property in a government-nominated board
of directors whose job was to prepare the sale) was presented to
Parliament in January 1986. The White Paper setting out the way in
which the water undertakings would be privatised was published in
the following month. One and a half million TSB shares went on the
market in September. The four and a half million applicants for shares
in the bank were just the beginning of the rage to buy into the privatised utilities; in December, there were four million applications for
shares in British Gas.

The flotation of British Airways began in January 1987 and, after
almost a year's respite at least from the initiation of new privatisation
proposals, the government then announced its intention to sell the
electricity supply industry. British Steel was offered to the public in

November 1988. The enabling Bill making possible the privatisation of the water industry was approved by the House of Commons in July 1989, and the ten municipal water undertakings were offered for sale in the following November. The issue was oversubscribed by almost 600 per cent.

It would be comforting – and, in part, true – to claim that it was easy for the government to drive on with such an obviously popular initiative. But even when the policy seemed likely to founder, the Conservatives' resolution never faltered. In the autumn of 1987, £50 billion was wiped off the share values in a single day. The City – terrified of what might follow a 10 per cent fall in the total of all quoted prices – begged the government to postpone the last tranche of the British Petroleum flotation. The government refused. Margaret Thatcher's capacity for choosing the right enemies was balanced by a willingness to antagonise friends in what she regarded as a good cause. The best cause of all was the pursuit of the idea on which all the government's policy was built.

The idea, although pursued with passion, was not always implemented with absolute consistency. The Bill to abolish the Greater London Council, published in March 1985, was justified as a measure to make local government more immediate and therefore more representative. The end of the GLC (in March 1986) was marked with the promise that the individual London boroughs would be far more sensitive to the electors' wishes, and that, by making them the sole municipal authority, power was being passed back to the people. In the years that followed, that argument became more and more difficult to sustain as rights and responsibilities (which were historically delegated to town and county councils) were abrogated by central government. But in the heady days of high-Thatcherism, ministers really believed in decentralisation – particularly for those bureaucracies which boasted a virtually permanent Labour majority. The same paradox – confusion, contradiction or downright double standards – applied to the abolition of the Inner London Education Authority, announced during the summer of 1987. The intention (or so it was claimed) was to give the boroughs the right to run the sort of education system which they chose. The decisions were taken in the name of parent power, in fine disregard of the undoubted fact that an over-whelming majority of London parents wanted the ILEA to remain. The high hopes of local autonomy were eventually to be dashed by increasing central government domination, which began with the hurried imposition of the National Curriculum and ended with off-the-record briefings that a Conservative government might make education a wholly national, rather than a locally administered service. But in the early 1980s, the watchword was 'choice'. In education, 'choice' was the euphemism for competition – the sovereign remedy to every problem.

Choice, in education, said the gurus of the 'intellectual' right, was provided by vouchers – the allocation to each family of 'cheques' or 'credits' with which parents bought, for their children, a place at the school they preferred. Good schools would be over-subscribed and able to select the pupils which they preferred; bad schools would be publicly humiliated into improvement by the general knowledge that they had empty desks. In consequence, they would be shamed into improvement. Esteem would take the place of profit in stimulating greater efficiency. The market principle (with all its mystical benefits) would, in consequence, be introduced into education.

The theory of choice by voucher was not put into practice until the government used it – in an attenuated form – to provide 'universal nursery education' in 1993. Margaret Thatcher – ideologue as well as party leader and Prime Minister – would gladly have employed it to emancipate the parents of secondary-school pupils, but none of her advisers could tell her how the scheme would work. Would every pupil qualify for a voucher of equal value, or would recipients be means tested? Would each school place be equally priced? Would parents be able to supplement vouchers with additional fees in order to 'buy' a place in a 'better' school? And, perhaps most important of all, could individual schools effectively change themselves into educational supermarkets which, as well as competing for customers, took charge of their own accounts and made all the decisions which are required of an independent entrepreneur? Keith Joseph, the Secretary of State for Education and philosopher of the libertarian right, told the Conservative party conference that, although he was 'philosophically' in favour of vouchers, the idea was 'technically flawed'. Despite his intellectual pretensions, he had forgotten John Stuart Mill's judgement that, when a theory cannot be applied in practice, the theory is of no value. And there was a second question about voucher schemes which philosophers would wish to ask: how did it differ from the assertion, enshrined in the 1980 Education Act, that parents have an absolute right to choose the school at which their children are educated?

However, the idea of competitive education was destined to bubble on. During the next half-dozen years it was promoted – covertly rather than by open advocacy – through the publication of league tables by which the performance of secondary schools was measured, and the encouragement of 'grant-maintained schools' which, in theory, offered a superior product. Perhaps the greatest change in school governance was the introduction of 'local management', which obliged head teachers and school governors to balance individual budgets by making, and implementing, their own decisions about staffing levels and procurement policy. The ideologists mistimed the revolution. If the order of the reforms had been reversed – beginning with the local management of schools – the subsequent introduction of vouchers would certainly have been possible and, in the mood of the late 1980s, the voucher scheme would have certainly become a crucial feature of secondary education.

Local management was intended to separate the schools from the (usually Labour-controlled) education authorities and was, as a result, exalted as another victory for individuals over institutions. But the war against the over-powerful state was less easily waged on the battle-ground of social security. The principles still applied. Indeed, the state – which good Conservatives believed intruded intolerably into private lives and expropriated far too great a proportion of personal earnings – was at its most intrusive and most extravagant in the administration of what was euphemistically described as 'welfare'. If the frontiers of government were to be driven back, the retreat had to begin with social security policy. The urgent need was financial as well as ideological.

By 1985 – the high water-mark of Thatcherism – North Sea oil production had risen from its first-year production total of 38 million, to 122 million tons. The price per barrel had increased from $13.60 to $27.60. As a result, oil produced 5.8 per cent of GDP and provided 12.2 per cent of government revenue. It was as near to a gift from providence as anything that a government has ever received. Most of it was squandered on meeting the high cost of unemployment.

What was more, there were urgent problems which needed to be addressed in order to avoid an immediate breakdown. A major social security policy revision was unavoidable. It provided a heaven-sent opportunity to impose New Conservative philosophy on what even old Conservatives regarded as the most revanchist of all government departments. Two social security reviews were launched. One examined the problem of early withdrawal from occupational pension schemes, and the ways in which the government could encourage the development of personal 'portable' pensions – two issues which (as well as being close to the hearts and wallets of the middle classes) offered much scope for the promotion of individual self-reliance and 'citizens' capitalism'. Before the review was fully under way, the future of the State Earnings Related Pension Scheme (SERPS) was added to its agenda. It was claimed – falsely, as it now seems – that by the year 2100, the ratio of national insurance contributors to pensioners entitled to receive SERPS would be 1.8:1, compared to 2.3:1 when the scheme was inaugurated. In fact, the re-examination of the pension supplement was largely prompted by ideological considerations. In the view of Thatcherites, it was the state's job to provide a basic pension as a safety net. Individuals should use their own initiative to augment it, if they chose (and could afford) to do so.

The second review ploughed over more familiar ground: supplementing benefits and assistance for low-income families with children. The most urgent part of its task concerned 'the rent rebate scheme' – a system of subsidising the housing costs of low-income families which, because of its complication, was taken up by only half of the potential recipients. Rent rebates – according to The Times, 'the biggest welfare fiasco in the history of the welfare state' – provided the worst example of a general problem. In 1980, the new government, convinced that bleeding-heart social workers would invariably be over-generous, had abolished the system of discretionary grants by which the sick, the old and the unemployed received (on the judgement of a DHSS officer) extra payments for fuel, special diet, essential furniture or necessary clothing. The discretionary grants were replaced by rules – rigid criteria against which the requests for assistance were measured. According to the Policy Studies Institute, the rules were too complicated for either the claimants or the DHSS officers fully to understand. The results were, for a civilised society, horrific. Three-fifths of adults on benefit lacked the basic necessities for minimum comfort – a warm coat, a change of shoes, essential underwear. Half were in debt – usually to the local gas or electricity boards. Almost as many ran out of money before the end of most weeks – not as a result of incompetence or extravagance but 'because of the routine expenses of normal living'. Even the payments which were the recipient's right, and should have been made automatically, were not taken up. Three-quarters of families entitled to receive extra payments did not understand the system which was supposed to help them; half the eligible families did not even know that the extra payments scheme existed.

Yet it was not the neglect of the poor which stimulated the government into urgent action. The mid-1980s – as well as being the age of market conservatism – was the era of law centres and advice bureaux. All over the country, and particularly within the decaying inner cities, professional social workers and concerned volunteers began to advise and persuade potential claimants to exercise their rights. Forms, filled in by eager activists in derelict high-street shops, were signed by grateful applicants who were not sure how or why the money would come their way. The government believed that if all the poor were to exercise their rights under the 1980s legislation, the cost of social security would be higher than the nation could afford. The 1980 benefits had been designed to be taken up only in part. Since there was a real danger that the poor would be encouraged to claim all the benefits to which they were entitled under the scheme, the scheme had to be changed.

The change was built around a new name. Supplementary Benefit became Income Support, and the formula on which it was based provided increased assistance to families with children, but reduced the help available to childless couples, the unemployed and the under-25s. Family Income Supplement was replaced with Family Credits. And a single means-test formula was used to determine the eligibility of all classes of claimant. The same principle – less generous but more easily understood and implemented – was applied to the revision of housing benefits. The government claimed that it had saved money without creating hardship and, at the same time, by concentrating extra help on families rather than individuals, had begun to open up a gap between welfare and work.

The gulf between rich and poor was certainly widened. The mandatory special-need grants which had replaced the discretionary payments had, because of a claimants' campaign, themselves become too expensive. They were, therefore, replaced with discretionary loans from what was called the Social Fund. Families who needed (but could not afford) warm winter clothing, basic furniture and a change of bedding were required to borrow money from the government – assuming that the government thought that their need was great enough to qualify under the scheme. The fund was kept to manageable limits by the natural reluctance of the very poor to mortgage their meagre future incomes. And in order to protect public funds from a sudden reckless demand for second-hand top coats and water-tight shoes, the Treasury invented an absolute safeguard against the profligacy of the poor: a specific sum was allocated to the Social Fund each year. After it had been exhausted, there were no more loans – no matter how desperate the deprivation.

SERPS, however, survived, albeit in an attenuated form. For SERPS investors and recipients were – unlike the very poor – target voters, the sort of people who make and break governments at General Elections. Receipts, instead of being based on 25 per cent of earnings during the best twenty working years, were to be calculated on 20 per cent of lifetime income. Only half, rather than all, the pension was passed on to widows, and there were generous tax incentives to contract out of the scheme. The result, at least according to the forecasts, was a 50 per cent cut in the cost of the scheme from £25 billion to £13 billion in 2033. By 1993 half a million men and women had opted out of SERPS – many of them were making a short-term and short-sighted decision for the second time in half a dozen years. They had left safe and generous occupational pension schemes and joined highly unreliable private alternatives which the government's deregulation policy had allowed high-pressure salesmen to persuade them to take out. Like the mortgage-holders with negative equity a decade later, they were numbered among the victims of the competitive society.

Health Service reforms began with new regulations which were prosaically consistent with the government's philosophy. Contracts for cleaning, catering and laundry services were to be put out to open tender, so that the breeze (if not the full blast) of competition could improve the efficiency of the nation's hospitals. Roy Griffiths, an expert in the marketing of retail groceries, was invited to examine what the government believed to be a surplus of manpower. Griffiths, a Health Service enthusiast, judged that the problem was not so much labour as management. His incisive report, and his subsequent appointment as health-care adviser to the Prime Minister, marked one of the great turning-points in NHS history. Thanks to him, the government was utterly convinced that, sooner or later, there would have to be another major reorganisation. The next shake-up would have to involve not boundaries, duties and names but the fundamentals of organisation and control.

In fact, the government was edging towards its fundamental reform – the introduction of cure-all competition into both the family doctor and the hospital service. And it was moving towards its goal in characteristic style, neither consulting nor attempting to placate the doctors and nurses whose lives would be changed by the revolution. A Green Paper – utterly opposed by the British Medical Association – proposed a 'good practice allowance' for GPs who innovated and modernised, and a system of patient registration which made it easier to change doctor. At the same time, a larger share of family doctors' income was to come from capitation fees, and payments for specific services (inoculation and immunisation) were to be introduced. The BMA condemned the whole document as 'containing proposals which, if implemented, could undermine the whole basis' of the

Health Service: they meant the introduction of market forces into the provision of a service which should not be governed by supply and demand. The Green Paper was quietly forgotten, but its principles took root. The 'policy advisers', lurking in the back rooms of Downing Street, were not to be denied. After the Green Paper, it was only a matter of time before competition came to the Health Service. The problem of community care was to be solved in an equally ideological but more practical way: the title of the service was changed and the cost reduced. 'Care in the Community' sounded like a less institutional (and therefore more humane) way of helping the incurably dependent. The phrase created a mental picture of contented pensioners sitting in peace and comfort by their family hearths. However, the problem was that the community did not or could not care enough. There were not enough welcoming homes to accommodate the chronically sick, particularly those who suffered from psychological disorders, so derelicts of every sort sat lonely and neglected in public places. But public expenditure was cut.

While Margaret Thatcher was mounting what she believed to be a social and economic revolution, Her Majesty's Opposition was engaged on other business. Of course, it observed the rituals of Supply Day debates, Prime Minister's Question Time and ten o'clock divisions. Its principal spokesmen even occasionally made speeches in the country. But the Labour Party's real concern in the 1980s was the Labour Party. The problem was not only the Liberal–SDP Alliance. Labour was being infiltrated from the wilder shores of politics. Members of single-issue pressure groups – Greens, gays and pacifists – were not difficult to accommodate. They were accepted in a doomed attempt to initiate the 'rainbow coalition' which had done so much damage to the American Democrats during the years when George McGovern and his ideas dominated that party. Most of the pressure groups' ideas were absorbed into party policy – producing, in the 1983 election manifesto, 'the longest suicide note in history' – without much evidence of ideological indigestion. The problem was not the new recruits who joined up to promote specific causes such as animal rights, permissive abortion laws and female emancipation, it was the political parasites who posed the real problems. By sucking the party's blood, they sapped its vitality and, because it was obvious that they had infected the body politic, made it far too unattractive ever to be elected to office.

Not all the extremist organisations attempted to burrow their way into the Labour Party. The International Marxists and the Socialist Workers chose to remain fiercely independent. Sometimes they took over Labour rallies and demonstrations, pushing their way to the televised front in order to display their trademark banners. On other occasions they attempted to disrupt, or even destroy, a march or meeting by either provoking violence or reacting to threats and abuse of their far-right counterparts. But their attempts to impose their brand of socialism on society were outrageously public. It was the Trotskyite Militant tendency which attempted to subvert by stealth and, for a while, had immense success in its efforts to infiltrate the Labour Party.

Militant's attempt to organise 'a party within a party' began sometime during the 1970s. By the middle of the decade, Reg Underhill, Labour's National Agent, had compiled a report which described in formidable detail the way in which the infiltrations worked. Paid agents were organising (or attempting to organise) subversive cells in every constituency. Their efforts were financed by devotees who donated part of their wages to the cause, and their ideas were promoted by the newspaper – itself called *Militant* – which believers sold on street corners at weekends. Militant was formidable not so much because of its numbers as because of the absolute commitment of its adherents. At a moment when Labour was riddled with self-doubt, it was undermined – in some places taken over – by a faction which was absolutely certain about the truth of its philosophy and the necessity of its programme. Faced by such a formidable enemy, the Labour leadership of the 1970s (with the notable exception of Jim Callaghan himself) had been stunned into inactivity. After the 1979 defeat, when Michael Foot assumed command, inertia was elevated into a democratic virtue.

Foot could not or would not believe that anyone who was happy to be called a 'socialist' should be excluded from the party. It was an honourable enough attitude, based on a liberal distaste for what, in the *argot* of the time, came to be called 'witch-hunts'. The legitimate left took up the chorus: nobody should be expelled, and no organisation should be proscribed on the evidence of ideas and ideology. No enemies to the left! Whatever the libertarian merits of that cry, it represented what was – at least for a party which still aspired to government – a disastrous abdication of philosophical duty.

Fortunately for Labour's reputation, by the end of 1981, Michael Foot was persuaded that Militant's conduct warranted investigation. But he was still not prepared to judge them on the policy of promoting Trotsky's hope of achieving 'continuous revolution'. But, splitting the thinnest of conscientious hairs, he was prepared to condemn, if proven, the organisation of 'a party within a party'. That was already an offence against the Labour constitution. A week before Christmas 1981, the Labour Party National Executive agreed to inquire into the activities of the Militant tendency. Six months later, the report concluded that Militant was a 'well-organised caucus, centrally controlled, operating within the Labour Party'. Nothing daunted, Militant continued to organise. Indeed it was so blatant in its attempts to subvert Labour that, by February 1983, even the hesitant National Executive Committee was prepared to take decisive if belated action. Five members of the *Militant* editorial board were expelled from the party.

Militant continued to flourish. It was particularly successful in Liverpool, where Derek Hatton – the most flamboyant of Militant sympathisers – became deputy leader (and effectively leader) of the City Council. In 1983, two constant participants in Militant campaigns were elected to Parliament. It was the Liverpool Trotskyites who did the Labour Party's reputation most damage. All over the country, Labour councillors were agonising about how to react to the government's assumption of powers which had historically been exercised by local government. Liverpool chose what the city described as resistance rather than surrender. Unfortunately, the casualties were not in the government but on Merseyside.

Disputes continue about Militant's popularity within Liverpool itself. They still get credit for an exemplary house-building record, for example, but they are also condemned for totalitarian excesses – the creation of a security force which acted as a private army, the appointment of often unqualified supporters to key city jobs, and the absolute refusal to countenance policies which conflicted with their Trotskyite prejudices. Liverpool's famously progressive churchmen (Roman Catholic Archbishop Warlock and the Church of England's Bishop David Shephard) publicly condemned the persecution of working families' attempts to create a housing association and the insistence that only the council could provide low-rented accommodation.

For two years the government tightened the screw, until county and city councils were required by law to set a rate within the limits stipulated by Whitehall. As the tension between local and national government grew, the National Executive of the Labour Party pleaded for reason and offered to conciliate. The Liverpool council's response (to Neil Kinnock no less than Margaret Thatcher) was outright defiance. Starved of an adequate government grant, it would (they claimed) be unreasonable to levy a rate of any size. Instead they chose to test the government's nerve. They were prepared to watch the City of Liverpool slump into bankruptcy. They gambled on the Tory Cabinet – which they claimed to despise – acting with more concern for the welfare of Liverpudlians.

There is still argument about whether what followed was bluff or capitulation. Faced with literal bankruptcy, the Liverpool City Council began to sack staff. An accountant would have warned that, at least in the short term, it cost rather than saved money, for there would have been vast compensation bills to meet. So it may well be that the redundancy notices were just for show. But whatever the reason that motivated the policy, by preparing to add thousands of workers to the Merseyside dole queue, the Militant majority gave Neil Kinnock the opportunity to destroy them.

The Labour 'movement' – party and trade unions – was prepared to watch while (during the 1978–79 'Winter of Discontent') Trotskyite grave-diggers refused to bury the dead. It was willing to see the Corporation jobs reserved for unqualified supporters of the ruling caucus. It chose to do no more than express its disapproval when the law, requiring a rate to be set and municipal bills to be paid, was openly flouted. But sacking good trade unionists was going too far. In his speech to the party conference at Bournemouth, the Labour leader struck the lethal blow:

I'll tell you what happens with impossible promises. You start with far-fetched resolutions. They are then pickled into a rigid dogma, a code, and you go through the years sticking to that, out-dated, mis-placed, irrelevant to the real needs, and you end in the grotesque chaos of a Labour council hiring taxis to scuttle round a city hand-ing out redundancy notices to its own workers. I am telling you, no matter how entertaining, how fulfilling to short-term egos – you can't play politics with people's jobs and with people's services or with their homes. Comrades, the voice of the people – not the people here; the voice of the real people with real needs – is louder than all the boos that can be assembled. Understand that, please, comrades. In your socialism, in your commitment to those people, understand it. The people will not, cannot, abide posturing. They cannot respect the gesture-generals or the tendency-tacticians.

The spell was broken. There were still party members who believed that there were 'no enemies to the left', but majority opinion was in favour of cleaning out Liverpool.

The process, such as it was, took a full year. Militant – despite its professional contempt for 'Tory laws' and 'capitalist courts' – fought a legal battle against its supporters' exclusion from the party. Labour's constitution (written in a less litigious age, as a friendly agreement to describe the shared beliefs of comrades and friends) was interpreted as requiring (in the name of natural justice) the full National Executive to consider every proposed expulsion individually and then make a recommendation for endorsement or rejection by the annual confer-ence. So, day after day, the party leadership met in semi-judicial state, heard the charges of 'forming a party within a party', listened to the defence, weighed the evidence and came to a considered judgement on what to recommend. Because of time, it was impossible to do more than examine the conduct of the Liverpool Militant leadership. 'Members' – Militant insisted that they were only readers of the news-paper – were left to cause continued but unco-ordinated disruption in individual trade union branches and ward parties.

The 'purge' was a highly successful as well as urgently necessary operation, but it contributed to Labour's reputation as a party on the fringe of politics. It was, of course, applauded by the general public and given a qualified welcome by the press, who thought that it did not go far enough. But it also helped to create the impression that Labour was in a political backwater, far removed from the mainstream of issues which affected the nation's health and prosperity. While the government was wrestling with the level of public borrowing, promising to cut taxes, reorganising the Health Service and creating a share-owning democracy, the Opposition was taking evidence from unknown Liverpudlians – one of them a young woman of nineteen – about the meetings they had attended during the last two years and the articles they had written for a journal which was not available on any news-stands. And that was not the only problem which the assault on Militant created. In one other crucial respect, it did even more profound damage to the Labour Party. In those days, the leadership subscribed to the doctrine of 'only so much' – the notion that the rank and file could only be pushed a limited distance. As a result, essential policy changes were postponed or abandoned. In the constituencies – disheartened by both the Tories' continued popularity and Labour's apparently wilful impotence – the feeling began to develop that somehow 'we' ought to become more like 'them'. But the urge to remain a party of the left persisted. The result was that fashionable radicals took increasing refuge in what they hoped was 'penalty-free socialism'.

The talk around dinner tables was of policies which were united by one common feature. They cost, or were believed to cost, nothing. In consequence, they could be implemented without setting off a chain reaction which started with higher levels of public expenditure and ended with increased taxes and certain election defeat for the party which proposed them. All the policies were good in themselves, though, for a genuine socialist party, they could not take the place of a drive towards redistribution of power and wealth. Candidates for inclusion in the miraculous manifesto included homosexual law reform, women's rights, environmental protection (in so far as it could be achieved by prohibiting the use of aerosol sprays rather than by introducing a pollution tax), revisions in the electoral system, embargoes on arms sales to Chile, the incorporation of the European

Convention on Human Rights into British law, sanctions against the apartheid regime in South Africa, a freedom of information act, the banning of circuses and blood sports and unilateral nuclear disarmament. And the greatest of these was unilateral nuclear disarmament.

The unilateralist cause had been given a major boost by the announcement in June 1980 that American-owned ground-based Cruise missiles were to be located in United States Air Force bases at Greenham Common in Berkshire and Molesworth in Cambridgeshire. In September that year, sixty thousand marchers took part in Britain's biggest anti-nuclear demonstration for twenty years. Michael Foot, a founder-member of CND, became leader of the Labour Party in November of that year and the 'Gang of Four' included Labour's dubious defence policy in their list of reasons for founding the SDP. As always, the government inflamed its critics by brushing their arguments aside with what sounded like contempt. The Prime Minister described the nuclear protestations as exhibiting a 'disagreeable streak of anti-Americanism', and in March 1982 her Defence Secretary illustrated quite the opposite attitude by announcing that Britain was going to buy US Trident II ballistic missiles. Inevitably, the protests concentrated on and around the nuclear base at Greenham Common. In December 1982, twenty thousand women had encircled the perimeter wire and clasped hands in a gesture of peace and friendship. From then on the anti-nuclear demonstrations – not all of them so pacific – became a regular feature of Berkshire life. In April 1983 CND supporters had again joined hands – that time in a fourteen-mile human chain that linked Greenham to Aldermaston and Burghfield, the two nuclear research stations. Two months later, the police arrested 752 protesters during a four-day vigil outside the Upper Heyford USAF base.

Fears of nuclear annihilation were not allayed by President Reagan's announcement that his Strategic Defence Initiative – 'star wars' – would create a shield across America which would protect it from nuclear attack. His claim that the system was purely defensive and would render nuclear weapons 'impotent and obsolete' were hugely unconvincing to anyone who understood the theory of deterrence. If the boasts were justified, the nuclear balance would be totally destroyed by the creation of one wholly invulnerable participant in the Cold War. The Soviet Union might choose to strike before the United States defences became impregnable, or America might attack Russia from behind the safety of its screen. Most likely, in the opinion of CND, some terrible mistake would happen. To them, every technological advance increased the risk of holocaust by error.

Labour fought the General Election of 1983 on the policy of nuclear disarmament – part of its manifesto which helped to guarantee humiliating defeat. Neil Kinnock, elected leader on the promise that defence policy would not change, confirmed his commitment in the month when he became Leader of the Opposition. On 22 October 1983, a CND demonstration in London attracted a crowd which was variously estimated at 250,000 and 400,000 protesters. Before it spilled out of Hyde Park and halted London traffic for two hours, Neil Kinnock told the rally, 'This is the movement for life.'

It was a movement which, in keeping with the spirit of the time, grew increasingly violent. Three hundred demonstrators – mostly women – were arrested *en masse* as they attempted to force their way into Parliament as a protest against the arrival of Tomahawk missiles at Greenham Common. But, already, although few people noticed it at the time, the international mood was changing. The Soviet system was – in the words which Karl Marx used to predict the demise of a more enduring economic order – collapsing under the weight of its own contradictions. By 1985, when Mikhail Gorbachev – a professional Communist administrator with no record of liberalism or reform – became General Secretary of the party, the empire which was run and ruled from Moscow was already doomed. But Gorbachev – at fifty-four the youngest member of the Politburo – accelerated the process. In November he met President Reagan in Geneva for discussions which ended with the promise of mutual arms reductions. The aim was a cut of 50 per cent in both nuclear arsenals and an eventual agreement on the deployment of medium-range missiles. Gorbachev told the press conference which followed the meeting that the world had become a safer place. In January 1986

Gorbachev talked – wildly, the West believed – of eliminating all nuclear arms by the end of the century.

The thaw continued and the improved temperature was confirmed by Gorbachev's domestic policy. In his speech to the 27th Communist Party Congress he attacked the country's bureaucracy and admitted that his predecessors had been responsible for 'years of economic stagnation'. It was, despite the lip service paid to 'socialist self-criticism', the first occasion in which a Soviet leader had admitted failures in the system. The hope of real relaxation was encouraged by the eventual admission that the explosion of the nuclear reactor at Chernobyl in April 1986 had exposed much of the surrounding area to high levels of radiation – an almost unique example of open Communist government. The path to permanent peace was temporarily blocked when, in the autumn of 1986, arms control talks in Reykjavik ended without agreement after President Reagan refused to abandon his SDI ('star wars') programme. But Gorbachev continued to initiate domestic reforms. Two days before Christmas 1986, Andrei Sakharov, the leading Soviet dissident, was released from gaol. A month later he made his frontal assault on the repression which had characterised half a century of Soviet Communism. The Communist Party itself – indistinguishable from the apparatus of the state – was told to accept 'greater control from below' and embrace genuine democracy. Two Russian concepts, *perestroika* (reconstruction) and *glasnost* (openness), were discussed with varying degrees of scepticism in the British newspapers.

British politicians were, in general, reluctant to accept that the world had changed. The Foreign Office, seeing advantage in the global stability which two equally balanced power-blocs provided, were slow to recommend a major shift in Britain's international policy. Labour fought the 1987 General Election on an old-fashioned policy of unilateral nuclear disarmament which was unrelated to the modern realities of defence and détente. The government – which regarded its nuclear capability as more of a status symbol than a deterrent – was reluctant to be forced into a change of strategy which might result in a reduction in its imaginary superpower status. And the British people loved the bomb. So, for one reason or another, British defence policy remained unchanged for more than a decade after the nuclear thaw began. By 1992, it was taken for granted that no party that could be accused of 'neutralism' or 'pacifism' could win a General Election. Labour became multi- rather than unilateral and in 1997 (with Nato deprived of its enemy) the two major parties were still united in their belief that Trident submarines were essential to the security of the United Kingdom.

If Britain was slow to understand or act upon the changes in the Soviet Union, both people and politicians remained pathetically anxious to detect signs of an easy resolution of the perpetual crisis in Northern Ireland. Throughout 1983 the murderous violence continued, but in January of the following year, Dr Garret Fitzgerald – the active and imaginative Taoiseach – proposed what he described as 'cooperative measures', designed to detach law-abiding Catholics from the IRA gunmen. Not surprisingly, Margaret Thatcher rejected both the suggestion that Gardaí from the Republic should patrol the nationalist areas of Belfast and Derry and the proposal that Irish judges should sit with Ulster justices in Belfast courts. But the British government put forward (as its alternative proposition) the idea of a Joint Security Commission. Encouraged by the hope that the Dublin government would repeal Articles 2 and 3 of the De Valera Constitution – and thus abandon its claim to sovereignty over the Six Counties – Britain looked forward to real progress towards a solution. But on 12 October 1984, an IRA bomb exploded in Brighton's Grand Hotel – the Tory party headquarters during the Conservatives' annual conference. Five delegates were killed. Had the bomb been planted only feet away from its hiding place, the Prime Minister and half the Cabinet would have been killed. The inevitable result was a temporary halt in even secret negotiations between London and Dublin. Margaret Thatcher was not prepared to risk the accusation of negotiating under duress.

The Taoiseach, without the constraints which limited the Prime Minister's manoeuvres, continued to press for a new initiative. At each meeting of the European Council he made new proposals for progress and confirmed that, although a change in the Irish Constitution was too difficult to consider, he was prepared publicly to agree that no change to Northern Ireland sovereignty could possibly come about without the consent of the people of the province – a guarantee that Ulster would remain in the Union for the foreseeable future. The result was the Anglo-Irish Agreement signed by the two heads of government on 15 November 1985.

Margaret Thatcher affected (and perhaps even felt) surprise at the reception with which the Agreement was greeted by 'loyalists'. The promise that the Union would only be dissolved after a majority of the province had expressed a wish to break the historic link was not sufficient guarantee of status to convince them that the policy was not a concession to the republicans. A general strike was called. The level of violence increased in loyalist areas. The Orange tactics were both indefensible and self-defeating, for they undermined the sympathy which the British public felt for patriots whose only wish was to remain subjects of the Queen. But their judgement was entirely correct. When the Agreement was published as a White Paper, the document was rightly described as having 'green edges' – not because (in the colour conventions of Westminster publications) its contents were not yet firm government policy, but because they represented a substantial step towards the 'all-Ireland solution' which Unionists feared. And Margaret Thatcher must have known it. But she clutched at the hope that it would accelerate progress towards the day when Northern Ireland was no longer a constant distraction from the serious business of building an enterprise economy.

The Agreement was built around the principle that London and Dublin should work together to bring peace to the North of Ireland – itself the concession that the Republic had a legitimate claim to be involved in the future of the province. Meetings of the Anglo-Irish Governmental Conference would consider proposals from both governments. Naturally enough, the Taoiseach placed greatest emphasis on 'confidence-building measures to end the alienation of the Catholic minority' while the Prime Minister insisted that 'the real question was whether the agreement would result in better security'. Both hopes were dashed. Garret Fitzgerald – who lost his majority in the Dáil – made claims about the Agreement's contribution to an 'all-Ireland solution' which (although they could not be justified by the text) infuriated loyalists in the province and Unionists at Westminster. When his government collapsed in March 1987, Charles Haughey's Fianna Fáil party was elected. Haughey had been a bitter critic of the Anglo-Irish Agreement. But still Margaret Thatcher clung to its generalities as the best hope of removing Northern Ireland from her agenda – even though the level of violence escalated to new heights of horror.

On Remembrance Day 1987, a bomb – planted close to the Cenotaph at Enniskillen – killed eleven and injured over sixty civilians. Worse horrors were to follow. On 6 March 1988 the SAS shot dead three Irish terrorists as they prepared to detonate a bomb in Gibraltar. No serious doubts remain about the terrorists' evil intentions, but it is still uncertain whether or not they could have been arrested rather than killed in the street. The three 'active service volunteers' were given martyrs' burials in Northern Ireland, and thousands of republicans crowded into the Milltown Cemetery for the burial. A 'loyalist' gunman opened fire on the mourners. Three were killed. As their funeral cortège passed through Belfast, two British army corporals – out of uniform and travelling on unrelated business in a private car – inadvertently crossed the procession's path. They were dragged from their vehicle, stripped and beaten to death. The bombing went on and on and was extended to mainland Britain. But the Prime Minister continued to insist that the Anglo-Irish Agreement was still the best hope of progress.

A few cynics convinced themselves that Margaret Thatcher was as anxious to dispose of Northern Ireland as she had been to disentangle herself from Rhodesia. It was even argued that just as her traditional support for Ian Smith and the whole minority had enabled her to impose majority rule upon them, her close association with the Unionists would allow her to insist that they conceded enough republican demands to guarantee a permanent end to the urban terrorism. But Margaret Thatcher did not make a habit of encouraging her friends to see sense or – as white Rhodesians and Ulster Unionists might have put it – selling them out.

Margaret Thatcher was the only senior minister in the Heath government to visit South Africa. And, in government, the Prime

Minister left no doubt about where her sympathies lay. She was the last leader of a democratic Western nation to accept that there could be no compromise with apartheid and, on 2 June 1984, President P. W. Botha became the first South African leader to visit Britain since the winds of change blew his country out of the Commonwealth. It was two years – and several periods of martial law – before the crucial issue of sanctions against the white Pretoria regime came to a head. For years it had been possible to invent lame excuses for refusing to impose a genuine trade embargo: black leaders did not want it; the United Nations did not demand it. The prospect of changing either the government or its policy were negligible. Then, in April 1986, Bishop Desmond Tutu called for international economic quarantine. A month later, one and a half million black workers went on strike in Johannesburg – according to President Botha, provoked by 'revolutionaries supported by the African National Congress'.

In preparation for the Commonwealth Prime Ministers' conference in August 1986, Mrs Thatcher repeated her intractable opposition to sanctions – an attitude which one newspaper claimed sources within Buckingham Palace said had 'dismayed the Queen'. A week before the Prime Ministers assembled, thirty-two countries withdrew their teams from that year's Commonwealth Games in protest against Britain's refusal to take the one step which Commonwealth leaders believed could end apartheid. The Prime Ministers' meeting ended with Britain alone in its opposition to mandatory sanctions, but in the following month, the House of Lords actually passed a resolution which called upon the government to accept and impose the proposed embargo. The pressure was beginning to build up. At the end of 1986, Esso and Barclays Bank (conscious of international opinion) announced their intention to withdraw their investments from South Africa. The Prime Minister, believing that she had weathered the storm, turned her attention to domestic policies.

That year, Margaret Thatcher was at the height of her powers – the undisputed, if not universally loved, leader of her party and country. With two election victories to her credit, and a third in almost certain prospect, the assumption of the right to rule without challenge or question would have been a temptation which even a more humble woman would have found hard to resist. Mrs Thatcher did not even try to accommodate the opinions of her critics.

The assault on trade unions and the emasculation of local government were all part of a conscious determination to destroy institutions which, under Britain's informal constitution, acted as checks and balances on and against the arbitrary power of central government. A by-product of her instinctive authoritarianism was the government's implacable opposition to the diffusion of powers which, in other democracies, were shared between executive and legislative. Not for her either a genuine relaxation of the Official Secrets Act or effective parliamentary control over the security services. And civil servants who broke the rule of silence were pursued without mercy.

In January 1984, Sarah Tisdall, a 23-year-old clerk employed in the Foreign Secretary's private office, was prosecuted under the Official Secrets Act for sending to the *Guardian* newspaper a document which set out the programme for the arrival in Britain of Cruise missiles. She was convicted and sent to prison for six months. In August, Clive Ponting, a senior civil servant in the Ministry of Defence, was charged under the same act for sending a Labour MP a truthful account of the sinking of the *General Belgrano* during the Falklands War. It proved that the government had deceived Parliament: the Argentine cruiser had not been attacked under the original 'rules of engagement' set out by the Commander-in-Chief. Having decided that the ship must be sunk, the rules of engagement had been changed to legalise the sinking. The prosecution obliged the government to admit that it had 'lost' the log of HMS *Conqueror*, the submarine which had fired the lethal torpedo. Reinforced by the knowledge that Ponting had done no more than expose the government's deceit, the jury at his trial in early 1985 ignored the judge's discretion and acquitted him on all charges. He was, nevertheless, sacked by the Ministry of Defence.

It was at least arguable that, whatever the merits of the case, efficient government requires civil servants to put aside their own feelings and act with unquestioning loyalty to the government which employs them. However, a journalist's undoubted obligation is to print the news and comment upon it according to his or her judgement. When the BBC series *Real Lives* recorded an interview with Sinn Féin's

Martin McGuinness, Margaret Thatcher bullied the Board of Governors into abandoning its 'interview with a senior member of the IRA'. Worse was to come. In January 1987, the Director-General of the BBC banned the broadcast of *Britain's Secret Society* because of the damage the government had claimed would be done to national security if the programme went ahead. *Britain's Secret Society* revealed that the Ministry of Defence was developing the Zircon surveillance satellite, with the intention of intercepting civilian and military radio communications. Censorship alone did not satisfy the government. A Special Branch raid on the BBC studios in Glasgow ended with the confiscation of two van-loads of material. Much of it was never returned – even though the police announced that there were no grounds for prosecution – nor was there either explanation or apology. Before the 1987 General Election, what the Opposition described as a combination of 'illiberalism and incompetence' had turned into farce. Peter Wright – an eccentric retired intelligence officer – published his memoirs in the United States. They included, among other dubious claims, the admission that, during the 1960s, the author had taken part in an attempt to destabilise Harold Wilson, then Prime Minister. Publication of the book, freely available in America, was prohibited in Great Britain. During attempts to extend the legal ban to Australia, the Cabinet Secretary giving evidence in court admitted that sometimes it was necessary to be 'economical with the truth'. The case was lost. But, for a time, the government succeeded in keeping from the British public information which was freely available to the Soviet secret service. The *Sunday Times* was indicted for contempt of court after publishing extracts from the American edition of *Spycatcher*, and an injunction forbade the BBC to broadcast a programme which examined the constitutional implications of the government's attempt to suppress British publication of a book already on sale abroad. At the end of the year, Mr Justice Scott – who was to appear again on the political stage almost ten years later – refused to make a permanent injunction prohibiting for ever the revelation of the *Spycatcher* allegations of security service misconduct. The press, he said, had a 'legitimate and important role' in disclosing wrong-doing.

At the time, the British press was altogether sure what its role should be. With the exception of the Mirror Group, bought by Robert Maxwell for £113.4 million in July 1984, and the indestructibly radical *Guardian*, it had no doubt about its loyalty to Margaret Thatcher or its enthusiasm for the ideas which she represented. Most loyal of all was Rupert Murdoch, who had (as a half-hearted Labour supporter) acquired the *Sun* during Harold Wilson's premiership and had added *The Times* and *Sunday Times* to his empire when (as an enthusiastic Thatcherite) he had been allowed to acquire the titles without the inconvenience of the monopoly enquiry which the law required. With the *News of the World* also in his possession he was in a peculiarly strong position to influence both the course of British politics and the character of British journalism. He chose to give strident support to the Tory government and to drive the nation's newspapers so far downmarket that, within a decade, some of them were barely newspapers at all. The stories about royal peccadilloes, scandalous behaviour of television personalities and the social lives of rich vulgarians — which have increasingly typified the British popular press — are Rupert Murdoch's legacy to the land of Shakespeare and Milton.

For a moment — in the early months of 1986 — it had seemed that there was a hope of the British press moving in the opposite direction. Eddie Shah, a free-sheet proprietor from Warrington, had launched a new tabloid which he called *Today*. In itself, the paper was not a journalistic sensation. But the middle-market tabloid — printed in part in colour — was thought to typify two essential features of a thriving newspaper industry. It was produced by 'new technology', and the workers were not constrained by the restrictive practices on which the London-based print unions insisted. It seemed that the newspaper industry had found the magic formula for which the whole economy searched — a better product which could be sold at a lower price.

By the end of the year a second news daily, the consciously superior *Independent*, was on sale. Meanwhile, Rupert Murdoch had transferred production of *The Times* and *Sunday Times* to 'Fortress Wapping', where printers — not members of the old craft unions — worked behind barbed-wire-topped walls with a speed and efficiency which their Fleet Street forebears would have regarded as class treachery. Even sentimentalists who sympathised with the old hot-metal craftsmen felt some guilty pleasure at the thought of how newspapers might increase in variety and improve in quality as costs fell.

Quite the opposite happened. *Today* no longer exists. Other new papers – the *Sunday Correspondent* and the *News on Sunday* – came and went in months. The *Independent* (and its Sunday partner) teeter on the edge of financial collapse. A Gresham's Law of newspapers forced even the best broadsheets downmarket as they struggled to meet the increasing cost of newsprint. The result (increasingly prurient and trivial tabloids, and broadsheets which fight for circulation by cutting prices and organising competitions) was the inevitable outcome of proprietors regarding their papers as a product to be sold by whatever means was most likely to increase circulation. For almost a full decade the British people had been encouraged to admire material (and often meretricious) success. Margaret Thatcher had hoped to build a land fit for the new middle classes who read the *Daily Mail*. Readers of the *Sun*, the *Star* and the *Mirror* were also her children.

They were the voters who carried her, triumphantly, through the 1987 General Election, with her majority barely reduced. And they were the consumers who supported her because (above all other reasons) she gave them tax cuts. In the 1986 budget, the Conservative government reduced the standard rate of income tax by 1p. In 1987 (election year), the reduction was 2p. Another 1p reduction in 1988 brought the standard rate to 25p in the pound, compared with 33p when Labour left office in 1979. Combined with the total abandonment of hire-purchase controls and the deregulation of banks and building societies, the result was a consumption-led boom that guaranteed Conservative popularity – at least for a while. The object, a Conservative election victory, was achieved. But the price had to be paid in the last two years of the decade. At the time it seemed so high that few people believed the Tory party would ever be forgiven for running up such a bill.

The pre-election boom – largely stimulated by increases in consumption expenditure – was substantial, though not sustained. The average return on assets of industrial and commercial companies, 4.3

per cent in 1981, rose to 10 per cent in 1988. Over the same period, the savings ratio fell from 13.5 to 5.7 per cent. Credit was uniquely easy. In 1980, new house buyers borrowed, on average, 76 per cent of the purchase price. By 1988, the average mortgage was 86 per cent. The ratio of consumer debt to personal income doubled over the same period; the increase in borrowing increased and was in turn increased by a rise in asset values. House prices doubled in four years – typifying the tragedy of the age. What seemed to be an unprecedented increase in the wealth of owner-occupiers turned – when the boom burst – into financial catastrophe as family after family discovered that, with the sudden collapse of house prices, they owed more to the building society than the value of the property which they owned.

In the two years which began with the 1987 General Election, consumer expenditure actually grew more quickly than the gross domestic product. But the good times could not and did not last. In 1987, consumer expenditure was £15.6 billion higher than it had been in the year before. In 1988, it rose by £23.4 billion. In 1989, the unavoidable cut-back began: the annual increase had decelerated to £10.8 billion; in 1990 it was only £2.1 billion. A year later boom had turned into bust. Consumer expenditure fell, year on year, by £7.6 billion. At the same time output was falling, unemployment was increasing.

During the 1987 election campaign, Tory ministers had denounced as irresponsible and unconvincing propaganda the suggestion that the current account deficit might rise as high as £10 billion. As consumption escalated and domestic industry failed to meet the new demand, the current account (which had been in rough balance in 1986) showed a deficit of £15 billion in 1988 and £20 billion a year later. The inflation rate – once more driven by unsatisfied demand – began to rise again. And in 1989, the floating pound depreciated by 22 per cent. The necessary, though painful, result was an increase in interest rates. In the summer of 1988, short-term rates were 8 per cent; by the autumn of 1989, they were 15 per cent. And so they remained for the last year of the decade. The effect debilitated the whole economy. Industrial investment was 15 per cent lower in 1988 than it was in 1992. Home prices fell even more, and the process was accelerated by the number of repossessed properties which went on the market when the mortgage-holders fell behind with their repayments.

The only excuse the government could offer was the rise in German interest rates – the direct result of reunification of the FRG and the GDR after the collapse of communism. The cost of creating one Germany was incalculable, but immense. And the Federal government made clear that it was not prepared to meet it by increasing West German taxes. The Bundesbank responded by increasing interest rates to their highest level since the war. Britain – unavoidably influenced by its strongest European partners and competitors – could only finance its external deficit by keeping interest rates above those prescribed by the Bundesbank. The problem should have been eased by Britain's membership of the Exchange Rate Mechanism, which Margaret Thatcher agreed to join in October 1990, but once again political prejudice took precedence over economic judgement. And ERM membership became a liability, not a protection.

10

No Such Thing as Society
The Triumph of the Middle Classes

—•·—

The Local Government Finance Bill received Royal Assent on 29
July 1988. Its purpose was to replace the rates – the property tax
which had financed local government in England and Wales since the
nineteenth century – with what Margaret Thatcher was determined
to call the 'Community Charge': a flat-rate levy which, in the jargon
of the time, required both dukes and dustmen to make the same contribution to the cost of services which they shared. It was, and it came
to be called, a poll tax. The government struggled mightily to avoid
the use of its proper name – the first concession that the Conservative
party was no longer certain that the ruthless pursuit of inequality
won votes. It was a poll tax which had ignited the Peasants' Revolt of
1381, and each subsequent attempt to impose flat-rate levies had
ended in disaster. True to its heritage, the Community Charge was
the most unpopular political proposal in post-war history. It brought
Margaret Thatcher's career to a reluctant end.

It had taken almost fifteen years for the poll tax to burrow its way
into law. In 1974, Margaret Thatcher (then Opposition Spokesman on
the Environment) had promised to abolish the rates. Every party was
dissatisfied with the rating system which, according to the objection
most often quoted, fell equally on the lonely widow and the family
with three working adults which lived in the identical house next

door. But only the Tories announced the intention of abolishing rates before deciding what to put in their place. Later, Margaret Thatcher claimed that Edward Heath had insisted that she made the precipitate announcement. But, wherever the responsibility lay, it made the Tory party look ridiculous. Throughout the five years which followed the thoughtless pledge, the problems of financing local government by a property tax increased, as towns and counties spent more and more on the services they provided.

Under Labour, most of the cost was borne by central government which, through Treasury grants, finance more than two-thirds of council expenditure. In the financial year 1974–75 – at the beginning of Harold Wilson's last administration – local authorities controlled 30 per cent of all public expenditure. The Conservatives (re-elected in 1979) were not willing to allow largely Labour town and county councils to exert such a massive influence over the Public Sector Borrowing Requirement. Council powers were reduced year by year, progressively denying them the right to determine their own spending patterns, their own rent levels, their own building programmes and eventually the level of local taxes. Although the government claimed that it was restraining 'spendthrift councils', rate bills remorselessly increased as the Treasury's contribution to local expenditure fell each year. In 1975–76, Whitehall financed 67 per cent of council expenditure. By 1990–91, the figure had fallen to 36 per cent. The 'rate burden' rose because central government believed that councils, forced to finance most of their own spending, would choose to cut services rather than increase taxes. Councillors of every political persuasion chose to protect services. The poll tax was introduced as the ultimate deterrent. Council spending would, under the new system, be financed equally by rich and poor.

Two full Parliaments separated the Tories' first announcement that the rates system would be abolished and its replacement by the Community Charge. The party's 1979 election manifesto took a conscious step back from the promise of 1974 with a glorious non sequitur: 'Cutting income tax must take priority for the time being over the abolition of the domestic rate system.' There followed six years of retreat. In 1981, a Green Paper included a poll tax among one of the several theoretical alternatives to the rates, and the 1983 election manifesto did not even mention the idea. But in 1984 hard reality and the fantasies of free market ideology combined to encourage Margaret Thatcher to take the most suicidal political decision since the imposition of the Corn Laws. A rate revaluation in Scotland – a periodic necessity with any property tax – produced assessments which would have more than doubled the payments levied on some households; most of them middle-class families on whom the Tory party relied. Ideology and expediency combined when the Adam Smith Institute, one of the Prime Minister's favourite sources of inspiration, returned to the theme of a flat-rate levy as a way of convincing local authority voters that if they wanted lavish local services, they would have to pay for them.

For the next three years, a series of Cabinet Committees and a succession of ambitious junior ministers tried to translate free market theory into workable practice. By February 1987, the government felt sufficiently confident in the progress which it had made to announce that the Community Charge would be introduced in Scotland in April 1989, and that the phasing-in of the new system would begin in England and Wales one year later.

The more that the government worked on the details of the poll tax, the more disastrous its political application was found to be. Even before the new policy was in place, officials had warned ministers that (other things being equal) the new local government levy would require 50 per cent of households to pay more than they had paid under the old rating system. By the spring of 1989, new estimates suggested that the original forecast had underestimated the average level of poll tax which was necessary to meet local council bills. The typical 'community charge' throughout the country was likely to be more than £300 per head. By the autumn the forecast was even more gloomy. Between 73 and 89 per cent of families would be worse off than they were under the rating system. So, true to Margaret Thatcher's record and psychology, the government decided to push ahead more swiftly. In England and Wales, the poll tax would not be 'phased in gradually'. It would completely replace the rates by April 1990.

Once again, the Conservatives were fortunate that Labour provided an inadequate opposition. Only once during the long and angry House of Commons debate was the government's majority tested, and that was when Tory back-benchers – defying the spirit of the new tax – proposed special relief for low-income families. Defeat in the division lobbies was the unavoidable result of the parliamentary balance of power which had been set in the 1987 General Election. Labour's inability to settle on an agreed alternative was less excusable. Some of the party's most senior spokesmen supported the retention of the rates; others called for a local income tax; another influential group proposed a hybrid solution which they believed combined two conflicting principles – assessment of property values adjusted according to family income. It was derided by the Tories as a 'roof tax' and then, when the poll tax was dumped in 1992, adopted as government policy.

The greatest damage was done to Labour's reputation not by arguments about policy but by the way in which a faction within the party insisted on opposing the new proposals. The principled opposition to a tax which reduced the local government levy on the rich and increased it for the poor was compromised by the association of some Labour supporters with the damaged, but not yet destroyed, Militant tendency. They believed that the proper response to the poll tax was fiscal disobedience, and showed every sign of really believing that, if enough people could be persuaded not to pay, the whole scheme would be dropped and a bankrupt government would be forced to resign. Had the fantasy of a forced election come true at any time between 1988 and 1990, the government would almost certainly have lost. The poll tax – both in prospect and in reality – would have been the greatest single reason for the defeat. But the Tories' almost unique level of unpopularity – confirmed in local, European and parliamentary by-elections – had other serious, if supplementary, causes. Chief among them was the reorganisation of the National Health Service. The government believed that it could improve efficiency and cut costs by applying the remedy which – despite the evidence of the previous ten years – Tories still believed would cure all economic and social ills. The market principle was introduced into health-care. A corresponding education reform allowed secondary schools to 'opt out' of local authority control, in the hope that the grant-maintained schools which they became would introduce competition into the system. It was opposed by almost everyone who took an interest in teaching the young, but the general public have never been included in that category. It is the treatment of the Health Service alone that pricks the British conscience.

Throughout the 1980s, the National Health Service had struggled to match its resources to the demands made upon them. Year after year, the struggle was lost. NHS expenditure showed an annual increase in real terms. But Sir William Beveridge's 1942 prediction that an increasingly healthy population would need less and less medical care proved to be diametrically wrong. As life expectancy improved, an ageing population was kept fit by new and expensive medical developments. Not surprisingly, voters resented any hint of health-care rationing. They wanted the government to finance all that the NHS could offer – without any compensating increase in taxes.

The government did not oblige. Hospitals, unavoidably, tightened their spending controls and improved their efficiency. But, at the end of most financial years, they simply ran out of funds. The deficit was kept to a minimum by closing wards and postponing the payment of bills. The result was an accrued financial deficit, an extended waiting list, and a boost for private medicine among those who could afford to insure against the months when their local hospitals were running at half capacity. In February 1987 the usual winter increase in demand for hospital beds was greater (and came earlier) than the hospitals anticipated. And 1987 was the likely election year. Managers were told to avoid bad publicity at all cost. More bills than usual were left unpaid to reduce the number of beds that were taken out of commission. The new government had a financial crisis to face – of its own making.

For some months John Moore, the new Secretary of State for Health and a convinced Thatcherite, chose to take no action, presumably working on the assumption that increasingly stringent financial targets would force the Health Service into achieving a level of productivity which would make it viable. He did, however, make a speech to the Tory party conference which referred to 'our health-care industry' rather than the National Health Service – a choice of words which was generally assumed to signal his enthusiasm for private medicine. When he contracted pneumonia, he became the first health minister since the creation of the Health Service to be admitted to a private hospital. The growing enthusiasm for health insurance was confirmed by Edwina Currie, one of his junior ministers, who suggested that sensible families spend their money on BUPA rather than Benidorm: 'If people have the money, I would urge them to seek their health-care elsewhere' than the National Health Service, she said.

Meanwhile, the financial crisis deepened. One suggestion for its solution was saving £170 million by the imposition of charges for eye tests and dental inspection. After a Tory back-bench revolt, the plan to charge for eye tests was dropped. Calls for a general enquiry were ignored or brushed aside until the Prime Minister was challenged on *Panorama* about the government's inactivity. To universal astonishment – and to the consternation of the health ministry – she announced that an enquiry was to be set up. Three days later it was.

The enquiry, if not exactly secret, was certainly private and, because it was conducted by politicians of a free market inclination, it was primarily concerned with the Health Service's structure. John Moore himself was determined to examine ways in which more private money could be devoted to health-care. He had read an OECD Report which showed that Britain spent less on medical services than any other advanced European nation, and noticed that the shortfall between the British performance and those of the country's competitors was more than made up by the extra private funding in continental Europe. As is often the case with inadequate ministers, having assimilated one fact, it dominated his thinking. Nigel Lawson, the Chancellor of the Exchequer, wanted patients admitted to hospitals to be charged for their keep. The Prime Minister vetoed the suggestion as political suicide, but proposed tax allowances on medical insurance premiums. There was even discussion of allowing 'contracting-out' – the payment of rebates to families and individuals who make independent provision for their health-care. The idea was dropped when it was explained that the offer would only be taken up by 'the healthy wealthy' and the NHS would lose revenue without enjoying a consequent reduction in the burden of care. In the end, tax allowances were agreed for pensioners who took out private health insurance – a decision which had virtually no bearing on the financial crisis. Searching for a more permanent solution, Margaret Thatcher asked about the 'internal market'. She was told that it would take four years to put into operation.

The idea of the internal market had certainly been around for years. In 1984, the Nuffield Provincial Hospital Trust had commissioned Alain Enthoven, an American economist, to examine its applicability to the National Health Service. He recommended that hospitals be allowed to buy and sell services, both from each other and the private sector, rather than attempt to be self-sufficient. The result, Enthoven wrote, would be 'the best combination of cost, quality and convenience'. Unfortunately, his report lacked detailed discussion of how the scheme could be operated within a Health Service that grouped its hospitals in regions under the financial control of 'boards' and applied the strict principles of Treasury accounting. The concept was, however, profoundly attractive to free market Tories, since it separated the producer from the consumer and, theoretically at least, gave the consumer the freedom of choice which guarantees efficiency. David Owen – as joint leader of the Liberal–SDP Alliance – had actually adopted the idea during the 1987 election campaign. Tory ministers, when asked for their views, had affected ignorance of Enthoven's work.

The two other essential constitutional changes which were needed to give reality to the idea of the internal market were devised by the Centre for Policy Studies, a free market think-tank, after the basic ideas had been adopted by Kenneth Clarke, the new Secretary of State for Health who had been reshuffled into the job after John Moore retired hurt. The market would be extended to general practitioners who would be 'offered' the opportunity to control their own budgets and 'buy' (according to their own choice and judgement) the operations, drugs and out-patient care for the families on their lists. Family doctors who chose to become fund-holders were promised grants which would allow them to buy rather better services than those which were available to colleagues who remained under the aegis of the local practitioners' committees. The same sort of financial inducement had proved remarkably unsuccessful when it was used to persuade state secondary schools to 'opt out' and take the direct grant.

The third element which completed the competitive triangle was 'hospital trusts' – self-governing institutions which, like the London teaching hospitals before the foundation of the Health Service, managed their own finances. Once again, 'trust status' was a voluntary condition for hospitals to choose or reject according to taste, but it was hoped that political pressure and financial incentive would ensure that the change was willingly accepted.

There is no doubt that many doctors in both hospitals and general practice welcomed the prospect of greater freedom and responsibility. But the BMA Executive (by a small majority) and the full membership (by a massive vote in a postal ballot) rejected the proposals and launched a bitter campaign which – although directed against the internal market – called into question the government's entire commitment to the National Health Service, which the battling doctors described as 'underfunded, undermined and under threat'. The government – foolishly it seemed at the time – chose to heighten rather than reduce the temperature. Doctors – who were also engaged in a routine renegotiation of their contracts – were accused of 'nervously fingering their wallets' whenever improvements in the Health Service were in prospect. The BMA responded by loftily reiterating that its only concern was patient care. In a war between doctors and politicians, the general public does not even have to pause to think before it decides which side it is on. Polls confirmed that an overwhelming majority of voters (including 50 per cent of all committed Conservatives) were opposed to the changes and regarded them as the first steps towards dreaded privatisation. In a Mid-Staffordshire by-election, Labour captured the seat from the Tories with a swing of 21 per cent – the biggest recorded shift in voting allegiance for more than fifty years.

For once, Margaret Thatcher's nerve failed, and she suggested that the whole Health Service reorganisation be postponed until after the election. Fortunately – for the Tory party, if not for the country – bolder spirits insisted that she carried on. The Conservative party's strength, throughout the 1980s, was the courage with which it held its convictions. There was never any hope that its health policies, however benign, could be made more popular than Labour's alternative. Labour, 'the party of the NHS', had created Britain's favourite institution and, even when Labour leaders were trusted with nothing else, they were trusted to protect medical care. But although the Health Service was inviolable Labour territory, the Conservatives could perform upon it in a way which illustrated their confidence and continued ingenuity. By December 1990, there were 57 'hospital trusts' and, four months later, 1,750 general practitioners had become fundholders. Both totals gradually grew, and after a couple of years of outright opposition, the Labour Party began to edge towards acceptance of a variation on the internal market which it had once described as typifying Tory callous unconcern for the old and the sick. The 'socialist ratchet', which Keith Joseph had once identified as keeping in permanent place the changes made by Labour governments, had wound down. It had been replaced by a free market wedge which, once driven into less competitive forms of organisation, was impossible to shift.

The internal market reforms were not the only change in social policy which the government contemplated in the late 1980s. The care of the elderly and infirm 'in the community' had proved disastrous – at least for thousands of bewildered geriatrics who received no help from the government. The trick, which was bound to be found out in the end, saved money by the pretence that sending psychiatric patients on to the streets to sit in parks and sleep in shop doorways offered a more intimate and humane service. Incompetence had compounded callous lack of concern. The Audit Commission had published a damning condemnation of the way in which the responsibility had been transferred from the Health Service to a variety of other agencies – none of which was sure of its responsibilities, and all of which were short of funds. The government's internal report proposed that local authorities should take sole charge, but that they should act not as 'providers' but as 'enablers' which bought care from private contractors. The idea appealed to Tories who thought of county and city councils as agencies who sub-contracted their work, and to Labour councillors who thought it would give them something to do. To make sure that the allocated funds were spent exclusively on community care, the government decided to pay local authorities a specific grant which could only be used for that purpose. Then the Treasury thought about the total cost. And the new (uncontroversial) scheme was (unlike the contentious Health Service internal market) postponed for two years. It came into force in 1993.

It was during the late 1980s that the churches – Catholic, Anglican and Non-Conformist – began to speak out against poverty and social deprivation. *Faith in the City*, the Church of England's testament against unemployment and urban decay, was the most famous of the calls for compassionate government. David Shephard, Bishop of Liverpool, had published *Bias to the Poor* in 1983, and for the rest of the decade he and like-minded clergy challenged the popular assumption that the casualties of competition had to be accepted as the price of all that a free market could provide. David Jenkins, Bishop of Durham, went further. As well as offending against the tradition of the established Church by questioning basic doctrine, he openly allied himself with striking miners and single mothers. During Margaret Thatcher's last years in Downing Street, the Church – particularly the Church of England – rediscovered its social conscience.

The neglect of the old and feeble caused barely a stir outside the organisations which were professionally committed to their welfare, but for a while it seemed that the combination of concern about the Health Service and hatred of the poll tax would guarantee a Tory humiliation in the General Election which was bound to be held during 1992. The only practical alternative was a change of policy. However, Margaret Thatcher – despite her uncharacteristic reluctance to press ahead with the Health Service internal market – refused to alter course. The Prime Minister might well have continued to chart her straight line towards defeat had she not, with the arrogance of years in power, treated her most influential supporters – and their most passionately held beliefs – with open contempt. If there was a single political issue which brought Margaret Thatcher down, it was Britain's relationship with the European Community. But beneath the thin policy veneer there were more visceral reasons for the Tory party's rejection of the woman who had led them to three consecutive victories. The strident style had grown intolerable to colleagues who had been happy to accommodate her arrogance as long as it was attractive to the British people. When her personality combined with her politics to make 'the iron lady' unelectable, the Conservative party dumped her. Margaret Thatcher's attitude towards the European Community – what the *Daily Mail* called 'her inability to unite the party over Europe or even to convince that she is doing her best to keep it together' – was the Tory party's excuse for dropping its pilot. Margaret Thatcher's real offence was changing from winner to loser.

Margaret Thatcher's attitude towards the European Union was certainly capricious. Although she was later to deny all responsibility, she had been an enthusiastic supporter of the Single European Act, which had been forced through the Commons with the aid of a guillotine. The object of the Act was, as its title made clear, the implementation of the treaty which broke down non-tariff barriers to trade within the Community. The 'harmonisation' of standards and regulations was essential to the creation of genuine competition within the common external tariff, and therefore was enormously attractive to Margaret Thatcher's free market ideology. However, she did not realise, or chose to ignore, the unavoidable connection between political and economic integration, so the Prime Minister either claimed authorship or brushed aside the aspects of the treaty which extended the Community's political identity. The creation of machinery to co-ordinate foreign policy (always attractive to Prime Ministers) extended the role of the European Parliament, itself an obvious step along the path to political integration. It also embodied the first, formal, imprecise, but explicit, reference to economic and monetary union. The Act substantially increased the areas of Community action which could be determined by majority voting – a development which was subsequently described by the Foreign Secretary as a 'manifestly federal aspect' of the treaty on which the Single European Act was based. Later, the British signatories to the agreement were to argue that they believed that the so-called 'Luxembourg Compromise' (by which European member states could veto proposals which they regarded as against their national interest) would remain unchanged and that, in consequence, Britain's position was protected. If so, they were remarkably ignorant of the Community and its ways. The Luxembourg Compromise was an informal arrangement which was always dependent on the mood of the Community. That mood changed with the development of a single market and the Luxembourg Compromise was abandoned and forgotten.

It was the subsequent argument about the Single European Act which brought into sharp focus the hopes for Europe which Margaret Thatcher came to typify. The most famous expression of that view was her 'Bruges Speech', which asserted that 'willing and active cooperation between independent sovereign states is the best way to build a successful European Community'. But the resurrection of De Gaulle's Europe of the States was only one part of her limited vision. Margaret Thatcher believed that Europe should be a custom's union – a *Zollverein* which did no more than organise the free market within its boundaries. But that is not the Europe of which the other member nations dreamed. They wanted, and still want, a genuine Community with co-ordinated social and economic policies. Margaret Thatcher wanted, and those who now follow her still want, the other nations of Europe to fall into line with a uniquely British view of its future. Europe is unlikely to oblige.

And there was another reason which hardened Margaret Thatcher's opinion against European integration: Germany. The British Prime Minister's relief that her old friend Ronald Reagan had, in 1988, been succeeded by his Vice-President, George Bush, was moderated by the fear that under its new leadership America 'saw Germany as its main European partner in leadership'. During the summer of 1987, flushed with her third election victory, Margaret Thatcher had visited Washington and expressed her doubts about President Reagan's disarmament proposals. Part of her concern was the risk that, if Nato abandoned its intermediate-range land-based missiles, it would lose its capacity to mount a 'flexible response' to aggression. But what she really feared was 'decoupling' – the adoption of a strategy which separated the defence of Europe from the defence of the United States. The 'special relationship' – interpreted as Britain being the United States' most favoured European nation – was emotionally important to her. By the end of 1989, she had begun to fear that the Mother Country was being elbowed aside by the Fatherland.

That awful possibility was immensely increased by events in what to the rest of the world was the *annus mirabilis* of 1989, when the impossible happened in the Soviet Union's Eastern European empire. In June 1989, Solidarity won the first free election in Poland for fifty years. To universal surprise, General Wojciech Jaruzelski, the Communist leader, accepted the result. When, in October, Erich Honecker was deposed in East Germany, it was generally accepted that Mikhail Gorbachev had certainly endorsed and probably inspired what amounted to a liberal revolution. On 10 November, demonstrators began to dismantle the Berlin Wall. In December Václav Havel was elected President of Czechoslovakia and, in the same month in Romania, Nicolae Ceauşescu was first deposed and then shot. While the world was spinning on its axis, Margaret Thatcher was telling Gorbachev in Moscow that she shared his opposition to the reunification of Germany. Once it had happened, her view on the European Community was prejudiced by the view that 'Germany is more rather than less likely to dominate' it, 'for a reunited Germany is simply too big and powerful to be just a player within Europe'.

It was no surprise that when, in retrospect, Margaret Thatcher examined the reasons for the economic catastrophe of the late 1980s – inflation into slump, record interest rates and a stock-market crash – most of the blame was heaped upon the Chancellor of the Exchequer's decision to 'shadow the Deutschmark', the manipulation of the exchange rate to make sterling gain and lose value in line with the strongest currency in Europe. It is hard to believe that a Prime Minister – living next door to the Chancellor and the width of Downing Street away from the Treasury – had no idea that the honest

British pound was trailing along behind the greedy German mark. But that was her claim. Some commentators have found it surprising that the Prime Minister did not know or ask about the basis of the government's monetary policy. The discovery, albeit belated, that Germany was the malign force behind the government's economic difficulties was entirely predictable.

The last enemy, and the opponent whom Margaret Thatcher chose with less than her usual care, was, however, French – Jacques Delors, sometime socialist minister and President of the European Commission. He had a grand design for the future of the Community and pursued it with the passion of a man who wanted to make his federal mark on history. The plan which came to bear his name proposed remorseless, if not swift, progress towards economic and monetary union. The ultimate goal was a single European currency, managed by an independent European central bank. It was to be accompanied by a common monetary policy and the 'convergence of economic performance' – that is to say similar rates of government borrowing and levels of inflation. The first stage of the process was to be the creation of an Exchange Rate Mechanism, which all countries of the Community would join. Each national currency would be given a fixed parity which, when necessary, would be supported by its friendly neighbours. Inevitably, the parities would be heavily influenced by the value of the Deutschmark.

Conservatives were divided over the idea of an ERM. Fixed parities were inconsistent with the belief in floating exchange rates – the 'market' in sterling that the devotees of competition thought essential. On the other hand, an independent central bank, constitutionally obliged to make the eradication of inflation its first priority, had a special appeal to Thatcherites who thought that 'honest money' was a government's overwhelming objective. The federalist implications of the scheme seem hardly to have been an issue. In the absence of Cabinet agreement, Margaret Thatcher (herself undecided) chose to prevaricate. Britain would join the ERM 'when the time was right'. Nobody knew when that would be or how it would be recognised.

It is impossible to guess how long the indecision would have continued had the Spanish government – in the chair of the European

Community for the first time – not determined to move things on at the 1989 Madrid summit. The Foreign Office feared that Britain, without either moorings or bearings, would be bypassed and left behind. Geoffrey Howe, Foreign Secretary, and Nigel Lawson, Chancellor of the Exchequer, decided that the moment had come to move policy on. A joint memorandum, proposing the acceptance of ERM membership on appropriate conditions, was sent to the Prime Minister. She rejected it. On the eve of the Madrid summit the two most senior members of the Cabinet – Lawson and Howe – sought audience. Unless the Prime Minister announced Britain's commitment to the ERM in Madrid, they would resign. A number of face-saving provisos – known as 'The Madrid Conditions' – were cobbled together to avoid the admission that the iron lady had bent. For the first time in ten years, Margaret Thatcher had been defeated by a Cabinet revolt. The ERM commitment was made. But the Prime Minister neither forgave nor forgot the indignity which had been forced upon her. Within months, she began to wreak her Pyrrhic vengeance.

The first victim was Geoffrey Howe who, Margaret Thatcher was convinced, had become the creature of the diplomatic service. On 24 July 1989, he was replaced as Foreign Secretary by the then little-known John Major. Howe was offered either the Home Office or the Leadership of the House of Commons. After a day's agonising he chose to lead the Commons with the additional (and purely honorific) title of Deputy Prime Minister. The Chancellor of the Exchequer lasted three months longer at the Treasury, then he resigned from the government and was in turn replaced by Major. Lawson's pretext was the Prime Minister's refusal to dismiss Sir Alan Walters, her personal economic adviser, who persisted in expressing public opposition to Britain's membership of the ERM. Walters certainly disagreed with the Chancellor's policy, and his insistence of saying so revealed, as it was intended to reveal, that the Prime Minister was out of sympathy with what he described as 'the pressure from Europe and the British Establishment to conform and join the Exchange Rate Mechanism'. Lawson's resignation letter explained that 'the successful conduct of economic policy is possible only if there is full agreement between the Prime Minister and the Chancellor of the Exchequer' and that 'recent events have confirmed that this essential requirement cannot be satisfied as long as Walters remains your personal economic adviser'. All true. But in reality the Chancellor chose to make a clean break rather than submit to the months of public indignity which Geoffrey Howe had endured.

Margaret Thatcher, with John Major as her new Chancellor, continued her rearguard action against monetary union. In December 1989, the European summit in Strasbourg voted in favour of amending the Treaty of Rome to include monetary union as one of Europe's objectives. The motion was carried by eleven votes to one. Margaret Thatcher described the suggestion that Britain was isolated as 'absolute nonsense'. At the Dublin summit in June 1990, Britain again stood alone. According to Thatcher, Jacques Delors' single currency plan disregarded national sovereignty and failed to reconcile the irreconcilable differences in Europe's economies. Both the new Chancellor of the Exchequer and Douglas Hurd, the new Foreign Secretary, shared the views that their predecessors had unsuccessfully tried to press on the Prime Minister. They argued the case with such determination that Thatcher, unable even to contemplate another major Cabinet rift, agreed that Britain should take what the rest of Europe regarded as the first step towards economic and monetary union – membership of the European Monetary System and the formal alignment of individual national currencies.

John Major made the announcement on 5 October 1990, but the Prime Minister's personal crusade against the European Community went on. At the Rome summit, three weeks later, Margaret Thatcher remained utterly intransigent about the prospects of a single currency. The rest of the Community agreed to aim at what they called 'Stage Two of Delors', a European central bank, by January 1994. Stage Three was to be agreement to irrevocably fixed exchange rates, which must have made Mrs Thatcher wonder if she had been right to accept even the concept of an irreversible alignment three weeks earlier. The single currency was accepted as an aspiration which, it was hoped, would turn into a prospect by the end of the century. From Mrs Thatcher's point of view, things could have been much worse.

But she still thought it necessary to announce that Britain would never accept a single currency. Parliament would never pass the essential legislation. During the summit meeting, the Prime Minister had been obdurate but calm. Back in the House of Commons, she reported the outcome of Dublin in the measured language of a statement which had been drafted by the Civil Service and agreed with more temperate ministers. But during the questions which followed, she abandoned all restraint. The end of the pound? A single European currency? 'No! No! No!' The three words ended her political career.

By then, the Labour Party's European pendulum was about to swing for the sixth time in ten years. So when John Major announced the application for Britain to join the ERM, Labour leaders – in some disarray since, at the time of his statement, delegates were on their way home from the annual conference in Blackpool – supported both the decision and the government's choice of the exchange rate which, once in the system, Britain would have to maintain. The parity was, they knew, far too high. But far ahead in the opinion polls and hopeful of soon being in government, they were afraid of being accused of 'selling sterling short'. The confidence with which they supported a Conservative decision to integrate the European monetary systems showed how much progress the party had made since the 1987 General Election.

The improvement had begun with an escapade which the leadership had feared would have quite the opposite effect. The leadership challenge mounted from the left by Tony Benn in 1988 (with Eric Heffer, an honest but undoubtedly self-regarding socialist, as the candidate for deputy) was never a threat to the incumbents. Neil Kinnock, at the nadir of his popularity, and the trade union leaders who supported him, did their best to avoid a contest – fearing both a distraction and a demonstration of disunity. But they had failed. For the first time, Labour conference delegates, voting in the electoral college, were encouraged to ask the opinion of rank and file party members. The result was near humiliation for the candidates of the left. From then on, Tony Benn, and all he stood for, ceased to be a force in Labour politics.

Ironically, the event which the leaders hoped would herald the beginning of a new era turned into an embarrassing anti-climax. A 'statement of aims and values' – asserting Labour's long-held belief in the mixed economy and defining socialism as based on the pursuit of equality rather than the extension of public ownership – was accepted, by the same Labour party conference which re-elected the established leadership. But it was approved not so much by acclamation as by indifference. Labour is only interested in ideology when it is in its extremist mode, so the torpor was itself a reassurance. It enabled Neil Kinnock, with the change in the international atmosphere to justify his conversion, to edge himself and his party away from unilateralism. The new policy – perversely accepting the need to retain the deterrent at a time when deterrence was no longer necessary – became official on 2 October 1989, when Labour's annual conference accepted a swathe of policy documents which revised the programme on which the party had fought and lost the General Election two years earlier. One of them contained the most enthusiastic support for an integrated European Community that Labour had ever expressed.

Labour's transformation into a, indeed *the*, European party was entirely rational. The party changed its mind when the Community changed its character, and came to have meaning and importance to the typical Labour supporter. In the early days of the Common Market, critics could speak of a 'bankers' Europe' based on the Treaty of Rome's explicit endorsement of capitalism and rejection of 'planning'. The bankers' Europe evolved into a Community which kept food prices artificially high by organising a farmers' cartel called the Common Agricultural Policy, regulated steel production by closing British plants and – despite its willingness to feather-bed some industries – was essentially dedicated to the free market and deregulation. Then Jacques Delors became President of the Commission. Monetary union was not his only ambition. He came to represent the aspiration for a 'people's Europe'. The idea was French as well as socialist. At the 1989 meeting of European socialist leaders, President Mitterrand had told the British delegate that he would veto the implementation of the Single Market in 1992 if Margaret Thatcher refused to accept the Community's 'social dimension'. Predictably, she would not endorse and he did not veto. But at the Trades Union Congress on 9 September 1988, Jacques Delors set out a vision of Europe which earned him a standing ovation and confirmed the Tory leadership's worst fears. European union might one day become a vehicle for reinstating all the apparatus of socialism – consultation, consensus and regulation – which Margaret Thatcher had laboured for ten years to dismantle in the United Kingdom.

Delors told the TUC 'a strong commitment to workers' rights and conditions is essential to the success of the internal market in 1992'. More significantly, he did more than describe what was needed: he set out the way in which the objective could be achieved. He proposed European legislation, binding on all member nations, which would enforce 'basic workers' rights' – defined more extensively than the General Council of the TUC would have dared to suggest. The Delors package included better health-care, improved safety standards, the chance of life-long education and – absolute anathema to Mrs Thatcher and her free enterprise government – the duty of employers to enter into collective agreements with their workforce and the opportunity for employees to serve on the boards of the companies for which they worked. 'Nineteen ninety-two,' said Delors, 'is much more than the creation of an internal market abolishing barriers to the free movement of goods, services and investment. Social dialogue and collective bargaining are essential pillars of our democratic society.' Norman Willis, the General Secretary of the TUC, gave the speech no more than a cautious welcome, urging delegates to 'make the most' of what was on offer. But Ron Todd, Chairman of the International Committee, General Secretary of the Transport and General Workers' Union and, in his time, a bitter opponent of the Common Market, was so enthusiastic that he urged his colleagues to spend their spare time learning a second European language. The resolution which endorsed the Delors view of Europe and the world was carried unanimously.

The 'social dimension' which so enthused the Labour Party became, in Margaret Thatcher's mind, an even greater objection to European integration than the creation of a single currency or the domination of a unified Germany. She described it as socialism by the back door or, in her party speeches, 'socialism by the back Delors'. And she was, of course, right. Tories had loved the Common Market before it had become an Economic Community. Their attitude – support for little more than a free trade area – was the exact opposite of Labour's belief that Europe must be more than a customs union. Once it ceased to be a *Zollverein* and accepted a responsibility for its citizens, which went far further than providing them with the boon of a free market, Conservatives began, understandably, to fear that it had turned into what they regarded as the interfering 'nanny state'. Within the terms of their philosophy, the Tories were right to turn against Europe. And Labour was right to think of it as an institution which – by applying the social politics which were accepted even by continental Christian Democrats – might move Britain to the left without the necessity of Labour winning a General Election.

In early 1990 – with mortgage rates rising to over 15 per cent; hospital waiting lists lengthening to almost one million; opposition to the poll tax escalating from civil disobedience to rioting; inflation accelerating back to double figures; and a £1.8 million current account deficit recorded in a single month – Margaret Thatcher (leading the most unpopular government since the war) needed another of the enemies who had previously appeared at such fortuitous moments. At first it seemed that Europe – either its federalist politicians or Brussels bureaucrats – would fit the bill exactly. By early summer, a better candidate had begun to emerge.

On 24 June 1990, Saddam Hussein – Ba'athist dictator of Iraq – began to mass troops on the border of Kuwait. By the end of the month, an army of 30,000 men was in position. Hussein had, for some years, been preoccupied with his war against Iran – a conflict in which he had been supported by America and the West with both overt and covert arms sales. But he had always insisted that Kuwait was really an (oil-rich) part of Iraq. The refutation of his claim was slightly complicated by the origins of both countries. At the end of the First World War, the Great Powers had drawn arbitrary lines on the map of what was known as Arabia. Kuwait and Iraq were two of the names

358

which had been written in the spaces before the virtual ownership of each new country had been handed over to the various warlords who had supported the Allies against the Turks. Iraq had replaced its feudal ruler with a brutal tyrant. Kuwait, although immensely rich, was the Sabah family's medieval fiefdom.

On 2 August, Iraq invaded Kuwait, claiming that it was retaliating against the 'theft' of oil (worth £2.4 billion) from a disputed field. The following day, the United Nations Security Council called on its members to impose economic sanctions. For the next week, total war was waged on the world's television channels. President Bush warned Saddam Hussein not to cross the Saudi Arabian border. Hussein called on Gulf Arabs to rise up, depose the Sheiks who ruled them and free Mecca from the 'spears of the Americans and Zionists'. On 12 August, a British businessman trying to cross the Iraqi border into Saudi Arabia was shot dead by Hussein's troops. But for the next couple of months, the battle was characterised by bluster rather than blood. Hussein announced that he was ready formally to end the ten-year war against Iran with a peace treaty which conceded all Iran's demands. Iraqi soldiers in Kuwait took eighty-two British citizens prisoner and held them hostage against Western intervention. On television, Hussein told the captives that they were 'heroes of peace' who had averted a Middle East war. Four days later, the women and children among the hostages were released. Saddam was playing cat and mouse.

In the last week of September, the United Nations tightened the trade embargo and agreed (by fourteen votes to one) to warn Iraq of the 'potentially severe consequences' of the continued occupation of Kuwait. Eduard Shevardnadze, Foreign Minister of the reformed but still not democratic or divided Soviet Union, supported both resolutions. The years when Moscow Communists blocked every United Nations peace-keeping or military initiative were over. That was a month before the Rome summit of the European Community, and had it not been for the Prime Minister's reaction to that (far from epoch-making) occasion, she might have sailed in triumph to the victorious conclusion of the by then inevitable Gulf War. The familiar pictures – scarf flying as she sat in the turret of a speeding tank surrounded by obviously adoring soldiers, or at sea with the Senior Service – would all have reappeared upon our television screen. But fate and Geoffrey Howe decided otherwise. In the House of Commons, her cry 'No! No! No!' had been a betrayal of their agreement and proof of her increasingly unpredictable temperament. Howe agonised for a day and resigned from the government. His resignation speech was the parliamentary sensation of the decade:

> The tragedy is – and it is for me personally, for my party, for our people and for my Right Honourable Friend herself, a very real tragedy – that the Prime Minister's perceived attitude towards Europe is running increasingly serious risks for the future of our nation. It risks minimising our influence and maximising our chances of being once again shut out. We have paid heavily in the past for late starts and squandered opportunities in Europe.

There followed an emotional passage about 'conflict of loyalties', a problem with which Howe admitted to having 'wrestled for perhaps too long'. But the real issue, for him, was Europe. For most of the rest of the Tory party, what mattered was Margaret Thatcher and her ruinous unpopularity. Howe provided the opportunity for the political assassination. Michael Heseltine, who had resigned from the Thatcher Cabinet four years earlier over the Westland affair and was widely regarded as the leader of progressive Tories in exile, decided that his moment had come. He announced, 'I am persuaded that I would have a better prospect than Mrs Thatcher of leading the Conservatives to a fourth election victory and preventing the ultimate catastrophe of a Labour victory.' Claiming that he had already received support and encouragement from over a hundred Tory MPs, he declared that he was a candidate for the party leadership.

The first ballot in the election was held on 20 November 1990 – only six days after Heseltine had accepted the nomination. Margaret Thatcher won a clear majority – 204 votes to 152 – but it was a hollow victory. The arcane rules which governed Tory leadership contests required a 15 per cent majority for victory on the first ballot, and the Prime Minister was four votes short. Had Margaret Thatcher fought a serious campaign, she would undoubtedly have won the extra votes which were needed to ensure her survival, but she regarded campaigning as beneath her dignity, and the sycophants who surrounded her – most of the politicians of quality having been driven out of her entourage – assured her that she was invincible. The Prime Minister was in Paris when the result of the first ballot was announced. Before she consulted any of her supporters in London she appeared in the forecourt of the embassy, snatched a microphone from the hand of a BBC television journalist and proclaimed her intention of fighting the second ballot – and fighting to win. She was nominated and seconded by Douglas Hurd, the Foreign Secretary and (after some persuasion) by John Major, the Chancellor of the Exchequer.

At last she began to take the election seriously. Each member of the Cabinet was seen separately and alone and asked to make a pledge of loyalty. A majority – at the most flattering estimate, twelve out of twenty-one – told her that she should go or could not hope for enough votes to enable her to stay. Most of those who agreed to support her did so with undisguised reluctance and out of duty rather than conviction. When the man she had asked to manage her campaign told her that the time had come for her to stand aside, Margaret Thatcher observed that it was 'a funny old world' and announced her resignation as leader of the Tory party. The Conservative instinct for survival had transcended all other emotions. In three years, Margaret Thatcher had evolved from invincible warrior-queen to lame-duck and liability.

So it was John Major – not quite elected to the Tory leadership on the first ballot, but near enough to make his opponents withdraw from the second – who was destined to take the decisions about whether or not and how Saddam Hussein should be expelled, by force of arms, from Kuwait. It was not the most onerous duty ever imposed upon a British Prime Minister. All he could do was endorse and support the decisions taken by the United States of America. They possessed both the power and the will to 'liberate' Kuwait. While the government had been preoccupied with its internal problems, a multinational force – legitimised by United Nations resolution – had begun to build up in the Gulf. Both land and sea forces were predominantly American, but Britain was there to emphasise its status as partner in the peace-keeping process and (more importantly) so were troops from other Arab states. The West could not afford the war against Saddam Hussein to become a Christian crusade against Islam. On 29 November 1990 (the day after John Major became Prime Minister), the United Nations Security Council set 15 January 1991 as the date by which Saddam Hussein must leave Kuwait. After that, the multinational, United States-led forces would be free under UN law to expel him by force. Iraq responded by accepting those United Nations demands which did not require evacuation from the occupied territories. Three thousand four hundred hostages, taken when Kuwait was captured, were released. The British among them arrived home with stories of looting and plunder: almost every valuable item of portable property had been shipped out of Kuwait and to Iraq.

By Christmas war seemed certain, and in January 1991 National Health Service hospitals began to prepare to receive the 7,000 casualties which, intelligence sources estimated, might result from a battle in which Hussein would use chemical and bacteriological weapons. The last-ditch effort to avert war – a meeting between the United States Secretary of State and the Iraqi Foreign Minister – failed. On 16 January American F-117 Stealth fighter-bombers flew under Saddam Hussein's radar and destroyed Iraq's communications centre. At the same time, Allied planes and Tomahawk missiles hit Iraq's air bases, bridges, power stations and missile launching sites. Operation Desert Storm had well and truly begun.

The Iraqis fought a dirty war. Millions of gallons of oil were released into the 'Persian' Gulf, in what the United States rightly called 'environmental terrorism'. Scud missiles, fired from mobile launchers, were targeted on residential districts of Haifa and Tel Aviv. Hussein's hope was that Israel would retaliate with a force and ferocity that would unite the Arab world against its Zionist enemies. America – on whom Israel were still dependent for military and economic support – just managed to persuade the Jerusalem government to be satisfied with bellicose statements about its undoubted ability and frustrated intention of destroying the Scud installations.

The war, as is the way with wars, briefly increased the Prime Minister's standing in the country, even though he had played little or no part in its conduct. A small group of doubters, among them a dozen Labour MPs, argued that the consequences of a ground war would be the deaths of millions of innocent civilians – slaughtered not for territorial integrity but oil revenues. There was a brief moment of outrage when it was reported that a not-so-smart bomb had mistaken a suburban bomb shelter for a Baghdad command bunker and killed 400 old men, women and children. But next day's opinion polls showed John Major to be the most popular political leader for ten years – transcending even Margaret Thatcher's standing at her moment of glory in 1982. When, a week later, President Bush told Saddam Hussein to 'withdraw from Kuwait or face a full-scale land attack', the Iraqi dictator responded by setting the captured oil-fields on fire. The Allied ground attack was launched on 24 February 1991. Within forty-eight hours, two divisions of Saddam Hussein's elite Republican Guard had surrendered. Forty-eight hours later President Bush told the American people, 'Kuwait is liberated. Iraq's army is defeated. I am pleased to announce that at midnight tonight . . . all US and coalition forces will suspend offensive combat operations.' One hundred and ninety-two Allied servicemen and women had died. Sixteen British soldiers were killed – nine of them by American 'friendly fire'. The best estimate of Iraqi casualties was 50,000 dead and 100,000 wounded.

The Gulf War is one of the few modern conflicts which became more controversial when it was over than it had been when it was in progress. Kuwait was returned to the Sabah family and, after the clearing-up was finished, the oil began to flow again. But Saddam Hussein was not deposed by his defeated generals, as his Western critics had prophesied. Much of his army remained intact – allowed to withdraw into Iraq, because of the West's proper reluctance to anni-hilate retreating soldiers. The Kurds – the racial minority within Iraq which Saddam Hussein had persecuted for years – were still bombed and gassed in their northern marshland homes. The British plan of herding them into 'safe havens', protected by the United Nations, proved entirely ineffective. Economic sanctions, imposed against Iraq under the United Nations mandate, caused immense suffering to its already tyrannised citizens without destabilising the Hussein regime.

John Major's Gulf War popularity was short-lived. Within a week of President Bush declaring victory, the Conservatives lost the Ribble Valley by-election to the Liberals. At the 1987 General Election, the Tories had won the seat with a majority of almost 20,000. The 'ghastly economic legacy' which, in Edward Heath's words, Major had inherited from Margaret Thatcher combined with the poll tax to give the Labour Party a 10 per cent lead in the opinion polls. Recklessly, in the first week of January 1991, John Major had announced that the poll tax would remain. Three months later (almost certainly without realising the hostage he was giving to fortune) he promised, during a visit to Bonn, that under his leadership Britain would be 'at the very heart of Europe'. That week, the clichés competed for headlines with hard news: unemployment had risen back above the two million mark, and fighting had broken out between Saddam Hussein's troops and Peshmerga Kurdish guerrillas. But Major's promise, and its implications, haunted his premiership long after unemployment began to fall again and the Kurds were forgotten as just unavoidable casualties in the war for oil.

In the early months, the new Prime Minister must have thought that the European Community – not yet a Union – would have an entirely benign influence on his future. It approved and supported his plans to create 'safe havens' in northern Iraq, and it agreed that majority rule was so near in South Africa that the trade embargo which the British government so hated could be lifted. Even Jacques Delors seemed willing to accommodate Britain's special position. In early May he suggested that the treaty which implemented European Monetary Union should contain a clause which enabled the British Parliament to decide the date on which the United Kingdom accepted 'Stage Three' – the ultimate goal of complete integration. But Tory MPs remained dissatisfied and resentful. One hundred and five of them – led by members of the Bruges Group, founded to support Margaret Thatcher's opposition to any hint of 'federalism' – signed a House of Commons motion which called for the rejection of any further move towards EMU. A fortnight later, a Bruges Group memorandum (leaked to newspapers) described John Major as 'too frightened' to veto the EMU treaty. He retaliated with an attack on politicians who were 'skulking on the fringe of talks about the destiny of Europe'. Margaret Thatcher, unable to keep out of the act, denounced the folly of attempting 'to create a new artificial state by taking powers away from national states and concentrating them in the centre'. Heath then denounced her. The Conservative party's European civil war had begun.

It rumbled on into the summer, and the autumn conference season, occasionally restrained by the prospect of an imminent election and sometimes intensified by a speech from a European Commissioner or politician which the 'Eurosceptics' (as they came to be called) regarded as proof that sinister forces were preparing to suck Britain into a federal state. The mood changes quickly within the councils of the Community. Twice a year the 'presidency' passes from one member state to another, and inevitably the new incumbent wants to make a mark with a new initiative. Each initiative reflects the particular view of the presidency – usually only slightly moderated by the knowledge that colleague countries might take a different view.

In the early months of John Major's administration, it seemed that the Luxembourg presidency was developing a plan for progress that Britain could accept. The idea was described as a Union built on three pillars. One – the European Community itself – would be bound together by treaty. The other two – foreign policy (including defence) and internal security – would be, in the jargon, 'inter-governmental'. Decisions would, therefore, be taken by agreement between sovereign states. Douglas Hurd, the Foreign Secretary, had himself announced that 'Europe has to take on more responsibility for its defence'. But other pressures were at work both at home and abroad. In London, the Confederation of British Industry was complaining about new 'social affairs directives', which would impose additional social obligations on industry. Britain, the CBI insisted, was the only European member state to have accepted (and honestly implemented) the eighteen directives presently in force. It must not accept the draft regulations on maternity rights and maximum working hours. Then Holland (the next president) presented heads of state with a draft of a new treaty which described the members of the Community as pursuing 'a federal goal'. The worthless declaration was swiftly dropped in a pointless concession to those countries (Britain among them) who were as worried by the wording of the treaty's declaratory passages as they were by the substantial changes it made to the Community's constitution. The scene was set for the Battle of Maastricht, in December 1991. It was the political equivalent of the Somme: massive casualties were inflicted on both sides and, when it was over, no one was sure who had won.

The outcome of the 'inter-governmental conference' was, in its way, happily similar to the 'three pillars' approach which had once seemed the government's favoured outcome. The European Union – a new name and a new concept – was to embrace both the European Community (with strengthened responsibilities and powers) and a new structure in which co-operation on foreign policy, defence and international security was governed by independent treaty and could not, therefore, be enforced by decisions of the European Court of Justice. There was also a declaration on the meaning and purpose of 'subsidiarity' – a doctrine invented by the Community to determine the boundaries of Community jurisdiction:

> In the areas which do not fall within its exclusive jurisdiction the Community shall take action in accordance with the principle of subsidiarity, only if and in so far as the objectives and purposes of the proposed action cannot be sufficiently achieved by the Member States and can therefore by reason of the scale of the proposed action would be better achieved by the Community.

The fact that John Major placed so much importance on that entirely ambiguous declaration illustrated how apprehensive he was about the reaction to the deal which he had struck in Maastricht. Clearly the words can be used to justify the Community doing everything or prevent it from doing anything – according to inclination. The Prime Minister came to realise that undeniable fact during the next half-dozen years as the arguments about Community competence continued, item by item. But, at the time, he claimed – as he insisted on Britain's right to decide its own immigration policy, conceded an extension of majority voting and extended the powers of the European Parliament – that the 'doctrine of subsidiarity' protected Britain from unwelcome intrusion by officious Brussels bureaucrats and continental federalist politicians. The longer the Maastricht debate went on, the fewer people believed him.

In effect, Maastricht moved Britain into Europe's slow lane. The draft treaty set out a timetable for implementing the second and third state of economic and monetary union. It nominated 1999 as the year by which a common currency should be in circulation within all those countries which met the 'convergence criteria'. Among them was the obligation to hold inflation down to a target which, according to the government, Britain (alone among all Community members) would be able honestly to meet. The more important (and, for Britain, the more onerous) obligation was the duty to contain the public sector deficit at no more than 3 per cent of gross domestic product and total public debt at no more than 60 per cent. The government spent little time speculating about whether those targets were desirable or attainable. For John Major negotiated an 'opt-out' – or at least the right to opt out when the time came.

A 'protocol' provided that Britain – and Britain alone – would not be required to move to Stage Three until the Union had taken a specific decision endorsing British participation in the common currency. That formula was, John Major declared, a triumph for his negotiating skills. Britain was simultaneously free to take its own decision about the final implementation of EMU and participate in the decisions which preceded and prepared for 1999. The Prime Minister insisted that 'in or out' of EMU, Britain would be profoundly affected by the creation of a single European currency, and therefore had the strongest vested interest in influencing its character and development. He insisted that he had achieved the best of all possible worlds by ensuring that Britain helped to negotiate an agreement which would bind every other EU country except the United Kingdom.

There is a perfectly rational argument in favour of waiting until the last minute to decide on the merits of Britain joining a single currency – though it was reasonable to expect a Prime Minister to make clear whether or not he hoped that the circumstances of the time would make it possible. Because John Major claimed to be absolutely agnostic, his sincerity was immediately in doubt. With a General Election less than a year away, the critics within his own party muted their criticism, but every examination of the draft treaty's details revealed concessions to centralism which John Major had not thought it necessary to mention in his statement to the House of Commons. The agreement that Britain could postpone a decision about joining the single currency was to haunt the Prime Minister for the full five years of the next Parliament, as more and more of his own backbenchers demanded – with varying levels of vehemence – that he should rule out membership at once.

The paradox of the Tory sceptics' position was clear to anyone who considered the Maastricht Treaty on its merits. The case against a single currency, if it exists, is based on an essentially socialist theory of economic management – the need to stimulate exports by constant depreciation in the pound, the importance of stimulating consumption and investment by deficit financing, the necessity to borrow in order to finance public spending, and above all the belief that unemployment is a greater social evil than inflation. Yet it was the Tory party from which the revolt against Maastricht came. The objection was largely romantic, and based on a misunderstanding of 'sovereignty' – which they defined as freedom from the constraints of a supranational authority. In fact, sovereignty (like liberty itself) depends on the *practical ability*, not the *theoretical right*, to choose the desired course of action. Britain inside the EMU is more likely to be able to sustain the optimum interest and exchange rate than it would be were the country to remain 'independent'. Yet, after Maastricht, there were few politicians who were prepared to say so. The Prime Minister was afraid to speak too warmly of Europe (at least in Britain) for fear of further alienating his back-bench critics. The Labour Party – though enthusiastic converts to British membership – enthused about other parts of the Maastricht Treaty. So the economic case for monetary union largely went by default. Not surprisingly, the result was the slow disenchantment of the British people. By the mid-1990s there was barely a popular majority for continued membership. Support for closer integration fell from a significant to a negligible minority.

Ironically some of the greatest proponents of an integrated Europe were the trade union leaders and left-wing Labour politicians who had, back in the 1970s, fought most fiercely against Britain even joining the Common Market. They argued, with some justification, that it was Europe, not their principles, which had changed. Because of their support for a 'people's Europe', they became the bitterest critics of the Prime Minister's second negotiating 'triumph' at Maastricht – the removal of the 'Social Chapter' from the body of the treaty and its reinstatement as a 'protocol' which was signed by the other eleven Union members but not the United Kingdom.

The European Community had a social dimension from the very beginning. Even the Treaty of Rome, which created the competitive economy of the Common Market, proclaimed that member states 'agree upon the need to promote improved working conditions and improved standards of living for workers'. To that end, Article 118 charged the Commission with promoting 'close co-operation' over a range of social policies, which included 'labour law and working conditions . . . the prevention of occupational accidents . . . the rights of association and collective bargaining'. Although Article 118 was little more than declaratory, the Single European Act of 1987 allowed the Council of Ministers to adopt (by majority voting) legally binding directives on health and safety. In 1989, Community nations, with the exception of Britain, signed the charter of the Fundamental Social Rights of Workers. Although it had no legal force, it was more proof that the rest of Europe was determined to expand the social dimension. The Social Chapter of the Maastricht Treaty was designed to give force to the declaration of 1989; all of its provisions were to be included in the legally binding treaty. Some (employment contracts, collective agreements, employment subsidies for areas of high unemployment) could only be implemented after the Council of Ministers had given their unanimous agreement. Others (health and safety, 'equality between men and women with regard to labour market opportunities' and 'the improvement of the working environment') needed a 'qualified majority' – endorsement by two-thirds of the twelve member states. In consequence, an agreement among other members of the Union might force Britain to re-regulate most of the activities which Margaret Thatcher had deregulated. John Major was immovable.

By opting completely out of the Social Chapter and securing the right to decide, in 1999, whether or not to enter the economic and monetary union which Britain would nevertheless help to create, the Prime Minister had, he claimed, 'won game, set and match'. He had certainly bought enough time to see him through the General Election. But General Elections are not won and lost on arguments about 'abroad' – even when the decisions taken in foreign capitals have a crucial influence on life in Britain, so the historic events in the world beyond Western Europe had little effect on the pattern of British voting in April 1992.

In Moscow in August 1991, a coup had almost toppled Mikhail Gorbachev and his reforming government. In Downing Street, John Major equivocated about whether or not he would do business with the hard-line Communists who might take over. It was the second blow he had dealt to Russia's nascent democracy: the British government – together with the other G7 countries – had refused Gorbachev the economic help he needed to sustain his popular revolution; instead he was given a lecture on the merits of free enterprise. Gorbachev survived the putsch, the Baltic republics won their independence and the Soviet Union disintegrated. When Gorbachev went, his successor, Boris Yeltsin, was also a democrat of sorts. Russia, detached from what had been the other 'socialist republics', rushed towards a market economy. Living standards fell from even the level that the Soviet centralised economy had been able to maintain.

In South Africa, a series of miracles – which began in February 1990 with the release of Nelson Mandela from prison on Robben Island, and ended with a real political partnership between the black majority and their historic oppressors – created a new democracy. The mystery of why the National Party – so long in oppressive control – agreed to hand over power to the black majority may never be solved. It was certainly not thanks to any pressure exerted by the

British government. The African National Congress – whose members Margaret Thatcher's government had dismissed as terrorists – won the first non-racial election in April 1994 and their banner replaced the Voortrekkers' green, white and orange tricolour as the flag of the new democracy. When President Mandela addressed the two Houses of the British Parliament, Margaret Thatcher – who had denied him help throughout his imprisonment and constantly sustained the apartheid regime – sat in the front row.

The British people sighed with relief and gasped with admiration as the world became more safe and free. But having rejoiced and marvelled, they turned to the more homely considerations of the General Election campaign. It was generally assumed that Labour would win. John Major had replaced the hated Community Charge with a property tax which fell more heavily upon the rich than on the poor, but the memory of the poll tax lingered. House prices had fallen so low that many mortgage-holders were trapped in negative equity and owed more to building societies than the value of their mortgaged property. Commentators confidently predicted that, for the first time in twenty years, the key lower-middle-class voters would desert the Conservative party. Some of them did – but not enough to defeat the government. On 9 April 1992, the Conservative government was returned to office with a majority of twenty-one.

Labour's failure was initially blamed on the Sheffield Rally – an American-style demonstration held a week before polling day. Its triumphalist tone, particularly Neil Kinnock's speech, was said to have alienated millions of voters who watched the performance on television. That absurd explanation was then replaced with an equally implausible analysis. John Smith, the Shadow Chancellor, had published an 'alternative budget'. Everyone earning less than £22,000 a year stood to gain from its proposals, but Smith's critics claimed that his tax plans encouraged the Tories to make wild claims about the cost of Labour's programme. Even some of his Labour colleagues judged that it 'gave the Tory propaganda legs'. In fact, had Smith not opened his mouth throughout the campaign, the Conservative party would still have invented something like 'the double whammy' – the wholly bogus claim that a Labour government would increase everybody's income tax by a thousand pounds a year. The claim was taken up and reported as fact by half a dozen Tory newspapers – particularly the downmarket tabloid which (with its 3.6 million circulation and virulent anti-Labour propaganda) was proud to claim, after the votes were counted, 'It was the *Sun* wot won it.'

The *Sun* (and the Tories' other allies, the *Daily Express* and *Daily Mail*) did apply the crucial pressure which levered the government back into office. But the big push was not so much against policies as the personality of Neil Kinnock, the Leader of the Opposition and the Labour Party. No politician in modern history had been subject to such a vicious and sustained assault on his character. Once the idea that he was not up to the job had been established in the public mind, it was easy to portray everything he said as proof that he had neither the intellect nor the experience to become Prime Minister. In truth, the Labour leader would have led the country with great courage and determination. The campaign of ridicule and vilification made him, and the party which he led, unelectable.

But there was an underlying reason – perhaps more important than the destruction of Neil Kinnock – for Labour's defeat. The British people had ceased to care – or at least to care enough to risk their new-found and, as they imagined, precarious prosperity by supporting policies which helped the poor. Britain had developed its own version of J. K. Galbraith's *Culture of Contentment*. The new middle classes liked what they had achieved and acquired since the war, and they were not in a mood to lose any of it. National insecurity had taken a different form from that which afflicted the country during the loss of Empire, the stagnation of the economy and the reluctant acceptance of the status appropriate to a medium-sized European power. The nervous motto of the middle classes was 'what we have, we hold'. They held their gains remarkably successfully during the Thatcher years. During the 1980s, middle-income families increased their weekly earnings from between £137 and £155 to between £174 and £204. Because of the acceleration in executive earnings and reduced direct taxes, families higher up the income scale did even better. Average weekly earnings in the top decile rose from £316.90 to £507. But families at the very bottom were (after housing costs had been taken into account) actually worse off. Their weekly income fell from £69 to £61. For the first time this century, the poor had got poorer – in absolute as well as relative terms. The Thatcher government had redistributed wealth far more effectively than any other government in history, but the redistribution was from the poor to the rich. The British people were, in 1992, in no mood to change that view of the good life. Naturally enough, some Labour Party members sympathised with the new affluent morality, for the Labour Party was changing too.

The case against Neil Kinnock included one charge which reflected those changes. At the time the party chose him to lead them out of the 1983 election disaster, Kinnock had been a unilateralist, anti-Common Market advocate of public ownership. Had he not been all of those things, he would not have been elected leader. By 1992, he had learned to love the European Union and abandoned both unilateralism and the hope of ever renationalising the privatised public utilities. Had he not changed, he could not have shepherded Labour back into the mainstream of British politics. The convictions which secured him the party leadership, although discarded, denied him the premiership. For the change opened him to the charge that he had either disguised his beliefs to deceive the voters or abandoned them in order to secure election. In fact, he had done no more than move with the times. And the Labour Party had moved with him.

Within four days of the 1992 election being won and lost, and while John Major was still forming his government, Neil Kinnock resigned the leadership of his party. He was replaced in July by John Smith, the author of the alternative budget on which so much was blamed. Smith, who won over 90 per cent of the vote in the electoral college, was in the classic tradition of Labour leaders – a firm advocate of collective security, a supporter of a closely integrated European Union, and a strong believer in the mixed economy who took for granted that Labour would wish to regulate the market in order to balance efficiency with social justice. He also believed in the absolute necessity of building a more representative Labour Party. He was leader for less than two years, but he takes credit for the most important reform in the party's post-war history – a change far more significant than anything that the revisionists of the 1960s had achieved, and more significant than the constitutional amendment that made the 'modernisation' of the mid-1990s possible. Smith established the principle of 'one member, one vote' by insisting that future leadership elections be held on that basis. He was impatient with what he regarded as frivolous reforms – in particular the re-writing of the generally ignored (public ownership) Clause IV of the 1918 constitution – and he was passionate in his belief in the trade union partnership. But without the single constitutional amendment to which Smith set his hand, the changes which subsequently made 'New Labour' possible would not have come about.

Immediately after the 1992 election was won and lost, nobody of any consequence within the Labour Party openly advocated the changes which were, after John Smith's death in May 1994, to create New Labour. Instead, the party leadership got on with applying the old principles to new circumstances – confident that, with a uniquely popular leader in Tony Blair, victory would be certain in 1996 or '97. It was not – as it has been subsequently represented – the policy of 'one more heave'. For Smith was determined to modernise his party. But he wanted to bring the old principles up to date, not replace them. He looked for intellectual improvements, not ideological alternatives. And it seemed that, by a combination of incompetence and ideological confusion, the government was ensuring that Smith's improved model of democratic socialism would soon be tested in government. John Major lost the 1997 election during the high summer of 1992.

At the beginning of the 1992 campaign, Labour – lulled by opinion polls into thinking that victory was at least possible – had prepared to survive the sterling crisis which was certain to follow the election of a new government. In any circumstances a run on the pound would have been unavoidable. Currency speculators always gamble against radical governments preserving the exchange rates which they inherit. But by 1992, Britain was a member of the Exchange Rate Mechanism, an institution which was designed to protect sudden fluctuations in currency values. The ERM might have been enough to see a Labour government through a hard first few weeks, had it not been common knowledge that sterling was overvalued. Labour secretly decided that as soon as it took office, it would negotiate a realignment of the ERM parities.

Labour lost. John Smith, a Europhile, was one of the few parliamentary survivors of the sixty-eight Labour MPs who had defied the party whip and voted for British membership of the EEC twenty years before. He had also been the Shadow Chancellor who had endorsed British ERM membership at the target rate of DM 2.95. Like every other rational observer, he knew that so high a parity could not be sustained.

The government stubbornly rejected all thought of realignment. That was the necessary public posture. Unfortunately it was also the government's private position. Interest rates were increased in order to attract 'hot money' into the country and Britain's own reserves were used in the futile hope that, by increasing the apparent demand for sterling, its value would rise. Once again, the healing powers of the market proved inadequate. Almost £10 billion, 40 per cent of the reserves, were squandered before the government accepted that it could not buy sterling's way out of trouble. Interest rose three times in a single day, eventually settling uneasily at 15 per cent. But the haemorrhage continued. At 7.40 P.M. on the evening of 16 September 1992, Norman Lamont, Chancellor of the Exchequer, announced that Britain had 'temporarily' left the ERM and, for the time being, the pound would float. It has floated ever since.

Reasons were immediately invented to explain and perhaps even excuse the greatest economic fiasco in modern British history. The real cause was the government's insistence on treating the pound like a status symbol rather than a currency. But the Prime Minister and the Chancellor chose to blame malicious foreigners and the ERM itself. Doubts about the outcome of the French referendum, which was necessary before President Mitterrand signed the Maastricht Treaty, were said to have unnerved the markets. Speculators, it was claimed, feared that a 'no' vote would cause the whole agreement to fall apart. Dollar depreciation, pulling the pound down behind it, was later added as a supplementary cause of the catastrophe. Germany, always a reliable scapegoat, was cast in the role of villain because the high interest rates – the consequence of the reunification of Germany – attracted funds to Frankfurt which might otherwise have ended in London. The President of the Bundesbank was excoriated for failing to come to Britain's rescue.

The national reaction against Europe was unreasonable but inevitable, and even the Labour Party, using the government's refusal to endorse the Social Chapter as its justification, voted against ratification of the Maastricht Treaty. A handful of Conservative 'Eurosceptics' joined the Opposition in the 'No' lobby – providing a preview of the internecine warfare which was to split the Tories for the next five years. But Europe and the government survived, by 316 votes to 319. But John Major's administration was already doomed. The ERM fiasco only increased the British people's suspicion of Europe, but it fundamentally changed their judgement about the Conservative party. Until September 1992, whatever the relative standing of the parties in the opinion polls, the Tories were always adjudged to be 'best able to run the economy'. After the ERM débâcle, the Tory party never occupied that position again – not for a single week in a single opinion poll. John Smith, knowing that his opponents had lost their most precious asset, began to prepare for government – even recklessly telling his parliamentary colleagues, 'There are some things that we must do, simply because they are right.' By 1993 the country took it for granted that, whenever the election came, Smith would be the next Prime Minister and that, fifty years after Attlee's post-war victory, Labour would be back in office with a substantial majority. John Smith died on 12 May 1994. Two months later, Tony Blair – aged forty-one – was chosen to replace him.

EPILOGUE

FIFTY YEARS ON

———◆———

The first of May 1997 marked a turning point in British history. In truth, it was no more than a symbolic date. For Britain had begun to change at least five years earlier, when the country had demonstrated a clear disenchantment with the Tory party but returned it to office because the key voters – the million or so men and women who determine the result of General Elections – had found the alternative even less attractive. In 1997, Labour no longer threatened the prospects and prosperity of the floating voters, so they flooded towards Labour on an overwhelming tide. The recent converts showed a far greater enthusiasm for victory than the traditional supporters – in the decaying areas of inner cities and on the council estates – chose to display. Tony Blair, and the New Labour Party which he had created, had found a natural constituency. The voters for whom the appeal was greatest were the men and women who – because they swung between election and election – held the political future in their hands. As a result Labour had become irresistible.

It took more than fifty years for Labour to discover its new identity. In 1945, the paradigm of Labour's good intention was the serviceman who had come home from the war determined to build a better Britain for his children. He could remember the suffering and hardship of the Depression, and he believed that if the politicians planned the peace as they had managed the war, the defeat of ignorance, sickness and poverty would be as comprehensive as the victory over Nazi Germany. Old Labour seemed to offer the collective solution to the problems which had been caused by selfish individualism.

The idea of improvement by co-operation lasted for thirty years. Then, after a sudden lurch towards the new libertarianism of small government and unrestrained competition, opinion settled around a typical British compromise. The people – particularly the opinion-formers – wanted improved welfare at lower cost and compassion without increased taxes. The new standard-bearers of Labour's philosophy were a young family in a semi-detached house on an owner-occupied estate. They were worried about the cost of their mortgage, the quality of their children's education and the availability of good medical care. The poverty which they saw around them – the homeless teenagers in shop doorways and the pensioners on park benches – caused them to feel genuine regret. But they felt no moral duty to contribute towards alleviating suffering which had been caused by the inadequacy of professional politicians – a profession for which they felt a healthy contempt. One of the attractions of New Labour was its obvious rejection of the conventional political posturing and its promise to govern without the handicap of class connection or inherited dogma. Tony Blair – who believed what they believed – was their natural leader. Their support almost certainly guarantees New Labour a permanent House of Commons majority, under any electoral system.

Perhaps, in 1997, Labour would have won without their mass conversion. What is certain is that many of them would never have voted for the old party of redistribution and equality. Paradoxically, they were the beneficiaries of the policies which, back in 1945, had been built on those ideals. But they had not so much kicked the egalitarian ladder away as allowed it to fall into disrepair because they believed that it no longer had any value. They believed that social and economic mobility allowed the industrious to prosper. When Tony Blair embraced the ideas of meritocracy, he became their man, and they turned what was almost certainly his inevitable victory into a landslide.

Their support confirmed and guaranteed government of, for and by the new social strata in society – first-generation graduates with company cars, boundless ambition and what they believed to be progressive opinions. The middle classes – their origins changed with the years but their addiction to property and status identical to their pre-war equivalents – were firmly and perhaps permanently in command.

They do not take all the credit or blame for Labour's 1997 landslide. Theirs was the positive contribution to the party's success. Just as important, in terms of seats won and lost, was the national distaste for John Major's Conservative party. Dislike of the government guaranteed that Labour won a majority of 179 – with a popular vote of about the same size, and a share of the poll 3 per cent less than Harold Wilson secured to achieve a majority of 96 back in 1966. The new middle classes had found their true home in Labour. In the rest of the country, voting patterns changed because even traditional Tories rejected the Conservative party – and there were a multitude of reasons for them doing so.

Elections are said to be lost by governments, not won by oppositions, and the cause of defeat is usually thought to be the failure to maintain or increase real disposable income. John Major left the British economy in what Kenneth Clarke – his last Chancellor of the Exchequer – never tired of calling 'good shape'. The national debt doubled during the last five Tory years and the overall (as distinct from direct) tax burden increased. But the national debt, although talked about in public houses, does not determine the outcome of General Elections, and income tax was reduced – predictably including a cut of 2 per cent during the last budget before the election. Inflation was more or less stable at 2–3 per cent a year, unemployment was falling (though not as fast as the statistics suggested), and the increase in output was modest but sustained. Unfortunately for the Conservatives, the British people stubbornly refused to 'feel good'. The government, they believed, was a failure – divided, incompetent and corrupt. It was during John Major's last four years that the word 'sleaze' passed into the political vocabulary.

It was the civil war on his back-benches which did John Major most damage. British political parties have always made a habit of tearing themselves apart over the question of relations – particularly trading relations – with European powers and Commonwealth countries. The Tories, because they have been in office for so much of the last two hundred years, have fought among themselves in government. The Corn Law disputes of 1846 and the Tariff Reform debates of 1906 sent them into the political wilderness for a generation. The Ottawa Agreement (and the return to Imperial Preference) in 1932 was managed more successfully because Ramsay MacDonald's National Government had such a large House of Commons majority that the dissidents and potential defectors were no threat to its survival. John Major did not enjoy the same security. Perhaps, if he had possessed a natural authority or had commanded the respect of the Tory Eurosceptics, he would have been able to call their bluff. But most of the back-benchers who opposed his promise to 'put Britain at the heart of Europe' were old Thatcherites, who voted for Major to succeed their heroine in the belief that he would carry on her policies. The discovery that he was not Margaret Thatcher's ideological heir turned them from half-hearted supporters into bitter opponents who believed that they had been betrayed. Many of them were looking for trouble. The Maastricht proposal for the creation of a single European currency provided the ideal opportunity.

Perhaps there was a case for postponing a decision on Britain's membership of a single European currency until immediately before its creation. But, because John Major was being buffeted from pro to con by the factions on his back-benches, his refusal to express even a preference looked like (and probably was) not statesmanlike caution but the abdication of leadership. The formula did not even keep his party at peace. The Eurosceptics constantly demanded the outright and immediate rejection of the single currency, and the more the Prime Minister attempted to placate them by slowly moving in that direction, the more blatant both their rebellion and their contempt became. When the Prime Minister sought to re-establish his position by resigning from the Tory leadership in June 1995 and offering himself for re-election, John Redwood, Secretary of State for Wales, left the Cabinet and challenged him. Major won easily, but the impression of a divided government had been stamped indelibly on the public's mind. For the first time since the disputes which followed the Suez conspiracy in 1956 the question (which had so damaged Labour's prospects) was asked about the Conservatives: 'If they can't agree among themselves, how can they hope to run the country?'

The attempt at government by equivocation was not John Major's only unforced error. Prompted by what his friends insisted was a deep personal commitment to conventional virtue, he launched a campaign for the revival of 'family values'. The gods that punish the sanctimonious immediately struck back. A succession of Tory MPs were accused of (and eventually confessed to) a variety of sexual mis-demeanours. The world having grown more tolerant of such behaviour, the government might well have survived the tabloid front pages unscathed. But in October 1994 two junior ministers admitted that they had taken payment from lobbyists in return for asking par-liamentary questions on behalf of the firms which they represented. Sexual peccadilloes were forgivable, financial impropriety was not. The 'cash for questions' scandal was only one of the revelations which put the government's integrity in public doubt. The prosecution of two executives of the Matrix Churchill machine-tool company was abandoned after the prosecution admitted that the arms sold to Iraq, in defiance of the government embargo, had been despatched after ministers changed the sanction guidelines without telling Parliament or public. Two judicial enquiries followed. Lord Justice Scott found that 'the guidelines did not remain unchanged' but the changes 'were kept secret'. The Attorney General, who had advised ministers to sign orders which requested the suppression of evidence on grounds of national security, did not resign. Lord Justice Nolan – examining the propriety of Members of Parliament accepting 'outside financial inter-ests' – concluded that all MPs should declare subsidiary earnings which might be regarded as related to, or consequent upon, their Membership. Individual MPs were left to decide for themselves which of their outside earnings came within the less than precise definition. So it was generally agreed that a minority of MPs continued to be paid for services which they were not prepared to reveal. It was Tory MPs who had taken 'cash for questions' and it was Tory back-benchers who were assumed to have been less than frank when making the declarations required by the Register of Members' Interests. The government party was, the public judged, irredeemably corrupt.

They also concluded, with even more justification, that it was also incorrigibly incompetent. Rarely, at least in this century, has a government fallen because of the unpopularity of its agricultural policy. But the BSE crisis – or at least the way in which it was handled by ministers – so savagely undermined the government's reputation that it was, in itself, a major reason for the massive and inevitable defeat. However the BSE epidemic began, it was undoubtedly extended by the doctrinaire decision to 'deregulate' animal foodstuffs. True to Thatcherite policy, farmers and the livestock industry were 'freed', to allow them to decide what should be fed to cows and sheep. They agreed, because it was cheap. Everybody made more money when dead sheep were fed to sheep and dead cattle to cows. The result was a spread of infection in both species and a European assault on one of the most symbolic of British exports – the roast beef of old England and Scotland's Angus steaks. The European Union used its legal powers to prohibit all British beef exports. Ministers reacted with wild oscillations between bluster and capitulation. A mass slaughter was arranged to propitiate the avenging gods of the European Commission. The export ban remained in force. Huge sums were devoted to compensating the farmers whose (often healthy) cows had been slaughtered and burned in power-station furnaces. The farmers remained understandably angry. John Major announced that he would block all European business in the Council of Ministers until the Commission changed its mind. The Commission stood firm. The Prime Minister did not. Normal business was resumed, but the ban was not lifted. The government had, fatally, made itself ridiculous.

Only once, and then briefly, did the Prime Minister look like a statesman. Ireland – so long the bane of British politics and politicians – provided a fleeting opportunity for John Major to re-establish his reputation and regain his lost esteem. On 14 December 1993 – after months of careful preparation – the Prime Minister and Albert Reynolds, the Irish Taoiseach, signed the twelve-point Downing Street Declaration, asserting their 'common view that it is now possible to end violence for good' in Northern Ireland. All parties in the House of Commons agreed. Even Gerry Adams – leader of Sinn Féin, 'the political wing of the IRA' – thought that it might be 'the beginning of the end' for the years of death and destruction. A cease-fire followed. It lasted for over two years. During that time there were endless constitutional talks at Stormont. Sinn Féin, who had 'refused to renounce violence', were excluded. No progress was made towards a settlement. John Major, having lost every by-election held in his last Parliament, became dependent on the Ulster Unionists to guarantee his House of Commons majority and was, as a result, suspected of accepting a secret Orange veto on the progress of the talks. The IRA, claiming to lose patience, decided to remind the world that they still existed. Bombs did immense damage, though caused few deaths, in London and Manchester. As always, the leaders of Sinn Féin refused to condemn the outrages. John Major's attempt at statesmanship slowly foundered and was swiftly forgotten.

So, almost eighty years after the Easter Rising, the governance of Ireland remained the anxious preoccupation of Westminster and Whitehall. So did sterling – potentially part of a single European currency – fifty years after John Maynard Keynes had hoped that he had solved Britain's currency problems at Bretton Woods. In other ways, the United Kingdom had changed almost out of recognition. Neither politicians nor people still believed that the NHS could provide comprehensive health-care free at the point of need. The parties agreed that social security could no longer protect the citizens of the welfare state from cradle to grave. The public utilities – including coal, which Harold Macmillan (in his 'family silver' speech) had ironically complained could never be denationalised – were generally regarded as best left to private enterprise and the profit motive.

The peace of the traditional British Sunday was being shattered by petty thieves, vandals, ram-raiders and ill-named 'joy-riders' – many of whom had consumed dutch courage in the public houses which, thanks to 'more liberal' licensing laws, were often open all day. The notion that crime is frequently the product of poverty – although documented and demonstrated to the satisfaction of anyone who took a serious interest in the subject – was dismissed out of hand, since it was incompatible with the individualistic spirit of the age. A nation of generally responsible adults was to be made safe for a sophisticated civilisation by punishments which were severe enough to provide a real deterrent. The speed and certainty of conviction was to be improved by changes in a judicial process which had, for far too long, shown a bias towards the criminal classes. Noisy families were to be threatened with eviction. Beggars (about whom nobody had thought for most of the half-century, because they did not exist for the forty years which followed the war) became objects of hatred rather than of pity. The gulf which separated the prosperous from the poor widened rather than first narrowed and then disappeared as the optimists of 1945 had once predicted. All thought of 'redressing the balance' – redistributing from rich to poor to compensate for the way in which the Thatcher government had redistributed from poor to rich – was dismissed as morally indefensible and socially corrosive. Families who could stand on their own feet believed that a way must be found of making their less fortunate neighbours survive without assistance from the state – or their taxes.

In fact, if destiny had consciously prepared Britain for the gentle reforms and ruthless efficiency of New Labour, it would have built a nation very much like that which Tony Blair inherited in May 1997. Disillusion, perhaps even disgust, at the way in which Britain had been governed for the previous five years combined with the hope that a young man, leading a reinvigorated party, would begin the long process of national renewal which so many people wanted but so few could define. The idea of New Labour – which Blair's advisers insisted was hit upon by chance – proved to be the catalyst of Labour's whole campaign. It did more than dissociate the party from the bad old days of public ownership and planning. It gave credence to the promise that Blair offered an entirely different sort of politics, free from the encumbrance of class bias and dogmatic preconceptions. The new middle classes liked the offer of a sweeter, cleaner, more competent government which inspired hope not because it set its heart on an ideological goal but because it focused its attention on objectives which 'all right-minded people' supported. Tony Blair created a political party which was free from the taint of party politics.

The transformation which he brought about within the Labour Party was, in part, the product of his will, at last, to win – a characteristic which came to personify the hopes of even old-fashioned socialists who shared neither his philosophy nor his background. It was also the direct result of the attribute which, to the surprise of traditionalists, he boasted about in all his early speeches as party leader. Tony Blair was not Labour born and bred. Had he known it better or loved it more, he would never have attempted to use it as the surrogate mother of a new and different party. He was the soldier who crossed a minefield in confident safety because he did not know that the mines were there. Because he neither knew nor cared about what Labour had once stood for, he was able to lead the most remarkable revolution in modern political history. The prophets of New Labour succeeded where the Militant tendency had failed. They took over an established political party and re-created it in their own image. The panache with which they operated was breathtaking, and they created an election machine which fought a brilliant, single-minded campaign. But the ideas which had inspired a century of democratic socialists were ruthlessly discredited. They had survived since Attlee's day and were, therefore, by definition too ancient to be of any value in New Labour's brave new world. New Labour was no less sceptical than the Tories about the virtues of equality. The good life was prosperity and security for 70 per cent of the population and a sigh of regret for the families which remained at the bottom of the social heap. Decent governments, New Labour insisted, showed proper respect for people's property, whether it was recently purchased shares in the privatised utilities or 'positional goods' (like private health-care and education) which illustrate the social superiority of those who possessed them. The radical party in Britain embraced what Karl Marx – no longer feared, hated or talked about very much – would have described as 'bourgeois values'. The sceptred isle was firmly under the control of the suburban middle classes.

INDEX

———•———

Abel-Smith, Brian, 208, 209
abortion, 177
Acheson, Dean, 32
Adam Smith Institute, 341
Adams, Gerry, 383
Adenauer, Konrad, 53, 114–15, 145
Africa, 56–8, 89, 121–4, 150, 231
African National Congress, 332, 371
Airports Authority, 312
Al-Ahram, 97
Albania, 34
Aldermaston marches, 137, 138
Aldrich, Winthrop, 107
Alexander, A. V., 6–7, 39
Algeria, 142
Allsop, Kenneth, 92
Amalgamated Engineering Union, 139
Amery, Julian, 94–5
Amin, Idi, 56
Anderson Report, 127
Anglo-American Productivity Councils, 24
Anglo-Irish Agreement (1985), 330–1
'Angry Young Men', 92–3
Antelope, HMS, 289

apartheid, 123, 174, 259, 326, 332, 371
Apprentice Boys of Derry, 197, 200
Arab Legion, 97
Arabs, 96, 113, 228, 362
Aramco Corporation, 95
Arbuckle, Constable Victor, 201
Ardent, HMS, 289
Argentina, 20, 286–90, 333
Armagh, 198, 203
Army Bureau of Current Affairs, 4
Arnold, Matthew, 55–6
Asia, 89, 150
Asquith, H. H., 65
Assam, 26
Astor, David, 111
Aswan Dam, 96, 98, 99
Atlantic Alliance, 89, 116, 120, 258, 282
Atlantic Charter, 12
Atomic Weapons Research Establishment, 137
Attlee, Clement, 67; 1945 election, 2–4, 6, 61; Morrison tries to depose, 3, 85; American loan, 13; welfare programme, 15, 41; economic policies, 16–17, 23; and Indian independence, 27–9, 30–1;

386

Smith, John, 371, 373–4, 375, 376
Soames, Christopher (Lord Soames), 222, 282
'social contract', 255
Social Democratic and Labour Party (SDLP), 248
Social Democratic Party (SDP), 226, 280, 293, 320, 326, 345
Social Fund, 318
social security, 14–15, 236–7, 269, 270, 316–18
socialism: after Second World War, 7; New Labour and, 385
Socialist Workers, 321
Solidarity, 281, 351
South Africa, 123–4, 150, 174, 183, 185, 187, 259, 326, 331–2, 364, 370–1
South-East Asia Treaty Organisation (Seato), 86–7
South Georgia, 286, 287
Southern Rhodesia, 122, 123, 181; see also Zimbabwe
sovereignty, 36–7, 224, 232, 368
Soviet Union, 23; Second World War, 5; and the 1945 election, 4; and the Marshall Plan, 33; Berlin blockade, 34–5, 48; post-war territories, 34; Cold War, 35–6; and the Middle East, 97; and the Suez crisis, 107; suppresses Hungarian uprising, 108–9; space race, 120; nuclear weapons, 136; shoots down US spy plane, 143; spies, 154–5; arms control, 258; under Gorbachev, 327–8; collapse of, 327, 351, 370
Spain, 352–3
Spanish Civil War, 4
Special Branch, 334
spies, 154
Sputnik, 120
Spycatcher (Wright), 334
Stalin, Joseph, 34, 35, 108
Stalinists, 295

Stanley, Oliver, 47
Star, 336
State Earnings Related Pension Scheme see SERPS
Steel, David, 233, 293
steel industry, 60, 69–70, 81
sterling: convertibility, 11–12, 13, 22; exchange controls, 25–6; exchange rates, 45–7, 67–8, 132, 162, 227–8, 251, 254, 267, 268, 291, 351, 354, 374; devaluation, 45–7, 58, 68, 159, 164–5, 206, 228, 251; balance of payments crises, 158–66; and Britain's EEC membership, 223–4; IMF crisis, 250–4, 259; shadowing the Deutschmark, 351–2; and the Exchange Rate Mechanism, 352–5, 374–6
Sterling Area, 10–11, 12, 52
Strachey, John, 21, 22, 58
Strategic Arms Limitation Talks (SALT), 258
Strategic Defence Initiative (SDI), 326–7, 328
Strauss, George, 3
Street Offences Act (1959), 127
strikes, 65; miners', 44, 217–21, 228–9, 295–6, 297–302, 303; dockers', 44–5, 164, 214, 216–17; seamen's, 172–3; 'In Place of Strife', 193–6, 214; trade union reform, 214–21; 'Winter of Discontent', 215, 217, 259–62; National Health Service, 238
Suez Canal, 93, 94, 95–6, 98–9, 100, 104, 105, 113, 164, 174
Suez crisis (1956), 69, 98–107, 109–15, 129
Summerskill, Dr Edith, 84
Sun, 259, 335, 336, 372
Sunday Correspondent, 336
Sunday Times, 334, 335–6

taxation, 76–8, 79, 80–1, 82, 129–30, 132, 161, 207–8, 236, 266–7, 336, 371–2, 379